Praise for Robert Weintraub
The Victory Season

"Robert Weintraub loads the bases with the kind of entertaining anecdotes, minutiae and quotes that separate baseball—and baseball writing—from other sports, and he skillfully captures the facts and texture of the '46 season with meticulous research and a conversational style. Weintraub is a big-league storyteller."

—Don Oldenburg, *USA Today*

"*The Victory Season* leaps off the page like a newsreel."

—Allen Barra, *Chicago Tribune*

"Robert Weintraub recounts the game's joyous reacclimatization, duly honoring the fine record of service of many players, shedding light on veteran returns and underscoring significant contemporary events. . . . Admirably wide-ranging."

—Maxwell Carter, *New York Times Book Review*

"A meticulously researched and elegantly written chronicle of what happened in 1946. . . . From start to finish, *The Victory Season* is a home run."

—David Martindale, *Fort Worth Star-Telegram*

"Weintraub tells myriad good stories. If you want generous context for a great season of baseball when it was still the national pastime and the country was in fascinating flux, Weintraub is your man."

—Dennis Drabelle, *Washington Post*

"Even if you think you know the history of baseball, Weintraub will surprise you with many gems from his meticulous research. *The Victory Season* is an important work featuring an all-star cast."

—James Miller, coauthor of *Those Guys Have All the Fun*

"In the tradition of Robert W. Creamer's classic *Baseball in '41*, Robert Weintraub's *The Victory Season* doesn't merely revisit a pivotal baseball season, it places that season in a larger historical and cultural context. It is a season—and a book—to be relished, as America returns to a very familiar place: at home, at peace, and ready to follow DiMaggio, Musial, Williams, and their compatriots across another glorious summer."
—Michael MacCambridge, author of *America's Game: The Epic Story of How Pro Football Captured a Nation*

"As Robert Weintraub's measured, elegant prose illustrates, *The Victory Season* makes an irrefutable case that baseball's golden age begins in 1946. Grade: Grand slam."   —Mark Hodermarsky, *Cleveland Plain Dealer*

"A beautifully written paean to the 1946 baseball season, when normalcy returned to the national pastime."
—Mike Vaccaro, *New York Post*

"There was more to baseball in 1946 than Ted Williams and Stan Musial marching home from war. The tectonic plates were shifting beneath the game's surface as the color line developed its first cracks and greedy team owners unwittingly inspired baseball's labor movement. With a Halberstam-like sense of purpose, Robert Weintraub captures it all in *The Victory Season*."
—John Schulian, coeditor of *At the Fights* and author of *Sometimes They Even Shook Your Hand*

"We see a lot of baseball books each spring, but few will be more supremely entertaining than *The Victory Season*....Impossibly charming....A winning account."   —Matthew Price, *Newsday*

"An entertaining read....Scattered among those big stories are little gems about players most of us have never heard of."
—Casey Common, *Minneapolis Star Tribune*

★★★ *The* ★★★
VICTORY SEASON

*The End of World War II
and the Birth of Baseball's Golden Age*

ROBERT WEINTRAUB

BACK BAY BOOKS
LITTLE, BROWN AND COMPANY

New York   Boston   London

For Arthur Weintraub and Peter Gibbs—may this book
at last heal the pain of the Dodgers leaving Brooklyn.

Back Bay Books / Little, Brown and Company
Hachette Book Group
237 Park Avenue, New York, NY 10017
littlebrown.com

Originally published in hardcover by Little, Brown and Company, April 2013
First Back Bay paperback edition, April 2014

Back Bay Books is an imprint of Little, Brown and Company, a division of Hachette Book Group, Inc. The Back Bay Books name and logo are trademarks of Hachette Book Group, Inc.

The publisher is not responsible for websites (or their content) that are not owned by the publisher.

The Hachette Speakers Bureau provides a wide range of authors for speaking events. To find out more, go to hachettespeakersbureau.com or call (866) 376-6591.

"Leave Us Go Root for the Dodgers, Rodgers": words by Bud Green / Ted Berkman / Dan Parker, © 1943 Jewel Music Publishing Co., Inc. Used by permission. International copyright secured. All rights reserved.

Library of Congress Cataloging-in-Publication Data
Weintraub, Robert.
 The victory season : the end of World War II and the birth of baseball's golden age / Robert Weintraub.
    p. cm.
 Includes bibliographical references.
 ISBN 978-0-316-20591-7 (hc) / 978-0-316-20589-4 (pb)
 1. Baseball—United States—History—20th century. 2. World War, 1939–1945—United States. 3. United States—History—1945– 4. United States—Social life and customs—1945–1970. I. Title.
 GV863.A1W416 2013
 796.3570973—dc23   2012040155

10 9 8 7 6 5 4 3 2 1

RRD–C

Printed in the United States of America

Contents

Introduction

IT LOOKED AS if a bomb had been dropped on Yankee Stadium.

No, the South Bronx didn't resemble the moonscapes of Dresden or Tokyo, and surely not the atomically ravaged wastelands of Hiroshima and Nagasaki. But baseball's biggest and most famous arena lay in ruins, looking perhaps like a London block during the Blitz.

Unlike the wartime air raids, this wound was self-inflicted, and the mastermind behind it was leading a pack of reporters to view the damage. One of them, John Drebinger of the *New York Times*, captured the demolition at the House That Ruth Built: "With everything blasted out from under the stands and rows upon rows of seats removed from the lower and mezzanine levels, the premises looked as if somebody had been conducting experiments with a new type of blockbuster."

The loudly dressed (checkered suit, wide purple-striped tie, two-tone shoes) gent leading the tour on this frigid mid-January day in 1946 was Leland "Larry" MacPhail. The man known far and wide as "the Roaring Redhead" for his shock of crimson and his top-volume monologues had been implementing various aspects of his pioneering vision since entering baseball in the early 1930s. Now, he was running the number one franchise in all of sport, and he intended to use that position to wrench baseball into a new postwar era.

When it came to maximizing profit for the moguls of the game, that is. MacPhail was a forward-thinker in ways intended to fatten his wallet, but in other areas, he was not nearly so progressive. And the year ahead, the first full baseball season since the end of World War II, would see Mac and his fellow owners straining to retain the status quo when it came to matters of hue—green, as in the money they would make, in direct contrast to the players returning home from war, and black, as in the color line that was threatened by a breakaway member of the cozy group that ran the sport.

MacPhail was certainly spending long green on renovating Yankee Stadium—$600,000 to be exact (roughly $7 million in today's dollars), the most that had ever been dropped on the renovation of a sporting ground. The whole barn was being repainted in several shades of blue and green, "with overlays of silver paint everywhere," according to the *Sporting News*. The fresh paint job would soon become a symbol of baseball's postwar renewal, if not proof that the sparkling palace indeed was, as MacPhail's propaganda machine insisted, "The Home of America's Finest Baseball."

Light towers, the largest and most reflective in the game, were going up over the main grandstand. The first base side was gutted to make room for a new two-story concession building. Seating areas were being torn up across the Stadium, as MacPhail was set to implement exclusivity into the fan experience, building the first corporate boxes, Stadium clubs, and private dining tables baseball had known. Perhaps most important, the Stadium's toilets were undergoing a thorough classing up. If you had to urinate in the House That MacPhail Built, you were going to go in style.

When we look at history's long sweep, it is correct to say that the United States moved from victory over Germany and Japan in World War II into a long period of peace, prosperity, and global hegemony—the key years of Henry Luce's "American Century." But there was a painful interregnum that is generally ignored by history, a year of wrenching reorientation from a militaristic society geared for war to one that required the reabsorption of millions of servicemen and -women into a country grossly unprepared for such a change.

The year 1946 saw a United States swept by nearly unprecedented labor disruption, paralyzed by spiraling prices and massive shortages of crucial goods and services, hit by social unrest, and nervously worried about the looming threat of Soviet Russia, the nascent atomic age, and the ever-present potential for the resumption of the prewar Great Depression. "I find peace is hell," President Harry Truman, who as 1946 began had been in the job for all of eight months, remarked bitterly to his diary as his first year in the Oval Office slogged on. "It was a cruel time to put inexperience in power," wrote journalist Richard Rovere.

Just months after the two nations had combined to defeat the German war machine and were co-prosecuting Nazi war criminals in Nuremberg, America and Russia already seemed headed for a war that would dwarf the one just concluded. "There is no 'misunderstanding' between Russia and the West," opined *Life*. "There is conflict." Truman set his frustration down in his diary on the fifth day of the new year. "I do not think we should play compromise any longer....I am tired of babying the Soviets."

In February, a State Department figure based in Moscow, George Kennan, had set out his worries about the Russians in the fabled "Long Telegram," an eight-thousand-word diatribe that would set US "containment" policy for the next four decades. "It reads exactly like one of those primers put out by alarmed congressional committees or by the DAR, designed to arouse the citizenry to the dangers of the Communist conspiracy," Kennan said wryly about his effort.

Less than a month later, as baseball opened spring training, former British prime minister Winston Churchill gave a speech at Westminster College in Missouri, a couple of hours from St. Louis, warning of an "Iron Curtain" descending across Europe, "from Stettin in the Baltic to Trieste in the Adriatic." Afterward, at a dinner given for him by Luce, the publisher of *Time,* Churchill pigged out on caviar. "You know, Uncle Joe [Stalin] used to send me a lot of this," Churchill quipped. "But I don't suppose I shall get any more now."

Still, for many Americans, crises overseas played second fiddle to the situation on the home front, as sudden peace caught the nation as off guard as sudden war had in 1941. Truman wanted to slow demobilization, keep the armed forces at a state of readiness, and continue mandatory service for all who were eligible. Instead, relatives of deployed soldiers bombarded their representatives with telegrams, demanding their fathers and sons and brothers come home now, while demobilization riots swept Europe and the Far East. Congress ignored Truman and General Dwight D. Eisenhower and reduced the US Army's fearsome combat power to a measly pair of divisions by mid-'46. Senator Elbert D. Thomas, the chairman of the Military Affairs Committee, in describing the incessant demands, said, "Constituents are on our necks day and night. The pressure is unbelievable. Mail from wives, mothers, and sweethearts demanding that their men be brought home is running to almost 100,000 letters daily" (new mothers sent baby booties to DC). Truman had to give in—had he halted the boys' coming home, he'd have likely been impeached.

Nearly a million and a half men were discharged each month starting at the end of 1945 and continuing throughout 1946. The result was a severe nationwide housing shortage. In Atlanta, for example, two thousand people answered a single "apartment for rent" ad. Chicago alone had a hundred thousand homeless vets on the streets. Meanwhile, Truman wanted the Office of Price Administration (OPA) to continue the wartime practice of capping inflation and ensuring that goods came to market at a fair price, but after years of selling little at low cost, suppliers were eager to build demand. So manufacturers and producers indulged in profiteering, as hundreds of everyday goods, from meat to milk to automobiles to underwear, were kept out of stores. A massive black market took over, making Main Street USA resemble the dark alleyways of postwar Berlin, where illicit goods were sold at exorbitant prices in every quarter of the German capital. Asked at a press conference where one could legally find a shirt for sale, Truman was embarrassingly forced to answer, "I don't know."

The cost of living skyrocketed some 18 percent as price controls were removed. Unfortunately, wages weren't raised in conjunction, and as a result, labor felt severely underpaid. With the specter of depression still looming over the country, conditions were ripe for an outbreak of strikes, and they came with a vengeance. From coal miners to railroad workers to coffin makers and barbers, employees in seemingly every industry walked off the job at some point in 1946. In all, five million people struck, and an estimated 107,476,000 working days were lost. In the main, workers got their desired result—wages went up, in some cases significantly.

But an unintended consequence was another fracture of the national bond that had seemed so strong in the wake of the defeat of the Axis powers. "Newspaper headlines daily proclaim the unfortunate tensions and dissensions which beset our nation," said Attorney General Tom Clark in a speech designed to recharge the country's patriotism. "The idealism that permeated our people during the war has yielded to the practical philosophy of 'every man for himself'!" Mere months after America's finest hour, the country was riven by cynicism, lawlessness, and disillusionment.

"Nineteen forty-six is our year of decision," Truman said in early January. "This year we lay the foundation for our economic structure which will have to serve for generations." The president, a huge St. Louis Cardinals fan, wasn't talking about baseball, but he easily could have been.

★ ★ ★

In that first year after the war, the game too was beset by threats to its basic architecture. Baseball players had no union to negotiate higher salaries for its membership or to call for a strike should their demands fall on deaf ears. That was a situation a Boston labor attorney named Robert Murphy tried to change in the summer of '46. Murphy was appalled at the conditions players toiled under, given their earning potential.

Since clubs first began paying people to hit and pitch, the basic contract every player had signed was a ridiculously imbalanced one. The club held all the cards. Salaries were negotiated without the benefit of an agent, almost always for far less than market value. But the player had little recourse, thanks to a nasty little codicil in the contract known as the Reserve Clause. It held that the club retained an option on signed players for the following year, regardless of circumstances. There was no such animal as free agency. Players were locked to their club in perpetuity, until the team decided to cut ties. Any player could be released with only ten days' notice, and could be sold to any other team with no notice at all—with all profits from the sale going to the team, not the man who was exchanged for cash against his will. It was indentured servitude of a sort that would not have been out of place in the Middle Ages—and that had been put in place in the Gilded Age, specifically 1879. The Supreme Court essentially halted any challenges to the Reserve Clause by ruling in 1922 that baseball was an "amusement" rather than a monopoly conspiring to keep player costs down, and was thus immune to antitrust laws.

Murphy's unionizing was but one front of a postwar assault on baseball's status quo. A Mexican millionaire named Jorge Pasquel led a determined raid on the underpaid talent in the majors, wooing away a number of American players to play in Pasquel's Mexican League and seriously tempting many more, including the superstars of the sport, with a seemingly limitless payroll. Although conditions in Mexico were markedly inferior to the big leagues, the mere idea of another suitor for their caged talent unnerved the owners, who saw in Pasquel a major challenge to the Reserve Clause.

And that wasn't all. Threats of de facto free agency and unionization were bad enough, but when a black player named Jackie Robinson was signed to play triple-A ball in '46, with a promotion to Brooklyn imminent if he could hack it, the moguls were met with a challenge they would be hard-pressed to resist. The unofficial color line that had been in place for virtually all of baseball's history was buttressed by firm ramparts that were part racism, part economics, and all fear. But the color line was about to be circumvented as decisively as had another line thought impregnable before the war, the Maginot Line.

The war years and the tumult that followed were momentous times, but everyday folks were still living their lives within the onrushing history. And one of the best ways to escape the reality of homelessness, shortages, strikes, and the Soviets was entertainment. That was where baseball proved invaluable.

They played ball during the war, but few thought it anything but a placeholder for the real thing. Some five hundred major leaguers traded in baseball uniforms for service uniforms, and their absence was keenly felt. The wartime version of the game pitted "the tall men against the fat men at the company picnic," in Frank Graham's matchless description of baseball from 1943–45, and the public was starving for the greats to get back on the field. Soldiers denied Americana they had taken for granted returned home to revel in the simple pleasures, which often included a cold one on a warm summer day at the ballpark.

Ted Williams, Stan Musial, Joe and Dom DiMaggio, Bob Feller, Enos Slaughter, Pete Reiser—the varsity was back in action in '46, and the fans were back too, in droves. Attendance figures skyrocketed. The per-team average leapt an incredible 71 percent, from roughly 675,000 to 1.7 million paid bums in seats. Minor league baseball set attendance records across the country. Even with disposable income at a premium, the populace found its way into ballparks in every nook and cranny of the nation.

The season they witnessed in 1946 would be one of the most exciting ever played, featuring a breathless pennant race that wouldn't be decided until the first-ever playoff series broke the National League tie, and a historic World Series that pitted the two league MVPs against each other—one that would come down to the final game and a mad dash around the bases that may (or may not) have been aided by an epochal gaffe.

MacPhail realized that fans would be coming to Yankee Stadium in unheard-of numbers, and he endeavored to combine the sport's mass appeal as an inexpensive form of unscripted entertainment with the promise of something extra for those willing to pay for it. MacPhail had turned the fortunes of struggling franchises in Cincinnati and Brooklyn. Now that he was playing the palace, the riches were really going to tumble in, especially when he raised ticket prices before the season. He employed any number of methods to get more people passing through the gates, and he became the first owner to regularly employ air travel, at first to get the team playing more profitable exhibition games, then to ease travel costs, both financial and physical.

At the same time, the Yankees signature superstar, Joe DiMaggio, was being paid the exact same $43,750 he had received before he left for the service after the 1942 season. His brother, Dominic, assumed the war had terminated his contract with the Boston Red Sox, only to rudely discover otherwise—he too was expected to simply pick up where he had left off, salary-wise. It was inequity (and outside agitators tempting them with the promise of something better) that would kindle the flame of conflict between players and management. As the *Sporting News* put it, baseball was "passing through social upheaval, along with bread baking, wheat growing, coal mining, railroading, and meat production." The game was a deep part of the national fabric. As such, the wrenching changes America went through were intertwined with the pastime. As Dave Egan wrote in the *Boston Herald,* "It is getting so lately that a sports columnist who does not write about trade unionism and set himself up as an authority on national and international affairs is considered nothing but a punk."

Despite the difficulties the new peace brought, on the horizon was a golden age, both for the country and baseball. *Life* saw a people "probing relentlessly for the outlines of a more amiable way of life. It is conceivable that a great many Americans never expect to work quite so hard again in the drab routine of mass production." Industry was retooling from its wartime footing to advance breakthroughs wrought by the war. Airplane plants were churning out passenger craft powered by jet engines, automobile manufacturers swapping out jeeps for fancy roadsters. The giant munitions plant in Muscle Shoals, Alabama, was reusing all the ammonium nitrate on hand to generate massive quantities of chemical fertilizer, which greatly advanced food production on American farms.

Baseball was part of that new vision of the future too, and the tension of 1946 between management and labor was pure power dynamics. Many ballplayers had seen action during the war, and many more had seen its effects. They returned with a new perspective on life—both in terms of its value and in terms of their place in it. They had seen firsthand how existence could be short, and cruel. That put a premium on maximizing their earning potential today, while they could, especially with interest in their game so high.

But things weren't so simple. The moguls had wielded complete control over the players before and during the war, and had gotten rather used to things just the way they were. They would be damned if the fight for the world's freedom resulted in more of it for baseball players. And when push came to shove, while the times may have been ready for the players, the players weren't quite ready for the times.

Chapter 1
THE "MATURE TED WILLIAMS"

THE WAR WAS over, but there were nothing but jitters among the hordes assembled for spring training in camps across Florida. The Sunshine State hosted teams for the first time since 1942—wartime travel restrictions had kept matters close to home the three previous springs. Never had so many been after so few jobs. Nobody felt safe. For every position on every team, it seemed, there were half a dozen guys with a shot at the gig.

Among the hopefuls were the established players who had been away two or three years and wondered if they still had the skills required for the majors. There were all the rookies who were on the cusp of the show when they'd been called up to the service rather than the bigs. And there were the wartime replacements who were out to prove they belonged in the postwar game. The hustle and double-timing on the spring fields was noticeable. "In the old days," wrote *Time,* "if a player got his sweat shirt damp by working too hard, it usually took him a leisurely hour in the clubhouse to change; now the men were back on the field in five minutes."

As if the times weren't strange enough, there too was the most irascible diva in baseball—"the skinny slugger with the cucumber build and the red pepper personality," as United Press described him once—all smiles and handshakes down in Sarasota, where the Boston Red Sox held spring training.

The 1946 season would be, in many ways, defined by Ted Williams. His ability to return to the major leagues after three long years away from the game was the sport's number one talking point that spring. Once the season began, every high and low moment the "Splendid Splinter" encountered would be refracted through the mirror of his wartime experience, his emotional maturity (or his inexplicable lack thereof) attributed to the time spent in the service of his country.

Ted had gone through a PR nightmare over his draft status in 1942. Before the season, he had claimed he was the sole supporter of his divorced mother in San Diego, which got him reclassified from 1-A status. For that, the press painted him as an unpatriotic coward, hounding him relentlessly, and the fans in Boston let their displeasure be known, as did Quaker Oats, which pulled its $4,000 endorsement contract. Finally, Williams enlisted in May, though he wouldn't have to report until the end of the '42 season. In retrospect, the treatment seems harsh, even by the standards of a Boston press corps and fan base that treated Ted as its whipping boy. But the war was going against the Allies on all fronts in 1942, and the picture of a star ballplayer refusing immediate service was bad optics. This was especially true when compared to the early enlistments of stars like Hank Greenberg and Bob Feller.

When Williams reported in the fall for duty with the navy ("my gal thinks I look sweet in Navy blue" was how he explained his choice of branch), he wanted to fly. Charles Lindbergh had spent much of his early days on the forefront of aviation in San Diego and he was Ted's first hero. Williams knew the mathematics of the job would be a challenge, but he preferred that to some "soft berth teaching gymnastics." Attacking the fine art of combat flying as he had the demanding ritual of hitting a baseball, he excelled, earning a 3.85 GPA in pilot training classes and working his way up to instructor status.

"He made the transition from civilian life to the service amazingly well," said fellow navy serviceman and ballplayer Johnny Sain, a pitcher for the crosstown Boston Braves, after the war. "What I noted chiefly about him as an airman was that he was never satisfied with himself. Ted was always trying to improve his technique. I imagine that is what makes him such a great hitter."

He got his wings as a marine aviator on May 2, 1944, and married "his gal," Doris Soule, the same day. He spent the war teaching newbies how to master the SNJ, the main navy training warplane. "Ted could make a plane and its six machine guns play like a symphony orchestra," remembered fellow aviator and Red Sox teammate Johnny Pesky. Williams had over a thousand hours in the air by then, and though he was en route to the Pacific when the Japanese surrendered, he would see plenty of combat a few years later when he left baseball for a second time to fly missions over Korea.

Williams played a little ball during his time away from the majors. He hit a bit with the Chapel Hill "Cloudbusters" while training in North Carolina (a fellow trainee named George H. W. Bush saw him play there). He and Babe Ruth took part in exhibitions at Fenway to raise money for the war effort. And he played on the Hawaiian Islands while awaiting combat orders that never came. Howard Alley, a fellow navy aviator based at Pearl Harbor, remembered that Williams was "aloof" while there, and certainly that had been his prewar reputation.

When it came time to return to his peacetime vocation, the self-described "Best Damn Hitter That Ever Lived" was worried that the cruddy wartime baseball itself would affect his hitting. He could tell, even from afar, that the ball being used in the major leagues while war raged was terrible for hitting, mainly due to the ersatz rubber used in the core. The real thing was too valuable to go to baseballs, but the replacement was dead. "Wouldn't it be something to grab the East Indies back from the Japs and get that good rubber again?" he mused in 1943. "Give the 'balata' [the name of the substitute ball] to the Japs, I say."

The East Indies were back in friendly hands, but the rubber was still scarce. And, as spring training began in Sarasota, Williams was walking into a great unknown. Like Muhammad Ali a generation later, Ted was a consummate athlete who had missed several years of prime performance due to war, albeit for far different reasons than Ali. As great a hitter as Ted was, would he really be able to simply stroll back into a ballpark and start walloping major league pitching once again?

Why, yes, as it turned out. He sure as hell could. On his very first swing in Sarasota, he launched a towering home run to right field. Still, during the spring, Williams wasn't convinced of his ability to regain his prewar excellence. "My legs are in bad shape and my arm is still sore," he complained to the *Sporting News.* "It stands to reason a fellow is not going to improve by remaining out of the game for three years. And now I come back, and I'm hitting against pitchers I've never seen before, and I don't know what they throw." But confidence bordering on arrogance was a key part of his athletic makeup; inwardly, Ted knew he'd always be able to hit. As such, Williams placed a series of bets regarding his 1946 performance with a buddy on the Tigers, Dick Wakefield. Commissioner Happy Chandler ordered the players to call off the wagers, but the bets spoke to Williams's faith in his ability to rake.

Before Ted reported to camp, a friend had dared Williams to show up at the ballpark in street clothes and demand a chance to try out. He responded, "No, they'd say I was screwy again," and said it would be all dignity from there on out.

This was the "Mature Williams," a grown man now supposedly made whole by his wartime experience, even though he hadn't faced live fire. The spring was free of the usual Teddy Tempest—the cruel and foul language directed at fans, the bat tossing when he didn't get a hit, and the endless battling with his foes in the press, the "human crows who perch on the rim of the ballpark and make typographical errors," as Austen Lake of the *Boston American* described his fellow writers, as Ted saw them. He ran hard after every fly ball, and accepted making outs at the plate with equanimity. His teammates orbited him, sucked in by his personable gravity. The writers were astounded—and, it should be noted, impressed. While some wondered openly just how long this "New Ted" could possibly last, most were eager to accept the idea that Williams could be great and take pleasure in his work at the same time, that he had gone to war and emerged with a new perspective on this silly game.

The Sox were managed by Joe Cronin, a former star shortstop who had been Boston owner Tom Yawkey's prized purchase, for a then-staggering $275,000, in 1935. A towering figure in the game's history, Cronin was a longtime player-manager, leading the Washington Senators to the 1933 championship in that role, and later going on to serve as GM of the Sox and president of the American League. Cro was a popular Irishman in a Gaelic-tinged city, and admirers lavished gifts upon him for years—he received more Irish setters than he could possibly house. But the Sox underachieved on his watch, and the fans turned on him. Cronin got the "groundball jitters," becoming error-prone in the field. He started to kneel in front of grounders rather than stay on his feet, a habit that came to be called the "$275,000 Squat." He became a subject of derision. "If you're gonna miss 'em, miss 'em like a big leaguer!" was the catcall from fans and enemy dugouts. His jovial personality took a maudlin turn. Cro's wife once showed a visitor around their house. "This is Joe's Crying Room," she said, pointing to a bedroom. "He's used it a lot this summer."

But Yawkey worshipped Cronin, and felt vested in him, so he kept him on as manager after the player part of the hyphenate fell away. In that role, too, he had been subpar. "His big chin was a breakwater for complaint," wrote Harold Kaese in the *Saturday Evening Post*. It was a line from a long piece entitled "What's the Matter with the Red Sox?," a several-thousand-word opus that exploded upon the placidity of spring training like a hand grenade.

Kaese was a beat reporter for the *Boston Globe,* and he spent most of his time baiting Williams, Cronin, and Yawkey for good copy. Williams pointed to a line Kaese wrote as the sparking incident for his poor relationship with the Boston writers. In 1939, Ted's parents had separated, and he decided not to go home to San Diego after the season, as it would have been rather painful. He sent his mother a large chunk of his paycheck and stayed in Boston. The next time Williams displeased Kaese in some manner, the *Globe* reporter wrote, "Well, what do you expect from a guy who won't even go see his mother in the off season."

In the *Saturday Evening Post,* Kaese unloaded on the whole organization, blaming Yawkey for spending money recklessly and unwisely. "He is stubborn, wealthy, and loyal," Kaese wrote. He also painted a memorable portrait of Cronin as an overmatched skipper who couldn't make the transition to the dugout. He was what we would call today a "player's manager"—his team loved him, but he was seen as missing the icy unfriendliness thought necessary to win in pro sports. Kaese quoted the great former Bosox slugger Jimmie Foxx as saying Cronin didn't know what he was doing, a message that put Cro squarely on the hot seat, especially with the stars back in the fold.

Cro was from San Francisco and was thought to favor West Coasters when making his lineup. With Williams and his center fielder, Dom DiMaggio, it was an excusable bias. Dommie, aka "the Little Professor," was charming and bubbly, a far cry from his famously remote older brother.

A catchy song parody of the day went—

> *Who's better than his brother Joe?*
> *Dom-i-nic Di-Mag-gi-o*

—and while that may not have been accurate, Dommie certainly wasn't coasting by on his surname. An excellent fielder and the fastest player on the team, DiMaggio was a key piston in the Sox engine.

Dommie was the youngest of nine DiMaggios born to Giuseppe and Rosalie, and like his brothers Joe and Vince, Dom gravitated toward baseball over the protests of his fisherman father, an immigrant who thought the game frivolous. They grew up in the North Beach section of San Francisco, with the whiff of the Pacific filling their nostrils when the strong winds off the bay ceased. Dom was a wee lad, myopic and brainy enough to fancy a career in chemical engineering before the crack of the bat turned his head. He starred as a pitcher and shortstop at Galileo High School, and was snapped up by the San Francisco Seals, the Pacific Coast League team that had launched his brothers to the majors.

Dommie quieted the cynics who felt he had been signed for his name alone by excelling in the PCL, despite the thick glasses he wore on the field. He was the MVP of the league in 1939. The Red Sox bought him for $75,000 after the season. DiMaggio was an All-Star by his second season, having earned the nickname "the Little Professor" for his studious mien and his 168 pounds (at 5'9"). The youngest DiMaggio had an exceptional 1942 campaign, despite the fact that his attention was mainly focused on gaining entry into the service. "I had to fight my way into the Navy," said DiMaggio. "They rejected me because of my eyesight, and for the longest time, I told them I wanted to be in the Navy. I was not about to sit out the war." He was 4-F, but through persistent wheedling managed to enlist despite his classification. The navy wouldn't put Dom in harm's way, but recognized his value in terms of propaganda and baseball. He played for the powerful Norfolk Naval Training Station nine, as well as on foreign diamonds across the Pacific.

DiMaggio was a potent hitter, but it was in center field that he truly shined, covering huge swaths of terrain with the same effortless grace as Joe, with an even stronger arm. He played extremely shallow, causing enemy fans to snicker when a liner was smacked over his head. But Dommie would race toward a predetermined spot on the grass, turn his head, and uncannily snare the ball at shoulder level. Unlike most outfielders, Dom would crouch sideways before the pitch, "with my left foot facing the plate and my right foot parallel to the center field," he explained to *Baseball Digest,* adopting a stance that resembled a runner anticipating the starter's pistol. It gave him an advantage getting to bloop hits and grounders as well as balls hit over his head. "I've never seen anybody else do that before or since," said Charlie Silvera, a catcher on the Yankees in the 1940s and '50s. "He played more like an infielder in the outfield," remembered Sox second baseman Bobby Doerr.

Williams was more than happy to let the swift gloveman to his left handle the majority of the balls hit their way. "The wolves in left field were always yelling about how Dom was playing his position and mine," Ted wrote in his memoir, *My Turn at Bat.* He left little doubt about how he regarded his outfield neighbor when it came time to pen a foreword for Dom's own memoir, *Real Grass, Real Heroes.* "There is no finer person on earth than Dom DiMaggio," Ted wrote.

Dom's relationship with the game's other moody superstar was more fraught. He and Joe alternated brotherly love with sibling rivalry, and Dom struggled to escape the Yankee Clipper's considerable shadow. "It's been a struggle all my life. . . . I was always Joe's kid brother," he admitted to the *Globe,* and he refused to let his two sons get into baseball, to spare them the comparisons to their uncle. But later in life, long after the spotlight faded, Dom became a fierce protector of his brother.

Two other key members of the Sox hailed from the left coast: Oregonian shortstop Johnny Pesky and second baseman Bobby Doerr of California. "Doerr, not Williams, is the key to the Boston offense," opined no less an expert on the game than Babe Ruth, and indeed, Doerr was the best combination of batting average and power at his position in the game. Pesky was just that, a slap hitter who excelled at getting on base and scoring runs.

Third base, catcher, and right field would be platoon positions, as Cronin had several players of varying abilities to fill those slots. The lack of definition at so many positions was the usual reason cited by prognosticators who picked Boston to finish below perennial favorite New York and Detroit in the standings. In Sarasota, Cronin himself joked about heading over to nearby Ringling Brothers to see if they had trained seals he could use in right and behind the plate.

The other regular was a newcomer to Boston, "part first baseman, part Cherokee" Rudy York. He had come over from the Tigers with a reputation for hitting the ball nine miles, and hitting the bottle just as hard. York heard all manner of un-PC cracks from fans and rival players, even in the mainstream press. "York reputedly has been heap big troublesome when heap full of fire water down through the years, but he is one of Boston's most highly esteemed citizens," was Lawton Carver of the International News Service's idea of a compliment.

York managed to miss military service thanks to good fortune and bad knees. He was one of the baker's dozen of players to appear in the opening-day lineup for each of the war years. York had a deep gravelly voice, as if he were sick all the time. When he spoke in the clubhouse, that low timbre gave his message greater impact.

York would be an important veteran voice in Boston, as well as another big bat, though he could be his own worst enemy. As if to seek out the danger that he had avoided during the war, York had a terrible habit of getting soused and falling asleep holding lit cigarettes, thus starting blazes in hotel rooms. As Sox reserve Eddie Pellagrini put it, "One year with Detroit [York] led the league in homers and RBIs. One year with us he led the league in fires."

Boston's pitching staff was considered the team's weak link. Dave "Boo" Ferriss had won twenty-five games in 1945, but that was written off as considerably aided by the weak wartime competition. Only twenty-four, he was still a rather unknown commodity, though he had just signed to an endorsement contract with Gillette—"Use Gillette Blue Blades—5 for 25 cents," he advised shavers across the country. Tex Hughson, a big rawboned slab of beef, had also dominated wartime hitters, then missed the 1945 season when the army changed its policy to begin calling up fathers over the age of twenty-five. He was a nonstop talker, with a country patois that bordered on the inscrutable. Generally, Tex worked blue, favoring constructions like, "He couldn't look more like you if you had pulled him out of your asshole with a chain."

Mickey Harris, Joe Dobson, and Jim Bagby filled out the staff. They would be backed up in the bullpen by a tall, lanky pitcher, whose first words upon arriving in Sarasota were, "Which way is right field? I've been away so long that I've almost forgotten."

Earl Johnson had landed at Normandy with the 30th Infantry Division and fought across Fortress Europe. "We were a replacement unit," Johnson told the *Providence Journal* after he returned from the war. "The wreckage [on Omaha Beach] was still there, the burned-out tanks and half-sunken ships and assault boats that were just so much twisted steel." Johnson was a rifle platoon sergeant, and on several occasions, he came across scores of dead bodies, from both sides of the fight. He also witnessed the immediate aftermath of the infamous Malmedy Massacre in Belgium, where the Nazis executed nearly a hundred American prisoners of war during the Battle of the Bulge.

Johnson received a Bronze Star for retrieving a truck filled with vital radio equipment back from enemy territory, and got clusters added to it when he hopped aboard a tank, drove through a minefield, and wiped out a German machine gun unit that had his men pinned down. Johnson added the Silver Star for bravery under fire during the Battle of the Bulge. But his war stories were mostly self-deprecating. He liked to tell a story about a time his unit was under attack from German armor. He tossed a couple of hand grenades, which missed badly. A kid in his platoon who had never so much as held a baseball tried next and scored a direct hit, destroying the in-nards of a German tank. "If only I had that kid's control," he would say wistfully.

To the *Providence Journal,* Johnson added, "I'm proud that I served my country, but prouder still to have made it home alive. What General Patton said is true: war isn't about dying for your country; it's about making the other poor, dumb bastard die for his country. I was one of the lucky dumb bastards who made it home safely."

Johnson was given the job of bullpen fireman, ready to leap in whenever the starter got in trouble. He figured to be a busy man.

On April 12, four days before the season began, a pitcher named Clem "Icicles" Dreisewerd reported to the Sox after a brief stint in the navy. Thus, Boston became the last AL team to "clear its service list," or have all its players (thirty at the high-water mark, well below the forty-four of the A's or forty-two of the Yankees and Tigers) re-turned from service and playing ball for the organization. It was the "first time in five seasons the American League did not have players farmed out to Uncle Sam," according to the Associated Press.

But two AL teams, Washington and Philadelphia, could never fully clear their service lists. The only two major leaguers to die in combat in World War II represented those clubs.

Chapter 2
THE FALLEN

ELMER GEDEON WASN'T really supposed to be in the pilot's seat. He was the operations officer for the 394th Bomb Group, the "Bridge Busters," and thus, his duties kept him mainly deskbound, in England, planning the attacks his group of B-26 bombers would carry out on bridges in Germany and Occupied France. But Captain Gedeon wanted to maintain flying proficiency, and he didn't like the idea that he planned missions that others would fly. So, on April 20, 1944, the twenty-seven-year-old from Cleveland took to the air from Boreham Field in Chesterfield, England. The destination was a construction site in the woods outside Esquerdes, France, near the country's southwest coast. The target was a launchpad for the V-1 rocket, aka the "Buzz Bomb," the first of Hitler's terror weapons that would be launched against England in the coming months. Elmer's B-26 and thirty-five other Marauders were being sent to destroy the area, part of a concerted effort to attack V-1 launch sites, known collectively as "Operation Crossbow."

Gedeon had been a three-sport star at the University of Michigan, one of the best athletes to grace the playing fields of Ann Arbor in the 1930s. He was ticketed for the 1940 Olympics in track and field, but the Summer Games, slated for Tokyo, were canceled. Elmer turned to baseball instead and signed with the Washington Senators. He got 17 plate appearances in 1939, with 3 singles, a single run, and 1 RBI in five games. Elmer spent the 1940 season in the minors and was drafted in January 1941, almost a year before Pearl Harbor.

He transferred to the Army Air Corps in October, barely scraping under the two-hundred-pound weight limit for fliers. Elmer was assigned to bombers, and he began flight training in North Carolina in 1942. One August morning, Elmer was the navigator aboard a B-25 that had difficulty lifting off. The plane scraped the pine trees at the end of the runway and plunged into a nearby swamp. Suddenly, the aircraft burst into flames. Elmer groped desperately at his restraints, managing to free himself and crawl out, despite three broken ribs.

As he gasped at the fetid swamp air, Elmer heard a call from inside the plane. It was crewmate and friend Corporal John Rarrat, who had broken his leg and was unable to move. Without hesitation, Elmer went back into the burning wreckage and pulled Rarrat free. Sadly, his bravery was for naught—Rarrat died from his injuries, as did two others from the flight. Gedeon spent twelve weeks in a hospital in Raleigh, recovering from severe burns, some of which required skin grafts.

Elmer lost fifty pounds while recovering, got a medal, and returned to the air. He told his cousin afterward, "I had my accident. It's going to be good flying from now on."

Elmer was assigned to the 394th Bomb Group and given a new bomber to master—the B-26 Marauder. Its unfortunate nickname, "The Widowmaker," gives some idea of the dangers in flying the plane. Its wings were so short and heavily laden by engines that it was also called the "Flying Prostitute," as it had no visible means of support. Gedeon and the 394th's ladies of the evening arrived in England in February 1944.

One of Gedeon's duties as operations officer was to assign crews to planes, so it was easy to put himself in the pilot's seat for the sortie against the V-1 site, in charge of six other crewmen. The flight lifted off in a hazy dusk. Elmer assumed the number two position in the flight, behind the leader as they formed up over the English Channel.

At around 7:30 p.m., the bombers arrived over the target site and encountered intense—and accurate—antiaircraft fire. Gedeon's Marauder had just dropped its bombs (most of which were determined to have missed the target) when flak ripped through the undercarriage. The plane burst into flames.

Normal procedure called for the crew to bail out through the bomb bay doors, but they wouldn't open. So the crew rushed forward to the cockpit to eject through the hatches above Elmer and his copilot, James Taaffe. Taaffe noticed that Gedeon was motionless, slumped forward over his controls. His clothes on fire, Taaffe had no time to check on Elmer, who may have been already dead, though Taaffe speculated later that he might have gone into shock, overcome by the trauma of once again being in a burning bomber.

Taaffe bailed out, blacked out, and came to on the ground, where he was surrounded by German soldiers. He exchanged fire for several hours before surrendering. After thirteen months as a prisoner of war, he was set free as the Allies overran his prison camp.

In the prison, Taaffe was told by his captors that his six other crewmates, including Gedeon, were dead.

Elmer Gedeon is buried in Arlington National Cemetery.

They had already been on Iwo Jima, as hellish a stretch of ground as existed in all of World War II, for fifteen days. Eleven days earlier, he had watched as the American flag was raised on the summit of Mount Suribachi, an image that stirred the world when the photograph of the moment was published.

But Harry O'Neill, once of the Philadelphia A's and now a platoon commander of the Regimental Weapons Company, 25th Marine Regiment, was still fighting a vicious, uncompromising enemy. The Japanese had forgone a standard defense of the volcanic island in favor of going underground, blasting an extraordinary system of tunnels, trenches, and gun positions out of the rock. Upon landing on the black sand beach, O'Neill and his fellow marines were on the far right flank of the assault, exposed to murderous fire from the front and sides. Now, they were slogging their way inland on an offensive, burning and shooting the Japanese out of their caves. It was nasty, incredibly dangerous work. The Japanese warrior code of Bushido held that surrender was not to be considered. So the remainder of the eighteen thousand Nipponese garrisoned at Iwo were fighting to the end. Only 216 would be captured alive—the rest were dead, many of them suicides.

O'Neill was no stranger to the epic savagery of the Pacific Theater. He had enlisted in the US Marines after Pearl Harbor, like so many of his fellow citizens. In the years of combat that followed, O'Neill had waded ashore and fought the Japanese at Kwajalein, Saipan, and Tinian. He had been wounded at Saipan when he caught shrapnel in the shoulder, getting a month at a San Francisco hospital for his trouble. It was nothing that would keep him from throwing out runners trying to steal on him when he got back home.

Harry Mink O'Neill was born in Philadelphia in 1917. He was a gifted athlete and went on to be one of the greatest sports stars ever at Gettysburg College. He led the school to Eastern Pennsylvania Intercollegiate championships in baseball, football, and basketball.

After graduation, a bidding war for his services broke out between the Washington Senators and his hometown Philadelphia A's. The grizzled Philly manager, Connie Mack, won out with an offer of $500 a month. O'Neill signed in June 1939. On July 23, the moribund A's, en route to finishing 51½ games behind the Yankees, were playing Detroit on a sweltering afternoon in the Motor City. The Tigers were winning 16–3. The game couldn't end soon enough. In the seventh inning, Mack gave starting catcher Frankie Hayes the rest of the day off and sent Harry in. Harry caught the final two innings but never got a chance to hit.

It was Harry's only game in the big leagues.

He spent the next two seasons in the minors, first with Allentown and then Harrisburg. He was still in Connie Mack's plans, but had taken a teaching and coaching job at Upper Darby Junior High School, just in case. Basketball season had just begun when Pearl Harbor was attacked.

On March 6, 1945, First Lieutenant O'Neill and his company were slugging their way across a narrow valley pockmarked by caves and small openings in the rock wall. It was a terribly exposed place, and sniper fire soon ravaged the company. O'Neill's men opened up with heavy machine guns and flamethrowers. One by one, the Japanese were flushed from their hiding spots and executed, or buried in place by explosives, or doused with flame and left to burn. But there were still plenty of the enemy about, well armed with mortars and machine guns.

The assault bogged down multiple times throughout the day, and by early evening, the fighting still raged near the infamous "Turkey Knob" area of the Japanese defenses. O'Neill stood next to a fellow marine, PFC James Kontes, in a deep crater that seemed to provide some cover. "We were standing shoulder to shoulder," Kontes recounted to the *Bucks County Courier Times* in 2009. "Harry was on my left. We were looking out at the terrain in front of us. And this shot came out of nowhere." The sniper's bullet pierced O'Neill's throat and exited out his neck. His spinal cord was severed. He died instantly.

"I think the guy must have been in a tree or something," said Kontes. "That was their favorite place to shoot from. They got Harry. They took him out because he was taller. He didn't suffer."

Harry's wife and high school sweetheart, Ethel Mackay O'Neill, wasn't told of Harry's death in action for a month. A few weeks later, his sister, Susanna, wrote a letter to the athletic department at Gettysburg College, where Harry had been larger than life. "We are trying to keep our courage up, as Harry would want us to do," she wrote. "But our hearts are very sad and as the days go on it seems to be getting worse. Harry was always so full of life, that it seems hard to think he is gone. But God knows best and perhaps someday, we will understand why all this sacrifice of so many fine young men."

Like Archibald "Moonlight" Graham, Harry O'Neill played in but a single game without coming to bat, but unlike Graham, O'Neill wasn't immortalized in print or on film. In 1905, the Japanese fleet destroyed a Russian armada at the Battle of Tsushima Strait. The naval victory emboldened the secretive, insular island nation to embark down a decades-long path of militarism, one that was about to reach a sudden, violent conclusion. That same year, Graham played half an inning in the outfield as a defensive replacement with John McGraw's New York Giants. He then quit the game, that half inning his sole contribution to baseball. He never came to bat or threw a pitch.

Moonlight became legendary as a character in the novel *Shoeless Joe,* by W. P. Kinsella, and the resulting film, *Field of Dreams,* starring Burt Lancaster as the ballplayer-turned–country doctor. Moonlight's poignant story of tasting the fantasy held by millions of American boys, to hit or pitch in the major leagues, yet being denied after that single swallow, hits a delicate nerve with anyone who dares to pursue his dearest aspirations.

Harry O'Neill was one of those boys. And because of O'Neill, Gedeon, and so many others like them, future generations of American boys were able to chase that same dream.

Chapter 3
KIDNAPPING THE KAISER AND OTHER ADVENTURES

ONCE, MUCH EARLIER, Larry MacPhail had a dream too, one of his first—he thought he could kidnap Kaiser Wilhelm II.

For any other man, that would have been a crazy fantasy. But the Roaring Redhead had shown an uncanny ability throughout his life to do exactly what he set out to do, regardless of difficulty.

He was a man who contained multitudes; a success who had run three major league franchises and a "MacPhailure" who left all three in disgrace; an outstanding judge of talent and a master showman but also a drunken bully and brawler. In his lifetime, he made a living as a church organist, an attorney, a department store executive, an automobile dealer, a banker, a building contractor, a Big Ten football referee, a baseball impresario, and a racing-stable proprietor. He was a knowledgeable musician and a first-rate amateur chef. And, of course, he was an army officer with a sterling record in two world wars.

Mac had been an artillery captain during the First World War, fighting the Hun in France. Appalled that Wilhelm II (a bombastic, hateful, mustachioed German leader whose dark place in history has been obscured by another bombastic, hateful, mustachioed German leader) had been given asylum after the armistice and allowed to live in Holland, MacPhail conjured an audacious plan to storm the Kaiser's office and capture him, ostensibly to take him to trial for war crimes. Incredibly, Mac and his squad of eight men got into Wilhelm's inner sanctum, but the deposed leader was not in. MacPhail swiped Wilhelm's monogrammed ashtray as a keepsake and escaped the court-martial that seemed sure to follow.

A quarter-century later, the Roaring Redhead was back in the service. While he saw combat in the Great War, Mac only served as a PR man in the Good War, which was fortunate, as he was fifty-two years old at the time he enlisted.

MacPhail needed to save his strength, for after the war, he would return to fighting against his greatest enemy—Branch Rickey. MacPhail and Rickey had a long history together—they were practically family. And, as with many family members, the years had torn them asunder.

MacPhail's first foray into baseball was owning a minor league team in Columbus, Ohio, which he sold to the Cardinals under Rickey's stewardship in 1931. Recognizing a fellow unorthodox genius, Branch would powwow over new ideas all the time with Mac, likewise a University of Michigan Wolverine. Two of MacPhail's pet projects, night baseball and air travel, were actually given soft opens in Columbus in the early 1930s. Later, Mac would bring both to the majors. He also invented the batting helmet, tried yellow baseballs ("stitched lemons") to make the game easier to follow, pioneered radio broadcasts in New York, thought up Old-Timers' Day, and even placed a microphone at home plate so fans could hear the arguments with umpires (an experiment that lasted exactly one game).

But an alcohol-fueled incident would terminate Mac's stay in Columbus and permanently stain his relationship with Rickey. Mac was closing down a hotel bar with the manager of the inn when drunken words were exchanged. Mac responded to some perceived insult by hammering on the doors of his players' rooms and demanding they all pack up and move to the hotel across the street, which they did in the wee hours of the night. Rickey, embarrassed, persuaded Cards owner Sam Breadon to fire MacPhail.

But Mac landed on his feet, taking over a destitute Cincinnati

Reds franchise and turning it around, at least at the box office. His introduction of night baseball to the majors in 1935 helped mightily. But a few years later, the dark shadows reemerged. Mac got sauced and ended up wrestling at a board meeting with none other than Powel Crosley Jr., the owner of the Reds and the man for whom the team's stadium was named. Unsurprisingly, Mac lost that gig too. But like many a troubled but talented ballplayer over the years, he was given yet another chance, this time with Brooklyn, another laughingstock. As the Reds had been, the Dodgers were in financial ruin when a bank, in this case Brooklyn Trust, approached MacPhail. The redhead had already earned a reputation as a quick-turnaround artist. "Every club I ever had," he once said, "I had for a bank; it was always a down club, a club that was in the sheriff's hands. My job has always been to get some bank out of the baseball business. I've always worked for a God-damn bank!"

Mac spiffed up Ebbets Field as his first step toward legitimacy, painting the old park, resodding the grass and adding seats, and making the ushers wear flashy green-and-gold uniforms; he hired a drillmaster to train them to stay in step. He also hired Babe Ruth as a coach to goose attendance.

Brooklyn's love affair with baseball and the sui generis scene at Ebbets Field during the 1940s and '50s date back to MacPhail's efforts to popularize the game in the borough. Winning helped, of course—Mac took over in 1938, and by 1941, the Dodgers had won the pennant. A year later, he was gone, his endless drama causing too much tsuris for the Dodgers board of directors. He was replaced at the helm of the Bums by—wait for it—Branch Rickey. Rickey promised to win with class and decency in Flatbush, a flat rebuke of his old protégé's boorishness. One of Rickey's new colleagues was his son, Branch Jr.—hired by MacPhail as a scouting director in a sign that underneath the bluster, he still cared for his mentor.

Mac's peripatetic career was due in the main to drink. As one writer described MacPhail, "He was an impossible man—loud, belligerent, unsteady, alcoholic. With no drinks he was brilliant; with one he was a genius. With two he was insane. Rarely did he stop at two." Red Barber owed his Hall of Fame broadcasting career to MacPhail, who first hired him in Cincy and brought Red to Brooklyn. Even he would duck Mac when the booze came out. "From then on I was always late for an appointment," Barber said. MacPhail's eyes were watery, and his freckled face blotched with red, sure signs of alcohol use and abuse.

Mac would drunkenly fire employees on a regular basis, only to rehire them in tears when he sobered up, none more often than Leo Durocher, whom Mac hired in a fit of brilliance to manage the Dodgers upon taking over the team. "There is no question in my mind but that Larry was a genius," Leo recollected. "There is a thin line between genius and insanity, and in Larry's case it was sometimes so thin that you could see him drifting back and forth." MacPhail once punched a newspaperman, then hired him to run PR for his team. He would thump people on the arm and chest to make his point, leaning in close and exhaling Scottish mist in their faces. He loved opera, and his life resembled a *tragédie en musique,* with his many successes offset by his volatile temper and inability to handle his liquor.

Both of Mac's sons, Lee and Bill, were in the navy, and when war broke out, Larry felt a call to duty in large part because of them. He had hardly been a model parent—when Bill was asked once to describe his father as a parent in one word, he responded, "miscast"—but now Mac felt it would draw him closer to his fighting children if he donned a uniform once more, beginning in late 1942. MacPhail's role in the army was as special assistant to Undersecretary of War Robert Patterson. Mainly, it meant writing letters and giving speeches exhorting the troops.

His prose was rather purple, as evinced by a letter he wrote for a wartime periodical called *Brief Items* describing the fight ahead:

The bunch you'll be stacked up against have as much conception of sportsmanship as the sons of rattlesnakes who mass-married a pack of black widow spiders. If they can find a way to use rusty razor blades instead of spikes they'll have them on their shoes for tomorrow's game. Every sack is 'booby-trapped' and every bean ball that skins your kisser didn't get there by accident—it was tossed that way, son, and don't ever forget it.

"I doubt I'll ever hold another job in baseball," Mac said upon entering the service, but it was the army that midwifed his return to the game. In late 1944, the estate of the recently departed owner of the Yankees, Colonel Jacob Ruppert, was looking to sell the team, and through bluff and bluster, and while touring the battlegrounds of France, Lt. Colonel MacPhail arranged to buy it. Of course, he didn't have nearly the cash to do so. He returned to New York to sign some papers in early 1945 and, naturally, stopped in at a corner watering hole—in this case, the 21 Club—to ponder his next move.

While Mac worked his way across the top shelf, through the saloon door walked a man in a marine uniform. He was Dan Topping, heir to a tin fortune and owner of the Brooklyn Dodgers—the National Football League version. He knew Mac from their joint use of Ebbets Field and had gotten to know him better during the war. MacPhail convinced Topping over drinks to help finance the purchase of the Yankees, and they subsequently recruited an even more liquid (in cash, not spirits) partner, Del Webb, a construction magnate from Arizona who built airfields for the army. Topping and Webb put up the dough (approximately $3 million), and Mac became the man in charge of the filet mignon of franchises—for next to no money down.

It was quite a coup. And now that he was in charge, Mac intended to fulfill the dream he had when he first heard the Yankees were for sale.

He would remake the team in his own image, for better or worse.

★ ★ ★

While MacPhail was pulling off his coup de main, his soon-to-be star player lay on a cot in Hawaii, his stomach in knots, his baseball career and marriage withering before his eyes.

Joe DiMaggio's war was spent raging against not the Japanese or the Nazis but the injustice of missing out on prime earning years. Even before he was called up, he was forced to walk a PR tightrope similar to the one Williams had. After Joe's astonishing fifty-six-game hitting streak in 1941, the Yankees incredibly didn't offer him a raise on his $37,500 salary. It was a slap in the face, couched in cynical patriotism (*You're lucky to be playing ball at all, Joe*). DiMaggio couldn't put up much of a squawk—after all, there was a war on (*You're going to bitch about money at a time like this?*).

DiMaggio squeezed forty-three grand and change out of the team, was jeered for most of the season, and the Yanks lost to St. Louis in the 1942 World Series. Like Williams, he realized that putting off enlistment was a losing battle, so he joined the Army Air Corps. His donning of the national uniform had a revitalizing effect on his marriage, at least for a spell. Joe was wedded to actress Dorothy Arnold, whom he had met back in '38 on the set of *Manhattan Merry-Go-Round*. They had a son together, Joe Jr., and DiMaggio's inattention to them both pulled the family apart. Dorothy had been spotted by the press journeying to Reno, quickie divorce capital of the world, before Joe was able to talk her into staying. Now, with Joe a flyboy, she suddenly was happy to play housewife in L.A. as DiMaggio went off to Santa Ana Air Base each day, mainly to drink beer and slug homers for the base team.

But come May 1944, the union had again hit the rocks, and Dorothy filed for divorce. She won a $14,000 lump payment and $150 a month in child support for Joe Jr. Days after this blow, the army sent Sergeant DiMaggio and several other top players to Hawaii. Army squared off against Navy in an ongoing series, while also playing local teams. Mostly, it was a great deal for the players—posted in paradise, no marching, plenty of privileges, and maybe a couple of hours on the diamond, at half speed. Forget combat—even compared to other rear-echelon types, it was a breeze.

But not for Joe. While Pee Wee Reese and Johnny Mize and Joe Gordon and Red Ruffing played ball in the tropical sunshine, accepted slaps on the back from wounded vets watching the games, and put away the scotch and steaks happy brass lavished upon them, DiMaggio stewed. His ex-wife was back in New York now, five thousand miles away and out at night, laughing it up at Joe's expense. Meanwhile, the Yankee Clipper was swatting ball after ball into the plumeria trees beyond the fence at Honolulu Stadium, and getting what—$50 a week for it? The fabled DiMaggio pride literally couldn't stomach the injustice.

It didn't help Joe's spirits that his parents were treated as enemies of the state. Giuseppe and Rosalie DiMaggio had come to America in 1904, but upon the outbreak of war, they were lumped in with thousands of Italian, German, and, more notoriously, Japanese immigrants, classified after Pearl Harbor as "enemy aliens" by the government. The DiMaggios were forced to carry photo identification at all times, and not allowed to travel more than five miles from North Beach without a permit. It wasn't as bad as being rounded up and tossed in Manzanar, as the local Issei and Nisei had been, but it did mean that Giuseppe couldn't ply his trade in San Francisco Bay, his boat having been seized by the government. At last, in late 1944, Rosalie became an American citizen, and a few months later Giuseppe did too.

Joe was torn up inside, an internal storm system that manifested itself as ulcers. He was in and out of the infirmary, and whether in his rack or a hospital bed, he spent most of his time totaling up the money he was missing out on making. He told his buddies he was going to stick it to the owners for the time he missed and hold out for a $25,000 raise. "Cost me three years," he'd grumble. "They're gonna pay for it." It was as if Joe was planning to send an invoice straight to Hirohito. He could still slug it—Howard Alley remembers a day Joe came out to give some tips to the swabbies and hit the first pitch he had seen in weeks miles over the center field fence, about "twice the length of the field itself." But he wanted to be compensated for his outrageous talent. "The war years never seemed to move at all," DiMaggio would rue long afterward.

In early '45, Joe used the ulcers to swing an early transfer stateside, and he was discharged by September. In that time, a miracle—he had apparently reconciled once more with Dorothy. They swanned about the Big Apple through the winter of 1945–46. DiMaggio had lost twenty pounds from the ulcers and seemed to need Dorothy for the first time. He wrote her letters and talked of a family home that would revolve around little Joey's happiness.

Uplifted, he reported for duty with the Yankees in St. Petersburg for the first time in three seasons. Immediately, MacPhail had the ball club up in the air, flying farther south, to Panama, of all places, to play exhibition games against local teams, servicemen, whatever could be drummed up. It was huge business, and DiMaggio was daily chased by Panamanian kids back to his hotel. But it was all a bit carny, beneath the dignity of the great Yankees. Joe professed to enjoy it, but privately he loathed MacPhail and his vaudeville style. Especially he hated the fact that his salary didn't increase for participating in these extra games.

The team then barnstormed its way through the South and mid-Atlantic, pulling in enormous crowds at every stop. A staggering 316,846 customers paid to watch Yankees spring games, "from Balboa to Brooklyn," shattering the old preseason record. MacPhail got an early sense of the nation's thirst for the return of big-time baseball while counting the profits, which came to about 150 grand.

DiMaggio struggled at the plate all spring, in contrast to Williams. "After you've been away from it a couple of years you have trouble," he told reporters in Panama. But, like the Splinter, the Clipper was all smiles and sunshine, making time for the fans and the press. To hear the papers tell it, the war was fought not to end tyranny but to offer Williams and DiMaggio a chance for some much-needed maturation. "Fans Just as Important as Hits to 'New' Dimaggio" read one headline. "To have dubbed prewar Joe a 'sour apple' would have been harsh but very close to the truth," wrote Joe Trimble of the *Daily News,* but this "New DiMaggio" was candy-coated. There remained a sense of calculation in his new openness. Few were as conscious of their public image. In New Orleans, kids jumped from the stands to besiege him for his signature. The local groundskeeper tried to stop them, but Joe waved him away. "I don't want them going off saying, 'DiMaggio was the kinda guy who wouldn't give an autograph,'" he explained.

Earning the extra cash from a World Series appearance was one thing that would make Joe genuinely happy, and there was every sense the Yankees would be in the 1946 Fall Classic now that DiMag was back, along with mainstays like shortstop Phil Rizzuto, second baseman Joe Gordon, and outfielders Charlie "King Kong" Keller and Tommy Henrich, who had missed a dozen seasons collectively to war. But a closer examination showed signs of fray. Two key members of the pitching staff were ancient mariners Spud Chandler, thirty-eight, and Red Ruffing, forty-one. The lineup was weak at the corner infield positions, and behind the plate, Aaron Robinson was the unlucky gent set to take over from legendary catcher Bill Dickey, who would move into a reserve role at age thirty-nine.

The Yanks were managed by the very successful, very sour Joe McCarthy. The skipper that led the late-1930s dynasty to four straight championships, and seven overall, McCarthy had accomplishments that spoke for themselves, which was fortunate, because he had little of interest to say for himself. He was respected, if not exactly beloved, by the team, though the younger players were devoted to him, mainly because of his willingness to play them—many of his colleagues shied away from the untested. He was a stout disciplinarian, squat of build, with a penchant for cigars as short and stubby as he was.

The stolid McCarthy couldn't stand the turbulent MacPhail from the first, and the feeling was mutual. Indeed, one of Mac's first moves was to try to hire Brooklyn coach Charlie Dressen to switch boroughs and manage the Yankees. Rebuffed, MacPhail steeled himself for a season of collision with McCarthy, who was noticeably hitting his ever-present scotch bottle particularly hard. That was the one thing the two men had in common.

But at least McCarthy was a known quantity. The championship favorite in the National League was beginning a new era with a rookie manager at the helm.

Chapter 4
REUNITED REDBIRDS

IN THE END, baseball meant more to Eddie Dyer than oil did.

He was a Cardinals lifer, a key cog in a top franchise. A star athlete at Rice University, Dyer was signed by Branch Rickey back in 1922, and Dyer was a pitcher for the Redbirds in the 1920s. He wasn't much in the bigs, with a lifetime record of 15–15, but he impressed Rickey with his smarts and baseball sense. Rickey hired Eddie to run the southern and southwestern minor league teams for St. Louis throughout the 1930s. Dyer was minor league manager of the year in 1942 with the Houston Buffaloes, then took over the job of running the entire minor league operation when Rickey left the Cardinals for Brooklyn in 1942.

But by 1944 he had tired of the game and hoped to make a little scratch down in Houston, his hometown. He quit the Cards to run a successful oil speculation business, and swiftly became a tycoon in both Texas tea and insurance. Dyer would quite happily have gone on being a Lone Star business mogul but for a wartime tragedy.

One of the best managers in Cardinals history was Billy Southworth. He guided the Birds to the 1942 and 1944 championships, and his career winning percentage (seven seasons in St. Louis, six in Boston) trails only Joe McCarthy. His son, Billy Jr., was in the Cardinals chain, a promising young outfielder. But then came Pearl Harbor. Billy Jr. signed up with the Army Air Corps. He flew twenty-five missions over Europe piloting a B-17 Flying Fortress, winning the Distinguished Flying Cross for his efforts.

Billy Jr. would write his dad in code, using baseball lingo to describe his wartime exploits. He named his plane "Winning Run," and on missions he wore his father's cap from the '42 season for good luck. He started a trend with that stylistic choice—bomber pilots were soon spotted wearing ball caps in their cockpits at airfields across Britain. He was a good-looking son of a buck, cutting a strikingly handsome figure in his bomber jacket. He once took a Hollywood screen test on a lark and was offered a movie contract. He also had a job waiting for him at Eddie Rickenbacker's fledgling aviation outfit, Eastern Airlines, when the war ended, if he wanted it. It was all pointed upward for young Billy.

Then on February 15, 1945, he took off from Mitchell Field on Long Island for a routine training flight to Florida. Immediately, his engines started to flame out. He tried to make an emergency landing at LaGuardia Field, but missed the runway, crashing into Flushing Bay. He was killed on impact.

Billy Sr. was destroyed. "It tore him up, wrecked his life," said Cards outfielder Harry Walker, who would later lose a son of his own. After a distracted second-place finish in '45, Southworth desperately craved a change of scenery. So he accepted a lucrative, almost fanciful offer from the Boston Braves, who paid him $60,000 for his services, far above the $16,000 he had been making in St. Louis. It tore him up to leave—this was a man who had the Cardinals logo inlaid in the linoleum on his kitchen floor. But staying put would have hurt even worse, so he decamped east, leaving a hole in the Cards dugout. Eddie Dyer was the first choice to fill it.

Dyer agonized over replacing Southworth, which would require leaving his comfortable life in Texas for the stresses of the National League, but in the end it was advice from his wife that swayed him. "You have had all the other jobs in the organization," Geraldine Dyer pointed out. "Now if you turn the big one down they will say you were afraid to take it." Practically double-dog-dared, Dyer took the gig.

Dyer was a shade under six feet, with an average build. His unremarkable looks would have made him an ideal wartime spy, as he didn't stand out in crowds. The biggest thing about Dyer may have been his prominent teeth, which snapped when he talked in a manner reminiscent of Teddy Roosevelt. He was friendly, upbeat, and self-effacing, greeting total strangers with "Hiya, pal!" and a firm handshake. He was a pure player's manager, not surprising since he had managed many of the Cardinals in the minors. "It's natural I sort of look after them," he said that spring. The writers had liked Southworth, but they worshipped Dyer—he gave them all the time they could want, and never grumbled. He had been a stud fullback at Rice, and he understood the needs of the sporting press.

No amount of hale fellow well met would be worth much if the team faltered. But given how much talent was on hand, it was hard to picture that happening.

St. Louis possessed what most considered the finest outfield trio in baseball. Center fielder Terry Moore had missed the last three years to the service and was getting up in years (he would turn thirty-four that May). But Moore could still run down fly balls with anyone in the sport. Flanking him were a pair of superstars back from the war, Enos "Country" Slaughter, the hard-hitting, hustling right fielder, and the incomparable Stan "the Donora Greyhound" Musial in left.

Slaughter, "a swift, bald man who combs his hair with obvious deceit," in the judgment of Jimmy Cannon, had only been discharged on March first after three years of military service, and he was less than thrilled to see that, financially anyway, nothing had changed since he left. "I was getting the same contract as before—$11,000," he recalled. "They said I was an old man. I was thirty." With the money, such as it was, Slaughter underwent a hemorrhoid operation, then "got me a pillow and drove to Florida." In one of his first training sessions, he badly strained a muscle in his throwing shoulder and wouldn't be able to throw normally until June.

Musial wasn't there when Country arrived in St. Petersburg. After a year spent repairing ships and playing ball at Pearl Harbor, he was discharged from the Naval Training Center in Bainbridge, Maryland. He caught a train to Philly, but was unable to get a bus to his hometown of Donora, Pennsylvania—everything was jammed up by discharged servicemen and -women. So he hitchhiked the three hundred miles, getting all the way across Pennsylvania in about a day, helped at the end when a motorist recognized the Cards slugger and hometown legend on the shoulder of the highway and took him to his doorstep. Due to the delays, Musial reported to camp a week late.

The Pulitzer Prize–winning war cartoonist Bill Mauldin captured the state of the nation's overburdened transportation system in a cartoon from about the time Musial was thumbing his way home. In the panel, a railroad man is running down the contents of a freight train to the conductor. "Car 29, mixed soldiers and poultry; car 30, frozenfruit; car 31, soldiers; car 32, mixed soldiers and farm machinery..." Stan, better known as "Stash" to his family and friends, would have seen plenty of other men in uniform on the shoulder of the road.

St. Louis was in good shape elsewhere in the diamond. Whitey Kurowski was an All-Star third baseman, Lou Klein solid at second. At shortstop was Marty "Slats" Marion, a string bean from Atlanta who was even more of a splinter than Ted Williams, packing all of 170 pounds on his 6'2" frame. As an eleven-year-old, Marion had fallen over the edge of a twenty-foot embankment and severely broken his leg. As a result, his right leg was shorter than the left one, which resulted in 4-F status but scarcely affected his grace between second and third. Marion was hyper, almost ADD at his position, always gadding about, beating his glove with his fist, or playing with the dirt. At the plate, he always drew a pair of Xs with his finger before stepping in to hit. With all that excess energy, it's no wonder Marion gave up a promising architectural career to play baseball. And he played it well—Slats made the All-Star team each year between 1943 and 1950, and won the NL MVP in 1944.

It was on the mound that the Redbirds truly separated themselves from their NL competition. There were so many arms in St. Pete that Red Barrett, who had led the league with twenty-three wins in 1945, wasn't even guaranteed a spot on the team. Barrett appeared on the cover of *Life* magazine that spring, which ordinarily would have been grand, except the theme of the accompanying story was how the stars from the war years were meeting stiff competition. Red would make the club but saw his workload drop from 284 innings pitched to 67, and his win total to three.

At least Barrett got to keep his address. The glut of pitchers in camp turned into a moneymaking bonanza for the team, who sold off a dozen of them to other teams, mainly Southworth's new squad, Boston (the Braves were laden with so many former Redbirds that they were nicknamed the "Cape Cod Cards"). Two first basemen were also sold off, to make room for a hot prospect named Dick Sisler, son of Hall of Famer George "the Sizzler" Sisler.

Some voices in the press cautioned the team against selling off so many players—after all, the season was a long one, and you never knew when depth would become critical. The advice fell on deaf ears, because the man pulling the trigger on all the deals was, by nature as well as background, a salesman.

The Cards were owned by "Singing" Sam Breadon, a native New Yorker who left Greenwich Village for the Midwest to make his fortune in automobile sales at the dawn of the industry. Sam became extremely wealthy selling Fords and Pierce-Arrows. The syndicate that owned the Cardinals had come to the "Dean of Missouri Automobile Men" for some solvency in 1917, when the franchise was on the verge of collapse, and over the years Breadon had put more and more money into the team, until it was practically all his.

The man he replaced as the franchise's top voice was Branch

Rickey, who had been manager and team president. Breadon's most canny move was keeping Rickey on to run the organization as business (now we would call it "general") manager. Rickey had spent much of the 1920s buying up minor league teams and tying them to the Cardinals, thus ensuring an uninterrupted flow of talent to the parent club. Breadon bankrolled Rickey's system, and it helped make the Redbirds a consistent winner. But the franchise wasn't big enough for their collective ego, and Rickey wanted to reap the financial benefits of his minor league setup—namely, a healthy cut when his players were sold to other organizations. When Breadon balked, Rickey left to run the Dodgers.

By the spring of '46, Breadon was an old man, spending nearly all of his time at the team headquarters. His office was crammed with photos of players and signed baseballs, and few fancy touches. He didn't smoke or gamble, rarely drank anymore, and had given up his favorite hobby, riding horses up in Fenton, Missouri, where he kept a country home. His main activity, other than singing ("Breadon will warble in his slightly off-key tenor at the drop of a highball glass," Dickson Terry wrote in the *St. Louis Post-Dispatch*), was taking long walks. "I like to be with my friends," he said early in 1946, "but nearly all of them are dead now."

"Though it breaks his heart, tight fisted Owner Sam Breadon will have to lose some good players," *Life* wrote, a claim that was ridiculous. A crucial chunk of the team's business model revolved around the hard-hearted selling off of extraneous talent. Breadon had a well-earned reputation for being a skinflint, lowballing his players in the secure knowledge that the Cardinals' minor league system would churn up plenty of replacements. In the spring of '46, that merciless method led to the sale of not just a herd of pitching talent, but also the team's redoubtable catcher, the best the league had to offer—Walker Cooper.

Cooper was a tough hombre, a guy who would spit tobacco juice on a batter's shoes and then ask, "What are you going to do about it?"

"When Big Coop was on your club," Musial remembered, "you didn't have to worry about squabbles with anybody else, because he was in all of them." The team called Cooper "Muley" out of respect for his great strength and endurance. It took him years in the minors to crack the big club—then he complained to the umpire about the very first pitch he saw in the big leagues.

Coop starred during the war years before finally going into the navy and missing almost all of the 1945 season. Now that he was back, he'd be damned if, à la Slaughter, he was going to play for the same salary as before he left, even though at thirty-one, he was a year older than the "old" Country. Cooper squabbled over his contract and found out the hard way that, despite his import to the team and his military service, he held no aces. The Reserve Clause tied him to the Cardinals until the team decided what to do with him. In this case, they sold him to Boston, as they had his less-ornery pitching brother, Mort, the previous spring. Walker fetched an extraordinary $175,000 ($2,085,666 today), one of the highest cash-only deals made at the time.

The team would surely miss such a bull behind the plate, the remaining pitchers most of all. It was a talented group, however. There was Alpha "Cotton" Brazle, the white-haired lefty known as "Old Boots and Saddles" for his laconic cowboy demeanor; Max Lanier, a tricky lefty; and Ken Burkhart, who had won eighteen games in '45.

And there was Johnny Beazley, who won the Rookie of the Year Award in 1942 and beat the Yankees twice in the World Series that year. After the Cards won, Beazley got a telegram from a recruiting office in Memphis, his hometown, that read, "If you can toss hand grenades like you pitch ball for them Cards, hurry up. The marines need you." Perhaps put off by the unimaginative sales pitch, he joined the Army Air Corps instead. One day, he pitched in a service game without any warm-up and hurt his arm. All spring he had been putting on a brave face, but he worried he was no longer what he had been before the war, and with so many quality hurlers about, he might be in trouble.

Righty Howie Krist didn't care about that. He was just glad to be pitching at all. After winning thirty-four games in three seasons for the Redbirds, he went into the army in 1944. While he hadn't been injured by enemy fire in France, Krist had hurt his neck diving into a foxhole and his leg carrying extra ammo on a long march. As it turned out, Fortress Europe was safer than home. When he was discharged in January 1946, he got into a bad car accident that fractured his jaw.

Murry Dickson had better luck. A right-hander with a potent fastball, Dickson loved to experiment on the mound, inventing so many variations of pitches that he was called the "Tom Edison of the Toeplate." A carpenter in the off-season, Dickson loved magic tricks and practical jokes, and he had a nervous habit of scooping up dirt before every pitch.

Dickson never said whether he had picked up the nerves in the European Theater, but he might well have. Sergeant Dickson fought across the continent with the 35th Infantry Division as a recon scout, a dangerous position with a job description of prowling behind enemy lines, wreaking havoc. He won four battle stars, including action at St. Lo and the Battle of the Bulge, went on a number of top-secret missions, and was among the first GIs to liberate Dachau.

Like many combat-scarred vets, Dickson preferred to focus on the lighter side of his service, such as the time he killed several chickens with a slingshot on Thanksgiving Day, 1944, so his patrol, deep behind German lines, could have a holiday feast without using gunfire that might give away their position. He loved to talk about the time a shell exploded nearby, causing him to jump into a foxhole. Another soldier landed on top of Dickson—when the pitcher looked up, it was General Patton himself! The two men got to talking, and Patton offered to make Dickson his driver, but Murry begged out of the assignment, worried that the "crazy" general would be the death of him. Dickson preferred to take his chances with the Wehrmacht.

He came home laden with souvenirs and a burning desire to rejoin the Cardinals and forget his combat service. Although physically unimposing (a mere 155 pounds), his unique repertoire gave him a leg up. Still, he seemed ticketed for the bullpen.

Two other smallish pitchers, lefties both, rounded out the staff. Howie Pollet was overjoyed to see Dyer take the managerial job. Eddie, a mentor since Pollet turned pro as a teenager, had hired him in the off-season to work in his oil-leasing business office. Pollet was a good Catholic boy, attending church regularly and preferring to talk fishing rather than head out on the town with the boys. He had two distinguishing characteristics, one public (he made a loud grunt while delivering every pitch, like a karate master splitting a board) and one private (he fell asleep with his arms folded across his chest like a mummy and never moved all night long).

Pollet served two years in the air corps, entirely stateside, playing with Country Slaughter in San Antonio for a spell. Pollet's good buddy Harry Brecheen was exempted from duty due to a childhood ankle injury. This was ironic, because his extreme agility and athleticism had earned Harry the nickname "the Cat."

Brecheen grew up in Oklahoma, the son of a lumber surveyor who was among the first to settle the town of Broken Bow. From the time he was young, Harry always held either a rifle, a fishing rod, or a baseball in his hand. He and Pollet spent off-seasons together in various woods and streams, pursuing their favorite hobbies. Brecheen owned a baker's dozen worth of bird dogs, and often resembled one when he leaned way forward to get the sign from the catcher, the bill of his cap low over his brow.

"Brecheen wouldn't give his grandma a good ball to hit," Terry Moore said of him. He outthought hitters, changing speeds masterfully, in the manner of future great Whitey Ford. Like Dickson,

Brecheen was wee—just 160 pounds of stripling. He was always told that his size would prevent him from making it through the long major league season, but he had won forty games over the previous three years. He made up for his diminutive frame with aggression, making copious use of brushback pitches, to the point that he would yell "Look out!" at batters who dug in against him.

It was a powerful team, and enthusiasm was palpable all spring, buoyed by the joy the locals felt at seeing the team for the first time since wartime travel restrictions had banned southern training camps in 1943. "Even the flocks of fat sea gulls that had waddled unmolested in Waterfront Park's left field for the past three years seemed infected with the excitement," *Life* noted. Groups of boys stripped down to patrol Tampa Bay for balls knocked into the drink. Caught up in the optimism, virtually every prognosticator that spring picked the Cardinals to win the pennant in a trot. Only Dyer himself sounded a note of caution.

"Things unforeseen happen to ball clubs that can greatly change the picture," the new manager said.

Not every Cardinal liked Dyer. Pitcher Freddy Schmidt felt the manager played favorites. "His guys from the minors got put forward," Schmidt remembered decades later, his bitterness still palpable. "The rest of us sat in the bullpen and never got a call." Then there was outfielder Harry Walker, who had been close with Southworth and feuded with Dyer. Perhaps that was because of Walker's infuriating habit of endlessly tugging at his cap before and after every pitch. Before the war, his teammates on the Cardinals called him "Cappy," but during the spring they hung him with a more lasting moniker—"the Hat." His habit of tugging on his caps meant he went through about twenty a season, and that got him in dutch with Breadon, who totaled up the money all those hats cost him and wasn't pleased. Dyer was asked if Walker's manic hat-pulling bothered enemy pitchers. "Pitchers?" Dyer responded. "Hell, it bothers everybody."

Walker had been a part of the 1943 team that won the pennant and lost to the Yankees in the World Series. He then went into the service, where he saw intense combat in Europe. But he also saw some baseball action while overseas, including an extraordinary series of games that took place in a most unusual setting.

Chapter 5

FROM HITLER TO HARDBALL

NOT LONG BEFORE, this site in Nuremberg, Germany, had been filled by National Socialists swearing fealty to the Third Reich. Now, the swastikas were painted over, brown shirts were considerably out of fashion, and the Stadion der Hitlerjugend (Hitler Youth Stadium) had been converted from a cauldron of hate to a place for uniquely American games. The US Army ran the show now, and fifty thousand Yank soldiers shouting and laughing and cheering over the decadent contest was the ultimate proof.

An endless number of doughboys of every rank and specialty poured into the newly built field: the infield finely crushed red brick, the outfield perfectly mown green grass. A brilliant sun warmed the faces of the GIs. Vendors sold beer and Cokes and peanuts, just like back home. The Stars and Stripes flew over the field, and a bugle corps played the national anthem before the cry of "Play ball!" Armed Forces Radio had a setup behind one dugout, transmitting the action to the boys throughout Europe and Africa who couldn't be there.

It might not have been a scene to inspire Leni Riefenstahl, but for these citizen-soldiers and smashers of the Axis war machine, it was paradise.

On his first night of combat in World War II, PFC William Jucksch of Missouri was, like the rest of his unit, "scared shitless."

Jucksch (pronounced "Jukes, like a jukebox") was from a small town near Joplin. He joined the army at age eighteen, and because he was a Boy Scout, and knew Morse code, "they made me a radioman," he said some sixty-eight years later. He was a forward observer with an artillery unit, and he landed in France on D-day plus five months. "We saw a lot of war," Jucksch said. "We shelled a lot of towns, trying to avoid their churches, but let's face it—we destroyed pretty much everything we saw." Slowly but surely, he became numb to the death and destruction that was all around him.

"You get immune to it," he admitted. "The human body is an amazing thing."

With war's end, the numbness gave way to "euphoria." "After the Japs surrendered it was so great," Jucksch recalled. "We took trips to Switzerland, Rome, wherever you liked." But sightseeing wasn't going to be enough to keep the hundreds of thousands of American boys still in Europe awaiting discharge from getting in trouble. After all, "the first thing we did was get the breweries going."

So a massive military athletics program was put in place. Now nineteen and a staff sergeant, Jucksch played some football, but it was baseball, America's number one sport, that attracted most of the servicemen's interest. To make a powerful statement, the brass decided to build a baseball diamond in the symbolic home of the Nazi Party—the Hitler Youth Stadium. "We had a conqueror's frame of mind," Jucksch explained. "The Germans had surrendered unconditionally, and this proved it."

It was renamed Soldier's Field, and soon the sound of lumber connecting with horsehide filled the Luitpoldhain. Come September, German prisoners of war were directed to erect removable bleachers for a special event to take place at Soldier's Field—the European Theater of Operations (ETO) World Series. It was the championship series for all service teams based on the newly liberated continent, and on September 3, 1945, it was the center of attention of the entire American war effort in Europe.

Beyond the center field fence was a long concrete strip where the Nazis used to parade, and all morning, and right up until first pitch, airplanes landed there, disgorging the panoply of generals, colonels, and majors eager to see the opening game of the Series. Jucksch, like most enlisted men, rode in a truck to Nuremberg, bouncing along on bomb-damaged roads from Austria. "When you're in a 6x6 [army truck] it sure felt like a long drive," he remembers.

One of the main dramatis personae of the Series was down on the field stretching, getting ready to play. Harry Walker was one of several former pros on his service team, the one representing the Third Army, General George Patton's fiefdom.

Walker was a southern boy, from Leeds, Alabama, and part of a baseball family—his father had pitched in the bigs, and his elder brother Dixie was currently starring with Brooklyn. Harry succeeded as a ballplayer more on grit than talent. Down in the minors, one setback after another had befallen Walker. Once, he complained of stomach pains and fainted in the clubhouse before a game. The trainer threw cold water on Walker to revive him, then informed the groggy, dripping player that no other outfielders were available, so he had to play. Walker gutted out both ends of a doubleheader, then went to the movies, where he collapsed with a burst appendix and needed emergency surgery.

The following season Walker was hit in the throat by an errant throw in warm-ups and couldn't speak for three months. This was considered a tragedy, as Harry was a great "barber," slang for talker, willing to chew the ear off teammates in the dugout, reporters on the train, or complete strangers wherever he met them.

After playing in the final game of the '43 World Series, Walker had risen before dawn the next day, appearing as ordered at the Jefferson Barracks Army Induction Center in St. Louis at five a.m. He was sent to Fort Riley, Kansas, for basic training, along with teammate Alpha Brazle. Before Walker could even load his first carbine, he contracted spinal meningitis. He was delirious, and placed in a straitjacket for his own protection. For six weeks, he teetered near death. "They said if I'd been sick only four years before, I would be dead," he recalled years later. "Only the advances in medicine during the war, particularly in sulfa drugs, saved my life." Ordinarily, he'd be sent home, but the army didn't want to be accused of going soft on ballplayers.

Walker recovered and spent several weeks training in jungle warfare. In classic army wisdom, he was then sent to the frozen forests of Europe. He was part of the 65th Reconnaissance Troop (Mechanized), a mobile unit that prowled in jeeps behind enemy forces (similar to Murry Dickson's wartime job). "Sometimes we'd be 30 or 40 miles behind the German lines, just like the scouts in the Old West. We wouldn't see our outfit for several days." Walker's unit lived off the land, swapping cigarettes for food and beer, and "fishing" with hand grenades.

The work was incredibly dangerous, even though Walker claimed he "got in at the dog race—before that the 65th was almost a suicide unit." One moonless night Walker rounded a corner in a road and found himself face-to-face with three German soldiers. They raised their rifles, but Walker was packing a .45 revolver he had bought, and he was handy with it. Harry the Hat got off five quick shots, killing all three Germans. "It was close," Walker said. "That rifle was only about four feet from me when I started shooting. What saved me was that he was trying to get his safety bolt off. He couldn't get it off before I was able to get him."

Soon after, Walker captured two dozen enemy soldiers after flushing them from their trucks. "They didn't want to surrender to the Russians, so they surrendered to us in droves," he said after the war. Walker killed many more men who wouldn't give up, however, often with the .50 caliber machine gun mounted in his jeep.

Walker received a Bronze Star, a Purple Heart for shrapnel he took on March 22, 1945, and several commendations for his service. He helped liberate several concentration camps, and the images of the wasted-away humanity he encountered haunted him for decades. "The war left a lasting impression on me," he told an interviewer. "But whatever price it took, it had to be paid."

When the Germans surrendered, Walker, the biggest star and most identifiable ballplayer in the Third Army, was tasked to find a way to help keep the multitudes of suddenly idle American soldiers occupied. Walker helped build the diamond at the Hitler Youth Stadium, and put together the Third Army league. He and the other ballplayers bused all over Germany and Austria playing games, until Walker went to the Third Army brass and managed to wheedle a B-17 Flying Fortress, *Bottom's Up,* to ferry the teams around.

Walker's team was the 71st Infantry Division "Red Circlers," so-called for the distinctive patch of the unit. The squad was a powerhouse, listing on its roster Johnny Wyrostek, an outfielder for the Phillies; Benny Zientara, an infielder with Cincinnati; Herb Bremer, a catcher with St. Louis in the late '30s; Pirates pitcher Ken Heintzelman; and Kenny's teammate in the Steel City, Maurice Van Robays, nicknamed "Bomber" for his on-field exploits, not his wartime specialty (he drove a truck during the fighting). In addition, the team was stocked with several top minor league prospects from the American Association and the International League. Most, including Walker, had been transferred to the unit by General Patton himself, to ensure victory for the pride of the Third Army.

The team's star pitcher was Cincinnati Reds hurler Ewell "the Whip" Blackwell, a 6'6" beanpole with a terrifying sidearm delivery. For right-handed hitters, Blackwell's delivery seemed to start from a few inches beyond their left ears. He wasn't particularly well known yet, having pitched all of three innings with the Reds in 1942 before joining up, but it was readily apparent to all who had to face him that this was a guy with a future. Indeed, Blackwell would make six straight All-Star teams upon war's end.

Blackwell had pitched a no-hitter in the Third Army championship series against the 76th Division "Onaways," and then a two-hit shutout in the decisive game. Now, the Red Circlers were taking on the champs of service teams based in France, a squad called the Overseas Invasion Service Expedition (OISE) All-Stars. They were huge underdogs to the Third Army juggernaut. The only major leaguers on the team were Russ Bauers, a mediocre right-handed pitcher who won twenty-nine games with the Pirates in the late '30s, and "Subway" Sam Nahem, who had been reduced to "the egregiously anonymous position of pitching batting practice to the batting practice pitchers," as he put it, in Brooklyn, St. Louis, and Philly before getting called up. Nahem coached the motley crew of semipro and low-level minor leaguers.

Subway Sam did have a secret weapon, however. Actually, two—one a slugging outfielder, the other a dominant pitcher.

They just happened to be Negroes.

Jucksch and his friends could sit wherever they liked in the massive stadium, the seating being general admission, and officers and enlisted men commingled in the stands. Gambling was reportedly widespread in the crowd, but Jucksch didn't remember much of it, possibly because he was too awed by the size of the venue. "Soldier's Field was a huge place," he recalled. "I had never seen anything like it."

At precisely 2:30 in the afternoon the game got under way. Blackwell pitched for the Red Circlers. "He sure was a whip that day," Jucksch remembers, as Blackwell made short work of the OISE Stars, fanning nine of them in an easy 9–2 win. Considering Blackwell was getting over a nasty case of strep throat, the dominance was even more impressive. The France-based side didn't make it too hard on the Third Army, committing seven errors.

Jucksch and his buddies may not have gotten much of a contest that day, but it hardly mattered. They were in the sun, drinking beer and watching a ball game. The long months of combat melted away in the heat. This afternoon with the National Pastime reminded them of what was coming, and soon—a return to their homes, and their families, and a life without war.

The second game was held the following day at Soldier's Field. It was September 4, Labor Day back in the States, and a holiday vibe infused the shirt-sleeved crowd. Jucksch wasn't at this one, but close to fifty thousand others were, with the huge majority pulling for the "home" team, the Red Circlers. This time, the visitors from France were winning, thanks to a sterling pitching performance from a man the *New York Times* identified as "Leo Day." His name was actually Leon Day, and he was hurling a four-hitter, all scratch singles, taking a 2–1 lead into the ninth inning.

The only thing more noteworthy than his performance was his skin color. The pitcher's mound wasn't far from the spot where Hitler and Goebbels and the other Nazi leaders had preached Aryan racial superiority. How they would have frothed had they been in the Hitler Youth Stadium on this afternoon, watching a black man, a *schwarzer,* shut down a team of whites!

Before surviving the war in one piece became the focus of his attention, Leon Day was a star hurler for the Newark Eagles of the Negro Leagues. In 1942, his last year of competition before the war, Day had fanned eighteen men in a single game for Newark and closed the Negro League All-Star Game by striking out five of the last seven hitters. In 1943, he enlisted. In 1944, he was driving an amphibious supply vehicle called a "duck" with the 818th Amphibian Battalion onto Normandy Beach.

He hit dry land six days after the initial landing, "scared to death," on June 12. "When we landed we were pretty close to the action because we could hear the small arms fire," he remembered to Negro Leagues historian James Riley. A couple of nights later, a wave of German fighters appeared over the beach, "dropping flares and [lighting] the beach up so bright you could have read a newspaper." Day evacuated his ammo-laden duck and jumped into a sandbagged foxhole, manned by a white MP. As the Luftwaffe strafed the beach, the MP shouted, "Who's driving that duck out there?"

"I am," admitted Day.

"What's it got on it?"

"Ammunition."

"Move that duck from out in front of this hole!" screamed the MP.

"Go out there and move it your own damn self!" Day replied.

Now Day aimed to continue his defiance of white folks while on the mound in Nuremberg. Coming up to the plate, trying to tie the game with one big swing, was Harry Walker.

Walker had been trying to get a read on Day all afternoon, managing a single in three trips to the plate so far. Day used a sneaky short-armed delivery, the precise opposite of Blackwell's, whose elongated arms made hitting him like facing a kraken. Day barely started his windup before the ball was shooting into the catcher's glove, its speed magnified by the suddenness with which it was upon the hitter.

Day tossed one of his stealthy fastballs in on Walker's hands, and the Cardinals/Red Circlers outfielder could only lift a harmless fly to center field. It was easily caught by a charismatic, powerfully built black outfielder named Willard "Home Run" Brown.

He had been the cleanup hitter for the Negro Leagues' best team, the Kansas City Monarchs. Pitcher Satchel Paige was the Monarchs best-known player, and he gave Brown his nickname after Paige watched his teammate outslug the Negro Leagues' Paul Bunyan, Josh Gibson. In 1947, playing for the St. Louis Browns, Willard would hit the first home run ever hit by a black man in the American League, his only major league tater. For now, he had to content himself with playing ball in between shifts on guard duty.

Some said he could have been as great as Gibson, if only he cared to be. Brown was ultra-talented but also what was known as a "Sunday player," one who gave his all when the stands were full but loafed it otherwise. His alternate nickname, Sonny, came from this trait—he didn't like to play on cloudy or misty days. Sometimes he would stay in the outfield while his team was at bat, promising to move if a ball came his way. Other times he would take a copy of *Reader's Digest* out to his position and check it out during play. But he also ran down drives and swatted tape-measure homers with ease, too, which contributed to the legend.

Brown knocked in OISE's first run of Game Two, and Nahem knocked in the second. Brown's Negro League rival-turned-service-ball-teammate Day polished off the Third Army team in the ninth. He finished with ten strikeouts, one better than the Whip had whiffed the previous day. The All-Stars won 2–1, evening the series at a game apiece. Years later, Day recalled that he "knew who [Walker] was but I never had any trouble with him or any of the other major leaguers." After all, he said, he "was bearing down" that day.

The OISE All-Stars may not have been the first integrated team in the service—other Negroes had played informally with whites throughout the war. But these were the highest profile games, by a huge margin, to feature blacks playing with whites. The biggest news from the games may have been the lack of comment Day and Brown's presence engendered.

If the doughboys on hand knew what was coming just over the horizon, they might have paid more attention. They were witnessing firsthand an out-of-town preview of baseball's new frontier.

The teams flew over to Reims, France, for the next two games. Three months earlier, Germany had formally surrendered to the Allies just a few kilometers west of the Stade de Reims, in a small schoolhouse that served as General Eisenhower's headquarters. With Hitler dead, Alfred Jodl signed the surrender documents for the Germans.

The All-Stars took a shock lead in the series with a 2–1 win in

Game Three, Brown doubling and scoring the first run in the lone rally against Blackwell. Thanks to the pitching of Nahem, those two runs were enough. In Game Four, Walker had his revenge on Day. He launched a two-run homer in the first inning to spur Patton's Men to a 5–0 win, tying the series at two-all.

A coin flip was held to decide the site of the decisive fifth game, and the toss was won by the Red Circlers, thus sending the teams back to Nuremberg. Once again, it seemed like everyone in the country with an American uniform and a pass turned out to watch. They would witness a dandy affair. *Stars and Stripes* would rave, "The game was so close all the way through that it kept the crowd of over fifty thousand on its feet cheering wildly and rewarding unfavorable decisions with sounds as wild as any ever to emerge from Ebbets Field or the Polo Grounds."

Nahem decided to start himself on the mound. A native of Bensonhurst born to Syrian parents, Nahem was a Communist, a Jew who spoke flawless Arabic, an atheist, and a lawyer who passed up the bar to play for the Brooklyn Dodgers. "An Attorney Who Obtains Injunctions Against Batters" was how he was once described in the *Sporting News*. Nahem was with the Phils when he entered the service after the 1942 season. He fought with an antiaircraft battery, and was put in charge of American baseball in France when the war ended.

Fortunately for his reputation, Nahem wasn't part of the GI squad that had lost to a local French team a few weeks earlier. The Fédération Française de Baseball fielded a team that was among the oddest-clad ever to take the diamond. Infielders wore blue shorts, aviation goggles, and coal miner's caps. The pitcher wore hockey pads; the left fielder, a steel helmet straight from the front lines. The right fielder was "an apparition in a tight one-piece bathing suit and straw hat that pranced out to occupy right field," reported an aghast witness. The umpire sported a World War I–vintage gas mask, and wore his wire mask not over his face but his groin.

Somehow, this bizarre collection of *batteurs* and *lanceurs* bested the Americans 5–3. The soldiers' excuse was no doubt that they were laughing too hard to compete at their best.

No one was laughing as the decisive Game Five of the ETO World Series proceeded. Nahem wasn't nearly as effective as he had been back in France. The Red Circlers scored an early run off him, then loaded the bases with no one out in the fourth. The "Brooklyn Barrister" was no dummy, so he took himself out, waving in Russ Bauers, the only other OISE All-Star with experience in the bigs. Bauers lived up to Nahem's faith in him, getting out of the jam in the fourth and holding the Third Army champs off the scoreboard the rest of the way.

Blackwell started once more for the Red Circlers, and was throwing darts again, though he also committed two errors in a sloppy game "replete with miscues and thrills," according to the *New York Times*. The game was still 1–0 in the seventh when the Negro players turned the tide. Day was sent in to pinch run after one of his teammates had reached base. He stole second and third, and came home on a short fly ball to tie the game. It was the sort of hard-charging ball that was on display every day in the Negro Leagues.

In the eighth inning, it was Brown's turn. With a man on first, he clubbed a double to the deepest reaches of Soldier's Field. Walker ran it down and relayed the ball in, but the runner beat the throw after a dramatic dash that had the crowd roaring. Walker hung his head out in center. He probably couldn't imagine that in a little over a year, he would be at the center of a similar play that would decide the next World Series.

Trailing 2–1, on the verge of being the victims of a monumental upset, Walker came to the plate hoping to start a rally and avoid a humiliating loss, and presumably a slap in the face from an outraged General Patton. Instead, he flied out. Moments later, Day, Brown, Nahem, and the OISE All-Stars were celebrating on the mound, having won the series three games to two. The crowd grumbled a bit in disappointment, then gave the teams a standing ovation for the outstanding show.

Back in France, the winners were feted by Brigadier General Charles Thrasher. There was a parade, followed by a banquet complete with steaks and champagne. Day and Brown, players who would not be allowed to eat with their fellow players in many places back in the United States, chowed down happily.

Meanwhile, Harry Walker stewed. He was more upset at losing than he thought he would be. The competitor in Walker was roused.

Back home, the Hat vowed, if he got another crack at a big game, he would come through.

Chapter 6
THE DODGERS TAKE DAYTONA

IN THE OPENING weeks of January 1946, Branch Rickey was walking to the Brooklyn Dodgers offices at 215 Montague Street when he felt a slamming pain in his chest. He was rushed to Brooklyn Jewish Hospital, where he was treated for a heart attack. Just a couple of months before, Rickey had been admitted with nausea, dizziness, and vertigo. He was diagnosed then as having Ménière's disease, which affects the inner ear. He lost a considerable amount of hearing on one side.

Now he had almost dropped dead on the streets of Brooklyn. "I just can't slow down," he admitted. "I'd rather die ten minutes sooner than be doing nothing all the time." The nonstop Antony & Cleopatra cigars he puffed probably didn't help. Nor did the stress of running the Dodgers, which he had taken over just as MacPhail had turned the perennial "Bums" into pennant winners. The pressure to not just succeed but exceed his former protégé was enormous. It was probably the reason Rickey always left games in the bottom of the eighth inning, regardless of score.

Wesley Branch Rickey hailed from southern Ohio, which is more Bible Belt than Rust Belt, and he carried the piety of a deacon throughout his life, refusing to drink or attend ball games on the Sabbath. He wouldn't play on Sunday as an aspiring pro, either, which helped submarine his career (as did his lack of elite skills) and drove him toward a career in the law, where, if anything, he was even more of a failure.

But he was friendly with the owner of the St. Louis Browns, Robert Hedges, who rescued Rickey from anonymity in 1911 by bringing him in to help with scouting. Thus began one of the more impactful baseball careers in the sport's history.

Rickey moved across the street to the Cardinals in 1917, becoming team president. He fought in World War I, like MacPhail, and returned to a team in financial distress. Rickey named himself manager to cut costs, the first decision of many that would get him labeled as extraordinarily thrifty. He was awful at the job and wisely kicked himself upstairs in favor of Rogers Hornsby in 1925. Hornsby promptly led the Redbirds to a championship the next year.

The Cards had little dough, but they had good scouts, Rickey first among them (it was often said he could spot talent from a moving train), so he played to that strength and created a widespread minor league system. It allowed the team, who couldn't outbid other teams for young talent, the ability to tie prospects to the big league club, use the cream of the crop, and sell off the rest for operating profit. "It wasn't the result of any innovative genius," Rickey told the *Sporting News*. "It is the result of stark necessity. We did it to meet a question of supply and demand for young ballplayers." The cutting-edge method utterly changed baseball in the 1930s and '40s, as the Redbirds stockpiled talent, dominated the National League, and remained solvent.

Rickey, like MacPhail, was a pioneer in several other areas. He had his pitchers use strings to define the strike zone in practice, to help with their control; invented the concept of sliding pits and batting tees; and was the first to implement classroom training to get all his players on the same page fundamentally. Later, he would hire the game's first dedicated statistician, Allan Roth, to give his team a numbers edge.

As the Cardinals' success grew, so did Rickey's profile. He became a regular speaker on the conservative circuit, as a forerunner to the kind of evangelical sportsman today defined by the likes of Tim Tebow. He was a close friend and supporter of Thomas Dewey, the Republican who became governor of New York and rival to then Senator Truman, even though Truman was a Missourian and rabid Cardinals fan.

He fell out with Sam Breadon over—what else?—money, and when MacPhail surprisingly went back into the service, Rickey leapt at a chance to replace him in Brooklyn. It was there he earned the nickname "the Mahatma," after sportswriter Tom Meany read a line about Mohandas Gandhi that described the Indian leader as a combination of "your father and Tammany Hall." Gandhi was known as "Mahatma"; thus too was Rickey.

The team Rickey had put together in Brooklyn gathered for spring training in Daytona Beach, where after a long day of drills, the players could go for a swim in the Atlantic, provided they avoided the hot rods racing on the tightly packed beaches of Daytona. (Within a year, the racers would organize themselves into a touring collective called NASCAR.) The swollen roster from all the returnees made life difficult for the team's traveling secretary, Harold Parrott. He had to scramble to find space for everyone. Some players lived four to a room. The Dodgers, like most teams, had told the players not to bring their families to Florida, but most ignored the order, especially those who had been in the service and already had been away from their loved ones for so long.

The most important Dodger back from the service was their fantastic, if injury-prone, outfielder "Pistol Pete" Reiser. Also back from a three-year absence was the team's steady shortstop. Harold "Pee Wee" Reese wasn't that small—at 5'10", 160, he was near average for players of the time, even a little big by middle-infielder standards. The nickname actually came from his time as a champion marble shooter during his Kentucky boyhood.

Reese was a scrappy and cannily effective player for the Louisville Colonels, a triple-A franchise, when the Red Sox took note (their farm director suggested Tom Yawkey buy the entire team to secure

Reese). But Boston had a shortstop—Joe Cronin, who inconveniently was also the manager, and Yawkey's favorite son. Cro checked Reese out, deliberately soft-pedaled his ability, and then dealt Reese to Brooklyn for a few bucks and some no-names. The Dodgers also had a player-manager at short, but he willingly stepped aside for the obviously superior Reese. Pee Wee would go on to become the Dodgers' longtime captain, a ten-time All-Star, and a Hall of Famer.

The critical pivot in Reese's career boiled down to the differing mentalities between the managers of Boston and Brooklyn. Joe Cronin thought himself irreplaceable until he had to be carried off the field on his shield. It was a superstar player's mentality. Leo Durocher, however, forged a career out of pure will. He approached every season—every game—as if it could be his last, for there was surely someone better coming along to take his job. And Leo wanted to win far more than he wanted the glory. If his team was better off with a new guy instead of him at short, so be it.

In the long, often-fantastic history of baseball nicknames, few have matched "the Lip" for pithy accuracy. Durocher talked a mile a minute, alternately harassing and cajoling players, umpires, writers, fans, and management. And, of course, women, who flocked to Durocher. He splashed on the cologne with two full hands and was always resplendent in $175 suits, custom-fit by the tailor to George Raft, star of *The Bowery* and *They Drive by Night*. Raft often played gangsters, and his real-life association with mafiosi helped inform his portrayals. Raft was also close pals with Durocher, an association that lent the skipper an aura of glamour and pizzazz.

Leo was ultra-intense, a forerunner to Billy Martin in many ways, mainly in his win-or-else attitude. He frequently humiliated his charges, such as pitcher Luke Hamlin, whom Durocher labeled a "gutless wonder" after Hamlin took a beating in a game. In 1943 Durocher's Dodgers had mutinied under Leo's unending abuse, threatening not to take the field unless Durocher eased up. The incident softened Durocher—a little. Second baseman Billy Herman nonetheless regularly fired balls from infield practice into the dugout, trying to nail Durocher.

Sportswriter Dick Young pegged the way most people in baseball felt about Leo. "You and Durocher are on a life raft," he wrote in the *New York Daily News*. "A wave comes and knocks him into the ocean. You dive in and save his life. A shark comes and takes your leg. The next day, you and Leo start even." Durocher's style could lift a team to heights unachievable under anyone else, but it could also cause blowback. Stan Musial said that Leo "tried to intimidate the other team, but I think it backfired on him more often than not. He was just stirring up a nest of hornets. When Durocher came to town, I was so charged up I could go up there and climb six fences. I wasn't the only one. Our whole team was up."

"Lippy" was a rogue, a hard-drinking, two-fisted braggart who loved to whip ass on the field and then tell anyone who would listen all about it. There was little pretense at playing nice or being a family-friendly guy. Even though he worked in the outer boroughs, Durocher was made for Broadway, and he wasted little time combining sports and nightlife in the big city. Latter-day lotharios like Mickey Mantle, Joe Namath, Joe Frazier, and Derek Jeter were merely following the blueprint Durocher had laid down.

He grew up in Springfield, Massachusetts, the son of a railway worker. His first sport wasn't baseball but pool, and his second was probably rock throwing. By the ninth grade, Leo had beaten up a teacher and been expelled. He played semipro ball for an electric company team and was spotted by fabled Yankees scout Paul Krichell, who had signed Lou Gehrig a couple of years earlier.

Durocher was in the bigs by 1928, a great glove man who made up for his lack of hitting ability with ultra-competitiveness. As a rookie, he once hip-checked a runner trying to leg out a triple. Said runner was a shrinking violet named Ty Cobb. "If you ever pull a stunt like that again," the Georgia Peach screamed, "I'll cut off your legs."

Instead of shying away from the oft-psychopathic Cobb, Durocher got in his grille. "Go home, grandpa!" he yelled back. "You're gonna get hurt playing at your age. You've gotten away with murder all these years, but you're through. You'll get a hip from me any time you come down my way, and if you try and cut me, you'll get a ball rammed down your throat!"

He would sometimes call time-out when in the field so he could stroll closer to the batter and insult him. Hank Sauer of the Cubs was a favored target. Sauer's prominent nose reminded Leo of a hood ornament, so he would yell "Pontiac" at the Cubbie, who would then call time to compose himself. Shocked by his audacity, his teammates were won over, save Babe Ruth, who relentlessly needled Durocher, calling him "the All-American Out."

Yet another nickname for Leo was "C-Note" in honor of his highfalutin lifestyle and his incessant need for cash. He was forever welshing on bar tabs and haberdashery bills, which would get him (a) the unwelcome attention of local legbreakers and (b) summoned repeatedly to the Commissioner's office. Such was his charm that even the grim moray Kenesaw Mountain Landis offered to give Leo a loan.

Branch Rickey hardly seemed the type to coexist with such a rampaging rake. But he brought Durocher to the Cards, telling Leo, "I have a firm belief that with you at shortstop we can win pennants. That's all I care about." A year later, Durocher captained the team to a World Series title. The Cards paid him $50 a week and gave the rest to his creditors. But it was MacPhail, not Rickey, who gave Durocher his first shot at managing, installing Leo as the Brooklyn skipper in 1938.

Managers dating back to John McGraw had dominated every aspect of their players' lives. After the war, this was no longer possible. Night games and swollen urban populations made curfews and tight control over the ballplayers folly. Players no longer accepted the fact that management could dictate their personal lives away from the ballpark. Meanwhile, social mores were changing, with women becoming more aggressive, showering constant attention upon the ballplayers, even ones not as famous as Babe Ruth.

Exhibit A: Kirby Higbe. Ol' Hig was a Dodgers pitcher from North Carolina with a taste for flashy cars and flashier women. Back in his hometown of New Bern, he once drove a yellow roadster for several blocks on the sidewalk, then got off with no penalty when he winkingly told the judge he had done it to avoid a woman driver.

His courtship of the fairer sex was equally tasteful. He flaunted the fruits of road trips, claiming that no less than thirty-five women once showed up to his hotel room looking for some action. "I was too obvious," he said years later. "I'd walk through the hotel lobby arm and arm with a blonde and a bottle of booze. Other guys would just have those things sent up." Higbe deserved to enjoy life, having served in both Europe and the Pacific Theater during the war. He spent the bulk of his time in the Philippines, arriving just as Leyte was recaptured. Ol' Hig spent most of his hitch selling American beer to the local Filipinos. After baseball he became a prison guard in South Carolina and was busted selling drugs to an inmate. He found religion as a result, becoming an acolyte of Billy Graham.

Higbe owed his place on the team to pinochle. He had been a career mediocrity when the Dodgers picked him up for loose change in 1941. Higbe and Durocher began a season-long card game, with Durocher swiftly establishing himself as the superior cardsharp. Leo then offered Ol' Hig a deal—he would knock two hundred points (at a quarter a point) off his lead every time Higbe won a game on the mound. Incentivized, Higbe won twenty-two games that summer, helped lead Brooklyn to the pennant, and wound up even at the gaming table.

The Dodgers were less affected by the war than many clubs, both in terms of key players going into the service and having them see combat. Durocher's 4-F due to a punctured eardrum was a typical good break in that department. But a squadron of minor leaguers who had been called up were in Daytona. Three of them were vying for a place in the Brooklyn outfield. One, Gene Hermanski, had served stateside. The other two saw action, and suffered for it.

Dick Whitman was, by most accounts, the best ballplayer ever to pass through the University of Oregon. A native of the Beaver State, Whitman was working his way up the Dodgers chain when drafted into the army. He was with an infantry unit in the Ardennes Forest during the Battle of the Bulge. Like so many other soldiers in that frozen forest, Whitman suffered frostbite to his toes.

But worse damage came when an enemy artillery blast detonated near him. The shrapnel flayed his back and neck, while grazing his ear. When asked of the moment after the war, Whitman could only remember falling into the snow with a hell of a headache. Not knowing how badly he'd been hit, he got up and asked the soldier behind him how it looked.

There was no one there. "He was carrying the tripod [upon which to mount a machine gun]," Whitman said. "But all I could see of him was his shoes; he was just blown all over." No, Whitman did not steal the name and identity of the soldier and become *Mad Men*'s Don Draper, but he did take home a Purple Heart, a Bronze Star, and three battle citations from the war. "His life really was the classic American story," said his son Richard upon Dick's death in 2003.

As was Carl Furillo's, in a different way. The son of poor immigrants from southern Italy, Furillo used baseball to escape the mines of his Pennsylvania hometown. Carl was from Reading, and he had a howitzer for an arm, so he simply had to be called the "Reading Rifle."

Like Whitman, Furillo was on the cusp of the bigs when he was called up to fight in the Pacific, with the 77th Infantry Division. He saw plenty of combat during his three-plus years in the service, and he was wounded in a mortar attack as the Allies closed in on the Japanese Home Islands.

Unlike his fellow outfield greenhorns, Furillo, whose sloth on the base paths earned him the nickname "Skoonj" that spring (short for *scungilli,* Italian for snail), hated Durocher. Rickey had offered a mere $3,750 for the season, and when Furillo went to Leo to gripe, the manager told him to "take it or fucking leave it." Furillo was young and idealistic, but he could hold a grudge, and he never forgave Durocher for his brusqueness.

Still, all three rookies were in camp and looking good to make the Dodgers, even with Reiser and star outfielder Dixie Walker around. "When I see these kids run, throw and hit for extra bases the way Whitman, Furillo and Hermanski have done," said Durocher, "I don't care if they've got famous names or none at all." Still, to most onlookers, the infusion of so many kids spelled a rebuilding season for Brooklyn. "The Durocher-Rickey Youth Movement involves employment of green hands who are going to commit errors of commission and crimes of judgement before they hit a major league stride," thought Red Smith in the *New York Herald Tribune.*

Brooklyn's pitchers weren't famous names, and that was the residue of Durocher's design. No manager was more flexible with his roster, and in particular, none was as adept at using his entire staff. Durocher was a pioneer in using the entirety of his bullpen, often in a single game. He thought nothing of using five or six hurlers to win one ball game, or matching lefty pitchers against lefty hitters long before that was de rigueur. Once he brought in a pitcher to throw a fastball, then removed him for a reliever whose task was to throw a curve. "I just get a feeling," he would say of his hunch plays. In the coming season, Leo would use 223 relievers over the 154 games, far and away the most exhaustive use of a bullpen in the league.

Aside from Higbe, the staff was fronted by a kid who had pitched decently against wartime mediocrities, lefty Vic Lombardi; relief ace Hugh Casey, who was best known either for throwing a spitter that catcher Mickey Owen missed on strike three, a play that turned Game Four of the '41 World Series in the Yankees' favor, or for brawling with Ernest Hemingway one spring in Cuba; and a promising newcomer, Joe Hatten, who was earning comparisons to Dizzy Dean with his sidearm delivery. Hatten was the subject of some tall tales around the dugout campfire. One went that while in the minors, Hatten had deliberately walked the bases full while leading by one run in the ninth, just to see if he could escape the damage. He then struck out the side.

Familiar hurlers from the "Boys of Summer" staff—Don Newcombe, Carl Erskine, Johnny Podres, Clem Labine—were not yet on the club in 1946. The most recognizable name two generations later belongs to Ralph Branca, who had been a spot starter the year before. Only twenty years old, Branca was a good prospect, but like so many other players that year, he chafed at the puny dollars he was supposed to make for entertaining millions of fans. Rickey offered Branca the same $3,300 he had made in '45. Ralph sent the contract back unsigned, then told the *Daily News* about the inequity of it all, how the owners were living in a 1941 world when the war had changed everything.

News columnist Jimmy Powers went off on Rickey, coining the moniker "El Cheapo" for the Dodgers' majordomo. Rickey was embarrassed into upping the offer to five grand. Branca signed the contract but remained unenthused. Rickey wasn't happy either, and he ordered Durocher to pin Branca to the bench. So baseball's master of the pitching change held one of his better hurlers to just five starts and twelve appearances before circumstances changed in August.

In most other training camps, the salary haggles would command most of the attention of the writers and fans. But not in Daytona. All eyes were trained not on the business office but on the satellite diamonds. There, the minor leaguers were drilling, hopes of one day making the big club oozing from their pores like sweat. One in particular, wearing number 9 down at second base, stood out, not because of his powerful build or pigeon-toed gait but because of his skin color.

Chapter 7

"THE RIGHT MAN FOR THIS TEST"

IT MAY HAVE happened while he absentmindedly threw lit matches into wastebaskets in his office, one of his more perilous habits. It may have happened while on the long daily subway commute between his home in Forest Hills, Queens, and his office in Brooklyn. It may have happened while at twenty thousand feet, at the controls of his Beechcraft plane that he flew around the country, scouting the next generation of Dodgers.

Wherever it happened is lost to history, but at some point at the end of the war, Branch Rickey decided the time was right to integrate baseball.

An entire separate book would be required to parse the precise motives behind Rickey's decision. Certainly there was some altruism in his soul, along with his Christian sense of right and wrong. But there was also a considerable financial benefit should Negro players do as he expected and vault the Dodgers to the top of the National League. Signing black players was a gaping market inefficiency waiting to be exploited. Between the huge number of new fans—of both colors—and the projected boost from playing more meaningful late-season games, there was a clear profit motive pushing Rickey to sign a black ballplayer. In this case the revolution could be monetized, though that hardly detracts from the courage it took to be the first one out of that particular foxhole.

Rickey made his feelings clear to Harold Parrott, telling him,

"Son, the greatest untapped resource of raw material in the history of our game is the black race. The Negro will make us winners for years to come. And for that I will happily bear being a bleeding heart, and a do-gooder, and all that humanitarian rot."

The original plan was to sign several Negro Leaguers at once and make the announcement in *Look*. But New York politics threatened to subsume Rickey before he could make his news public. Mayor Fiorello La Guardia and city councilman Ben Davis were proposing to make integrating baseball part of their election campaigns, so Rickey stole a march, ordering his top scout Clyde Sukeforth to bring him forthwith the name of the best-prepared black player for this daring venture.

Sukeforth returned with the name Jackie Robinson on his lips, and within weeks, Rickey decided to sign Robinson to a minor league contract with the Dodgers' top farm team, the Montreal Royals of the triple-A International League. Robinson's Negro League team, the Kansas City Monarchs, wasn't consulted or compensated.

From a purely baseball perspective, there were several far more qualified candidates to break the color line than Jackie Roosevelt Robinson. Jack had been a four-sport letterman at UCLA, perhaps the best all-around athlete since Jim Thorpe, despite a childhood bout with rickets. He led the Pacific Coast Conference in scoring twice on the hardwood; averaged more than eleven yards per carry as a football halfback; won the NCAA long jump title; won the conference golf championship; and even made the semis of a national Negro tennis tournament, after picking up a racquet for the first time just a few weeks earlier.

But while he was solid on the diamond, Robby was hardly a match for some of the players thought most likely to crash through the wall of segregation, like Monte Irvin. Irvin, a powerful outfielder who would lead the Negro Leagues in hitting in 1946 while with the Newark Eagles, was the choice of most blacks to be the first to play in "white folks' ball" (an honor few of them wanted), but before any inroads could be made in that department, Irvin was drafted. His three years of service in an engineering battalion in France and Belgium left him rusty, and he turned down overtures from Rickey in late 1945.

Regardless of his actual ability on the field, Robinson had something the other candidates didn't—experience playing college sports with, and in front of, whites. That counted for a lot, as did his maturity (Robinson was nearing twenty-seven in late 1945). Jackie was also engaged to a nursing student named Rachel Isum, whom he had met at UCLA. That domestic grounding helped further convince Sukeforth, and then Rickey, that Robinson had the right temperament for the role of race pioneer.

Robinson was born in 1919, in Cairo, Georgia, to the son of a sharecropper. His grandfather was a slave. But the Robinson family moved to Pasadena, California, when Jackie was young, after the family patriarch, Jerry, left one day when Jackie was six months old and didn't come back. His mother, Mallie, raised Jackie and his three brothers and one sister on her own, and they were the lone black family on their block. Nothing was easy; still, life on the West Coast was easier than it would have been in the Deep South.

Jackie carried a sizable chip on his shoulder. Some of it was the natural arrogance of a great athlete, some of it his background, and some of it pure pride. He could be tough to get along with, and he had a violent temper (although, to his credit, he seldom let Rachel see that side of him away from the diamond). "Due to his inability to cool it, we were worried about him making the grade," remembered Quincy Trouppe, a Negro Leaguer who played with Robinson during the winter of 1945. "I remember one day when [teammate] Felton Snow tried to talk to Jackie about the right way to handle a play at shortstop, and Jackie really talked back to him bad." "A lot of us knew that," said Negro sportswriter Wendell Smith, who always referred to Robinson as "the young man from the west." "But we didn't want to tell Mr. Rickey." Rickey was clued in almost immediately upon meeting Jackie, writing that he possessed "more and deeper racial resentment than what was expected or hoped for." He had quoted Giovanni Papini's *Life of Christ* to Robinson at that fabled first meeting, in August 1945, telling Jackie, "Only he who has conquered himself can conquer his enemies."

The press conference, on October 23, 1945, announcing the signing was a sensation. It was held in Montreal, and Rickey didn't attend. "I just want a chance to play, and I think I can handle the worst of it," Robinson told reporters. "I don't look for anything physical. I really believe we have gotten beyond that in this country. I know I'll take a terrible tongue beating, though. But I think I can take it. I know about that riding white players give one another, and I'm sure it will be much worse for me because I am a Negro. . . . I've had plenty of nasty things said about me from the stands, especially in basketball, where you can hear everything they shout. I think it made me play better.

"I think I am the right man for this test," he continued. "There is no possible chance that I will flunk it or quit before the end for any other reason than that I am not a good enough baseball player." Robby was signed to a $600 monthly salary, with a bonus of $3,500. The *Pittsburgh Courier* put it aptly when it wrote that Robinson had "the hopes, aspirations and ambitions of 13 million black Americans heaped upon his broad, sturdy shoulders."

Upon his signing, most promised to judge Robinson on his merits. However, many critics readied their quills. "The waters of competition in the International League will flood far over his head," opined the *Sporting News*. Jimmy Powers of the *Daily News,* who otherwise pushed hard for integration, thought Robinson "a 1,000–1 shot to make the grade." Many black players privately thought Robinson had been selected precisely because he wasn't that good—thus, when he failed, the cause of integration would be set back for years.

Such a cynical ploy might well have been dreamed up by some of the plutocrats of baseball. Baseball had long resisted breaking the color line for various reasons, most financial. The owners made quite a bit of money renting their parks to Negro League teams, and they feared an end to that gravy train if blacks were allowed in the majors. They also greatly worried that white fans would stay away from the gates in droves if Negroes were competing. So while they stayed off the record as Rickey upended the status quo, privately they were aghast.

Bob Feller, the Cleveland Indians star pitcher, had competed against Robinson the year before while barnstorming. He predicted Jackie's failure on account of his "football shoulders," which would make him vulnerable on inside pitches, or something like that, anyway. Robinson was puzzled by the remark, writing to Smith of the *Pittsburgh Courier* that fall,

> The few times I have faced Feller has made me confident that the pitching I have faced in the Negro American League was as tough as any I will have to face if I stick with Montreal. There is one thing I would like to have made clear; just what does Feller really mean when he says I have "football shoulders?"

If Feller's comments were aimed at getting under Robinson's skin, he misfired. Jackie had already been through a much more trying episode.

The success of black soldiers in the service emboldened the civil rights movement. How, went the common refrain, could Negro soldiers have fought for basic human rights when they didn't have them when they returned home?

Ironically, it was because of a terrible experience in the army that Robinson became Branch Rickey's choice to integrate the game.

Robinson was playing semipro football in Hawaii with the (integrated) Honolulu Bears in the winter of 1941 and working con-struction during the week. The season over, he embarked at Pearl Harbor on a ship back to California—on December 5, fewer than forty-eight hours before the naval base was attacked by the Japanese. Jackie joined up in early 1942, entering the army. Rachel took losing her boyfriend to war in stride. "All the men in my family were in the army," she said. "My father was gassed in France during World War One. So I knew the army life. We worried, but we were confident they would serve and come home safe. It prepares you—you don't wring your hands the whole time."

Indeed, Rachel too did her bit, becoming a riveter at the Boeing Aircraft factory in San Francisco at night, after a day spent studying nursing. Robinson started at Fort Riley in Kansas. He sent Rachel a box of chocolates every week. "My roommates always knew when to come and get their share," she says. While in Kansas, Robinson, responding to a company-wide invitation to dinner, placed a tele-phone call to an officer who had mixed up his seat. Unaware he was talking to Robinson, the officer asked, "How would you like to have your wife sitting next to a nigger?"

But things were worse at Fort Hood in Texas. He was with the 761st Tank Battalion, a superb unit that was preparing for combat in Europe. Robby was a second lieutenant, and by all accounts an out-standing officer. But an old football injury to his ankle was a piece of red tape the army didn't like. Robinson was ordered to get an exam for an injury waiver if he wanted to continue with the battal-ion. He was on his way back from the doctor aboard a military bus when he was told by the driver to sit in the back.

Service buses had already been desegregated by order of the Pen-tagon, but that command had not reached down deep in the heart of Texas. Robinson refused to move, and the driver backed down, but back at the fort the driver called the military police. One of the MPs dropped the *N* word on Robinson, who cursed him in return.

The commander of the 761st, Paul L. Bates, refused to court-martial Robinson, but an officer higher up the chain wanted to exact a pound of flesh from the uppity black soldier, so Robby was transferred to the 758th, and military justice got involved. Jackie was brought up on multiple charges—drunkenness (Robby didn't drink), insubordination, conduct unbecoming an officer, you name it. The NAACP wanted to furnish an attorney, but because there were so many pending cases (real or trumped up) against black soldiers, the organization couldn't spare one. Jackie Robinson was not, as yet, *Jackie Robinson.*

So Robinson defended himself. It wasn't a long process. He admitted he had gotten riled up, explaining that he was "a negro, not a nigger," and the word had set him off. He told the senior judge, a captain, that he would have cursed him too if the judge had used that word to describe Robinson.

All nine judges found him not guilty.

The episode was deeply distressing for Robinson, as one can imagine. But, in a circular way, it was critical to his later success. For after the court-martial, Robinson felt the patriotism leech from his system. He was sent back to the 761st, but even the battalion's impending journey to fight the Nazis couldn't rouse him. Robinson was no stranger to racism, but the court-martial charges had been different, more insidious, more upsetting. "He came to see me in San Francisco, and I could see he was ready to leave the Army," Rachel remembers.

So Robinson asked for a discharge. The army, eager to wash its hands of the whole affair, quickly agreed. He was transferred to Fort Breckinridge in Kentucky for a few months, then released. It was late fall of 1944.

Of Robinson's four sports, baseball was probably his weakest. But the NFL was a backwater, the NBA was yet to exist, and track only mattered every four years (and the 1940 and 1944 Olympics were canceled due to the war). So baseball was Robby's best bet for getting paid to play ball, and that meant the Negro Leagues.

In the black community, his name carried weight from his UCLA days, and the Kansas City Monarchs were eager to sign him up. His game was nothing special, and glory on the playing fields of Westwood didn't sell too many extra tickets. But there was some upside. Robinson got some reps out on the diamond, crucial extra seasoning that he needed.

More important, Sukeforth saw him playing, something that could not have happened had Robinson been in Europe fighting the Wehrmacht, or even stateside in a staff position. Because he was wearing a Monarchs uniform, and not an army uniform, Robinson was in the right place at the right time. Sukeforth, impressed by Robby's maturity and athleticism, recommended him to Rickey. And thus was history made—a civil rights breakthrough borne on the winds of prejudice.

Pee Wee Reese was on a troop ship headed back home from Guam when a sailor told him that the Dodgers had signed a black man. "I'd have to say the word he used was not 'black,'" Reese added.

Robinson spent the winter of '45–46 playing ball in Venezuela. He was a shortstop and roomed with Roy Campanella, his future teammate in Brooklyn. He returned to California in February with an engagement ring in his luggage. "He wasn't going to propose until he signed a professional contract somewhere," Rachel remembers. "It was a promise he had made to himelf." They married at the Independent Church in Los Angeles on the tenth. After a brief honeymoon, the couple arrived at Los Angeles Airport on the late afternoon of February 28. Jack wore a gray business suit, Rachel a long ermine coat with matching hat and an alligator handbag, all wedding gifts from her new husband. They boarded an American Airlines flight to New Orleans, en route to Daytona and a historic training camp.

Mallie Robinson, Jackie's mother, was there to see them off. She handed her son a shoe box, and Jackie was surprised to find it filled with fried chicken and hard-boiled eggs. Just what baseball's race pioneer needed—a boxful of stereotype! But Mrs. Robinson insisted. "I thought something might happen and I didn't want you starving to death and getting to that baseball camp too weak to hit the ball," she said later.

Jack and Rachel arrived in the Crescent City without incident. While waiting for the connecting flight to Pensacola, Rachel saw her first ever "Whites Only" sign. She deliberately drank from the water fountain reserved for caucasians and used the restricted ladies room. Their flight was departing at eleven a.m., but a few minutes before, they were told that they had been bumped and would have to take the noon flight. There was a flight every hour, and the couple was repeatedly bumped off for servicemen. Starving, they asked to sit in the airport restaurant but were refused. So they took a cab to a cruddy local dive that served blacks. "I was almost nauseated," Rachel recalled. "It was a dirty, dreadful place and they had plastic mattress covers [for tablecloths]." They despondently ate Mallie's chicken and eggs.

Rachel shouldn't have been too surprised, despite her West Coast upbringing and the shelter it brought from the South's ugly overt racism. Only two days earlier, an argument between a black navy veteran named James Stephenson and his white radio repairman escalated into a full-blown race riot in Columbia, Tennessee. Almost the entire black section of town was arrested. Two weeks before that, a former army serviceman named Isaac Woodward was taken off a bus in South Carolina by police and clubbed so hard he was blinded. An all-white jury would later acquit the officers involved.

At last, the Robinsons boarded the seven p.m. flight to Pensacola. It was scheduled to refuel and fly on to Daytona, but in the Panhandle, they were bumped again. As they left the plane, they watched two white passengers board. Jackie was already running late, and this was the last flight of the day, so the Robinsons dashed for a bus to take them the final 445 miles of the journey. It would take sixteen hours, so Rickey, covering, told the press that "bad weather" had slowed Jackie's trip.

The driver ordered them to the back of the bus, and, unlike at Fort Hood, Robinson was bound by his word to Rickey that he wouldn't cause any trouble. So he and Rachel sat in the cramped caboose, on seats that didn't recline, hungry and exhausted.

Later that year, Robinson would give a long interview to the *Richmond Afro-American* in which he freighted that discouraging bus ride with considerable long-term import. "I was the advance guard, so to speak," he said.

I was the force that had been chosen to establish a beachhead in hostile territory. I was to test the potency of enemy fire. And as I sat there in the rear of that darkened bus with my eyes closed, I decided to map out the strategy I would use. The jostling of the rickety vehicle wouldn't let me sleep, so there was plenty of time to think. That's when it came to me that my cause was sure to be a winning cause. I thought of the various weapons the enemy had used to prove that in the world my race was inferior to all others. One of those weapons was this senseless law which required my wife and me to sit on the backseat of buses in the South. We did it, we still do it, and except for a slight and temporary injury to our pride, nothing really serious comes of it. We suffer no physical harm and their only gain is a false sense of social security. And as I sat there thinking, I tore down each one of the enemy's antiracial weapons in much the same way—from his carefully hidden peonage system to the Jim Crow educational patterns which still persist all the way up to the steps of the Capitol in Washington. I can't help feeling that during the sleepless overnight ride from Pensacola, Jackie Robinson matured! By the time I stepped onto the practice field at Daytona Beach for my initial workout in organized baseball, I was ready for anything.

For her part, Rachel quietly wept in the dark.

Chapter 8
REALITY CHECK

AT LAST, ON Saturday, March 2, Robinson arrived for his first pro camp. A racially mixed crowd surrounded the Robinsons as they disembarked from the bus, including John Wright, a second black player, a pitcher, signed (to far less fanfare) by Rickey to co-integrate baseball, and Wendell Smith, the sportswriter from the *Pittsburgh Courier,* the Negro newspaper with the largest circulation in the country.

Smith and Rickey were coconspirators in this "great experiment" almost from the start. Small and trim, with a dapper mustache, Smith was one of several Negro sportswriters who had pushed integration for years, going so far as to poll National Leaguers in 1938 about the idea. To his surprise, 75 percent of those he queried had no problem with playing alongside blacks, as opposed to 20 percent that did. Smith knew from integration, as he was the only black student at Detroit's Southeastern High School when he attended. His father was Henry Ford's chef, and Smith sometimes played ball right there on the auto magnate's lawn. He was told by a scout that he had major league talent, but alas, couldn't be signed for "white folks' ball."

Rickey was paying Smith $50 a week, nominally to scout but really to be Robinson's body man, in particular making sure he had places to eat and sleep in the South. "This whole program was more or less your suggestion, as you will recall," Rickey wrote Smith on

January 13. "Most certainly I don't want to find ourselves embarrassed on March 1st because of Robinson's not having a place to stay." "The *Courier* is willing to pay all my expenses in connection with this service," Smith wrote back. "We are trying to render the cause of Democracy in this country, so ably championed by you."

"He was there at every juncture," Rachel remembers of Smith. "He gave us a feeling of stability. He was helpful but never dictating. He was both counselor and big brother."

Smith, Wright, and the Robinsons went to the home of black pharmacist Joe Harris and his wife, Duff, for the night. Jackie vented about his journey from L.A. that evening. "I never want another trip like that one," he said. He threatened to return to California and quit the whole venture but was talked out of it. It was dawning on Robinson that, in the South at least, his college athletic exploits and army service meant nothing. He was just another Negro.

The flood of returning servicemen and Rickey's superb scouting meant that a crush of nearly two hundred players were in Daytona. As such, Rickey decided to move the minor leaguers with no chance of making the parent club, including Robby, to Sanford, the celery capital of Florida, forty miles southwest. There, Smith arranged for the Robinsons to stay at the home of David Brock, a local black businessman. The prominent Mayfair Hotel had refused them, naturally. Smith, meanwhile, stayed with an old girlfriend from school, whose father was the local numbers kingpin.

On Monday, March 4, Robinson donned his Montreal Royals uniform for the first time. He reported for duty at 9:30 a.m. and was immediately besieged by reporters. "What would you do if one of these pitchers threw at your head?" was a typical question. "I'd duck," was the answer. Robinson had played only shortstop and a little outfield previously, but the club thought he'd be best suited at second base, provided he could learn how to make the pivot.

But Robinson was not long for Sanford. That night, a white man showed up at the Brock home. Smith met him outside. "You're chaperoning Robinson?" the stranger asked. When Smith nodded, he was warned, "You better get him out of town today." The man had just come from a meeting between the mayor of Sanford and a large group of angry white residents, who demanded Robinson leave forthwith. Not wanting to test the situation, Smith bundled the Robinsons into a car, and they drove back to Daytona. Jack threatened to quit again; again, he was dissuaded by Smith. "I knew Jackie would make it and if he did things had to open up," Smith wrote later.

Daytona Beach was more welcoming. The "liberal city on the banks of the Halifax River," in Smith's words, was a haven filled with prominent and welcoming blacks. Joe Harris and his wife, Duff, introduced Robinson to an assortment of interesting people, including the educator and activist Mary McLeod Bethune. The lively, charming Bethune, a spry seventy years old, had founded a school for black girls in Daytona in 1904, a school that had flowered into the coed Bethune-Cookman College. She had also taken on the Ku Klux Klan by registering black voters throughout the 1930s. Thanks to her political efforts and savvy, Daytona had attracted several Depression-era work projects that had rescued the town from financial collapse. It was her spirit that infused the beach city. Mayor William Perry declared, "No one objects to Jackie Robinson and Johnny Wright training here. We welcome them and wish them the best of luck."

Robinson felt the difference as well. One afternoon, a dyed-in-the-wool southern gentleman approached him. "I've seen every game you've played in," he said as Smith took notes, "and want you to know that I'm pulling for you to make good. In fact, everyone here feels the same as I do. We believe a man deserves a fair chance if he has the goods, regardless of race or color."

Life at the Harris home provided no respite from pushing up against barriers. "The Harrises were activists, and held political meetings at the house," Rachel says. "Daytona had no black bus drivers, and right there in the house they organized a challenge and forced the city to hire a few." Jackie and Rachel didn't necessarily partake—they were cooped up in their love nest, lost in each other. "Duff would call us down to breakfast by calling 'c'mon lovebirds, time to eat!'"

Still, Robinson was prevented from staying in the Riviera Hotel with the rest of the Dodgers, nor could he eat at the same restaurants. If he wanted to swim in the ocean, he could not use Daytona's main beach, but had to travel down to Bethune Beach, named for Mary. Unfortunately, it was close to an hour's drive away. Smith, too, felt Jim Crow's sting. He was treated as an equal by the horde of white sportswriters in town, but he could not socialize with them away from the park.

Meanwhile, Robby faced the not insignificant challenge of proving he belonged with the whites on the field. The other Dodgers weren't hostile, but neither were they especially welcoming. They had their own jobs to worry about. "It had nothing to do with color," explains Eddie Robinson (no relation), who played for the Baltimore Orioles of the International League in '46. "If some guys came in from Germany to compete for jobs, it would have been the same thing."

The lone exception was a top candidate to play second base for the Montreal Royals in 1946, a player named Lou Rochelli. Rochelli selflessly taught Jackie how to pivot on the double play, how best to hurdle oncoming runners, and how to angle throws so that the shortstop could turn two. The following season, Pee Wee Reese would get credit for being the first white Dodger to embrace Robinson and facilitate his transition to the majors. If it weren't for similar actions by the unknown Rochelli, Jackie might never have made it to Brooklyn.

Robinson started slowly. The big leaguers were on the white side of town, while Jackie, Wright, and the other Royals (all reimported from Sanford so Robby didn't seem special) practiced at Kelly Field, in the Negro section, to avoid any possible issues. Robinson strained his arm and worried about being sent to a lower-level minor league club. Rachel would soothe his arm at night with icepacks, and his nerves with games of gin and laughter.

On the practice field, Rickey would stand on the first base line, urging Robinson to bring some of the flair and dash of the Negro Leagues to his play. "Be more daring!" he'd yell. "Gamble. Take a bigger lead." Meanwhile, Robinson was trying to win over his new manager, a Mississippian named Clay Hopper. Hopper so exemplified the southern gent that he actually owned a plantation in the Rebel State. His initial reaction to Robinson's signing was to beg Rickey to change his mind. "I'm white and I've lived in Mississippi all my life. If you do this, you're going to force me to move my family and my home."

During one workout that spring, Robinson made a tough play in the field. Rickey was standing alongside Hopper and called the play "superhuman." Hopper turned and infamously asked his boss, "Do you really think a nigger is a human being?" Rickey was incensed, but restrained himself. In relating the encounter to Robinson, he told him, "I saw that this Mississippi-born man was sincere, that he meant what he said; that his attitude of regarding the Negro as subhuman was part of his heritage; that here was a man who had practically nursed race prejudice at his mother's breast. So I decided to ignore the question." Privately, Hopper told friends, "I'm glad my father isn't alive to see me managing a black player."

On Sunday, March 17, Robby played in his first actual intersquad game, one that pitted the Royals against the Dodgers. A huge crowd of four thousand showed up at City Island Ballpark, buoyed by the one thousand or so black fans who sat apart from the grandstand, as required by law. One man who wasn't there was Branch Rickey—not even Robinson's first game was enough to get him to break the Sabbath.

Jack took the field against Pee Wee Reese, Dixie Walker, and Leo Durocher, who already had stated that he welcomed Robinson, although some of his former players, like first baseman Ed Stevens, felt that was for public benefit only and that Leo didn't want Robinson. He went 0–3 but got aboard on a fielder's choice, stole second base, and scored. He also fielded his position well, a more notable effort given his struggles to learn the intricacies of second base play. He got a loud ovation as the game concluded.

In 1948, Robinson would reflect on this first game: "When I got home, I felt as though I had won some kind of victory. I had a new opinion of the people in the town. I knew, of course, that everyone wasn't pulling for me to make good, but I was sure that the whole world wasn't lined up against me. When I went to sleep, the applause was still ringing in my ears."

The only thing ringing in his ears a few days later was the clanging of a padlock around a chain, barring him from play. The Royals had come to Jacksonville to play against Jersey City, but Durkee Field was shut tight, barring Robinson from competing against whites, per city ordinance. "Jacksonville got more bad press banning Robinson and Wright than any city in Florida has experienced since the Jesse Payne lynching at Madison last October," Smith wrote from the perspective of the black media.

Bad press or no, the canceled games mounted. Jacksonville struck down two more dates, and Savannah and Richmond sent word that Robinson and Wright were unwelcome in their parks. On April 7, Montreal's game with St. Paul began in Sanford, but before the third inning started, the police chief stormed on to the field and threatened to prosecute Hopper if the blacks weren't taken off the field. Hopper did as he was ordered, and the game ended. Then, three days later, in DeLand, Florida, park officials canceled a game because the lights weren't working—although the game was scheduled for one p.m.

Even when Robinson got to play, there were challenges. During a game against Indianapolis, a former major league pitcher named Paul Derringer faced Jackie. Derringer was tight with Hopper, and he told Clay before the game that he was going to knock Robinson down, "to see what makes him tick." Sure enough, Derringer put Jackie on his behind in the first inning. Robinson got up and lined a base hit, which incurred a pitch right at his head his next time at bat. This time, Robinson retaliated by tripling to deep left.

After the game, Derringer approached Hopper.

"He'll do," was all he said.

Despite such successes, the stress (and repeated bruises from being hit by pitches) was getting to Jackie. His sleep suffered, and he slumped at the plate. When he finally got a couple of singles, including a perfectly dropped bunt, the agricultural college at Bethune-Cookman sent Rachel a chicken and fresh vegetables for a victory celebration. "It was a communal victory for sure," Rachel recalled.

Still, Rickey was forced to cancel the remainder of the exhibition schedule. "I didn't realize it would be this bad," Rickey confessed as spring training ended. "Next year we'll have to train out of the country." He thus decided to move 1947 training camp to Havana, away from the burden of Jim Crow. But from a larger perspective, the camp was a success. Robinson earned a spot playing second base with the Royals. Wright, too, would be on the opening-day roster. On April 15, Jackie, Rachel, Wright, and Smith boarded a special train with the rest of the Royals, bound for New York City and the beginning of their historic season.

Chapter 9

THE MOST INTERESTING MAN IN THE WORLD

EVEN BEFORE ROBINSON'S debut on Floridian fields, the benign tyranny of baseball's moguls was under threat. This menace came from, of all places, Mexico.

It all started with a workout.

Jorge Pasquel was ahead of his time when it came to physical fitness. Broad and strong, he jogged and lifted weights long before that sort of thing was fashionable. His Mexico City mansion was equipped with all manner of exercise gear, but when he was in New York, as he was in early January 1946, he frequented a health club, Al Roon's place at 46th and Lex, above a Horn & Hardart automat cafeteria. His regular trainer wasn't working that day, so a new one was assigned.

Pasquel was stunned to find Danny Gardella waiting for him by the weights. The New York Giants outfielder was working his off-season job helping others get fit. Few around baseball thought anything of the fact that most players needed to moonlight to make ends meet. But Pasquel was shocked.

After the workout, he invited Gardella and a bodybuilding pal of his from the gym, Bob Janis, up to his room at the Sherry Netherland Hotel. With no information to work with, Gardella and Janis assumed Pasquel was queer. "If he makes a move on us, I'll coldcock him," Gardella assured his pal.

The Mexican magnate had nothing on his mind but business. He told Gardella that he would pay him far better to come and play in Mexico, where Pasquel owned the national league, the Liga Mexicana de Béisbol. With the war over, he was looking to boost the level of play. Pasquel and his four brothers directly owned two teams, in Mexico City and Vera Cruz, and had heavy sway over the other six clubs. Gardella said he would think about it, and accepted a gift of a pair of shoes (he was allowed to choose one of Pasquel's fifty pairs). Janis walked out of the room with a new job, as bodyguard and man Friday for the unusual millionaire.

Jorge Pasquel had been the man to see in Mexico City since long before 1946. "Sure, you could say I'm a dictator," he told *Time*. "Whatever I order is done."

The thirty-nine-year-old was from a wealthy family, the scion of a shipping magnate, and, along with his quartet of brothers (Alfonso, Bernardo, Girardo, and Mario), dabbled in businesses across the country. He started with a tiny cigar factory in Vera Cruz, but soon was wheeling and dealing in banking, ranching, real estate, shipping, automobiles, and customs. He flaunted his wealth, keeping a fleet of Lincolns and building a fully staffed haberdashery in his mansion to ensure he was always at his dandified best. "What is money?" he would say with a shrug. "I have forty, fifty, sixty million . . ."

He was an expert on Napoleon, keeping a bust of the French dictator in his mansion. He worshipped other powerful figures from history, like Attila and Alexander. A large man, he was nearly two hundred pounds and powerfully built but was light on his feet. He had a pencil mustache and favored thin-framed sunglasses that gave him an underworld look. Jorge was going bald a little too quickly, and often it seemed he was perpetually angry about it. His handsome features would suddenly cloud over with temper, and his rage would fill whatever room he was in. Moments later, all would be forgotten. His generosity was legendary. It seemed that everyone in Mexico had a story of his giving away *dinero* and gifts to complete strangers who approached him with tales of woe. One writer likened him to Santa Claus.

As one might expect, he had fought a duel once, with a general in the Mexican army, over a woman, naturally. Both men turned up, weapons in hand, but at the last moment decided that gunfire was less appropriate than letting the woman decide for herself. She chose Pasquel.

Even more fitting to his image was a story (unconfirmed but with enough shades of truth) about a trip to Havana in February of '46. He spent an evening drinking rum with Ernest Hemingway, whose self-styled macho persona might have been based in part on Pasquel. Well into their cups, the men stripped to the waist and began to box on the lawn of Hemingway's estate, El Vigía ("The Lookout"). The referee was Gene Tunney, who knew a little something about the sport.

Alfonso Pasquel was there, drunkenly taunting Hemingway, letting him know that Jorge had "killed a man in a duel." Jorge's lover, the beautiful actress María Félix, was there too, and supposedly wagered $100 on Papa to best her *papi*. Both men landed a few heavy blows, then thought better of the brawl and jumped into the swimming pool to refresh.

In sum, Pasquel was the original "most interesting man in the world."

Gardella was an odd choice for a pioneer. Squat and muscular, he was purely a power bat. His glove was atrocious. When a fly was hit his way, "the more casual fans hoped that Danny wouldn't drop the ball, while connoisseurs prayed that he wouldn't get killed." Mainly, he was a character. He loved practical jokes, acrobatics, odd stories from the paper. He would backflip across the outfield, then break into a quality Italian aria. He once fell asleep on the bench, shoes untied. Suddenly called upon to pinch hit, Gardella pounded a home run, rounding the bases with his shoes flapping. Not all of his merriment was so spontaneous. Gardella once premeditated a cruel prank; he spent several days convincing his roommate that he was feeling suicidal, then slipped out to the balcony and let loose a terrifying scream, causing his roomie to become hysterical before Gardella revealed himself.

A few weeks after meeting with Pasquel, Gardella asked the Giants for a raise from the $5,000 he had earned in 1945. After all, he had hit eighteen homers. But Danny undercut any chances he had at more cash by missing the train for Miami and spring training. When he finally arrived, he showed up for a team meal disheveled and casually dressed. Team rules insisted on a suit and tie, but Gardella couldn't afford either. He was released and immediately headed south for Mexico. Pasquel picked up the wayward Giant in a limo jammed with willing women, took him to dinner at a hip nightspot where the fabled bullfighter Manolete was eating tamales, and offered Gardella $8,000 for the year, plus a $5,000 signing bonus that equaled his salary offer from the Giants. At that, Gardella was a Vera Cruz Azul.

He made the announcement to American reporters by presaging LeBron James's Decision. "The Giants have treated me shabbily," he said. "I have decided to take my gifted talents to Mexico."

Several players, many with Latino roots, followed Gardella's path, including fellow Giant Napoleon Reyes (whom Pasquel may have signed merely for his first name), Bob Estalella of the A's, Chisox pitcher Alejandro Carrasquel, and Brooklyn's Luis Olmo, aka the "Puerto Rican Perfecto," who hit .313 in 1945. But the Liga had yet to make a significant splash, despite much boasting from the Pasquels. The guys they attracted were mostly wartime-ball roster filler, expendable with the return of the varsity.

The first big fish to sign on with Pasquel was Brooklyn catcher Mickey Owen. He was best known for letting that fabled third strike get past him in the ninth inning of Game Four of the 1941 World Series, which led to a Yankees rally and eventual championship. Owen had made four straight All-Star teams, was a solid, dependable starter on a popular team, and when he turned his back on Rickey to sign with Pasquel, it got plenty of attention. Owen got $15,000 a year for five years, plus a $12,500 signing bonus. "He even offered to bring my mother down," Owen told reporters. Pasquel sealed the deal by winning over Mrs. Owen, flashing a sizable diamond ring at her while promising, "This is for you at the end of the season." Mickey was made player-manager of Vera Cruz, where Gardella would be his right fielder.

Owen's signature on the dotted line opened eyes across baseball, boosting the players while worrying ownership, who hadn't taken Pasquel seriously. "Offers are coming in every day and unless the owners realize what's coming up next year they may wake up without ball clubs," said Owen's now former teammate Augie Galan.

Horace Stoneham, the owner of the New York Giants, sure felt that way after three more of his squad took the bait. Second baseman George Hausmann was leaned on by his wife, who was struggling to find a place to live in New York City. When she heard that they would live for free in a spacious abode in Mexico, she practically signed the contract herself. Two of Hausmann's teammates came too. Rookie Roy Zimmerman wouldn't be heard from again. Pitcher Sal Maglie would. Two more hurlers, Ace Adams and Harry Feldman, followed a couple of days later.

Stunned, Giants player-manager Mel Ott called a team meeting to assure the remainder of his team that he, at least, would be staying at the Polo Grounds. The gathering had a timely soundtrack. A slightly deaf pitcher named Bill Voiselle was in the bathroom, having missed the call to take a knee. As Mel was talking about the defections, Voiselle was shaving and singing "South of the Border" to himself. A teammate had to be dispatched to the john to tell Voiselle to knock it off.

Then the Pasquels landed a true star. Vern Stephens had led the AL in homers in 1945 and RBIs in 1944 while playing a strong shortstop for the St. Louis Browns. But the Brownies refused to give him a raise, and when Jorge whispered in his ear about big, guaranteed money, Stephens listened. He asked for a five-year, $175,000 deal, and wonder of wonders, Jorge said yes straightaway. The departure of the sport's hardest hitting shortstop astonished everyone in the game.

But Stephens didn't stick around. He was good at baseball, but not so much at life—he was socially inept and not particularly curious about anything outside of hitting the hanging curveball. Bob Janis said Stephens was "afraid of his own shadow" and couldn't hack Mexico's hustle and bustle. He was thrown the first time he showered, when he discovered the hard way that the *C* on the faucets stood for *caliente,* not "cold." So Vern jumped back to the Browns after a couple of weeks.

His father had come to stay with him in Monterrey, and now Stephens's père drove him to Laredo, where Vern put on daddy's overcoat and hat, pulled the brim down low, and skulked across the International Bridge. "I was afraid they might do something to stop me," he told reporters back in los Estados Unidos, "so I just hustled out of Monterrey and got moving." The Browns gave him $4,500 more for '46 to smooth things over.

Pasquel issued a formal complaint with the State Department, but otherwise forgot about Stephens and began to hunt big game in earnest. He breakfasted with Feller, lunched with Williams, and supped with Hal Newhouser. His offer to the Splinter was so grand that Ted asked, "Are you going to give me four strikes, too?" Williams, whose mother and grandmother were Mexican, wasn't impressed by the gauche Pasquel. "[He] had diamonds in his tie and diamonds on his watches and diamonds on his wrist," Ted remembered. "Every time he talked, he kind of splattered you a little bit. I got a commitment from him, but never really gave him a tumble." Others did—Pasquel nearly made Hank Greenberg choke on his steak when he offered the Detroit slugger $360,000. The big stars were surely tempted, but remained coy—for now. They preferred to use Pasquel's bottomless checkbook to try to drive up their own rates to stay in America.

Pasquel also sent Bob Janis to Daytona to go after Robinson, but the muscleman didn't have much of a chance for a sales pitch—Janis was in the clubhouse headed toward Jackie when Rickey and Durocher appeared. Leo had a bat in his hand, and tapped it against his palm, readying for combat. "Stop stealing our players!" Rickey yelled, and Janis beat it.

But Pasquel wasn't intimidated. When he "accidentally" crossed paths with Reiser and offered him $100,000 for three years on the spot, Pistol Pete was tantalized. "If I thought this offer was free of all US taxes," Reiser said, "I would take it in a minute. It would take ten years or more at a good salary here to earn that much."

The Mexicans were exploiting a yawning gap between baseball's popularity and the financial renumeration for its players, one that had always existed but was particularly stark with the war won and the palpable thirst for their services on display nationwide, even before the season started officially. "We treat players right here, not like slaves," Pasquel said, for the first time framing his raids as a labor issue, rather than merely a vanity play. "U.S. players are bought and sold like so much cattle and have no control over the decision."

The pivotal recruiting pitch was put to Yankees shortstop Phil Rizzuto. The Scooter had served on a navy supply ship in the Pacific during the war, shuttling between New Guinea and Manus, and had spent nearly a year in the Philippines. When he returned to the Yankees, he wasn't the player he had been before the war, and he scuffled during the Yankees' wide-ranging spring training. He was also suffering from island-borne malaria, an ague that would plague him intermittently during the season.

Sensing an opening, the Pasquels wined and dined Rizzuto at the Waldorf-Astoria, along with teammate Snuffy Stirnweiss. "We met them upstairs in their suite," recalled Rizzuto. "They were packing guns, which scared me. They promised us Cadillacs, if we'd go with them. Maybe I wouldn't have been so receptive to them if I were hitting better. But I had just gotten back from two years in the service and I was having a tough time adjusting to curve balls and getting base hits. I wasn't sure of my ability anymore. I was thinking this might be the most money I'll ever make in baseball, but after we left, Cora [Phil's wife] said to me, 'No way we are doing this.'"

MacPhail took the Mexican threat and what it represented to the Reserve Clause and the treasured status quo more seriously than many of his fellow owners. After all, the raids were the sort of thing he would do, were MacPhail running an upstart organization and not the totemic franchise in all of sports.

So when Mac had caught wind of the Pasquels' interest in Rizzuto, he'd bugged their hotel room. This was a little different terrain than promoting night baseball, but it was right up the alley of the shadow warrior who almost stole the Kaiser out of house arrest. He had his dark arts, and he used them to full effect. The next day, he called Rizzuto and Stirnweiss into his office, played them the recording of their meeting with the Pasquels, and suspended them for two days, suggesting strongly they break off all contact with the Mexicans. The ploy ended the Pasquels interest in luring Yankees players.

MacPhail had ensured his team wouldn't be hurt. Now he went to work on the rest of the majors. He paid a visit to Commissioner Chandler, who MacPhail himself had championed the year before when few had thought of him as a worthy replacement for Kenesaw Mountain Landis. Mac had pushed the Kentucky senator into the job. Now MacPhail, doing his best Scotch-Irish version of Don Corleone, reminded Chandler of how he got to that particular post. Mac then noted that big money from the Pasquels was a strong inducement to jump, and that an even stronger reason not to go was needed to protect the integrity of the game.

On April 16 in Chicago, Chandler announced the reason. He banned jumpers from the majors for five years.

This was big news, but it got a little lost in the noise generated elsewhere. For Chandler had made his sweeping pronunciation on opening day, 1946.

Chapter 10
OPENING DAY

TUESDAY, APRIL 16, was sunny and cool in Washington DC. The morning papers were full of baseball talk, and an advertising campaign that trumpeted "THE STARS ARE BACK!" appeared in them all; indeed, the owners had paid to place similar ads in dozens of publications across America.

Yep, "real baseball" was back, and John Q. Public would have to pay for the privilege of watching the frolic on peacetime diamonds. Only five teams, notably including the defending champion Tigers and the NL pennant-holding Cubs, had kept ticket prices static. The rest had upped their rates from 50 to 100 percent, typically to between $2.00 and $2.50 for reserved-box seats, $1.25 for general admission, and about $.60–$.75 for the bleachers.

Ordinarily, already put-upon Americans might have responded to this indignity with some outrage. But such was the overwhelming hunger to see baseball at its highest level once again, and the joy that the game was back in all its glory, that stands were packed across the league. The eight inaugural games played that Tuesday drew 236,730 fans, the second-highest total in the sport's history to that point. All told, close to half a million fans attended the sixteen openers.

A crowd of 30,272 turned out to Griffith Stadium in the nation's capital to see the Senators host the Red Sox, including someone of particular importance—President Truman. Roosevelt in 1942 had discontinued the tradition of the president opening the season by throwing out the first pitch. He had more important matters to worry about that April, as the Japanese cut the Burma Road, invaded New Guinea and Sri Lanka, and captured Bataan in the Philippines, forcing some seventy-eight thousand prisoners to march south. Thousands died along what came to be called the "Bataan Death March."

Now, four years later, Truman received a large ovation as he strode through the stands to his box and prepared to throw out the ceremonial pitch. He was the first president to walk to his seat—all previous chief executives had been driven to their boxes. The First Lady, Bess, and Admiral William Leahy, Truman's chief of staff, flanked the president in his box, which was crammed with an entourage of thirty-two people, including General Dwight D. Eisenhower. A natural lefty who had learned to write and perform other tasks with his right hand as a youngster, Truman promised to throw out this pitch southpaw, to honor "the game's great left-handed hurlers."

But when the time came, he mistakenly began to throw it out with his right hand. Reminded of his presidential promise, "he switched the ball to the publicized duke, limbered it up with two short waves of the soupbone, drew it back behind his ear, and fired an overhand delivery about 50 feet into the cluster of players of both sides deploying for the throw," according to the *New York Herald Tribune*. A Sox reserve named Andy Gilbert caught the ball after it had caromed off a couple of Sens, and he had Truman autograph it.

The game was a command performance for the longtime baseball fan in the Oval Office. Hardly one to put on airs, the "accidental President" remained a Missouri good ol' boy even while living on Pennsylvania Avenue. Truman spent his downtime playing endless hands of stud poker with his "Show Me State" cronies, and returned often to his home turf, where he made a point of spitting in the Mississippi (a long-held tradition thought to bring luck).

To Truman, the return of the prodigal hardball stars was in keeping with the finest tradition of warrior-citizenship. His hero was Cincinnatus, the Roman general who returned to his farm when war ended, his nation served. True, Joe D. and his ilk hadn't seen much combat, much less battled it out with the Volscians. But regardless of actual dangers faced, Truman revered the likes of Williams, who had sacrificed three years of his career for his country. That was in the finest tradition of the republican ideals Truman treasured. It was in stark contrast to what he was starting to see day in and out. It was completely beyond his understanding how the United States could go so quickly from wartime sharing and belief in the common good to the breathtaking selfishness on display in postwar America. He was fit to be tied by the political obstruction he faced in Washington; as *Life* wrote about his pitch at Griffith that day, "It's the first time in months he's found anybody to play ball with him."

Williams came to bat in a scoreless game in the third inning. He'd been saddled by a sore throat for the previous few days, but announced in batting practice that he was at full health by catapulting several balls over the right field wall. Now Williams unloaded on a knuckleball from Roger Wolff to dead center, a home run that landed some 440 feet from the plate. It was among the longest shots in Griffith Stadium history, and even the home folks rose to give Williams a loud ovation in response to the sheer magnificence of the clout. Boston went on to win 6–3, backing up Truman's prediction of a Sox victory.

After the game, the housing shortage that gripped the nation was brought home when reporters learned that ten of the Senators players, unable to find a dwelling, had been living for over a week in the team clubhouse. The Sens weren't alone. The Chicago White Sox offered a season pass to anyone providing a lead that resulted in housing for twenty team members who had nowhere to live as of opening day. The homelessness partly explained the feeble effort the

Chisox put forth, managing just three hits off Cleveland's fireballer, Feller, in a 1–0 loss. Rapid Robert had a little something to do with it as well.

The demobilization had unleashed so many former soldiers on the country that the most basic of human needs, shelter, was an issue for millions. Real-estate salespeople exacerbated the shortage by jacking up prices and putting unreasonable demands on many properties, such as "No Children Allowed." Young couples with families were forced to crowd in with in-laws. Mauldin, the Pulitzer Prize–winning cartoonist, was spot-on and savage with his drawings lampooning the situation. One portrayed a statue of a soldier sleeping on a park bench, with the phrase *Semper Sans Cot* ("Always Without Cot") stenciled upon it; the cartoon was entitled "The Unknown Soldier, 1946."

Another pictured a former GI on a park bench telling the police officer rousting him, "You shoulda seen where I spent my nights last winter!" A third had a couple of veterans being accosted in a hallway by a shotgun–toting landlord. "If ya want character references," one says, "write to Signor Pasticelli, Venafro, Italy. We occupied his barn for seven weeks."

The satire was rooted in unfortunate reality. The housing shortage was so severe people slept all night at Turkish bathhouses. In Corpus Christi, Texas, the entire town turned out for a barn raising of sorts, a project that built an entire home for a veteran in a single day. The city of Greenwich, Connecticut, leased mansions that had been sitting empty to vets for $1 a year. The head of the government-housing department, Wilson Wyatt, authorized 250,000 military Quonset huts to be converted for private use. Meanwhile, he encouraged factories to turn out prefab homes, mobile units that could be laid down and built around. Early examples drew huge crowds in department stores, and orders were backlogged for months. In New York, a man named Henry Levitt took notice of the crying need for housing and developed plans for entire cities of prefab homes, to be known as Levittowns, that soon would dot the suburban landscape.

In the meantime, house hunters used all manner of chicanery to find a place to dwell. Some would approach the superintendent of an apartment complex and bet him $200 that there were no vacant units, hoping to lose the bet/bribe. Others gifted the women who took housing ads for the *Times* with nylons, perfume, or straight cash, anything to get a leg up on the new listings. "The girls, being of strong moral fiber, always turn these offers down firmly," the paper reported.

One corporate manager had an underling transferred west—then took his apartment. An investigator for the New York district attorney's office arrested a tenant—and moved into his vacated apartment. Chicago reported a shortage of NO VACANCY signs, though FOR RENT signs were going at half price.

The most common solution for the unsheltered was to trade something of value for an apartment: a Leica, a pet, a job. Automobiles were the most common trade bait. One fall issue of the *Times* had no fewer than forty-eight offers of cars-for-apartment trades in the classified section.

In one reported case, a woman was told that her Plymouth would land her a home in New Jersey, but for a place in New York City, she needed a Cadillac.

Williams wasn't the only star to get off to a good start. In Philadelphia, Joe DiMaggio also celebrated his return to action with a home run as the Yankees shut out the A's 5–0 behind Spud Chandler. The "New DiMaggio" celebrated with his teammates in the dugout with a demonstrative flair that had the press asking themselves, *Who is this guy?*

Up in New York, UN Secretary-General Trygve Lie, a Norwegian, attended his first-ever game, the opener at the Polo Grounds. Actress Dorothy Lamour was there too, "wearing a large white hat to avoid attention," in the words of John Lardner. They got to see another superstar, Ott of the Giants, go yard in an 8–4 win for New York over the Phillies. It was the 511th homer of Ott's storied career—and his last. In the next game, the thirty-seven-year-old Ott dove for a liner and injured his knee, essentially ending his career. Fortunately, he was the player-manager of the Giants, so he had a reason to come to the park every day. Not so for the pinup star from Hollywood—Lamour reportedly left after the first inning, an act, in Lardner's mind, "contrary to protocol, which called for the Phillies starter to leave the game first." Said starter, Oscar Judd, lasted into the second inning before he was driven from the mound, trailing 6–0.

In Boston, a mariachi band played "South of the Border" to taunt the visiting Dodgers over the loss of Owen, tossing pesos into the crowd when they finished. Then the Braves broke a 3-all tie with runs in the sixth and seventh to beat Brooklyn 5–3. Of more interest was the Brooklyn starting outfield. Despite the presence of Reiser and Walker, Leo made a point by starting the three rookies, Hermanski, Whitman, and Furillo. The manager was serving notice that he would use any player on his roster at any time.

Braves Field had looked good, as the stadium seats had been freshly painted before the game. Unfortunately, the weather was sharply cold in Beantown, and the paint hadn't dried well in the chill. Thus thousands of fans went home with green paint on their clothes. The team ran an ad apologizing for the miscue, offering to reimburse cleaning bills. Claims poured in from all over the country, many from people who were clearly looking for a quick score and obviously hadn't been in Boston on the sixteenth. The Braves paid all claims anyway, costing the team more than six grand. The day had a more lasting effect too. The positive reception to the rich green hue of the park would make an impression on the crosstown Sox, who would put the shade to use on the monstrous left field wall at Fenway Park the following spring.

About the only city unmoved by the occasion of opening day was, of all places, St. Louis. A touch fewer than fourteen thousand turned out to see the Cards drop the kickoff game to Pittsburgh on a chilly afternoon. There was no ceremonial first pitch, and little sense of occasion. The home team put three runs up in the very first inning, two on a double by heralded rookie Dick Sisler. Sisler was notable mainly for his odd habit of pirouetting his bat counterclockwise as the pitcher delivered, pausing briefly at the shoulder before starting his swing.

Pirates manager Frankie Frisch, a longtime Cardinal who knew from cold spring days in St. Louis, had his clubhouse boys forage for tinder before the game and build a fire in an old wheelbarrow in the back of the dugout. The Pirates warmed themselves by the blaze throughout the long game (it lasted two hours and forty minutes, a marathon by the standards of the day), while the Cardinals shivered. Sure enough, "Everything the Cards did after the first inning turned as sour as a week-old crock of clabber," noted J. E. Wray in the *Post-Dispatch*. Pittsburgh came back for a 6–3 win.

Chapter 11
JACKIE'S DEBUT

WARREN "LEFTY" SANDEL was a tough guy, a pitcher from the old school who thought nothing of brushing back hitters—or putting one in their ear if the situation called for it. He once plunked three straight batters who were attempting to squeeze a run home from third base, even though it cost him the game. He did it just to make a point. So he was surprised to have his own catcher question his manhood. With a 2–1 count on the hitter, Sandel's equally tough, tempestuous catcher, Dick Bouknight, trotted out to the mound and asked Sandel a rather direct question.

"Are you going to throw at this nigger or not?"

It was April 18, two days after the majors had opened their campaign. Now the minor leagues were beginning play, and there was a celebratory feel in the air on this Thursday afternoon in Jersey City, New Jersey. Mayor Frank Hague had closed the schools and declared a holiday for city employees—on the condition that they purchase tickets for the game that day between the Jersey City Giants and the Montreal Royals. Because of the edict, fifty-two thousand tickets were sold for the game at Roosevelt Stadium, a park that held about twenty-three thousand.

They could have sold that many tickets for the Thursday afternoon game, even without the Mayoral Holy Bull, thanks to the starting second baseman for the Royals that day—Jackie Robinson.

Roosevelt Stadium was named not for Teddy Roosevelt (whom Jackie was middle-named for), but for FDR. The art deco–style stadium was built as a Works Progress Administration project in the Droyer's Point section of Jersey City, at the intersection of Danforth Avenue and Route 440. Pregame, the park was festive, with two bands playing, tumbling acrobats cavorting across the outfield, and a huge throng of writers and photographers on hand to capture the action.

Clay Hopper wasn't planning to start Robinson, not yet fully believing in his new infielder/experiment, but when he caught wind of the hype being whipped up around Robinson's debut, he caved in. Hopper told Jackie he was starting that morning at the McAlpin Hotel, at 34th and Broadway in Manhattan, and Robinson crossed the Hudson anxiously awaiting his first day at integrating the game.

It took him five full minutes to work his way through the crowd outside to the clubhouse. Many black fans had turned out, of course, but there was a healthy mix of races and creeds, what Smith called, "A seething mass of humanity, representing all segments of the crazy-quilt we call America," in the *Courier*. "Wendell Willkie's 'One World' was right here on the banks of the Passaic River." Another writer, Baz O'Meara from the *Montreal Star,* called it "another Emancipation Day—a day Abraham Lincoln would like."

As the national anthem wafted across the field, Robby and John Wright stood ramrod straight, blue caps in hand, their faces blank. Smith put himself in their shoes:

> No one knew what they were thinking right then, but I have travelled more than two thousand miles with the courageous pioneers during the past nine weeks . . . and I feel like I know them probably better than any newspaperman in the biz . . . I know that their hearts throbbed heavily and thumped a steady tempo.

Indeed, Robby himself alliteratively described the "lump in his throat and my heart beating rapidly, my stomach feeling as if it were full of feverish fireflies with claws on their feet."

Mayor Hague threw out the first pitch, and the game was on.

Robinson batted second in the lineup, and came up in the first with one out. A huge roar greeted him. "Although I was wearing the colors of the enemy," recalled Robinson in his autobiography, *I Never Had It Made,* "the Jersey City fans gave me a fine ovation. And my teammates were shouting, 'Come on, Jackie, start it off. This guy can't pitch. Get a-hold of one!'"

The "Little Giants" were less welcoming. Sandel, the starting pitcher for Jersey City on this historic occasion, recalled to writer Rick Van Blair in the early 1990s that "Before Jackie came up some of the guys in the dugout were making all kinds of remarks like, 'Whoever don't get a hit tonight has to room with a nigger on the road.'" Sandel had grown up in California and knew Robinson some from Jackie's days on the West Coast. "I didn't have anything against him," Sandel said. "If he was better than me, more power to him." Thus, when Bouknight came out to demand that Sandel plunk Robinson, the pitcher refused. Bouknight, not liking that answer, went back to his squat, and when the next pitch came in outside, he returned it to Sandel—an inch or two from Robby's right ear.

Robinson took the count full and bounced out to short, a grounder considered unremarkable by most onlookers, but one Smith called a "sizzler to shortstop"; he wrote that Robby was "thrown out by an eyelash at first base."

Rachel Robinson was busy roaming the breezeway behind the stands, too nervous to sit still. "I didn't engage with the other players' wives at all," she remembered. "I was distant; I was paying too much attention to the field to be polite." Out at second base, Robinson couldn't bear to look at the crowd, "for fear I would see only Negroes applauding." The import of the moment threatened to paralyze the twenty-seven-year-old. "We all sensed that history was in the making," wrote Robinson, "that the long ban on Negros was about to come crashing down, setting up reverberations that would echo across a continent and perhaps around the world. I believe everyone in Roosevelt Stadium that day realized he was witnessing a significant collapse in the ancient wall of prejudice."

The Royals led 2–0 in the third when Robby came up to bat again. The flags on the foul poles fluttered lazily in the slight breeze. Two men were on base, so Sandel assumed Robinson would bunt. Indeed, Sandel said years later that he had stolen the bunt sign from the Royals dugout, so he let up a little on his fastball to get into a defensive posture a touch faster.

Unfortunately, Robinson had either missed the sign or ignored it, for he "swung with everything I had" at the chest-high pitch and was rewarded with a "crack like a rifle shot in my ears." The ball disappeared behind the left field fence, a shot estimated at 335 feet. The crowd at Roosevelt Stadium let loose with a bellow that scattered nervous wildlife across North Jersey.

It was an amazing moment, a theatrical blend of the historic and the sensational. Robinson rounded the bases, trying vainly to keep a broad smile off his face. The many black fans in attendance shouted, danced, and threw programs in the air. George "Shotgun" Shuba, the Royals left fielder, was on deck, and he "danced a mild jig," according to the *Afro-American*. He waited at home for Jackie. "You could see it in his face, how happy he was," Shuba recalled to the *New York Times* fifty years later. "You could see he was just overwhelmed with joy."

Hopper slapped Jackie on the back as he rounded third, and Shuba shook his hand as Robby touched home to make the score 5–0 Montreal. The following April, Dodgers shortstop Pee Wee Reese would famously shake Robinson's hand and put his arm around the besieged newcomer as he ended segregation in the major leagues. This moment is much less remembered, but it confirmed what Robinson had suspected all along—that winning and performance would far outweigh race on the athletic field, and he would be welcomed once he showed he belonged. "I didn't think anything of it," Shuba said. "A teammate had homered, and I shook his hand."

The whole team congratulated him in the dugout. "Deep southern voices from the bench shouted, 'Yo sho hit 'at one, Robbie, nice goin' kid!'" Smith later wrote. But up in the press box, Smith was too overcome by the moment to reflect on the culmination of his tireless efforts to promote the idea of the breaking of the color line. He could only look over to fellow Negro sportswriter and Robinson supporter Joe Bostic and smile broadly.

According to Sandel, however, Hopper was upset that Robinson had ignored the bunt sign, and he roasted his rookie between innings.

Phil Oates was in to relieve Sandel the next time Robby hit, in the fifth inning. He had played longball, and now Jackie showed the fans some of the flair the Negro Leagues were known for, what its practitioners called "tricky baseball." He bunted for a hit, stole second, and went to third on a groundout. What followed would become familiar to baseball fans lucky enough to see Robinson play. He teased Oates, dashing down the line and throwing on the brakes, shoulder-faking, and generally inciting the crowd to holler and Oates to come undone. Oates stopped in mid-windup to throw over to third, a clear balk, and Robinson trotted home with a run he had created by "running the bases like a wild colt from the Western plain," in Smith's phraseology.

Jackie was rolling. In the seventh, he singled, stole second, and scored on a triple. In the eighth, he bunted his way aboard yet again, scampered around to third on an infield single, and then flummoxed yet another pitcher, this time Hub Andrews, drawing another balk and scoring for the fourth time. That made the score 14–1, which would be the final blowout result.

Other than an error in the fifth that allowed Jersey's lone run to score, Jackie had been magnificent under immense pressure. Robby had gone 4–5 with 3 RBIs, 2 steals, and the 4 runs scored, and had made an indelible impression on everyone in the park. "He did everything but help the ushers seat the crowd," Bostic wrote in the *Amsterdam News.* Dink Carroll in the *Montreal Gazette* wrote, "He has the same sense for the dramatic as Babe Ruth, Red Grange, Jack Dempsey, Bobby Jones and others of that stamp. The bigger the occasion, the more they rose to it." "Jim Crow Dies at Second" was the headline in another paper.

The only ones not in Robby's thrall were the Little Giants, especially Sandel. He was incensed that Robinson had bunted for a hit with the game out of hand. "To me that was just fattening up his average because in that situation you have to hit away," he said. True to his nature, and the unwritten codes of baseball, the next time Sandel faced Robinson, he knocked him down with a fastball, and said "that was for bunting that last time."

But no one else was complaining, least of all the overflow crowd. Jackie later wrote, "I knew what it was that day to hear the ear-shattering roar of the crowd and know it was for me." At game's end, the throng rushed onto the field. Fans surrounded Robinson. Smith again captured the scene as Jackie tried to get off the field:

"Perspiration rolling off his bronze brow, idolizing kids swirling all around him, autograph hounds tugging at him . . . and big cops riding prancing steeds trying unsuccessfully to disperse the mob that cornered the hero of the day."

Red Durrett, a Royals teammate whose two homers on the day had been completely overshadowed, performed more heroics by wading into the mob and pulling Jackie to the safety of the clubhouse. There, however, Robinson encountered more bedlam. Flashbulbs exploded, reporters shouted questions, half-dressed teammates approached to slap his back or clap his shoulder. "Don't think I didn't like it," Robby told Lloyd McGowan of the *Montreal Star.* Someone thought to call Rickey, who was at his desk on Montague Street (the Dodgers were having their home opener that afternoon). "He's a wonderful boy," he said when informed of the remarkable events of the afternoon.

The sun was disappearing behind the park as the Robinsons left. Her face red from the slanting rays of twilight, Rachel turned to her husband and said, "You've had quite a day, little man."

"Yes, God has been good to us today," Jackie replied.

Chapter 12
TRIAL BY FURY

St. Louis righted its ship in Game Two of the season, a 6–0 shutout behind Max Lanier. The strongly built lefty was, like President Truman, adept with both hands. In Lanier's case, he pitched from the port side because he had broken his right arm twice as a youngster. Max was dominant during the war years, winning seventeen games in 1944, before finally getting called up in May of '45. He pitched for the team at Fort Bragg and happily saw the war end almost as soon as he got through basic training. Lanier still had plenty of time to serve, but was granted an unexpected, and controversial, discharge in October. The War Department was forced to investigate and cleared the pitcher for baseball duty.

Lanier held out for a time in the spring, battling for extra money from the notoriously miserly Sam Breadon. He got only a $500 bump from his 1944 rate, and a grudge began to build. Lanier was a rowdy-looking man from North Carolina, fast with a joke and a first-rate singer, but the disagreement over salary robbed him of some life. He was thirty and beginning to think about life after baseball for the first time.

On the mound, however, it was hard to see his distraction. Lanier baffled hitters by delivering from various angles, including sidearm, and using a wide repertoire of pitches. He used a very high leg kick and never pitched from the stretch, regardless of runners on base. He started the season 6–0, with two shutouts and a microscopic ERA.

In particular, Lanier could be relied on to best the Dodgers, winning eleven straight against the Bums at one point. That was important, because Durocher's team was looking far more formidable than predicted. After losing the opener in Boston, Brooklyn won eight in a row.

The strong play started on April 18, when 29,825 turned out for the first home game of the season at Ebbets Field, against Brooklyn's hated Harlem rivals, the Giants. As a male quartet sang under the stands and a lone trumpeter played a "brassy paeon of joy," fans swarmed Flatbush. Cops asked loiterers in the area if they had tickets—if not, they were turned in the opposite direction, away from the park. New York City Mayor William O'Dwyer, who loved the Dodgers almost as much as he loved the ponies, tossed out the first ball, "a weak blooper that plopped almost unnoticed on the grass." The Dodgers thence unloaded on Mel Ott's Giants, winning 8–1, even as Brooklyn's triple-A team was hammering New York's behind Robinson's heroics at exactly the same moment. Pete Reiser, the superstar returned from war, was in an unusual spot—third base, a position he hadn't played since he was a rookie in 1940. Durocher was determined to give the kids (Whitman, Hermanski, and Furillo) a shot in the outfield.

The game on April 23 had the Brooklyn faithful believing that this might be a special season along the Gowanus. The euphoniously named Ed Head no-hit the Braves 5–0 that afternoon. Head was a righty from northern Louisiana. He began life as a lefty, but one day when he was fifteen, Head was riding in a bus with his sweetheart. As kids that age are wont to do, he had his arm draped over her shoulders. She was in the window seat and thus had a good view of the bus that came up and plowed headlong into the one they were riding in.

She died instantly, but Head survived, his arm crushed. Amputation was recommended. But Head pleaded with the surgeon to telephone Ed's uncle, Dr. L. E. Larche. Larche had the only fluoroscope in all of the area, and an examination showed the arm could be saved. After many hours of surgery, Head kept his left arm. Unfortunately, he could no longer pitch with it. So he learned to pitch right-handed, and amazingly adapted well enough to get to the bigs.

Head hadn't pitched in two seasons, and his good wing was still sore from absorbing a recoil from an anti-tank gun at Camp Hood, Texas. And his mind was almost certainly elsewhere—his wife had given birth to a baby boy, Rickey, the day before. Maybe the distraction helped, for Head made short work of the Braves. "I knew I was going to do it all the time," boasted the proud papa. At the final out, fans deluged the field in celebration.

A few weeks later, Head hurt that expedient right arm again, and never returned to pitch in the majors.

But Brooklyn's biggest victory of April came off the field. The season before, Durocher had been arrested for beating up a heckler beneath the Ebbets Field stands. Now he went before a jury of his peers to account for the assault. The courtroom saga was judged by *Life* as "The most sensational trial held in Brooklyn since the smashing of Murder, Inc."

Accuser John Christian was a huge Dodgers fan, a star athlete at Thomas Jefferson High School in Brooklyn, and a veteran, with a sore knee that he hurt in a glider accident while in the army. Sitting at Ebbets Field with another former Jefferson High star, Dutch Garfinkel, Christian let fly with some choice words for Durocher at top volume. "His voice could carry two or three blocks," Garfinkel remembered. Durocher testified that Christian had called him a "bum" and a "thief" and had accused him of throwing games.

A security man named Joe Moore shoved his way to Christian and ordered the fan to come with him. Moore, a gargantuan fellow who pushed 275 pounds, was legendary at Ebbets Field for whaling on kids who tried to sneak into the park. The two men made their way to a small room behind the Dodgers dugout.

Here the accounts diverged. Christian said on the stand that Leo came back, took a "black object" (most likely Moore's trademark cosh), and knocked him down. "Then he punched me in the face while I was down.... Moore pushed me out and Durocher followed me and beat me again with his fists. I fell down again and Moore said 'I'm going to throw you outta the park.'"

Leo, unsurprisingly, remembered it differently. "Have you a mother?" he said he asked Christian. "Well, how would you like it if... I went to your house and called her the names you have been shouting out tonight?"

"You're still an asshole," Durocher testified Christian replied.

"I ran at him," the Lip continued. "I saw him fall against a wall. He fell into a water trough. I did not pursue him. I don't know what might have happened if... I had gotten my hands on him." Somehow, Leo managed to maintain a straight face during his time on the witness stand.

It took the all-male jury a mere thirty-six minutes to acquit Leo and send him triumphantly back to Ebbets Field, where curious reporters would search in vain for the alleged "water trough" that supposedly bloodied the plaintiff. The courtroom erupted in cheers at the verdict. Several weeks later, Durocher quietly paid Christian $6,750 to settle a civil suit, although it was rumored that actor Danny Kaye, a Durocher buddy, paid the settlement.

Brooklyn parlayed the fast start and its manager's legerdemain into a 15–7 record and a surprising two-game lead on the Cardinals by the time of its first matchup with St. Louis, a two-game set beginning May 14. The Redbirds had started much like Brooklyn—an opening-day loss, followed by seven straight wins. They had scuffled of late, but in Brooklyn served notice that they remained the pennant favorites. In the opener, the Dodgers gave away free nylons as a promotion, though the game hardly needed extra buzz. Thirty-one thousand packed the park, but went home unhappy when Marty Marion knocked in a pair of runs in the eleventh inning to win it for the Cards, 7–5. Sure enough, Lanier, the Scourge of Brooklyn, went the distance for the victory. By now, Durocher had decided to go with veterans in the outfield, and Hermanski and Whitman hit the bench, in favor of Walker and Reiser. Furillo got regular action, mostly in center field—though he would become an acclaimed right fielder in later years, he played only four games there in 1946.

The next day, Howie Pollet bested Dodgers starter Lew Webber 1–0, and the teams were tied for first. The game was most notable for an incident that took place in the fifth inning, when Webber brushed Country Slaughter back with a pitch. The Cards outfielder responded by bunting up the first base line and running over Webber as the pitcher tried to field the ball. The benches emptied, "indicating another free-for-all indicative of Dodgers-Cardinals relations," according to the *Post-Dispatch*. The crowd gave Slaughter a fierce hammering out in right in the bottom of the inning, but Enos shut them up by making a sensational catch and doubling off Furillo at first to kill a rally. The crowd was quiet after that.

It was the sort of old-school vengeance that endeared Slaughter to baseball lifers and new fans alike. Hall of Famer Bucky Harris would say of Country, worshipfully, "His name should be in school textbooks along with this country's most revered heroes. He never quit. He never will. He won't even let down."

As his nickname suggests, Slaughter grew up in the backwoods—in his case, a tiny cabin in Roxboro, North Carolina. His father, Zadok, was a farmer who played true country hardball, taking his catcher position in semipro games with no shoes and no glove! The bravery apparently was a hit with the ladies; as Slaughter wrote in his memoir, "I guess Ma figured that a guy who wasn't afraid to handle speeding baseballs without the protection of a catcher's mitt or even shoes had what it took to handle droughts, floods, and anything else that could get in the way of a farmer."

The Slaughters were poor, but Enos and his five siblings grew up happy. The farmwork built his wrists and back and shoulders. Baseball specific skills can be traced to his formative days too. He built up his arm strength hunting rabbits with rocks, killing them with a well-aimed throw. His future batting stroke was honed in communal wood-chopping contests. His keen eye came from shooting his rifle, which was seldom more than an arm's length away. There weren't many automobiles in Roxboro during those Depression years, so the extended Slaughter clan, up to twenty strong, hopped in "Hoovercarts"—engineless auto chassis pulled by mules. In this manner, they would make their way to civilization, represented by the Durham Athletic Park, twenty-five miles away, where the minor league Bulls played ball.

Enos was rangy and athletic as a teen, and was offered a scholarship for baseball and football at Guilford College in Greensboro. But Slaughter worried that his bumpkin mien wouldn't fit in at school, so he signed on to play second base for the local textile mill, where his brothers worked. Billy Southworth, then a Cards scout, spotted him at an area tryout and signed him in 1935. He also passed along a key tip. Enos had been running flat-footed, and Southworth told him to run on his toes. With that, Slaughter's speed increased dramatically.

When Enos had progressed to his first minor league team, in Columbus, Georgia, a more pivotal bit of advice was passed his way. Slaughter had a tendency to lope, if not loaf, especially on defense. His manager told him, "Listen, are you too tired to run all the way? If you are, I'll get some help for you." From that day forth, he hustled out every step once his uniform was on.

That manager was Eddie Dyer, the same man who was now Cardinals skipper.

Dyer also refined Slaughter's fundamentals. "You seem to think that your strike zone is over your head," he'd rage at Enos after he whiffed. "It isn't. Don't swing at the high ones." Dyer turned his right fielder's howitzer into a more accurate rocket as well. "An outfielder throws a ball low and on a hop to permit a cutoff. Stop throwing those high flies."

In double-A ball, at a different Columbus, this one in Ohio, his stellar play warranted a nickname, in the opinion of the sports editor of the *Columbus Daily Journal*. The paper held a contest to pick a winner. "Country" was the overwhelming suggestion, and Enos himself seconded the motion. Certainly, it fit the plainly unsophisticated Slaughter.

By '38 he was at Sportsman's Park, the summer home of the Cardinals; he was by now more fully developed, with thick muscle through his haunches, giving him a low-slung appearance. His "fairish amount of nose," in Red Smith's description, remained unchanged. By his sophomore season, he was getting MVP votes. On the field he was a classic success story, a guy who overcame his underprivileged upbringing to reach the pinnacle of acclaim in his profession. But there was tragedy away from the diamond. His first wife, childhood sweetheart Hulo, hated St. Louis from the first, missing the rural life in Roxboro. They divorced soon after Slaughter made the bigs, their marriage not helped by the loss of an infant daughter in 1936 after just six days of life.

In the winter of '39, Slaughter returned home for his annual Christmas-week rabbit hunt with Zadok. It was a Slaughter family tradition, one handed down since the family first settled in Roxboro generations earlier. Father and son were cutting up their haul when Zadok accidentally cut his hand. Unfortunately, one of the bunnies had tularemia, aka "Rabbit fever," and Zadok contracted it. He was dead within a month.

Just before the war, Slaughter remarried to a St. Louis woman named Josephine. (It was the second of five marriages Slaughter would accrue in his lifetime.) Then the Cards made the 1942 World Series, where they met the defending-champion Yankees. It was the first Fall Classic to be broadcast live to American troops overseas. After the fourth game, Slaughter was asked to speak to the troops by radio. "Hi fellows," he told them. "We played a great game today and we won. And we are going to finish this thing tomorrow. Then

I'm going to report for duty in the Army Air Corps and join you." True to his word, Slaughter homered to help win the Series the next day, then went to San Antonio to become a flyboy.

But the physical marvel had a flaw—he was color-blind. So he couldn't be a pilot, and he refused to be a bombardier—the idea of handing control over his fate to some other man while he was cooped up in the back of the plane sickened him. Instead, Slaughter became a physical education instructor. He never saw combat but went overseas to play ball in the South Pacific, island-hopping in the wake of Allied forces heading for Japan. Country was still Country, even in service ball. He would slide on the coral reef diamonds of Saipan without a care for the damage incurred by his trousers, and he always ran in from his position in the sweltering tropical heat. He was phlegmatic about the time he spent away from St. Louis too, insisting that "The three years I missed really didn't hurt that much." Indeed, after an early series in '46 against the Cards, Chicago Cubs general manager Jim Gallagher grumbled of Enos, "That big-rumped baboon goes into the Army, drinks beer for three years and comes out running faster than before."

The war may not have affected his stats or ability, but it cost him Josephine. It was a classic war divorce, the kind sweeping the nation in 1946. The return of so many millions of servicemen, who came home to women who had married in haste and gotten used to a life without that particular husband, caused the divorce rate to spike from 3.5 divorces per one thousand people to 4.3. Joe DiMaggio's very public divorce, along with those of several movie stars, took away some of the lingering national stigma attached to splitting up. Josephine filed for divorce in August, citing cruelty and stating that Enos had struck her.

She had grounds for adultery charges as well. During spring training in St. Petersburg, Enos met a war widow named Mary Walker, who had a two-year-old boy named Rex who never knew his father. Slaughter took up with her, becoming the man in Rex's life, and married Mary that winter after his divorce from Josephine was finalized.

The domestic upheaval didn't noticeably affect Country's play. After setting off the rhubarb in Brooklyn, Slaughter cracked skulls the next day in a more traditional manner, homering twice and going 4–4 with 4 RBIs. St. Louis beat Boston 9–8, winning in classic hustling Redbirds manner, on a steal of home in the tenth inning by pinch runner Joffre Cross.

The two games displayed the devastating blend of hitting, hustling, and heart the Cards were capable of. Despite Brooklyn's strong start, few Cardinals fans were worried. They were secure in the knowledge that St. Louis was still the bully on the block.

Chapter 13
THOSE SPLENDID SOX

ST. LOUIS HAD a history of success on its side. In Boston, a generation of fans had grown up without knowing a high-quality Sox team. So the Hub could be forgiven for being overenthusiastic when the Red Sox exploded from the blocks like an Olympic sprinter. They won their first five games, seven of the first ten, and finished April 11–3. Bobby Doerr had already knocked in seventeen runs. Dom DiMaggio was hitting .361, Johnny Pesky .360. Williams's on-base percentage was .493. And the pitching troika of Hughson, Harris, and Dobson were all 3–0. They might have been buoyed by the visit to Fenway Park on April 30 by an aspiring congressman who was running to replace James Curley in the 11th District—John F. Kennedy.

The sole frontline player to struggle out of the gate was Boo Ferriss. Boo was shelled in his first two starts, though the potent Sox lineup bailed him out in both games. It gave ammo to the critics who thought Ferriss a mirage who had fattened up against wartime mediocrity.

But on April 26, Boo shut out the A's, and he was off on a tear after that. He won ten straight decisions, not losing until mid-June, and lowered his ERA from 17.25 to 2.98. He had already established a reputation as an excellent pitcher in Fenway Park, his fastball sharp enough to prevent righties from turning on it and tattooing the nearby not-yet-Green Monster in left, the numerous advertisements that festooned the wall giving hitters a target to aim for.

Everyone had called Ferriss "Boo" since childhood, the result of his inability to say the word "brother." His youth was Rockwellian, a classic southern upbringing in Shaw, Mississippi, just south of the fabled crossroads at Clarksdale, where Highway 61 meets Highway 278, and where a fair country guitar picker named Robert Johnson mythically met up with a goat-tailed fellow one moonless night and sold his soul to become the greatest bluesman ever to emerge from the cotton fields.

Boo was born a decade after Johnson, in 1921. Practice and genetics were the key to his success, not satanic dealmaking. His daddy was a semipro player, manager, and umpire, and Boo grew up inhaling the game, playing pickup ball in the open lot alongside his house. There was no Little League in the tiny burg, so Ferriss was playing with the high school team in the seventh grade. One day, a bigger kid plowed him over and broke Dave's right wrist. Undaunted, he kept on throwing lefty and never missed a game. As Head and Lanier and Ferriss, among many others, proved, the ability and willingness of Depression-era kids to adapt to crippling injuries and keep on playing ball was remarkable.

Boston signed the strapping pitcher out of Mississippi State but was lukewarm on his progress until Bill McKechnie, the Cincinnati Reds manager and pitching talent guru, offered to buy him. Cronin refused, figuring that if McKechnie saw something in Ferriss, he was worth keeping. The Sox stood by Boo as he joined the Army Air Corps, playing ball in the San Antonio area against other bases, including one that featured Country Slaughter. To give an idea of Boo's elite athletic ability, he led the air corps league in not just victories but also batting average, edging out Slaughter .417 to .414. He came down with asthma early in 1945, and that won him an early discharge. Delta Dave was in Boston in time to win twenty-one games in 1945. Tom Yawkey was so happy with Boo's season he gave him a $10,000 bonus, typical of the owner's largesse toward players he liked. But such philanthropy had to be on his terms—Yawkey was an outspoken defender of the Reserve Clause.

Ferriss was a favorite of the writers, for whom he always made time, in stark contrast to the grumpier stars of the club. "He is serious but not humorless; imaginative, but not temperamental," judged Kaese in the *Globe*. Ferriss showed some imagination in his choice of superstition. After warming up, he would toss his glove in air. However it landed, face up or face down, he would have to leave it that way after every half-inning on the mound, or bad juju followed.

Clearly he wasn't paying attention to his glove on a chilly night in July 1947, when he tore some shoulder cartilage on the mound. Today, he might miss half a season, maybe two-thirds. In '47, he was rubbed down with alcohol and told by his doctors to "be sure to wear a coat." Leeches were not prescribed, fortunately, but regardless, Ferriss was never the same pitcher. He gritted his way to a 7–3 record in 1948, and had all of five appearances over the next two seasons before accepting the fact that his arm and career were shot.

Williams was the face of the Sox, York their muscle, Dommie DiMaggio their soul. But the beating heart of the team was the double-play duo of shortstop Johnny Pesky and second baseman Bobby Doerr, a pair of West Coasters who formed the finest middle infield in the majors.

Legally, Johnny Pesky was still John Paveskovich during the summer of '46—he didn't have it officially anglicized until after the season. His lineage was Croatian, and his old man was a cook in the Austro-Hungarian Navy. Jakov Paveskovich didn't think much of baseball, either as a game or as a career, and he let his boy know it. But Johnny couldn't stop hanging out down at the Portland Beavers ballpark a few blocks from the Paveskovich home. The Beavers were in the powerful Pacific Coast League, and Johnny saw all manner of good ballplayers pass through, including a seventeen-year-old hotshot with the San Diego Padres named Ted Williams. Pesky wrangled a job as a clubhouse boy, washing sweaty jock straps and other assorted sundries.

In high school they called him "the Needle," on account of his stiletto nose. Pesky was very active in semipro ball, and one of the teams he played on was the Silverton Red Sox, a timber mill–sponsored club. In an amazing coincidence, the lumber company was owned by Tom Yawkey, so Pesky could be considered Boston Red Sox property way back in the late '30s. He was signed by the real team soon after.

Pesky was a rookie in 1942, and while he was learning to navigate the American League, he was also taking classes at Mechanics Arts High School, learning the finer points of becoming a naval aviator. With him in the classroom was Williams, who got considerably more attention. The Splinter would remain the bigger draw, but Pesky proved he belonged in his company, hitting .331 as a rookie shortstop, trailing only Williams. He finished third in the MVP vote and would have won the Rookie of the Year, had there been such a thing.

Then he was off to war.

The navy cost Pesky three years of baseball productivity, but it gained him his wife. Johnny met Ruth Hickey in Atlanta, where he was serving as an operations officer and she was a WAVE (Woman Accepted for Volunteer Emergency Service). They would stay married for sixty years, until her death in 2005.

Like Williams, Pesky didn't see overseas duty, and he wasn't the pilot Ted was, either. Pesky enjoyed regaling others about his teammate's ability in the cockpit, though, especially once Williams left Pesky behind in *The Right Stuff* department and went to advanced training in Jacksonville, while Pesky stayed on the ground. "I heard Ted literally tore the sleeve target to shreds with his angle dives," raved the shortstop to anyone who'd listen. "He'd shoot from wingovers, zooms, and barrel rolls, and after a few passes the sleeve was ribbons. At any rate, I know he broke the all-time record for hits."

It was a hit Pesky supposedly had in 1948 that is his lasting legacy. Former Sox hurler and broadcaster Mel Parnell named the yellow divider between fair and foul ground in Fenway's right field "Pesky's Pole" in honor of a game-winning homer he said Pesky hit off it to win a game in 1948. Alas, the only homer Pesky ever hit at Fenway with Parnell pitching came in 1950, in the first inning, of a game the Sox lost. It was his only home run of the season, one of only six he ever hit at Fenway. Still, the honorific speaks to Pesky's lifetime of service to the franchise, and the Pesky Pole is an iconic part of the Fenway experience today.

Back when Pesky was a clubhouse boy in the PCL, one of the guys he ran errands and hung up laundry for was Bobby Doerr, who was only a year older than he was. Doerr was with the Padres, a teammate of Williams, and, like Ted, a native of Southern California. His father, Harold, who had played in the PCL himself, was a telephone repairman in Los Angeles and an early booster of Bobby's career. "He told me, 'If you want to play baseball, I'll cut the grass and be sure to get you to all the practices,'" Doerr later remembered. "He had a great bearing on my life. He was a great man." Harold spread the generosity around to other kids in the area, often buying them gloves, spikes, or sometimes even a meal.

In the winter of 1936, Bobby traveled to Oregon for a few weeks of fly-fishing for steelhead trout. One night, Doerr went to a dance at a local Civilian Conservation Corps camp across the river from his home. Later that evening, he got in an old rowboat to head back, and plopped down next to his future wife, Monica. "The seat next to her was all white from being cold," Doerr explained years later. "When I got in Monica put her coat down so I didn't have to sit in that old icy seat. I thought that was pretty nice. I fell in love with her that night." Oregon, too—Doerr would live there for the rest of his life when not in Boston (he and Monica lived in Newton, Massachusetts, during the season).

Doerr hit the big leagues in 1937, the opening-day leadoff hitter for Boston as an eighteen-year-old. He had some thump in his bat for a keystone sacker and was one of the best fielders in the game. He and Williams bonded from the start, mainly over their shared love of Westerns. "He'd call me up and say 'There's a Western movie on with Hoot Gibson' and we'd go," Doerr recalled.

At first, Doerr was exempt from the war, as he was a father. But come 1944, that was no longer enough to keep him out of the service. He was forced to leave in September, just as the pennant race began in earnest. Doerr also missed all of 1945, preparing to fight in the Pacific. He was about to ship out when the atomic bombs fell. "I was pretty glad Truman used them, let me tell you," he said nearly seven decades later.

Every guy on the Red Sox roster was a hero in those early days of the season. Eddie Pellagrini, a rookie utility guy who had played service ball with Pee Wee Reese and Johnny Mize, went in to his first game on April 22 against the Senators after Pesky was beaned. In his very first at bat, he clouted a home run off Sid Hudson over the high wall in left to win the game 5–4. "I still send Hudson a Christmas card every year," Pellagrini said years afterward. Three days later, Eddie had a double, triple, and homer against the Yankees. "I should have retired after that," he said. Pellagrini only appeared in eighteen more games all season.

Baseball already had achieved outsized importance on the national psyche, and in Boston, it was exponentially more significant thanks to the Sox's white-hot start. The city had a reputation as an upper-crust haven for stuffy WASPs, but in truth the streets of the Olde Towne were dominated by craftsmen, laborers, machinists, and mechanics. According to a census taken at the time, there were only 27,500 professionals in the city. Roaming knife sharpeners, who rode around on three-wheeled bikes that propped up lathes, were more commonly found than lawyers downtown.

The nearly 20 percent unemployment rate of 1940 had eased

considerably, thanks to the war, and while the census indicated that multiple generations still cohabited together, disposable income had returned to the family unit. A good chunk of that was used on the Sox. Just how big the team had become to the city was demonstrated on Sunday, April 21. Philly was in town for a doubleheader, and the Sox won the opener 12–11 after wiping out a seven-run deficit to win in the tenth, scoring six in the bottom of the ninth alone. That game took so long that the second game was stopped at 6:30 p.m., in keeping with local blue laws, with the A's ahead 3–0 after five innings. The game was the only one the Sox lost in the first week of the season. The outcry was so great that the law was changed immediately.

Chapter 14

BASEBALL FOR THE ONE PERCENT

YANKEE STADIUM OPENED its doors for the first time in 1946 on Good Friday, April 19. Neither the schedule makers nor MacPhail had factored in the New York chapter of Catholic War Veterans, however, a lobby that was at the height of its power so soon after the war. Because of their protest, Mayor O'Dwyer found himself suddenly with a conflict that afternoon, and thus didn't throw out the ceremonial first pitch. Ever the agile salesman, Mac found a Congressional Medal of Honor winner at the last second to substitute, and the Yanks edged the Senators 7–6.

Joe DiMaggio and the rest of the Yankees were in unfamiliar territory. As part of the massive renovation of Yankee Stadium, the home dugout was moved for the first time from its longtime spot on the third base side over to the first base line. There was a spanking-new clubhouse as well, completely redone from the original that had remained untouched since the place opened in 1923.

The players weren't the only ones with a sense of dislocation. MacPhail had instituted numerous changes to the ethos of the place. As Red Smith wrote, the Roaring Redhead had "celebrated the marriage of baseball and booze by transforming the Stadium into a genteel ginmill." Mac intuited that in New York, exclusivity was the name of the game. He ripped apart the innards of the park to build a pair of ornate rooms, and called the construction the "Stadium Club," where select season-ticket holders could bend their elbows and discuss world domination "away from the vulgar gaze of the hoi-polloi." In essence, it was a baseball-themed speakeasy.

The four hundred members were carefully screened for eligibility, and once inside the gilded few could hang out in air-cooled comfort, enjoy ritzy service from tuxedoed staff, and be amused by film and theater stars, singers, comics, and other entertainers Mac brought in, making the game itself seem trivial. The Stadium Club rolls included various military brass, politicians, sportswriters, and celebrities, along with popular former athletes like boxer Max Baer and, of course, Babe Ruth. At a stroke, MacPhail added roughly $450,000 to the Yankees coffers through the Stadium Club.

Next, MacPhail had turned his attention to the best seats with an actual view of the game. He rearranged the box seats, creating more and moving them around to maximize their views and ease of access and egress. He then priced them depending on how close they were to the field and how far they were from the ruffians in the general-admission sections. Everyone who bought a box got a brass nameplate to give the purchase a personal touch. Each seat was now personally identified. And, in a forerunner to the modern scourge of personal-seat licenses, those who paid top dollar for the box seats got first call for tickets to boxing matches and football games held at the Stadium, along with access to a private concession stand and fully stocked bar, and what the *Times* called a "magnificent feeling of aloofness." Mac sold all 2,500 boxes and probably could have peddled twice that number. In 1944, all of six season boxes had been sold.

Meanwhile, some fifteen thousand cheap seats were added to the grandstand and bleachers. They were several inches wider than the older seats, leading to increased comfort. The new double-decked restaurant was the hub of several concession stands that were added throughout the runways, so fans were never more than a short walk from a dog and a beer. The countertops were all new and gleamed with modernity.

When MacPhail first bought into the Yankees, the baseball world, accustomed to a staid if not haughty franchise in the Bronx, wondered how such a clownish figure would act in the sport's National Cathedral. "Wall Street might react the same way to the news that [World War II shipbuilder and future steel magnate] Henry Kaiser had been named senior partner of J. P. Morgan," thought *Fortune*. Mac's transformation of the Stadium calmed some fears among the moneyed set, but he couldn't resist dipping into his chintzy bag of tricks to lure and entertain the masses. He hired pretty girls to be ushers, staged weekly fireworks shows, and held mile-long foot races on the Stadium track before games. Barbershop quartets performed and roamed the aisles between innings. Ladies Night, a popular invention from his days in Cincy, was brought in from the sticks to the Big City and proved a hit with the sophisticated femmes of New York, as did Nylons Day. Mac announced that the Yankees would begin sponsorship of a daily symphony program on WQXR, leading one writer to wonder "what possible need Larry MacPhail has for a horn, not to mention a whole orchestra."

But marketing was a huge part of MacPhail's master plan to keep his team in the money, and things like Yankee tradition and understated class were not part of the program. Every inch of available space was used for advertising—Philip Morris, Lifebuoy, Calvert, Burma-Shave, Botany Ties, and the Bronx Savings Bank, among others, hawked their goods and services to Yankees fans. Prior to 1946 and MacPhail, advertising for specific games was usually limited to the basics—time, place, opponent. Maybe, *maybe,* the pitching matchup. But MacPhail hired an ad firm to begin teasing the newspaper readers of the metropolis with cliffhanger copy in the morning editions:

> Can Washington's famous "knuckleball" pitchers stop what experts call "the slugging-est team in the League"? Or will DiMaggio, Keller & Co. make mincemeat of the Senators' pitching staff? Come out to the ball game and see!

Wisecracks abounded at the cheesy come-ons, but no one laughed at the Yankees bankroll. The team broke its season attendance record by July 3, going over 1.4 million fans before Independence Day. For the season, 2,265,512 would pass through the turnstiles in the Bronx, roughly three times as many as had in 1945. And that was despite the fact MacPhail had raised ticket prices 7.5 percent before the season began. He was raking it in, to the point where he could magnanimously allow servicemen to get into the ballpark for free all season.

To call the action, MacPhail had tried to lure Red Barber from Brooklyn, offering him a three-year, $100,000 deal to become the Voice of the Yankees. In a spasm of spending quite unlike him, Rickey outbid his former liege, offering $105,000, and kept Red at Ebbets Field. The bidding war underscored Barber's excellence at the mike and importance to the Dodgers. Stymied, MacPhail came up with another innovation, bringing broadcaster Mel Allen on the road for the games, instead of re-creating them by wire. Shortly thereafter, that would become standard operating procedure for all the teams.

Alas, the team on the field was a far cry from the typical Bronx Bombers, the powerhouse that had captured fourteen pennants and ten championships in the previous quarter century. At a glance, they were inferior to Boston, without the depth in the lineup or the power pitching. They held a psychic dominion over their rivals up the Post Road, however, which the Sox needed to break if they were to achieve their destiny this season. And indeed, a 12–5 victory over the Yankees at Fenway on April 25 propelled the Sox on a fourteen-game winning streak, during which Boston scored nearly eight runs a game.

The Sox were 20–3 when they invaded the new-look Stadium on May 10. Inside, the liquor was flowing faster than the Harlem River down the street, the Stadium Club and boxes packed with the "business drunk"—executives who could afford to toast their own brilliance at four in the afternoon, along with the shot-and-a-beer rank and file that swelled the gate to 64,183 that sunny afternoon. The Yanks were hanging in, 4½ behind the jet-fueled Sox, and a series win would not only sugar those scarlet rocket engines a bit but reinforce exactly which team was the bully of the American League.

The visitors took the opener 5–4, scoring a pair of runs in the seventh off Yanks relief ace Joe Page. The Clipper knocked in all four pinstriped runs. It was Boston's fifteenth straight win. Saturday, "Tiny" Bonham, the ironically nicknamed Yankees right-hander with a "torso like a blacksmith," according to the *Sporting News,* threw a two-hit shutout to at last put one in Boston's *L* column and even the series. It was the first loss of the month of May for the Bosox. Sunday's rubber game thus became a critical juncture in the early part of the season.

The Bombers had on the mound just the man they wanted that day. Spurgeon Ferdinand Chandler hated his name, so when a writer called him "Spud," he embraced it. Chandler detested far more than just his name, however. The *Saturday Evening Post,* in an article entitled "The Yankees Angry Ace," called him an "explosive perfectionist," noting, "His blue eyes glower an almost visible hatred at the batsman. He snarls, and snaps his pitching arm, until it appears as though the arm will break off at the shoulder and wrist." When he surrendered a "distance whack" to the enemy, Chandler would walk off the mound in circles, screaming obscenities at himself. A writer named Milton Gross thought Chandler possessed "the emotional unbalance of a woman who has discovered her originally styled hat duplicated in a $2.95 model."

Unbeaten in five decisions on the season so far, Spud was eager to take the ball and spit venom at the Scarlet Hose, but was forced to wait for a pregame show that came straight from MacPhail's fevered imagination. The sixty-five thousand in the Stadium were treated to a fashion show, courtesy of Ohrbach's Department Store on 14th Street, a "mass seller of mass produced clothes for a mass audience," sniffed that publication for the masses, Life. Pretty models were driven around the field aboard fifteen marine jeeps, the ladies impressively keeping hands on hips in classic runway poses while standing on the backseats, at risk of being thrown from the vehicle at the feet of Joe DiMaggio and Ted Williams. The models showed off affordable lines of slacks, shorts, and bathing suits for the coming summer, while the "jeep drivers dutifully kept eyes straight ahead," according to Life.

When the game finally started, twenty minutes late, Spud was off his game, giving up three walks and a run in the first inning. He settled down, but was equaled by Mickey Harris, who held the Yanks to three hits. The game was decided on an error by Rizzuto. His boot allowed two unearned runs to score in the fifth, and that was enough for Boston to win the game and silence the huge crowd, who presumably consoled themselves by taking the subway down to Ohrbach's to stock up on cabana wear before Sunday dinner.

Chapter 15
CASUALTIES

BOTH TEAMS HEADED west after the game. The Sox trained as usual to Chicago. The Yankees embarked on a thirteen-game road trip, one that began in the far west, meaning St. Louis, the historic Gateway to the Frontier. Ordinarily, the team would have hopped on a train a couple of hours after the final out, off on a journey that would last roughly an entire day, give or take a couple of hours. Instead, MacPhail decided it was time for his team to fly.

It wasn't the first time Mac had flown a team of his from one park to another. He had experimented with the new mode of transport back in the thirties with Columbus and the Reds, and the Yankees had of course flown that spring to Panama. The press dubbed it "MacPhail's Flying Circus," and the owner soaked up the publicity. But this was different. Mac was making flight the preferred mode of transport on all road trips, save for northeast-corridor jaunts. To MacPhail, there was a decided tactical advantage to shortening a trip from twenty-four hours to five. The guys would get a good night's sleep in town and make their leisurely way to Sportsman's Park, rather than try to grab winks while rocking through the Midwest countryside.

The Yankees gathered at LaGuardia Field for the flight minus four players, including pitcher Red Ruffing and player-coach Frank Crosetti, who refused to fly (their train would then be delayed, and the quintet barely made it to Sportsman's Park on time). At the airfield, the team boarded the *Yankee Mainliner,* a forty-four-seat, four-engine C-54 converted cargo plane contracted from United Air Lines. Mac made sure the beer flowed aboard the plane, distracting anyone with pteromerhanophobia.

One could hardly blame Red and Crow for refusing to take to the air. Flying in 1946 was hardly for the faint of heart, and the nascent commercial aviation industry didn't inspire much confidence. "Like many other youthful veterans of WWII, commercial aviation is having difficulty finding civilian attire to fit," Alvin H. Goldstein wrote in St. Louis, the prewar industry center and Charles Lindbergh's spiritual home.

There was huge demand for flights, but a shortage of airworthy planes. The pace of refitting military aircraft for civilian use was painfully slow, and shortages plagued the airlines. Airfields were stacked with planes trying to land, but a lack of controllers often meant that planes spent as much time over the field waiting to land as they did on the journey itself. Only critical fuel situations hastened landings, and pilots often dumped gasoline en route to ensure an on-time arrival. Weather delays were endless, and a sizable percentage of commercial craft was unable to climb above the clouds to the smooth sailing in the stratosphere, subjecting paying customers to horrendous turbulence and frequent returns to the point of departure.

It was frustrating, for the papers were filled with new flying records and feats. One day, Transcontinental and Western Airways, soon to be renamed Trans World Airlines, operated its first international flight, connecting New York and Paris. The next, Heathrow Airport opened for business in London. One day, pilots landed in Cairo forty hours after taking off from Honolulu, 9,500 miles from island to desert. The next, a plane flew over the Arctic Circle, proving travel over the poles was possible. One day, a P-84 Thunderjet tore through the sky at 611 miles an hour, just shy of the record set earlier that same day in England, where an RAF pilot teased the limits of the sound barrier at 615 mph. The next, a mammoth navy Lockheed, nicknamed the *Truculent Turtle,* spent fifty-five hours in the air, traveling over eleven thousand miles, a mark that would stand until 1962.

But those same papers were also filled with reports of crashes, seemingly every day, one upon another. No carrier was spared. Eastern lost a DC-3 in Connecticut with all seventeen aboard killed, and two weeks later United suffered a similar crash in Wyoming, with twenty-one dead. A horrific crash killed all twenty-seven on board an American flight in the California desert in early March. A navy Privateer disappeared off the Florida coast with twenty-eight souls gone. The entire Lockheed Constellation fleet was grounded after a fire broke out on board a flight that crashed in Reading, Pennsylvania. Two hundred sixty-eight people lost their lives in fourteen separate crashes around the world in September alone.

Even the great aviator Howard Hughes fell from the sky, crashing an experimental reconnaissance plane onto the rooftops of several posh Beverly Hills homes on July 7. Hughes somehow survived, despite six broken ribs, a collapsed lung, and major burns. His British counterpart Geoffrey de Havilland Jr., renowned test pilot and son of the famous airplane designer and pioneer, was less fortunate, killed when his DH 108 broke up over the Thames estuary.

In one extraordinary incident, a pilot named Warren Berg was flying over Detroit when he was forced to bail out of his malfunctioning plane. As Berg descended, another passing plane became ensnarled in his chute and nosed toward the earth. Berg desperately deployed his reserve parachute, which slowed the plane just enough. It hit the ground roughly but not catastrophically. Incredibly, Berg's broken ankle was the sole casualty.

So while aviation was undoubtedly the future, train travel was still the present, and omnipresent it was. Sure, occasionally there was danger here too—in late April in Naperville, Illinois, the *Exposition Flyer* slammed into a parked train at nearly 100 mph, killing forty-seven and ushering in an 80-mph rail-speed limit. But for the most part, the nation relied on its trains.

New York's Penn Station and Grand Central Terminal were better known, but Union Station in St. Louis had emerged during the war as the most heavily used depot in the land, ferrying soldiers from across the nation's breadbasket to either coast for embarkation overseas. About 1.5 million tickets were issued there each year between 1942 and 1945. All trains backed into the station, a method that had failed only once, when a troop train had gone too far and crashed through the glass and steel wall that separated the platform from the midway. With that kind of traffic, trains were oversold and late all the time. As the English writer G. K. Chesterton put it, "the only way to guarantee making a train is to miss the one before it."

The long trip between St. Louis and the East Coast tested the baseball traveler's constitution, but it was hardly a forced march. As writer Roger Kahn recalled, it was a "24-hour hegira. You traveled in a private car and ate in a private diner, and a drink was never farther away than a porter's call button." Said porters wore immaculate white suits, serving steak and chops in large portions and of higher quality than most players would get at home. The tables featured white linens, fresh-cut flowers, and fine silverware.

There were other benefits granted baseball teams that the average rail passenger didn't get. If a train arrived at its stop late at night, it was usually sidetracked until breakfast, so the players could sleep in. Dining hours were extended, generally encompassing any time a player wanted anything to eat, and rules about merriment in the club car were overlooked when a ball club was on board.

An extraordinary set of circumstances the season before had illuminated the rivalry between the Cards and Dodgers, the vagaries of train travel, and Sam Breadon's penchant for squeezing out every last nickel, all at the same time. St. Louis and Chicago were battling for the 1945 pennant, with Brooklyn traveling to Sportsman's Park and then Wrigley Field, hoping to play spoiler. A game in the Land of the Cottonwood Tree, as St. Loo was called, was rained out, and rather than play an afternoon doubleheader the following day, as the rules stated, Breadon tried to pull in some extra gate by announcing a twi-night affair. As the Brooks were due in the Windy City the next day, they howled bloody murder. The late start meant that instead of traveling by sleeper train, the team would have to sit up all night in an uncomfortable freight car, the only possibility to avoid forfeiting the next day's game.

Leo was a hurricane of anger. Even though his team stunk, a wartime collection of hangers-on and happy-to-be-heres, he psyched them into playing like the '27 Yankees. "Look at that plush-lined bum up there in his private box," he fumed, pointing at Breadon, who looked every inch the feudal baron with his fur coat and long cigar. "Fuckin' Ol' Moneybags is making you risk your arms and legs. Go make him pay for it!" Which the Dodgers did, sweeping the key twin bill.

The team arrived at Union Station well past midnight to find a dirty collection of freight cars hauling produce, but with no dining cars. The players were hardly used to such low-class conditions, but their discomfort paled when the engineer, a Cubs fan eager to speed the team to Chicago, pushed his clunker of a train too hard. At Manhattanville, Illinois, it crashed into a fuel tanker, and the front of the train was an inferno. The team escaped out the back, but the engineer, Charley Tegtmeyer, was killed.

Out in the cold, Durocher's fury was palpable, the blaze highlighting the high fever in his eyes. "Breadon! He should be here to see what he caused," Leo spat. Ironically, the Dodgers limped into Chicago and were in no condition to best the Cubbies, who went on to edge the Cards and Breadon for the pennant.

Ballplayers being ballplayers, they often found the time for lounge-car fisticuffs, whether seriously or for the sheer testosterone rush of brawling. Losses at the gaming table often precipitated violence.

Guys would get angry and go after the winner, or merely rip up decks of cards, forcing someone to walk over to the club car for a new deck. "We usually ran out of cards on trips west," remembered Buddy Lewis, who played for the Senators in 1946.

Train travel was a breeding ground for superstition too; Durocher, for example, never, ever slept in the upper berth, a fact a traveling secretary named Ed Staples found out the hard way back in the early '40s. Nicknamed "Stables," he took Leo's bottom rack on the long trip out to St. Louis and sacked out, forcing Durocher to roust the conductor to find him a new cabin. When Ed finally awoke, Durocher unloaded upon him. "No wonder they call you 'Stables,'" he roared. "You're a horse's ass!"

Generally, long train trips were moneymaking operations for Durocher, whose prowess at the card table ensured that he always had money he could then blow when the team got to the next city. His personal pigeon was Roscoe McGowen of the *Times*. Durocher would bluff the portly, scholarly scribe down to his shoes, and McGowen would curse Leo out in Shakespearean meter. At heart, he didn't mind, for Lippy could be counted on to square things by picking up the tab at the bar or the nightclub.

Listening to music made the miles go down easier, and the Cards had an eclectic bunch of ears. Stan Musial loved boogie-woogie, while Red Schoendienst preferred Broadway hits like "Ah, Sweet Mystery of Life" and "Indian Love Call." Howie Pollet and Harry Brecheen were partial to classical, especially Brahms and Beethoven. Max Lanier was a country guitar-picking aficionado, digging mournful records like "There's a Chill on the Hill Tonight" and "I Pass the Graveyard at Midnight." "If I could hear my music while I'm pitching, the bastards would never get a loud foul off me," Lanier once said.

Pranking teammates was a timeless art, and every team had a jokester or two. Typical of the genre was a setup pulled by the A's on a trip back from playing the Browns in late June. There was a quiet country kid on the roster, a reserve who seldom played or made a peep. Some of the boys put a bottle of White Lightning in his bag. They arranged for a sheriff from some backwater along the way to board the train and pretend to arrest the kid for operating a still. As he was dragged away in cuffs (the sheriff being a Method actor), he screamed his innocence. The other A's, having satisfied themselves that the kid indeed could talk, laughed uproariously, then turned in for the night.

Since roster turnover had been so great after the demobilization, teams used the long train rides to get to know one another better and to talk about their wartime experiences. At least the guys who had it easy over there did; those who had seen serious combat were generally loath to talk about it with anyone who hadn't been under fire, if at all.

Red Sox players who had been around the season before (eight players saw at least some time in both '45 and '46) told the newcomers about the day in August 1945 when the one-legged pitcher shut them down. His name was Bert Shepard, a fighter pilot shot down over Hamburg in May of 1944. It was opening day of the 55th Fighter Group's baseball season, and the pitcher had volunteered to fly his thirty-fourth mission because it left at dawn, which would leave him enough time to get back for the game. He never made it. Instead, he took antiaircraft shrapnel in his right leg, and crash landed. A Luftwaffe surgeon named Ladislaus Loidl rescued Shepard from farmers armed with pitchforks and amputated his leg.

Wearing a prosthetic a fellow prisoner of war designed for him, Shepard returned to the States and set about playing ball. The Senators signed him when asked to do so by the War Department, and Shepard made several spring training appearances, his prosthetic awkward but manageable. On August 5, 1945, with the Sens trailing Boston 14–2, Shepard made his lone major league appearance, striking out the first man he faced, Catfish Metkovich, and pitching five and a third innings, giving up just three hits and one run.

The likes of Williams, Pesky, and DiMaggio must have had a good laugh at that, the peals ringing out over the passing countryside. Ol' Catfish would have taken some ribbing—struck out by a one-legged pitcher! Metkovich, who earned his nickname (bestowed by Casey Stengel) by stepping on a bewhiskered fish and embedding its fin in his foot, no doubt turned as red as his uniform from the catcalls.

Shepard wasn't on the '46 Senators, but Buddy Lewis was. A vet with a healthy appetite for hijinks, Lewis had signed up for the Army Air Corps early in the war. One of his first assignments before going overseas was to fly VIPs to and from Washington, and when he met with his now ex-teammates before flying back, he told them to watch out for his farewell. As the game that afternoon got under way, a plane shot right over home plate of Griffith Stadium, very low, in defiance of all manner of ordinances. It wiggled its wings and flew off past the center field bleachers. It was Buddy, saying sayonara.

Lewis went off to the China-Burma-India theater to fly C-47s. He was told if he was shot down over Burma and survived, he should carry a baseball; because of the Japanese love of the game, they might spare him. He also carried a sizable portion of cocaine, as the native Burmese would do all manner of favors in return for a sniff or two.

Lewis was too good a pilot to get shot down, perhaps as good as Ted Williams. He won a Distinguished Flying Cross for his ability to land in small jungle clearings, often behind enemy lines, and "crossed the hump," i.e., the Himalayas, numerous times. Crossing the hump was a particularly dangerous achievement, and only the best pilots made it routine. He flew an astounding 368 missions in his "Old Fox," a plane he nicknamed for Clark Griffith, the Senators owner. "Everybody agreed he was the best transport pilot in the CBI theater," Luke Sewell, then the manager of the St. Louis Browns, told the *Washington Post* in 1945 after flying with Lewis in Burma. "He set his big transport plane down on tiny strips that didn't look big enough for a mosquito to land on. And he did it while he was talking baseball to me."

Buddy still had his joie de vivre upon return, but he was affected by the conflict as so many others were. "When I came back from the war," he reflected years later, "my whole philosophy of life was completely different. I had changed so much that baseball didn't mean as much to me as it did before the war. I enlisted at 25, and came out a 30-year-old."

Lewis was a third baseman before the war, playing next to, and rooming with, shortstop Cecil Travis. Lewis was a solid player—Travis was a star, one of the best players in Senators history. A sweet-swinging lefty that no less an expert than Ted Williams called "one of the five best left-handed hitters I ever saw," Travis was a perennial All-Star, despite playing for the woeful Sens. In 1941, Travis hit .359 with 19 triples and 101 RBIs. Then he went to war.

Travis played ball while his unit, the 76th Infantry Division (the "Onaways" who lost to the "Red Circlers" in the ETO semi-finals), trained stateside, but once in Europe, he saw action. In January 1945, the 76th was rushed into combat at the Battle of the Bulge, fighting the onrushing 212th Volksgrenadier Division in the woods of Belgium. The extreme cold was as bitter an enemy as the Wehrmacht. It felled Travis, a southerner from rural Georgia who had rarely spent a day in freezing temperatures in his entire life.

"Heck, you was in that snow," he recalled some years later, "and you was out in that weather, and if you was lucky you got to stay in an old barn at night. The thing about it, you'd sit there in those boots, and you might not get 'em off for days at a time. And cold! You'd just shake at night. Your feet would start swelling, and that's how you'd find out there was something really wrong—you'd pull your boots off, and your feet is swelling."

Something was wrong, all right—when doctors got a look at his frostbitten feet, Travis was rushed into surgery. Fortunately, it was in time to save his feet—without the operation, they would have been lost. Yet he wasn't immediately discharged—Travis was transferred to the Pacific Theater, but the war ended before he shipped out.

Travis returned to baseball, but he wasn't the same player he was before the war. He had lost the ability to transfer his weight at the plate thanks to his operation, and nearly four years away from the game had robbed Travis of his timing. He hit only .252 in 1946. The classy, unassuming star retired after the 1947 season, but not before a "Cecil Travis Night" was held in the nation's capital, attended by several military luminaries, including General Eisenhower.

The Battle of the Bulge ended with the Allies beating back the Nazi counteroffensive in January 1945. Two months later, on March 7, 1945, the Allies launched "Operation Lumberjack," an effort to seize the Ludendorff Bridge at Remagen and establish a toehold on the other side of the Rhine. It was a critical strategic turning point in the invasion of Germany. The army got across the river and held the bridgehead, despite fierce bombardment from German artillery and air power.

On March 17, army engineers were swarming the bridge, trying to repair damage from the German shells, when the structure collapsed. Twenty-eight engineers were killed, many of them swept away by the Rhine current. Ninety-three more were injured.

One engineer was yards away when his fellow bridge builders fell to their deaths. This soldier narrowly missed becoming the third major leaguer to perish in action during the war. He survived to return to the Boston Braves, where he would win eight games in 1946, including a three-hit shutout of the Cardinals that presaged his future brilliance. His Hall of Fame career would begin in earnest in 1947, encompassing 363 wins by the time it was over, more victories than any lefty in baseball history.

His name was Warren Spahn.

Spahn grew up in Buffalo, New York, the son of a wallpaper

salesman, and made it to the Braves in 1942. He only tossed a handful of innings before his manager pulled him from a game for refusing to brush back Pee Wee Reese, who recently had been beaned. That manager, Casey Stengel, told Spahn he was "gutless," and sent him down to the minors while the game was still being played.

At season's end Spahn enlisted in the army. At first, he played baseball, hurling a no-hitter in a game at Camp Chaffee, Arkansas. But he shipped out to Europe with the 276th Combat Engineer Battalion in 1944. "Let me tell you," Spahn said, "that was a tough bunch of guys. We had people that were let out of prison to go into the service. So those were the people I went overseas with, and they were tough and rough and I had to fit that mold." Spahn brought a baseball mind-set to unit security. Hyperaware of Germans wearing American uniforms, Spahn would challenge anyone who approached his position. "Anybody we didn't know, we'd ask, 'Who plays second for the Bums?' If he didn't answer 'Eddie Stanky,' he was dead."

Spahn fought in the same frozen Belgian woodlands that did a number on Cecil Travis's feet during the Battle of the Bulge. He was hit by enemy fire, once in the head and once in the stomach, minor scratches both, albeit millimeters from being grievous if not mortal wounds. "We were surrounded in the Hertgen Forest and had to fight our way out of there," Spahn recalled. "Our feet were frozen when we went to sleep and they were frozen when we woke up. We didn't have a bath or change of clothes for weeks."

Spahn, after finally warming up and washing the stink off his body, moved on to the Ludendorff Bridge with the 276th. The battalion was responsible for ensuring that traffic flowed across the Rhine despite the missing parts and damaged girders. On March 16, 1945, a shell exploded near Spahn, and he took some shrapnel in the foot. Fortunately, once again it was a fairly minor wound. Spahn was out on the bridge the following day for a meeting during which his platoon was assigned the role of bridge security. He had just stepped off the main section of the span when it fell into the Rhine.

For Spahn's efforts under fire, he was awarded the Purple Heart and the Bronze Star. He was also the only ballplayer to be awarded a battlefield promotion, trading his staff sergeant insignia for a second lieutenant's gold bar.

Little more than a year after nearly meeting his maker on the Bridge at Remagen, Spahn, already bald with a bulbous nose, was back on the mound, a changed pitcher and a changed man. "Before the war I didn't have anything that slightly resembled self-confidence," Spahn told the Associated Press in August 1946. "Then I was tight as a drum and worrying about every pitch. But nowadays I just throw them up without the slightest mental pressure."

Spahn expounded on the easy transition back to baseball a few years later. "After what I went through overseas, I never thought of anything I was told to do in baseball as hard work. You get over feeling like that when you spend days on end sleeping in frozen tank tracks in enemy threatened territory. The army taught me something about challenges and about what's important and what isn't. Everything I tackle in baseball and in life I take as a challenge rather than work."

Spahn lost years of potential stats to the war, like the others who served, but unlike Feller or DiMaggio, who never let anyone forget the fact, Spahn was more philosophical. "I matured a lot in those [war] years," he said after he retired. "If I had not had that maturity, I wouldn't have pitched until I was 45."

Spahn's battlefield promotion meant that he had to stay in the service through May. Meanwhile, the American League race was being settled. The Yankees won in St. Louis the day after flying into town, but went 7–6 on the long trip despite the accrued air miles. Boston likewise won after the train trip to the Windy City, but went 5–5 on its road swing, so little had changed in the standings when the

Yankees returned to visit Fenway in late May.

Chandler was again tasked with stopping the Sox and was coming off a three-hit shutout in Cleveland, leaving him 6–1 with a 0.58 ERA. In the ninth inning against the Tribe, Spud had barehanded a sharply hit grounder, badly spraining his middle finger and leaving him in a splint that had him perpetually flipping the bird. It was announced that he would have to miss the start in The Hub.

But in the clubhouse before the game, Chandler dramatically ripped the splint off, flexed his hand a few times, and pronounced himself ready to go. Unfortunately, "he had no more business being in the box that Sunday [*sic*—the game was on a Saturday] than his youngest son did," according to the *Saturday Evening Post*. Little Richard Chandler was one year old. Rip Russell hit a colossal three-run homer in the fifth as Spud was driven from the Fens, surrendering all the runs in a 7–4 defeat. Chandler would finish 20–8 with a 2.10 ERA on the season, but against the Sox, he went 1–4 with a 4.38 ERA.

For the first time since the good old days when the Babe had sported the colors of the Olde Towne Team, the Sox were clearly better than the Yankees. After splitting a doubleheader the next day, Boston was six games clear of the Bombers, and, despite their pioneering use of air travel, things were trending downward in the Bronx.

The Red Sox contentedly listened to the rhythmic clackety-clack of the rails and went from town to town, bashing baseballs at every stop.

Chapter 16
MONTREAL

April 27, 1946

> *"If you don't take the field . . . you will be suspended from baseball for the rest of your life."*
>
> —Frank Shaughnessy, President,
> International League

THE TELEGRAM SENT to every International League team by Frank Shaughnessy was a preemptive blow that immediately quashed rumblings of a leaguewide walkout to protest Jackie Robinson's presence. It was one of the few times all year that management was able to prevent labor from striking. Between that and his opening-day heroics in Jersey City, Robinson could be forgiven had he relaxed and thought perhaps this wouldn't be such an ordeal after all.

The rest of Montreal's season-opening road trip cured him of any possible cockeyed optimism.

Baltimore was long considered the northernmost city in the South, and it had a long racist legacy. John Wilkes Booth had fomented his plot to assassinate Abraham Lincoln in Baltimore, and many of his cultural forebears came out to shout epithets at Robinson when the Royals arrived to tangle with the Orioles. Two virulent and leather-lunged types sat directly behind Rachel. Most of their sentences were punctuated with the phrase "nigger son of a bitch!" Black fans were forced to sit way out in the left field bleach-ers, where it was hard to yell loud enough for Robinson to hear their cheering. Only the knuckleheaded stuff reached his ears.

Robinson played poorly in the three-game series, two of which the Royals lost. Robinson felt the pressure anew. He made a couple of errors and didn't hit well either. His mistakes crushed him into a "deep depression."

Syracuse was even worse. As he came up to bat on April 24, a Chiefs player ran out of the dugout with a black cat, yelling, "Hey Robinson, here's one of your relatives!" Robinson then responded by doubling, whereupon he yelled, "I guess my relative is happy now!"

That was the way Jackie told it in his autobiography, anyway. A *Time* story from the next year said he had *tripled* with the bases loaded to win the game, to silence the feline lovers in the Syracuse dugout. Actually, according to the box scores, Robby didn't hit any doubles on that trip to 'Cuse, and went 0–4 in the first game there, an 11–4 loss. Indeed, he didn't have an extra-base hit all season at Syracuse.

What is true is that the Syracuse fans and players unloaded on Jackie with epithets, racial and otherwise. "We called Robinson some of the foulest names he'd ever heard, the worst things you can scream at another man," remembered the Chiefs second baseman, Garton Del Savio, to the *Syracuse Post-Standard* fifty years later.

The Syracuse catcher, Dick West, said, "I remember the first time he came up to bat, our whole bench was hollering at him, and he looked down at me and said, `You got some players from the South.'" West, who was from Kentucky, recalled, "I looked up and said, 'I don't feel sorry for you. You can go to hell.'" Before one game, many members of the Chiefs actually were about to run out to play the Royals wearing blackface when they were stopped by their manager.

There were some lighter moments. At one point, a Syracuse

pitcher hit Robby on the hand with a pitch, but the umpire ruled he was in the act of swinging. A Chief yelled, "Alright Robinson, stop trying to hit the ball with your hand!" and even Robinson broke up laughing. That night, he was feted by the local Elks club and treated to a steak dinner with all the trimmings. Robinson was still carrying a live rabbit a fan had given him for luck back in Newark. Robby considered giving the bunny to the cook to complete the feast but instead gave the little hare to a young fan.

As April turned to May, and the first signs of spring poked through the Canadian frost, the Royals came home to Montreal for the first time. They flew back from Baltimore in two large cargo planes, beating MacPhail to the punch by a few days. In the air, Jackie and Rachel were locked in deep conversation, not engaging anyone, according to Wendell Smith, who was traveling with the team (a coup that resulted in a six-figure boost to the circulation of the *Pittsburgh Courier*). Most likely, they were discussing a pressing problem that faced them upon arrival in Montreal, one that was shared by millions of Americans as well—where to find a place to live.

Local newspapers made appeals for readers to help find the Royals apartments for the season. Some of the players lived on couches, and at least a couple lived at the ballpark for a few weeks. Jackie was luckier, for he had Rachel as his real-estate agent. She toddled along on pregnant legs, tirelessly walking avenues and climbing stairs (mostly on the outside of buildings in the style in Montreal) of elevator-free buildings. It never occurred to her to look in a black neighborhood—Montreal's Negroes made up only two percent of the city's population, and what clusters there were tended to be poverty-stricken.

She found a nice duplex on the East End, at 8232 de Gaspe Avenue in the predominantly French Villeray District. A French-Canadian woman who was letting the apartment welcomed her inside and served Rachel tea, an act of simple kindness that warmed her heart after the less-hospitable weeks in Florida. The landlord insisted Rachel use her china and linens, a grace note that didn't go unnoticed. "What was nourished there in that house," she told the *Canadian Press,* "had widespread influence in our society." Rachel raced to sign the lease.

Upstairs, in the upper-level of the duplex, lived a family with eight children. The children would rush out of the house to help with grocery bags and heavy packages when they saw the heavily pregnant Rachel coming down the street. She reciprocated by leaving fruit for them on their way to school. "Little things [like] that turn into big pieces of your experience," she said much later. "They were friendly, they were protective, they were supportive and it was not something that I'd have expected." Other neighbors provided her with extra ration books for butter and sugar and sewed her maternity clothes.

Quebec was hardly a Negro paradise. While racism was far less overt than in the Jim Crow South, the local black population suffered from severe neglect, especially in education and health care. The first French word Rachel remembered learning was *noir.* The Robinsons were celebrities, and thus were given a more heartfelt welcome, but in general, Montreal's blacks were treated as outsiders, aliens to be stared at in wonder, like creatures in a zoo, if not outright persecuted. The best thing about the city, as far as its black population was concerned, was that language and culture, French versus English, were the main points of division. Race came in a distant third.

The Robinsons' apartment wasn't far from the Royals' home park, Delorimier Stadium, which was plopped into the block at the corner of De Lorimier Avenue and Ontario Street East. Royals fans had a penchant for gambling, and they and the park had a bad reputation because of it. Thousands of dollars changed hands at every home game. Fans hollered to players during games, promising payouts if they got a hit or stole a base. A fan once commandeered the

PA system to make an offer to a player. Undercover agents were put in the crowd, but that only slowed the action.

On May 1, Jersey City repaid the Royals' visit for the home opener. Nearly sixteen thousand fans filled the joint for the game on a sunny, glorious early-spring afternoon. Montreal's portly mayor, Camillien Houde, threw out the first pitch, and "There Will Always Be an England" was sung as the Union Jack was raised.

Jackie, resplendent in his home silver-and-blue Montreal uniform, singled and scored a run, but the Royals lost to the Little Giants 12–9. The crowd cared not a whit. Robinson posed for photos and signed autographs for nearly an hour on the field after the game, relegating the city's main sports legend, hockey star Maurice "the Rocket" Richard, who was at the game, to the shadows. He went "almost unnoticed," according to the *Sporting News*.

Wendell Smith took his leave of the Robinson beat after the game, after spending two months at his side. His final column from Montreal sounded a hopeful elegy for the "Great Experiment." "When I see (Robinson) attired in a Brooklyn Dodgers uniform and performing on the fertile turf of Ebbets Field—something which is not altogether impossible—I will regard this particular assignment and story finished and, in the parlance of the marines: 'Mission Accomplished.' For on that great day I will be able to truthfully say 'Mine Eyes Have Seen The Glory.'"

The Royals were 6–8–1 amid Jackie's coming-out debutante dance, but once the hoopla settled down a bit, the team steadily demolished the International League. It was a strong club, with quality players like Herman Franks, Les Burge, Spider Jorgensen, and Al Campanis. Even though the team's star from 1945, Roland Gladu, had jumped to the Mexican League, the Royals won seven straight and were 19–5 in May to seize control in the standings.

Robinson was earning his $600 monthly salary. Swinging hard from his pigeon-toed stance, he hit .349 in May, scoring twenty-three times and dominating games from the base paths. "Like plastic and penicillin, Robinson is here to stay," wrote Lloyd McGowan. Fans screamed *Allez!* as soon as he reached base, urging him to steal bases and wreak havoc. The Delorimier Stadium public-address announcer pronounced his name with a French flourish—*YACK-eeeeee RO-been-son!*—that Jackie would say allowed him to pretend to be someone else while playing, his Franco-American alter ego.

Away from the park, the Robinsons enjoyed the European flavor of Montreal. Rachel roamed the narrow streets and alleys of the city's old district, prowling in bookstores and music shops and sipping tea in cafes. She went to every home game, of course, but only occasionally traveled on the road with the Royals, preferring to languor in a place where she could simply disappear into the cultural fabric, instead of bearing witness to her husband running through the brick walls enacted to halt baseball's racial pioneer. That was exhausting territory, not to mention dangerous for a pregnant woman. She loved Jackie dearly, but she could be forgiven for wanting some time to simply escape into a book or walk down a street in peace or just stay off her feet for a while as Jackie Jr. grew inside her.

"Coming to Montreal at that time in our lives and the kind of reception we got was our honeymoon," she remembered. "We were still recovering from our experiences in the South, and we were deeply in love. We needed that time alone. It strengthened our relationship." The newlyweds were active in the city. Jackie was busy with charity appearances, often going to area hospitals and veterans' administrations with members of the hockey Canadiens, who were sporting royalty in Montreal. The couple became close friends with Montreal sportswriter Sam Maltin and his wife, Belle. They dined together frequently, with Belle letting Rachel in on some of her "trade secrets" to preparing good Jewish meals, and the foursome often went to concerts on Mount Royal, the ridge that overlooks the city.

Robinson wasn't particularly close with his teammates, who respected him but didn't hang out with him. One Royals fan, Alvin Guttman, recalled seeing a few players at the Chic-N-Coop restaurant, and congratulated them on having a fine second baseman. "Yeah, but it's too bad he had to take a job from a white man," came the reply. It was less racism than careerism. Like all minor leaguers, the players had a single goal—making it to the majors. They were after jobs in Brooklyn and were focused on that. Going out of their way to be humanitarians wasn't part of the equation. Robby was helping them win at present, so that was great. Otherwise, he didn't help any of them make it to Ebbets Field, so he didn't really matter. Shotgun Shuba, who had put paid to any idea of team unrest by shaking Jackie's hand in the opener, was gone after a few weeks, demoted to Mobile. In a great irony, the player Robinson was closest to was probably Campanis, who, on the television program *Nightline* four decades later, infamously would question the ability of blacks to run franchises, immolating his reputation.

In another oddity, Robby was not particularly close with the other Negroes on the '46 Royals, pitchers John Wright and, later, Roy Partlow. Wright was in a tough position, with everyone convinced he was on the Royals merely to be the "second Negro," Jackie's sounding board for all things black, as though the clubhouse were an ark that needed two of everything. Actually, Wright was an accomplished Negro Leaguer, once winning twenty-five games in a season, but he had control problems with the Royals and pitched rarely. A native of New Orleans, he spoke Creole French, and thus had a leg up on Robinson, who never learned the language. But Wright didn't adapt to the cool climate and European rhythms of Montreal, and in mid-May was sent to Class C ball at Trois-Rivières, a Quebec-based team seventy miles from Montreal.

Wright was immediately replaced by Partlow, a veteran in his mid-thirties who was signed from the Philadelphia Stars in the apparent belief that Robinson still needed another black teammate. Partlow was a firebrand, and thus a peculiar choice to help integrate the game. When he too was demoted after not getting much action ("I've got seven pitchers and not enough work for them," Hopper told the *Afro-American*), he disappeared for a spell, frightening the Negro press. The likes of Wendell Smith and Joe Bostic were still walking on eggshells, fearing that any misstep by any of the black players would sabotage "The Great Experiment."

When he finally turned up in Trois-Rivières, Partlow reeled off nine straight wins. Wright, too, played well once freed from Robinson's orbit. The two Negro pitchers played key roles in the Class C playoff run Three Rivers made that fall. Partlow scored the winning run in Game Five of the championship series against Pittsfield as Trois-Rivières captured the championship. "Wright and Partlow, now they were nice boys," recalled their manager, Frenchy Bordagaray, in a 1995 interview with the *Montreal Gazette*. "They were just perfect. They had to be. Otherwise, I was a dead duck, and so were they. Sure, it was a sensitive job. We were breaking down the color barrier."

But the kind words and the Class C title didn't do much for Wright and Partlow, who never sniffed a chance at the majors again.

While life in Montreal was grand, Robby and the Royals still had to cross the border and play in America, and their welcome continued to be a cold one. Race relations were not going to improve overnight simply because a black man was playing well in Canada, especially not in the Deep South. That fact was seared into the nation's consciousness on May 9, when the skies over Stone Mountain, Georgia, were lit up, reflecting the massive cross burning staged by the Ku Klux Klan to intimidate blacks planning to register to vote for the first time in the state's upcoming gubernatorial primary.

An exception was Buffalo, where Bisons fans cheered Robby and presented him with gifts that included watches, travel bags, and, sometimes, straight cash. Special trains from Chicago brought in loads of black fans, and they took advantage of Offermann Stadium's lack of segregation codes to get close-up looks at their champion.

But Baltimore continued to resist progress. On several occasions, Mobtown fans swarmed the field, rioting and requiring police interaction. Robinson would retreat to the dugout, his teammates forming a protective cordon until the boys in blue could quell the crowd.

On June 7, Robinson went hitless as the Royals beat the Orioles 5–2. After the game, according to the *Sporting News,* "a riot broke out. Fans swarmed the field. Robinson had already reached the clubhouse, but the rednecks waited outside until one in the morning. 'Come out here Robinson, you son of a bitch,' they taunted. 'We know you're up there. We're gonna get you.' Teammates Spider Jorgensen, Marvin Rackley and Tom Tatum stayed with him until the crowd went home."

Robby kept a lid on the magma that threatened to bubble over, but it was becoming more and more difficult to do so. The pressure was building, the season was wearing on him, and there were still months to go.

Chapter 17
THE BRAT

SOME MAJOR LEAGUE violence broke out in Brooklyn on May 22. With the Cubs in town and the game tied at one in the tenth inning, Chicago shortstop Lennie Merullo slid into Brooklyn second baseman Eddie Stanky with spikes high, and the two former teammates began swinging. A huge brawl erupted. Merullo got mixed up in the dirt with Reese, Pee Wee slugging him from behind and giving Merullo a black eye. Cubs pitcher Claude Passeau, a tough hombre who once whipped a ball in fury at Durocher in the dugout, came together with the manager and ripped Leo's jersey clean off. Order was finally restored, and the Brooks won it in thirteen innings.

The next day, ill will remained. During batting practice, Merullo approached Reese to show Pee Wee his new shiner and asked the Dodgers shortstop to hit him again, this time while Merullo was looking, so he could break Reese's neck. Dixie Walker overheard the tough talk and whacked Merullo from behind, getting in the second blindside hit on the Cubbie in as many days.

This one didn't work out so well. Merullo ran after Dixie, got him to the ground, and whaled on him as Walker's nine-year-old boy looked on, wailing "Daddy!" Merullo showed no sympathy, knocking out one of Dixie's teeth and breaking another. Both sides came together in another melee, with the police centering attention on Cubs first baseman Phil Cavarretta, the reigning NL MVP. "The husky Cub" took on several cops and half the Brooklyn roster, according to various reports, causing the *Tribune* to accuse the police of "protecting the Dodgers." He would later outrageously deny partaking in the fight, though when asked directly if he had slugged Durocher in the nose, Cavarretta fell silent and grinned.

When order was finally restored, five policemen were stationed in each dugout to prevent a rekindling of emotions. Half the players were ejected, and Reese, Walker, Cavarretta, and Merullo were fined. Most important, the Dodgers won in extra innings once again.

On-field brawls were unusual for Dixie Walker, but they were second nature for Eddie Stanky, whose very name invoked his character. He was perfectly happy to roll around in the filth if that's what it took to come out on top. Durocher, who saw plenty of himself in Stanky, summed up his worth to the team.

"He can't hit, can't run, can't field. He's no nice guy . . . all the little SOB can do is win."

Billy Herman, an aging star back from two years in the navy, started the season as the Dodgers second baseman, mostly out of respect, but Stanky was too good, or perhaps too much of a nudge, to be kept out of the lineup. He crowded the plate, so beanings were frequent. A particularly nasty one back in the minors had fractured his skull and kept him out of the war. Then in his very first at bat in the majors in 1943, he was conked on the melon once again. But he rose to play as hard as he could. That was the type of grit that earned him the loyalty of the hardscrabble Brooklyn fans, who honored him with an "Eddie Stanky Day" late in the '46 season.

They called him "the Brat from Kensington" at first, in reference to his Pennsylvania upbringing. But Stanky's persona was too irritating to be limited in scope, so he became simply "the Brat." Like his manager, winning was all that mattered to Stanky, and any and all behavior could be countenanced toward that end. He would grab

Boston Red Sox star Ted Williams was a marine pilot during World War II. His flying ability led him to become a trainer, and he wouldn't see combat. He flew missions during the Korean War, leaving baseball once again to serve his country. (Transcendental Graphics / theruckerarchive.com)

Joe DiMaggio (L) of the New York Yankees joined the Army Air Force. The discipline is for the cameras—Joe mostly played ball or nursed an ailing stomach during the war. (Transcendental Graphics / theruckerarchive.com)

Bob Feller served on the USS *Alabama* as a gunnery officer but managed to work in some pitching on various islands and atolls across the Pacific. (National Baseball Hall of Fame Library, Cooperstown, New York)

The Overseas Invasion Service Expedition All-Stars, the winners of the European Theater "World Series" of 1945. Negro Leaguer Leon Day is far right, bottom row; next to him is fellow Negro Leaguer Willard Brown. Jackie Robinson made his pro debut months after this integrated team took the diamond. (Courtesy of Gary Bedingfield)

The best of frenemies: Yankees co-owner Larry MacPhail with his mentor and rival, Dodgers president Branch Rickey. The men would clash over numerous issues, none more contentious than Rickey's signing of Jackie Robinson. (National Baseball Hall of Fame Library, Cooperstown, New York)

Mexican League majordomo Jorge Pasquel, whose raids on major league stars scared the owners into meeting some of the players' demands. He was known to suit up and manage teams when he felt the urge. Here he kibitzes Mickey Owen while holding Owen's distracted young son. (Transcendental Graphics / theruckerarchive.com)

Jackie Robinson, during his first spring training in Daytona, Florida. Robinson was chased out of Sanford, Florida, by hostile locals, so Branch Rickey moved all of Brooklyn's minor league prospects to Daytona. (National Baseball Hall of Fame Library, Cooperstown, New York)

The 1946 season gets under way as President Harry Truman throws out the first pitch in Washington before the Senators play the Red Sox. Opening-day attendance across baseball dwarfed previous records. (National Baseball Hall of Fame Library, Cooperstown, New York)

Rising to the occasion: Jackie Robinson crosses the plate after homering in his professional debut for the Montreal Royals against Jersey City. Teammate George Shuba shakes his hand. Robinson and the Royals would go on to win the "Little World Series," the top prize in the minor leagues. (AP)

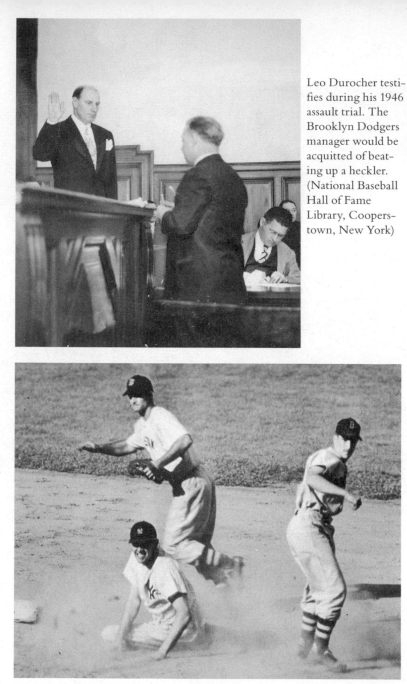

Leo Durocher testifies during his 1946 assault trial. The Brooklyn Dodgers manager would be acquitted of beating up a heckler. (National Baseball Hall of Fame Library, Cooperstown, New York)

The beating heart of the Boston Red Sox lineup, double-play combination Bobby Doerr (L) and Johnny Pesky (R). (Transcendental Graphics / theruckerarchive .com) runners by the belt as they raced from second to third, tag them in the face with extra relish, and accidentally-on-purpose drill runners with throws if they got too close.

He was well known for the "Stanky Maneuver," his habit of jumping up and down and waving his arms at second base in hopes of distracting the hitter. That was soon outlawed, as was a less-remembered stratagem. When on third base, Stanky would stand several feet behind the bag. On flies hit to the outfield, he would time the flight of the ball and sprint forward, hitting the bag just as the ball was caught, thus tagging up at full speed.

Offensively, Stanky's game was centered around drawing walks. To him, it was a battle within the greater war, and he delighted in frustrating opponents by getting on base after protracted at bats. In modern baseball, his grinder approach would be highly prized, as teams have learned the value of wearing down opposing pitchers. Back then, he was simply viewed as an irritant, if a highly effective one.

During a game in Pittsburgh in early June, Stanky drew three walks, then bragged to teammates, "I'll make 'em walk me again." He then taunted pitcher Johnny Lanning, dancing around the plate, crowding it, never remaining still in the batter's box. He fouled off pitch after pitch, working the count. The umpire warned him to behave, but Lanning was rattled by then. Finally, Stanky walked for the fourth time that afternoon. He then rubbed it in in his usual manner, carefully dropping his bat at the catcher's feet across home plate, and "trotted smugly" down to first. Pirates catcher Al Lopez broke his toe venomously kicking the bat off the dish. Stanky would come around to score the winning run in a 7–6 victory. As a rival player hissed to *Time,* "First you 'lose' Stanky [walk him], then you lose your head. First thing you know, you've lost the ball game."

He set a record by earning 148 free passes in 1945, when he also scored more often than anyone in the NL. In '46 he would draw 137 walks, which augmented his mediocre .237 batting average enough to allow the Brat to lead the league in on-base percentage at .436. It was just about the only department in which Musial wasn't tops in the NL.

If Stanky was beloved in Brooklyn, then Dixie Walker was worshipped. They called him "the Peeple's Cherce" ("the People's Choice" when translated from Brooklynese). Back in '41, when MacPhail ran the Dodgers, the team had splashed out for veteran slugger Joe "Ducky" Medwick, believing Fred Walker, aka Dixie, wasn't the answer. Dixie, his pride wounded, batted .308 to lead the team, while his clutch hitting delighted the Brooklyn faithful. Fans mobbed him wherever he went in the borough, cars driving up onto sidewalks to get his attention.

He was, of course, Harry's elder brother; more to the point, he was Ewart's son. The original "Dixie" Walker was a pitcher for the Senators in the first decade of the century. He passed along his athletic genes, but it took a summer in a Birmingham steel mill to fully infuse Fred with the desire to escape that life for baseball.

He was incredibly gifted and always being tabbed as the "next big thing," but it wasn't until he came to Brooklyn in 1939, after several years in the bigs, that he became a star. He had an excellent 1940, leading the team in hitting, though it was his dominance of the hated Giants that really endeared him to the Flatbush fans. The season was one of misfortune, though—his four-month-old daughter, Mary Ann, died of pneumonia that May.

He had knee and shoulder injuries that kept him from service, and Walker hammered wartime pitching, winning the batting title in '44 with a .357 average and the RBI crown in '45 with 124. He was back to raking the ball in '46—the day of his suspension for brawling, Walker was hitting .365 with 25 RBIs, second in the league in both categories.

Walker was now Public Enemy No. 1 in the Windy City. Two weeks after the brawl, the Dodgers visited Wrigley Field. Fans pelted him with rotten fruit and other assorted refuse. A set of false teeth was shipped to the visiting clubhouse special delivery, and a huge banner reading TOOTHLESS was unfurled when Dixie came to the plate.

A few days earlier, the Braves had come to Brooklyn for a doubleheader. In the second game, a Boston outfielder named Carvel "Bama" Rowell slugged one to right that smashed the Bulova clock that sat over the scoreboard. Shattered glass showered on Dixie. Bama was awarded a ground-rule double. The episode may have inspired the scene in the movie *The Natural,* where Roy Hobbs homers into the light stanchion to win the NL pennant for the New York Knights. The teams split the double-dip, and the Brooks closed out May with a 25–12 record, two games ahead of the heavily favored Cardinals.

Clearly, strange and beautiful things were afoot in the "Borough of Churches." More tangible positives abounded as well. The mortgage on Ebbets Field had just been paid off. Rickey was making money hand over foot. He took a healthy cut of player sales, which brought $250,000 to the team's coffers that summer. He sold TV rights to broadcast a handful of the team's games for $6,000, well more than the Yankees got. In all, the team's profit in 1946 was close to half a million bucks (a shade under $6 million today).

Rickey and other Lords of the Game should have been sleeping just fine. But then Jorge Pasquel opened his checkbook once again. And a dark shadow fell across the game.

Chapter 18
PARALYSIS

LATE ON THE night of May 22, St. Louis second baseman Red Schoendienst lay in his bed at the Knickerbocker Hotel in New York, talking with his roommate, who was pitching phenomenally well. He had started six games and won them all, going the distance each time, his 1.93 ERA explaining his record. Red prophesied that his roomie would have at least eleven wins by July 4.

Max Lanier thought otherwise. "I've pitched my last game for this club," he told the startled redhead.

Lanier was making $10,500, penny-ante stuff for a starter of his quality. On Breadon's roster, however, that qualified as rich. Musial was the highest-paid Cardinal, pulling down all of $14,000. Few squawked, for the farm system initiated by Rickey meant there were always two or three guys ready to step up and replace whoever didn't get with the program. "If you complained too much, you'd be back in Rochester," said Marion. After Breadon had sold off so many pitchers that spring, however, Lanier's hand was strengthened. He and Breadon had battled over salary all spring, with Lanier holding out for more than ten grand. Dyer even went to his owner to ask him to pay Lanier, a long limb for a new manager to walk out on. Breadon replied, "I'll give him $500 more. He can take it or go home."

Everywhere Lanier looked, workers were holding out for more money. In January, eight hundred thousand steel workers had paralyzed the nation's heavy industry by staging the largest strike in history. One thousand mills shut down across the United States. Two hundred thousand meatpackers were on strike, along with glass workers, electricians, machinists, telephone operators—name the job, and most likely some of its workers held a picket sign that year. Hawaii's sugar plantations were completely shut down by massive strikes. Back in St. Louis, schoolteachers walked, giving seventy thousand grateful kids a holiday. In Oakland, a minor picketing of a local department store inflamed when police broke up the rally and set up machine guns to intimidate sympathizers. It didn't work. Instead, nearly the entire city walked off the job, 130,000 of 200,000 Oaklanders. "These finky gazoonies who call themselves city fathers have been taking lessons from Hitler and Stalin," said one striker whose epithets were as colorful as he was steadfast. "They don't believe in the kind of unions that are free to strike."

On April 1 came another tremendous body blow, when John L. Lewis led the United Mine Workers in a shutdown, knocking out the steel and auto plants that needed coal to operate. Ford and Chrysler closed their plants, and electrical power was down 50 percent in some cities. The *Evansville Courier* called the strike "the most momentous event in the country's peacetime history." The Truman administration was seemingly impotent to stop it all. "We are doing everything we can," the president would meekly repeat week after week. According to David McCullough's 1992 biography, Truman wrote his mother saying he wouldn't mind going out on strike himself.

With no union to get his back, and no one to arbitrate his worth other than Sam Breadon, Lanier was stuck. Coming out of the service and with few career options other than playing ball, Lanier was forced to take the "take it or go home" offer, as so many other players had been.

But his superb start caught the eye of Jorge Pasquel. Pasquel had just convinced the Cards second baseman, Lou Klein, to jump, along with rookie pitcher Fred Martin. But Lanier, the best pitcher in the National League at the moment, would be a huge coup, and would make the press that had scoffed when Stephens returned to the Browns drop their cynicism. Pasquel asked Klein to help him recruit Lanier.

The second baseman did so enthusiastically, practically begging his teammate to go with him into the unknown. He brought Lanier over to see Pasquel at the Commodore Hotel (the Cards were in New York to play the Giants at the Polo Grounds), and the Mexican magnate laid it on thick. He offered Lanier double his $10,500 salary, a four-year deal, and a $30,000 signing bonus. Lanier, who like Klein was thirty years old and unsure how much earning power remained in his left arm, did the math in his head and realized that was more than he was likely to make over the rest of his career, regardless of how well he pitched. He agreed to jump.

"I went there for one reason," Lanier explained years later. "Money. I received it."

Back at the Knickerbocker, Schoendienst, who fell asleep figuring his roommate was joking, woke up to the harsh truth, courtesy of a note in the bathroom. "I'm leaving and keep hitting line drives. Hope to play against you. Max."

That wasn't the day's only bad news. The Cards managed to best the Giants to sweep a two-game series, but then the trouble started, courtesy of the Brotherhoods of Engineers and Trainmen.

The railroads that were so pivotal to the functioning of the country were operated by an amalgamation of twenty separate unions, all of which were hankering for better pay and working conditions. They asked for a raise of $2.50 and "perks" such as cold drinking water, awnings on cabooses to keep them out of weather, and not having to pay to clean their own official railroad watches. Eighteen of the unions had reached tentative agreements with the various railroad operators that employed them, but the Engineers and Trainmen were holdouts. Despite the intervention of the White House in negotiations, nothing was settled by the agreed-upon strike date, May 23.

So the Cardinals left Harlem for Grand Central, only to discover that there were no trains operating to take them to Cincinnati, their next stop. Traveling secretary Leo Ward reacted swiftly and managed to charter a flight the next day, ahead of the onslaught of people seeking planes when they realized the rails were shut down. The airlines were swiftly overloaded, and bus companies were too, despite "putting everything with four wheels" on the roads to serve the marooned public.

The train strike immediately shut down the country, making the steel workers' walkout look like a minor league fuss. More than 45,000 trains were idled by the 250,000 workers who walked off the job. Commuters were stranded with no way to get home. The final trains to run resembled cattle cars. *Life* ran a photo of the last train out of Grand Central bound for the New York suburbs. A woman was jammed headfirst into an open window, with only her heels and the bottom of her coat visible, the rest of her inside the train. Traveler's Aid stations were swamped, and hotels overrun. All mail immediately stopped. Steel, automobile, and other industries reliant on the trains to move freight shut down large facets of their operations, putting many thousands more out of work. Even *Life* was forced to temporarily raise its newsstand price, from ten to fifteen cents.

One seventy-two-year-old conductor had to hitchhike from Union Station in St. Louis to Ohio. An Asbury Park, New Jersey, man was stranded at the altar when his bride couldn't get a train to the site of the wedding. One airport clerk told the AP that a man offered her six pairs of nylons (worth far more than their weight in gold at that point) in exchange for a seat on a flight to Philadelphia. "If only he'd throw in a pound of butter I'd take him there myself," she said. Cabbies and enterprising civilians with automobiles were getting $25 to ferry folks from New York to Washington. Some passengers stuck in Indianapolis simply lived aboard their halted train for several days. Many thousands more sat down in train stations or, in more remote locales, trackside, and waited. The army deployed thousands of troops at rail depots across the nation, anticipating riots, while General Eisenhower was ordered back to the Pentagon from vacation due to the crisis.

Unlike previous strikers, whom the nation generally tolerated, if not sympathized with, the railroad unions were castigated far and wide. Truman compared their leaders to the "foreign enemy" that had attacked at Pearl Harbor. "It is painful to see these two railway brotherhoods, which have long enjoyed universal public respect, invite public opinion to turn against them," wrote the *New York Daily News,* and the *Times* concluded, "They are gambling with the entire future of the labor movement in this country, and it ought not to take many hours or days to convince them of that fact."

The entire labor movement was tarnished. "Labor is like a kid who gets too much money from their parents," thought one Des Moines dentist. A housewife in New Orleans was blunt—"My husband's a union man, but he's wrong." Veterans were particularly put out. "It looks like what we went through in the war was hardly worthwhile," one told a New York reporter. Another, overhearing, went further—"If we had Hitler here, there would be no strike." It seemed to many as though the blossoming Communist threat abroad had found a beachhead right here in the Great 48.

Baseball was affected right along with everything else. Half a dozen teams were stuck for hours before arranging to get to the next city. The Cleveland Indians were due into St. Louis to play the Browns after beating the Red Sox in ten innings on the twenty-third. They chartered a flight, but the plane was appropriated by the government for higher priorities, so they climbed on a bus early on the morning of the twenty-fourth. The team was still hours from Missouri at game time. The contest was officially declared a rainout, even though the sun shone over St. Louis.

Catcher Joe Garagiola had just been called up to the Cardinals, and the hometown hero hoped to join the team in Cincinnati but was stranded, unable to get to the show. Teams across the majors, like the Tigers, Cubs, and Pirates, hired fleets of cars to haul them to the next stop on their schedules. Umpires were told to stay where they were and officiate whatever games took place in that city.

Meanwhile, the Cardinals' charter raced toward Cincinnati. Ten players, including Pollet, Beazley, and Dickson, were deemed nonessential and were left off the plane. They found a bus and completed a twenty-seven-hour slog, thus missing the game of the twenty-fourth. They had it easy. The rest of the club flew in a DC-3, many of them in a plane for the first time. It was a typical flight for 1946—fifty miles short of their destination, the air turned violent, and thunderheads forced the plane down well short of Cincinnati about two hours before game time.

A group of ancient taxicabs was on hand at the airstrip, and the junkers raced for Crosley Field. Most made it without incident, but the cab carrying Musial and a few others, including Slaughter and Moore, had a faulty hood latch. The hood kept popping open, blocking the cabbie's view of the road. With an accident that would deprive the National League of its best player growing more and more likely, Musial told the cabbie that he should sit on the hood to hold it in place. Musial took the wheel, driving while sticking his head out of the window to see past his new hood ornament. The other guys stared at their shoes or gripped the door handles in terror as Stash sped into town and up to the ballpark. "I was laughing, but the guys were a little white," said Musial later. Somehow, they all arrived in one piece, and on time. Unsurprisingly, they were no match for Ewell Blackwell. The Reds won 5–1. The cabbie probably looked for a safer job.

Lanier, Klein, and Martin had a different madcap journey. They were headed for St. Louis to pack rather than Cincinnati to play, but the rail strike didn't discern. They found a bus to Baltimore, and were so worried about their big bonuses being stolen that they stored the cash bundles inside a big radio they had bought for the purpose of clandestine travel. They managed to get on board a plane to Chicago from Baltimore, but all the outgoing flights to St. Louis were booked solid. So they covered the three hundred miles by taxi, with Pasquel picking up the $400 tab.

A friend of Klein had somehow found a new car for his buddy, a Chrysler Windsor, even though automobiles were tough to buy. He had likely gone through the black market, which had sprung to life across the country in an instant as the OPA struggled to enforce price ceilings in the same way liquor agents had struggled to keep people from imbibing during Prohibition. "The black market cut through every stratum of American life" reported *Life*. In one celebrated case, a girl in Oakland bought a stick of penny candy and was forced to buy a $5 candy bar as well. Sugar that usually cost $.08 went for $1 a pound. The estimates of goods being resold at jacked-up prices on the black market were staggering—75 percent of automobiles, 70 percent of lumber, 75 percent of grain, 85 percent of bananas. Clothing, meat, liquor—if it could be sold, it was sold at a markup, accompanied by a muttered "you looking to buy something?"

Martin ventured south separately, but Lanier and Klein drove together in the Windsor. As they packed up, they talked with reporters. "We realize that we have no more than five years of ball left and for the sake of our families we figured we could not turn down the proposition," Lanier said. John Lardner wrote in *Newsweek* that he didn't understand "why the whole St. Louis team hasn't jumped to Mexico before now." Others in the press thought differently. "Has the USA reached the point where it can't match Mexican money?" asked Grantland Rice. "Has it become that cheap?" Writing from Cincinnati, the dean of St. Louis sportswriters, Bob Broeg, thought, "It wouldn't be surprising if Crosley Field just up and moved across the Rio Grande."

The defections stunned the Cards, who were tied for first when Lanier and the others signed on Pasquel's dotted line. "I felt like our pennant chances had been shot out from under us," Dyer moaned a short time later, and the team went into a tailspin, losing seven of the next eleven to close May. Breadon was nonplussed, pointing out that a pitcher named George "Red" Munger, a solid starter who still hadn't been discharged from the service, would soon be back to fill Lanier's spot. Munger, however, wasn't due back until August.

Howie Pollet, Dyer's favorite among the Cards, stepped up and volunteered to shoulder a heavier burden in Lanier's absence. "Give me a day's rest after I start a game," he told his manager, "and I can relieve if you need me. Then another day of rest and I can start again." Dyer said later, "Howie wasn't a robust fellow, but his heart was stout and I'll never forget it." Murry Dickson, who until that point was solely used out of the bullpen, also gained a prominent role in the rotation as the Cards tried to make up for the loss of their ace. Johnny Beazley took on more of a starter's role as well. Freddy Schmidt, however, remained glued to his seat in the bullpen.

Lanier and Klein became Vera Cruz Blues, joining Mickey Owen and Danny Gardella, and learned what the league was all about on their third day in Mexico. Vera Cruz led by two in the ninth inning, but the bases were loaded with nobody out. Pasquel, watching from his front-row box seat, pushed aside the silver platter of food he was wolfing down, called time out, and walked to the dugout. He ordered Owen to put in his new star pitcher. Owen shrugged in Lanier's direction, as if to say, "It's his money." Lanier, who hadn't pitched in over a week, struck out the side on nine pitches. Pasquel ran out to hug Lanier, yelling, "Max, I won this game, didn't I?!"

That was the high point of Lanier's time down south. He quickly became a clearinghouse for all the problems faced by *Yanquis* playing in Mexico. The water made him sick, the food made it worse. He mostly lived on canned tuna and peaches. His home had no air-conditioning, only overhead fans with slow blades that merely pushed the oppressive heat around the room. Lanier couldn't sleep and soon was so exhausted he could barely speak.

When he left for road trips, things got worse. Travel in the Mexican League was by bus or occasionally two-motor prop plane. Bus rides from city to city were terrifying affairs, as road rules were ignored and the loudest horn had the right of way. Air travel wasn't much better. Once, on a road trip to Tampico, the Vera Cruz plane landed in a cow pasture to pick up a passenger. Lanier would later vividly remember seeing the trees bending from the pressure of the plane upon takeoff.

Regardless of Lanier's travails, Pasquel's success with the St. Louis Three led him to go hard after other Cardinals, including Slaughter, Kurowski, and especially Musial. Jorge had Owen call Stan relentlessly, pitching him on the merits of La Liga. Then he sent Alfredo to St. Louis to meet with Musial at the Fairgrounds Hotel on June 6. Musial almost choked on the fat cigar he was puffing on when Alfredo spread five $10,000 cashier's checks on the bed and told Stan it was a bonus on top of the $125,000 they would pay him over five years. He later understated the obvious when he said, "All that money makes a fellow think before saying no."

"Musial to say adios" rumors swept St. Louis, leading to the city almost losing its collective shit after an innocent mix-up. Musial happened to be moving on the afternoon of June 6 to a bungalow in the southwestern part of town. A reporter called his soon-to-be-former home and Stan's son Dickie picked up. When asked what they were doing, the boy answered "packing." Naturally, the press jumped to the conclusion that they were leaving town for Mexico.

Musial put that story to rest but was still torn about whether to take Pasquel's riches. It was Eddie Dyer who sized up the situation and cut to the heart of Musial's true feelings. "Stan, you've got two children," Dyer said. "Do you want them to hear someone say, 'There are the kids of a guy who broke his contract?'"

That got Stan where he lived, and he told the Pasquels thanks but no thanks. Later, he intimated to the *Sporting News* that patriotism had outflanked avarice:

My dad came over from Poland. He worked in a steel mill in Donora, PA. He worked hard. But he never kicked. This was his dream, the good old U.S.A. . . . I want our little family to be together right here in America.

A shaken Breadon called Stan to his office and magnanimously awarded his superstar a $5,000 raise, bumping him to $19,000. It was still the best bargain in the game. The news didn't filter down to Mexico. Even as Musial was signing to stay in St. Louis, the public address announcer at the Verz Cruz–Puebla game told fans that Musial was en route and would play the next day against Lanier's Vera Cruz team.

Life noted that "Owners should have been happy, but they went around with harried, haunted looks, worrying which might be the next of their players to tear up his contract and jump to the fabulous Mexican League." But Musial's refusal to jump defanged the Mexican threat. His decision was closely watched by all of baseball. Had Stash crossed the border, many more were sure to follow. Instead, the players were mollified. If Musial was staying put, laughably underpaid as he was, then things down south must be not all they were cracked up to be.

Indeed, La Liga was quickly losing its "fabulous" sheen.

Chapter 19
FINITO

A FAMILIAR, IF flushed and heavily sweating, round face appeared in Jorge Pasquel's box during a Vera Cruz–Tampico game at Delta Park in May. It was "El Sultan del Bat"—Babe Ruth, in the flesh. *"Qué tal, amigos,"* the Babe mumbled to well-wishers. He had only two years to live, and the oppressive heat and smog was playing havoc with the Babe's constitution. But he was down south to send a message to the owners that were essentially blackballing him from the game. Since retiring from clubbing tape-measure home runs, Ruth wanted nothing more than to manage a big league team, but he was frozen out, partially because he was unsuited for the job, partially because the owners resented his outrageous salaries and bigger-than-the-game behavior while he had been playing.

So Ruth was reduced to flying to Mexico City and fanning rumors that Pasquel was set to make him commissioner. "I think the Pasquels are doing a fine thing for baseball and for their country," Ruth told the press horde. "Baseball is a game that should be played all over the world."

The owners were embarrassed, mainly because of the timing of Ruth's statement. MacPhail had led a lawsuit seeking to permanently stop the raids, and the owners' chest-thumping was overshadowed by the Babe's trip. MacPhail and his cohorts in the owner's boxes across baseball thought the law would be on their side, but in truth, it was a day in court the Mexicans looked forward to. "Monopoly is our defense," said Jerome Hess, the attorney for the Mexican League, "and it will be tried right down to the end, until every scintilla of evidence has been introduced."

Among Mexicans, baseball and the Mexican League had never been more popular. As the *New York Times* reported, the streets were full of talk of the game, while most reveled in the idea of "Saint Jorge" slaying the "dragon" of *Norteamericano béisbol*. It was seen as a small piece of revenge for the Mexican War of exactly a century before, a conflict that cost Mexico half of its territory to President James Polk's Manifest Destiny. As pitcher Tom Gorman, who leapt from the Braves to Mexican League ball in the spring of '46, said, "The Mexicans love to see a mere human dispatch a tremendous bull."

Back in America, those with a vested interest in the game did all they could to ruin the reputation of the man who threatened their livelihood. Stories abounded of Pasquel pulling handguns on reporters, or ignoring owed payments, or threatening players with violence after on-field mistakes. "He is viewed as a sinister, swarthy, and unscrupulous man of limitless means whose widespread agents operate on a Fu Manchu–like scale," reported *Time,* and that alien, vaguely Communist aura was exactly how the owners painted Pasquel to the public.

They had help from several coconspirators. American sporting-goods manufacturers, heretofore the sole suppliers of the Liga, refused to sell equipment to the Mexicans, under threat from the owners. The result was a shortage of bats, balls, and bases that forced the Mexican League to postpone its opening day by a week. Then a sympathetic congressman let slip that back in 1941, Pasquel had been blacklisted by the US government for illegally trading with Germany. Meanwhile, a judge in New York called the luring of players "malicious acts" and set a temporary injunction against the Pasquels approaching any of the Yankees. Pasquel responded by sending Commissioner Chandler a contract offering Happy $50,000 to come down and serve as commish in Mexico.

On March 21, opening day in the Liga, Vera Cruz dumped Mexico City 12–5 in front of thirty-three thousand at Delta Park. Outgoing Mexican President Manuel Avila Camacho threw out the first pitch. Gardella homered and doubled in the game but, true to his scouting report, also dropped a couple of fly balls. Pasquel ordered him to get his eyes checked. The first two dozen games on the schedule drew about seven hundred thousand fans, proving that folks in Mexico were every bit as eager to turn the page on the war as their neighbors to the north. Pasquel also had sold the 1946 radio rights for a cool $20,000—in 1942, Pasquel had paid for the broadcasts from his own pocket.

But there were warning signs that the good times were coming to an end. The Americans were having trouble adjusting to the mores of *béisbol Mexicano.* The lawless culture took them aback. Virtually everyone, or so it seemed, carried a weapon, brandishing it at the drop of a sombrero. "If some of those Mexican henchmen didn't think you were hustling to their satisfaction," said Mickey Owen, "they'd sidle up to you and stick a gun in your ribs. . . . It just scared the hell out of me." Fireworks and hissing skyrockets would be set off after good plays. "They're worse than Brooklyn," Owen exclaimed after being startled once too often.

The Sierra Madre chain provided an unforeseen problem for the jumpers. The altitude in Mexico City and the surrounding cities left players gasping for breath, while pitchers found that their curveballs lacked snap in the thin air. The *Times* reported on a player who hit a triple, then held up the game for five minutes while he attempted to catch his breath. The locally made bats were constructed of poor lumber and cracked unless hit perfectly sweet. The players called them "drugstore bats." Mosquitos were a constant nuisance, especially in hotel rooms that didn't provide screens. A sleepless night was a strong possibility if the bugs weren't kept at bay.

Tampico had a large, mostly modern park that seated thirty thousand fans, and Pasquel was said to be planning a $2 million stadium for downtown Mexico City. But most of the parks in the league were substandard. They didn't have showers or clubhouses, for one thing, necessitating players to change at their hotels, which often didn't have running water, especially outside of Mexico City. The dugouts were small and airless in the fearsome heat, and players mostly sprawled on the ground outside. In Vera Cruz, the dugout was sunk so far into the crowd the players had to lean way out to see the game, as if they were in a pillbox.

The infields were often grassless, rock-filled tracts, and outfields were seldom mown uniformly. In Pueblo, the groundskeeper had a secret weapon to control the grass—goats were let loose to eat the extra growth before games. Even Tampico's decent park had a railroad track that ran smack through center field. Right in the middle of a game, a whistle would blow, the gates would open, and the action would stop while a freight train ran across the field. Outfielders had to look down while tracking flies to ensure they didn't trip over the tracks.

Travel was mostly by overcrowded bus, filled to double capacity, ones where "people got on, but nobody got off." Max Lanier wasn't the only American scarred by road trips. Two decades later, Sal Maglie still shuddered when he remembered the trips over the mountains to and from Puebla, his team. "The buses were driven by madmen," he told *Sports Illustrated*. "They used to push those old wrecks as hard as they could on the narrow, winding roads in the mountains." Maglie started flying at his own expense to avoid the bus, but the local airplanes weren't much safer. Landing strips in a few towns were simply open pastures. "It was unnerving," Owen said years later. "Coming in for a landing we'd look out and see eight or ten of those big black Mexican vultures waiting for us. That's one of the things I remember best about Mexico—those vultures."

Nearly everyone smoked, and the haze obscured fly balls. Worse, fires started from wayward cigarillos were a constant hazard. Vendors sold seat cushions, enchiladas, and lottery tickets. Gambling was pervasive, with pesos changing hands after almost every pitch. Police with tear-gas guns lined the aisles, ostensibly to control the gambling, but they barely slowed the action. The best seats up front cost about $2—most paid far less. The fans, almost all of whom were male, yelled *"ciego!"*—"blind man"—at the umpires.

They played only three times a week, Thursdays, Saturdays, and Sundays, further disrupting the jumpers, who were used to far more regular action. The season lasted ninety-eight games. The players' average salary was about $200 per month—and that was including the Americans. There was no seventh-inning stretch, no pregame meeting to go over strategy, and hardly any "inside baseball"—hit-and-run plays and sacrifice bunts were rare. The outfielders didn't call one another off fly balls, and they didn't shift depending on what side of the plate the batter hit from. Pitching changes were rare and occasionally dangerous. An aptly named hurler known as Loco Torres once refused to be pulled from the game, until his manager prodded him off the mound by walloping him in the backside with a fungo bat.

In an ironic turn of events, the Americans who jumped were playing integrated baseball a year earlier than anyone outside the International League. Players from all over Latin America, including dark-skinned Cubans and Dominicans, and African-American players as well, all tumbled together and mixed with the whites from the majors. J. G. Taylor Spink, the publisher of the *Sporting News,* had pooh-poohed the Mexican threat on those grounds. "They can't get many of our players to join those mixed nationalities that make up the clubs down there," and some indeed stayed away because of that factor.

The Yanks who ventured south were in the main farm boys who, in a strange twist, wound up deeply envious of the more sophisticated black players. They spoke little Spanish, whereas the Negroes were mostly bilingual, at least conversationally so, thanks to years of playing ball in Latin America. It was a talent that set them up with the local ladies. The whites from the States were shut out of postgame "action," a not-insignificant fact in a world defined by locker room ethics.

The black players were also far more tolerant of the hardships of baseball outside of the majors. They were used to an itinerant hardball life, one that came with all manner of difficulties. They adapted—the major leaguers were hard-pressed to do likewise.

Max Lanier found out the hard way that the Negro Leaguers were tough outs. Lanier's first game after his exceptional relief appearance came against Monterrey, a team led by several Negro stars, mainly Ray Dandridge, a future Hall of Famer. Dandridge powered a home run (*jonron*) off Lanier. Afterward, Lanier asked Dandridge where he had come from. "We come from the same place you did, the U.S.A.," Dandridge replied.

"I never heard of any of you guys before," Lanier said.

"Well, we've been here," said Dandridge.

Mexico had always been a sanctuary for Negroes looking to play, such a well-known stop that boxer Joe Louis, when asked his plans after he pummeled Billy Conn in June, said, "I dunno—maybe go down to that Mexican League. They say I hit pretty good." But star players like Dandridge and Martín Dihigo resented the fact that the major leaguers were getting so much money and attention, even as the blacks and Latinos outperformed them on the field.

The specter of the Mexican presidential election hung over the season, and the major leaguers began to suspect that their recruitment was more about politics than pitching and hitting. Pasquel was close with candidate Miguel Alemán, of the Pardito Revolucionario Institucional (PRI), and he gave plenty of credit internally for the ballplayers jumping to Alemán, which helped him at the polls. The PRI controlled Mexican politics, and Alemán was the odds-on favorite to win, with or without Pasquel, but the good PR didn't hurt. Of course, that didn't mean Alemán and Pasquel left anything to chance. Lanier remembered a clubhouse boy telling him that "the election was yesterday, and I voted seven times!"

After the election, Pasquel attempted to cut salaries, including Lanier's. The resulting squawk changed Pasquel's mind, for a while at least, but Lanier, already put off by the food and Mexico City's pollution, was ready to jump back to the States.

He didn't do it, but his catcher, Mickey Owen, did. Owen had a pretty sweet deal. He was getting $120 per month for food, had a maid to clean his furnished apartment, and had a car and driver. He bought a sterling-silver set with his $12,500 bonus. He was exempt from US taxation, and Pasquel paid his Mexican duties.

But Owen was miles out of his element, and that outweighed his financial portfolio. He was a child of the Ozarks and hadn't counted on playing with blacks—or worse, being managed by one, Ramón Bragaña, who replaced Owen as the player-manager of Vera Cruz when Owen's limitations with the language proved him unfit to run the club. He was also handled rather easily in a fistfight with Afro-Cuban star Claro Duany. Then came a real insult—he was asked to play first base so a Negro League vet could catch.

Worst was the paranoia that set in—Owen complained to writers that "they" were following him, opening his mail, hiring detectives to watch his every move. He claimed that every evening at midnight, an agent of Pasquel's would pound on his door and make him sign a piece of paper signifying that he was home and in bed. Finally Owen went to Pasquel to complain about his intolerable situation, and Pasquel pulled out a pistol and pushed it across his desk to Owen. "Shoot me if you think you've been lied to or misled! Shoot me!!" A reporter from *Life* was in the room; he stormed out to vomit from the tension.

He was hitting .243 and getting booed by impatient fans. In Owen's mind, the day was rapidly approaching when one of those gun-toting partisans would open fire at him after a ground-out—heck, it could be Pasquel himself doing the shooting. He was done with this *mierde*. So Owen hailed a cab and paid $250 for a lift over the border to Brownsville, Texas. His wife hadn't even had time to pack most of her clothes. When he talked ill of his experience to American reporters, a Mexican paper warned, "It would be wiser for Mr. Owen not to get too close to the international border after his remarks."

Owen imagined he would be exempt from Chandler's ban, and Rickey certainly was willing to bring him back for the pennant race. "The Mahatma of Montague St. . . . who seemed to think it was quite alright to take Jackie Robinson away from the Kansas City Monarchs, is waiting on the Dodgers doorstep with outstretched arms," wrote the *Los Angeles Times*. Brooklyn's argument was that Owen had never signed a contract for 1946 and thus hadn't really "jumped." The contrary argument from St. Louis was made in a loud voice. The Cards had turned down repeated offers from Rickey for one of their young backstops and didn't want to see a major positional advantage over their heated rivals overturned on a technicality. Chandler held firm, and Owen was out of luck. "When Owen makes an error, it is a beaut," snickered *Time*.

Other Americans were proving equally sour on the Mexican experience. Only Nap Reyes hit anywhere near what was expected from him, and the pitchers weren't acclimating to the small ballparks and thin air. Their attitudes went south as well. Former Dodger Luis Olmo dozed off in the outfield in the fourteenth inning of an interminable game. As he snored, a hit came his way. Awoken by the roaring crowd, and thinking the winning run had scored, Olmo turned and fired the ball over the fence in disgust. Only then did the runner, who was held at third base, trot home to win the game.

Time summed up the situation—"The Mexican gold rush is no El Dorado."

While the Americans were having buyer's remorse, the Lords of the Game outflanked Pasquel. Breadon, with tacit approval from MacPhail, who was emerging as an ironic leader of the baseball establishment, made a surprise visit to Mexico in late June. He took in a game with Jorge, fended off rumors he was selling the Cardinals to the Pasquels, and watched his former hurler Freddie Martin lose a poorly pitched game.

Afterward he talked up the Pasquels. "They are real people," he beamed, "who will keep any promises they make." Most presumed that meant Breadon had secured a deal ensuring the Pasquels would stop raiding the Cardinals; others broadened it out to include the entirety of the majors. That viewpoint took on further currency when Chandler, who had made a great show of fining Breadon $5,000 for his "unauthorized" trip, quietly rescinded it. Whatever the truth, the raids stopped. The owners heaved a sigh of relief, though the raids had exposed many of them as outlandishly cheap. The Depression was over, and the nation's tolerance for cries of poverty from the moguls was wavering.

The demise of the Mexican League and Pasquel's dream was nigh. Pasquel's money had been a crucial factor in the jet-propelled rise of the enterprise, but the appearance of stability was almost as critical. Owen's defection and Breadon's side deal had made Pasquel look like a petty tyrant of a banana republic. He hadn't helped matters with stunts like managing teams himself on a whim, or becoming official scorer to make decisions that allowed him to welsh on performance bonuses. He remained as majordomo of Mexican baseball until 1951, when an irate fan beaned him on the head with a stone thrown from the stands. Enraged, Pasquel sold his stake in the Liga and turned to safer pursuits, notably big-game hunting in Africa. He was killed in 1955 when his private plane crashed in the Mexican mountains.

But if the owners thought they were done with challenges to their economic foundation, they were sadly mistaken.

Chapter 20
STRIKE OUT

June 7 was a warm evening in Pittsburgh, and a single question was on the minds of the shirt-sleeved fans, 16,884 in all, in the stands of Forbes Field—would they see their Pirates take the field to play the Giants that night? Perhaps a few in the crowd recognized the potential historic import of the evening—history that would ironically be made only if their Pirates chose not to play.

With game time just minutes away, the answer was very much in doubt. The home clubhouse was locked tight. Reporters stood on ladders and piled trunks to steal a glimpse inside through the single square window. In the hallway that led to the field, a slightly built man in his mid-thirties paced back and forth, awaiting the result of a momentous vote taking place in the locker room.

His name was Robert Murphy, and he was the other half of the tag-team combination that was terrifying MacPhail and the other owners that summer.

Murphy was a lawyer from Boston, in the employ of the National Labor Relations Board, ironically as a management expert. He loved baseball and, in the course of regularly attending Braves and Sox games, got to know a few players. He heard them complaining about salary issues with ownership, and would always tell them, half in jest, "Form a union."

But the more Murphy thought about it, the more it made sense. He vividly recalled an incident from back in 1933, when Jimmie Foxx, the slugging "Double-X" who had just won consecutive MVP Awards, was "offered" a salary cut by Connie Mack, from $18,000 to $12,000, and Foxx had little recourse. That had struck Murphy as insane at the time, and now, with a law degree from Harvard and several years' experience in labor relations in hand, it seemed even crazier. "I could talk for three days on some of the injustices done to ball players by the club owners," he said. Murphy saw that stage and screen entertainers were unionized. Why were ballplayers any different?

The first tilt toward player solidarity had come way back in 1885, when John Montgomery Ward, who was a lawyer as well as a New York Giant, attempted to organize his brethren, to little lasting effect. Then, a "Player's Fraternity" formed in 1912, in the wake of Ty Cobb's suspension for beating up a fan. Not the most sympathetic of causes, perhaps, but a large majority of the players signed up, in part because the leader, a lawyer named Dave Fultz, studiously avoided the use of the word "union." Fultz once called for a strike (a settlement was reached the day before) and applied to the American Federation of Labor for inclusion. AFL boss Sam Gompers turned the players down, however, and World War I, with its "work or fight" ultimatums, killed off the Fraternity.

Now, in the wake of an even bigger war, Murphy was spoiling to try again. He wasn't a baseball man—the only athletic endeavor he took part in was running some track while at Harvard—and that made him suspect in some people's eyes within the game. But what he had to say outweighed their cynicism.

His stated goal was "a square deal for players, the men who make possible big dividends and high salaries for stockholders and club execs." He then sat in Boston as the fourteen other major league teams came to town, and spoke to the visiting players in his soft New England accent about the absurd conditions they were agreeing to without representation. Before the war, his words may have fallen on less-willing ears, especially during the Depression, when the prevailing opinion among baseball's rank and file was that they were lucky to have a job at all, much less one so fun. But now, with the stands bursting and the excitement for the game palpable, the players were more receptive to his message. Everyone, it seemed, was making more money from the game—except them.

As he put it early in the season, "We lost 15 or 20 players to the Mexican League already, and we may lose even more. If they had been satisfied [in the US], they naturally would have remained. It's our aim to improve salaries, player conditions, and contracts so that players will be satisfied." Murphy's hardest task was selling the players on dues of fifty cents a week.

Murphy proposed an American Baseball Guild, with him as director. The Guild's platform would contain six main negotiating points:

1. Half of the purchase price of any player sale would go to the player (at present, the sold player got zilch).
2. The players should have the right to an arbitrator to settle salary disputes.
3. That there would be no maximum salary.
4. That the minimum salary would be $7,500 a year.
5. Bonuses and insurance should be a standard part of every contract.
6. Contracts must not be one-sided.

It was that last vague-sounding point that struck the most fear in the heart of any management type who heard about it. Without saying so outright, it challenged the Reserve Clause, which was the very model of a one-sided contract. Even though Murphy went out of his way to say that he wasn't after abolishment of the Clause ("the wealthier clubs would corner the player market" is what he told the Cardinals when he met with them in May), everyone knew that would be the inevitable result, if not immediately, then in the very near future. After all, as he told the Redbirds in their meeting, "the validity of baseball contracts makes me laugh. An owner can do as he wants with a player on a ten-day notice." The player, meanwhile, was bound to the club forever.

While many in the press made jokes about a "Second Basemen's Local 307" and overtime pay for extra-inning games, Murphy would have seen that the winds were at his back. In the spring, a navy vet named Al Niemiec returned home and went back to his old job, that of infielder with the Seattle Rainiers of the Pacific Coast League. He was cut after a handful of games, and sued to get his gig back under the GI Bill, which guaranteed veterans they would be able to return to their old positions. Judge Lloyd Black agreed.

"Baseball is no different than a store or a machine shop," he wrote. "The law is simple. A veteran rates his old job back. . . . Since it is argued correctly that baseball is the great American game, certainly it ought to bear its share in meeting obligations to servicemen." Then, using language that had to set Murphy's hair on fire, Black wrote that the Reserve Clause was patently illegal, and "reminiscent of chattels."

Murphy, a bachelor, made the Guild his consuming passion that spring. He claimed that he had signed up members on at least eleven of the sixteen teams, and that he was ready to work on the minor leagues and the six thousand or so players down on the farm next. He certainly got the attention of the Lords of the Game. Already buffeted by Pasquel's raids, the last thing they needed was a shit-stirrer fomenting labor trouble in their clubhouses. "The owners were no longer laughing; they were panicky," wrote *Newsweek*. Clark Griffith, the tightwad owner of the Senators, screamed about the ridiculousness of Murphy's demands. "Collective bargaining in baseball would be utterly impractical," he said. "There is no production line in this game. It's a matter of individual ability."

Some in management were more sympathetic than others, or at least more pragmatic. After Murphy had held secret talks with the Boston Braves about holding a strike vote, team president Lou

Perini somehow got wind of Murphy's intent and flew to Chicago, where the Braves were playing the Cubs, to talk it over with his players. As a result, he agreed to stop scheduling doubleheaders after night games, increase the minimum salary to $6,000, and begin payments during spring training.

If the moguls were hoping that the press, whom they fed and liquored and (mostly) transported and sheltered on road trips, would be sympathetic toward their side, they were surprised. Most in the press saw the situation as absurdly tilted toward management, and wrote as much. Dave Egan, "the Colonel," nominated Murphy for instant enshrinement in the Hall of Fame. Even Westbrook Pegler, the staunch right-winger (but a former baseball writer), took a line that sounded decidedly leftist. "The owners will have some of themselves to blame," he wrote. "Not all, but enough of them, have been harsh and arrogant, mean in money matters and completely ruthless in imposing on the youth of great players."

By summer, Murphy was feeling cocky enough to call for a team to strike. He decided on Pittsburgh as his test case. The Pirates played in a strong union town with a heavy industrial base. Among others on the team were ETO World Series vets Ken Heintzelman and Maurice Van Robays, both emphatically pro union, their wartime experience giving them perspective on the shackles they served under at home. Then there was backup catcher Bill Salkeld. He had hit .315 in 1945, but received a mere $500 raise, to $6,000. Unable to find a place for himself and his family to live, due to the nationwide housing shortage, he had to put them up in a hotel, which broke him financially. Finally, he was forced to put his wife and kids on a train to California so they could live with his in-laws, going hat in hand to his teammates to borrow the $500 required for the tickets. The trial turned him into a hard-core proponent of Murphy's guild and anything that would help ballplayers on the margins cope.

Then Pirates owner William Benswanger got involved, browbeating his players into rejecting the outside agitation. Some players, with little education and no entitlement history to fall back on, were reticent to challenge ownership too strongly, despite their strong feelings about the financial situation they were in and the odiousness of the Reserve Clause. Baseball culture had conditioned them to revere the owners as proud, if stern, fathers.

Al Lopez, the team captain, liked what he heard from Murphy, but his response captured the mind-set of most players, who simply weren't mentally prepared to recognize themselves as being taken advantage of. "I thought Murphy's ideas made sense," Lopez told *Baseball Digest* in 1951, "but I also knew Bill Benswanger, our boss, was a thoroughly good guy." The contradiction between "boss" and "good guy," with its implicit understanding that a nice man wouldn't take advantage of the players, was the gulf that Murphy had to leap. Besides, as everyone told them, "you should have seen the old days." "The Pasquels got us thinking about big money," said slugging Pirates rookie Ralph Kiner, "but none of us ever thought we would get out of baseball law [the Reserve Clause]."

Murphy was confident that he had made enough inroads with the team to win a strike vote, though, and set a date—June 6, which happened to be two years to the day after the invasion of Europe began. Twenty-four hours before the strike date, Murphy met with Pirates management. The team tried to convince Murphy to kick the issue until the end of the season, when they could properly hash things out. Murphy was having none of it. "Letting this thing slide isn't going to help us one bit," he snapped. "By that time, half the players might be in Peoria." The meeting grew heated, and nothing was settled. On his way out, Murphy snarled that he was looking forward to telling the players "just what kind of bosses they've got." Some observers thought Murphy himself was to blame for the lack of progress. Red Smith, who strongly believed that the players were being taken advantage of, called the union organizer "red faced, inclined to belligerency, and equipped with a sneer that must be the envy of all sneerers."

At the last moment, the team voted to play on the sixth, putting off a potential strike for twenty-four hours. Murphy upped his vitriol. "I guarantee that there will be a strike tomorrow night unless the club comes across. We're going to get tougher. If it goes another day, we're not only going to ask for recognition, we're going to start making actual demands. If a club can change a contract and not the players, what kind of contract is it?"

Back in 1912, when Cobb had been suspended for his psychotic rampage into the stands, the Detroit Tigers were faced with a sympathy strike by Cobb's teammates before the next day's game. To avoid a forfeit, the Tigers fielded a squad of replacements, including a forty-eight-year-old coach, a boxer who happened to be in town, and several local university students. Needless to say, they lost to Philadelphia 24–2.

Thirty-six years later, the Pirates prepared with a similar strategy. In case of a strike, they would field a team consisting of the team's two "loyalists," pitcher Rip Sewell and infielder Jimmy Brown, along with a whole bunch of local sandlot players. Manager Frankie Frisch told reporters he would "play second base myself. And I'll put Honus Wagner [seventy-two years old at that point] in at third, too."

The Congress of Industrial Organizations in Pittsburgh supported a strike, as did a majority of fans polled by newspapers in the city. Many others, however, were far too wearied by the country's unceasing strikes to get behind ballplayers walking off their "jobs." President Truman was asked if he planned to nationalize the Pirates, as he had threatened to do with the rail workers (which had the effect of settling the paralyzing walk-off after forty-eight hours). "Then I could have two good teams in St. Louis," he laughed, writing off the Browns, as most people did.

Come game day, no one knew for sure which way the team would vote. Murphy urged the players to act. "Fellas, we strike tonight!" he yelled before he was kicked out of the clubhouse. (Benswanger had insisted the team ban him from the voting process.) For two long hours, the Pirates talked strike in the clubhouse, while Murphy waited outside. In the stands, fans bought beer and hot dogs, adding to Benswanger's take even as the possibility was strong the scheduled game was about to be replaced by farce. The Giants warmed up, not knowing if they would be facing scheduled starter Ed Bahr, or some yokel plucked from the stands at the last moment.

Suddenly, the clubhouse door flew open, and out came the Pirates, dressed for action. The strike vote had been twenty for, sixteen against, several votes shy of the needed two-thirds majority. The team was back in the baseball business. They raced to the field, no one even looking at Murphy. One Pirate told a reporter "the strike is over for keeps."

Although no one knows precisely what was said in the clubhouse, apparently Sewell and Brown had convinced enough of their peers to avoid a walkout. Years later Sewell said that at a crucial moment, he stood up and said simply, "We all have signed contracts, and it is my night to pitch. I'm going out to pitch." (It wasn't and he didn't, actually—Sewell didn't take the mound but did enter the game as a pinch runner and scored a run. Jimmy Brown had 3 hits and 2 RBIs.) The Pirates beat the Giants that night, 10–5, and strike talk was shelved for good. Although they got to see the regulars, the crowd wasn't totally thrilled with the vote. Sewell and Brown were booed throughout the game, and Brown was knocked around in the parking lot after the game by some union toughs. Murphy approached Sewell after the game. "He told me he was going to get somebody to do something or beat me up," Sewell remembered. "I said 'you'd better see that you do a damn good job of it, because if you don't buddy, you know what you're going to get.'" Happy Chandler, by contrast, sent Sewell a gold watch in thanks.

"We played a dirty trick on Murphy," admitted Pirates third baseman Lee Handley afterward. "We let him down, and I was one of those who did it. We are not radicals. We don't want to be affiliated with any labor organization."

Murphy vowed to press on. "The mere fact that the Pittsburgh members of the Guild did not choose to use an economic weapon does not mean that we shall not continue to fight here and elsewhere," he insisted. The truth was, his call for a strike vote without the sure knowledge that it would carry revealed his inexperience, both in baseball and as a labor organizer. "He was ignorant of, or overlooked, sound union technique," wrote Paul Gould in *The New Republic*. Still, Gould had to concede that "Murphy has made a definite contribution toward bettering the ball player's lot."

That was mainly due to concessions won through his efforts. One, a per diem for the players during spring training, when they usually had to shell out for themselves, is still called "Murphy Money" even today. And his talk of a pension plan fired up interested players to arrange one on their own.

But Murphy's failure would have a lasting impact on the players, who were somehow surprised when they found themselves continuing to grumble at the unfair advantage management held over their lives. Any unwritten promises to change things were conveniently forgotten. "The country was in such an uproar, maybe we were too distracted to do anything," remembered Freddy Schmidt. Just four years later, the duplicity of ownership was apparent for all to see, moving Dick Young to write an essay calling for "another Bob Murphy" in *Baseball Digest*. One was "certain to pop up and haunt major league moguls, unless they quickly restrain their dollar-squeezing greed. He won't be named Bob Murphy, perhaps, but he'll find a more sympathetic audience among ballplayers than did the ill-fated organizer."

Murphy told the AP that he was hardly finished, and indeed, planned "to do something for hockey players" over the winter. Alas, he rapidly faded from memory, his efforts to unshackle the players from bondage and earn them a greater share in baseball's massive profits tossed aside for a generation, until another outsider with a labor background, the late Marvin Miller, picked up Murphy's mantle and changed the game forever.

Chapter 21
HERE COMES "THE MAN"

IN EARLY JUNE, Stan Musial reported to Sportsman's Park a few hours before first pitch, and was surprised to find a first baseman's glove in his locker, rather than his usual outfield mitt. It was Dyer's passive-aggressive method of telling his superstar that a position change was in the offing.

The kid, Dick Sisler, wasn't working out at first base, hitting .270 with just a single homer and a puny .668 OPS through the end of May. "Sisler stuttered when he talked," said Schmidt, "so he had trouble communicating with the other infielders. And he dropped a lot of balls at first. So Terry Moore went to Dyer and told him we wouldn't win with Dick at first." Just as his best pitcher and starting second baseman had gone AWOL, Dyer was faced with another crisis. He loathed to break up the game's best outfield, but it made sense to move Musial to first and play Harry Walker in left, even though Walker had started slowly and Dyer didn't particularly like the Hat or his quirks. Other options at first base weren't good. So Stan took some grounders, broke in the new glove, and pronounced himself ready to watch the game unfold from a whole new angle.

It was typical of the game's least Type A superstar. Musial seldom made a fuss over anything.

Musial's unlikely path from Donora, a typical western Pennsylvania steel mill town, to the top of the baseball pyramid is well chronicled.

The son of a Polish father and a Czech mother, he was born Stanislaw, and his name was only anglicized when he enrolled in school. Most folks around Donora called him "Stash" throughout his childhood. He was a local boy through and through, marrying the daughter of the neighborhood grocer, Lillian "Lil" Labash. He was also a dominating pitcher, once striking out thirteen adults at the age of fifteen in semipro ball. That got him signed by the Cardinals, and in the minors Musial would play outfield when he wasn't pitching. One August afternoon in 1940, he fell heavily while going for a line drive and injured his shoulder. His resulting dead arm sidetracked his pitching career, and he was dumped down to Class C Springfield. For a while it appeared Musial would be just another washout.

But his manager at Springfield, Ollie Vanek, saw potential in his hitting, and encouraged Musial to forget the slab and concentrate on being a full-time position player. He set about destroying the Western Association, hitting .387, and was quickly promoted to Rochester, the Cards' top farm team. He was so good that he was called up late in the 1941 season, as the Redbirds chased Brooklyn for the flag, which the Dodgers would win by 2½ games. Many Cardinals players complained afterward that if Musial had been brought up sooner, they would have won the pennant.

He batted with a peculiar, soon-to-be iconic stance, a peek-a-boo over his shoulder with his back almost square to the pitcher. "He looked like a kid peeking around a corner to see if the cops are coming," said Hall of Fame pitcher Ted Lyons. Author Tom Meany described it thusly: "The bent knees and the crouch give him the appearance of a coiled spring, although most pitchers think of him as a coiled rattlesnake." "Once Musial timed your fastball," thought Warren Spahn, "your infielders were in jeopardy." The word "automation" was coined in 1946 by an engineer at Ford Motor Company named Delmar Harder. He was talking about the Ford assembly line that cranked out an engine every fourteen minutes, but he might just as easily have been describing Musial's robotic lashing of line drives.

Stan and Lil had a son, Dickie, so Stan was exempt from the early stages of the war. It wasn't until 1945 that he finally had to go. Pete Reiser tried to talk Musial into joining the army and Pistol's Fort Riley team. "I told Pete, 'Naw, I'm going into the Navy,'" Musial told author Frederick Turner. "I just liked the Navy for some reason—the water and all. You know where a lot of those guys wound up who were at Fort Riley? At the Battle of the Bulge." Musial wasn't likely to have been sent to that frozen forest, given his ballplaying status, but his navy hitch still cost him, at least in the lifetime numbers department. Musial would have been a cinch for 500 homers and 2,000 RBIs had he not missed the season.

But there was a serendipitous benefit to his service. While in the navy, Musial tried to hit more home runs to give the swabbies and gyrenes watching something to remember. He crept closer to the plate to do so. When he returned to action, Musial found that he was standing closer to the plate, whereas before the navy, he had stood uncommonly far back in the box. He was thus less susceptible to outside pitches, and he would always smile when remembering his navy days as a result.

Smiling was Musial's default setting. Unlike so many superstars of his time and earlier, there wasn't a trace of cantankerousness to Stash. *Post-Dispatch* photographer Louis Phillips had to deal with just about every player in the majors in his long career taking snaps for the paper. The rotund and bespectacled shutterbug mostly hated the job, but he loved Musial. "He's not like the hammerheads of other years," Phillips said in a *P-D* profile in mid-'46. "Those other players always gave me a pain in the neck. Like as not, when I'd ask them to pose, they'd say 'what's in it for me?' But this guy Musial is different. He smiles and asks 'what kind of pose do you want?'"

His idea of rowdiness was to shake hands and leave a fake thumb behind in the palm of the startled handshakee. He studied magic in his off-hours, thanks to a local insurance man named Claude Keefe, who had gotten him hooked. He was a big sports fan, talking about boxing and football with anyone who'd listen, but he also kept abreast of world affairs and enjoyed arguing politics on long train rides. He loved bowling, and would go on to own a number of lanes in St. Louis, and he surely noticed the invention in 1946 of the automatic pin spotter, which revolutionized Tuesday-night bowling leagues across America and led to the dismissal of thousands of pin boys.

He and Lil had had a second child, daughter Geraldine, in '44, and the family had finally moved full-time to St. Louis after years of splitting time between there and Donora. Now that he had actually squeezed a raise out of Breadon, a move to first base seemed like the least he could do. Aside from the team's struggles so far that season, and a twitchy knee he had banged on the sandy dirt of Waterfront Park that spring, all was good in his world.

The training home of the Cards had an iffy reputation in terms of field worthiness, but it was just a spring camp. Sportsman's Park, home to the Cardinals and the AL Browns, on the other hand, was the worst field in the majors. The infield was lumpy, the outfield a haven for rocks, the pitching mound unkempt and scarcely higher than the batter's box. The old barn had terribly unsanitary conditions and virtually no parking spaces.

The two-tiered pile sat on the corner of Grand and Dodier, several blocks west of downtown, where the major urban renewal projects that erected Busch Stadium and the Gateway Arch were still two decades away. Baseball had been played on the location since at least 1866. The grounds were turned into a proper baseball park by a saloonkeeper named Chris Von Der Ahe in 1882, and the place had retained a speakeasy vibe ever since. During Prohibition, a nightclub, complete with striptease acts, operated just beyond the outfield wall. A goat was used to trim the grass during the Depression.

In 1946, there was a new penthouse for swells to watch the game, built by new Browns owner George Muckerman, who channeled a bit of Larry MacPhail's mojo. But it was tough to class up this joint. Under the stands, the scene resembled a county fair, a "garish midway" with dozens of booths selling all manner of goods, from fried dough to shoe shines. The main concessionaire was named Blake Harper. Red Smith totted up his offerings before a game in '46:

Hamburgers, hot dogs, innumerable brands of beer, spring water, pop, pennants, mini hats, plastic baseballs bearing Cardinals autographs, record books, a history of the Cardinals, peanuts salted in the shell, peanuts salted outside the shell, peanuts unsalted, pop corn, crackerjack, cigars, cigarettes, milk, coffee, orange juice, candy, Red Bird rattles and other noise makers, mechanical pencils—but no beefsteak. However, Mr. Harper recommends his beef, veal, and pork "super hot dog" whose ingredients, he says, come from Syria, Australia and Canada and are individually "tenderized 48 hours in pineapple juice."

Vendors also sold cushions, and repeat customers carried their own into the park, as the seats were uncomfortable at best. The twelve-foot-high outfield wall was unpadded, and a scoreboard towered over it in left. In right field, a thirty-three-foot-high screen prevented cheap home runs and favored lefties with uppercut swings. There was no hitter's background, so when the stands were full, it was tough to pick up pitches—a handicap that seldom bothered AL visitors, as the Browns rarely sold out.

The center field seats were particularly hard to sell in summertime; they were in direct sun for afternoon games, roasting in temperatures over one hundred degrees. Upper grandstand seats were the sole province of Negro fans, as Jim Crow laws remained in effect at Sportsman's Park until the 1960s. Advertisements sold Griesedieck Beer ("No Finer Beer In All The World") on the right field fence, while Lifebuoy Soap dominated the center field wall. "After the Game Enjoy A Lifebuoy Bath. The Cards and Browns Do. Stops B.O." Sportsman's Park was the only stadium to have ad space on top of the visiting dugout, and the only spot in the majors where sponsors shilled their goods over the stadium loudspeaker.

When Cards superfan Mary Ott, a leather-lunged shrieker nicknamed the "Horse Lady of St. Louis" for her braying screams, was at full cry, even the loudspeaker was drowned out. Ott was a Sportsman's Park fixture for twenty-five years, wrecking the eardrums of opposing players and umpires with her bloodcurdling shouts. "I like scientific rooting," she said in describing the method to her mayhem, "something that helps the home boys win and makes the other guys sore. I figure if I really work on 'em, I can knock a lot of them pitchers out of the box in three innings." "Her vocal cords lubricated with countless bottles of beer," wrote William Nicholson of the raucous Ms. Ott, "she particularly enjoyed making afternoons hideous for the Dodgers."

The "Mound City," so-called not for pitching rubbers but for the enormous Mississippi Indian temple and burial mounds that dominated the area when St. Louis was first settled, had seen explosive growth during the war. Rural whites and blacks alike came to town, attracted by factory work and cheap rents. The city was mainly populated by these blue-collar workers, who made up the majority of the fans that came out to watch the Cards.

The "Gateway to the West" was a city of opportunity, attracting transients and tourists alike with the promise of frontier riches just over the horizon. Denizens were often people who originally had planned to merely stop over en route someplace else, and wound up staying. That trend accelerated during the war, and the city's prosperity during the conflict emboldened city fathers to embark on a long-range plan to clear out the slums that had blighted the waterfront for years, in favor of a more modern urban center. Meanwhile, the docks had new bosses. In the summer of 1946, the papers were full of reports that the Kansas City mafia, disenchanted by the locals, had sent over some muscle to take control of the St. Louis gangland.

Despite its reputation as a great baseball town, St. Louis fans could be a tough draw, living up to the state motto, "Show Me." "The average Cardinal fan does not risk going down to the ball park unless Sam Breadon guarantees a no-hitter in advance and a diamond ring in every hot dog," wrote one fan to the *Post-Dispatch,* explaining low turnout during the '46 season. The Cards' attendance numbers were not that bad—they drew 1,061,807 fans, good for seventh in the majors and nearly double from the year before. The small ballpark also held the numbers down. Still, given their perennial contention, there was a sense that the city had other things on its mind.

Fortunately, Mary Ott made enough noise to offset the fans who stayed home.

The most pressing concern that afternoon with Stan at first base and the Phillies in town was a musical number. Harry Walker, looking for any method to shake the team from its funk, recalled that back in the summer of '42, the Cards rolled to a pennant after changing the pregame music from Kay Kyser's version of "Jingle Jangle Jingle" to a goofy Spike Jones tune called "Pass the Biscuits, Mirandy." Snag was, the copy belonging to team trainer Harrison Weaver (known far and wide as "Doc") had disappeared from his record collection at some point during the war. Weaver trolled the St. Louis record shops for another, but came up empty. The lack of team unity built through song showed in a lackluster 5–2 loss to Philly, with Musial going hitless in his first game at his new position. "We sang and played music all the time," recalls Schmidt. "We played for peanuts, all we had was singing!"

Desperate, Weaver called the team doctor, Robert Hyland (unlike Weaver, a licensed physician), who arranged with a local radio station to press a new copy for the team. Thus sustained musically, the next day the Cards clobbered Philly 7–0, with Musial clocking a two-run homer in the third and adding an RBI single later on. He had found a new home in the infield, where he would later say he "didn't want to play...I thought I would be there three or four days. I ended up playing there ten years."

Still, the Cardinals remained frustratingly inert. June had begun with a home sweep at the hands of the mediocre Giants, a three-game losing streak that had the *Post-Dispatch* calling the Cards "butter-fingered and inept." Part of the trouble was that the team was riven into two disparate cliques. The "College Kids" drank soda pop and eschewed gambling and were a genial bunch that slouched toward intellectualism even though, despite the moniker, hardly any of them actually attended college. Their number included Marion, Walker, Pollet, and Brecheen among others. Save Walker, they were pals with Dyer, and did what they were told.

The other group was the "Mean Bunch," a two-fisted crew that drank heavily and played ruthless card games on train trips. Kurowski and Slaughter were the leaders of this group, whose numbers were dwindling with the sale of Cooper and Lanier's departure. Still, the lack of chemistry in the clubhouse was palpable, and the press noticed without ever coming out and writing openly about it. (In Boston, the divisions would have been front-page news.) The only public notice of any rift was when several of the wives went to Dyer and insisted he ban the high-stakes card games, for their husbands were losing needed cash.

Musial was above such high school divisions—he was well liked by everyone, and his good-natured midseason switch to an unfamiliar position underscored his devotion to the team. And, of course, he was crushing the ball, despite the distractions.

The ultimate example of Musial's talismanic role, not just for the Cards but across the National League, came on June 21. St. Louis had come to Ebbets Field feeling better about themselves thanks to a four-game sweep of their pigeons in Boston. That didn't last, as

Brooklyn took two of three. It was hardly Musial's fault, however. He went 4–5 in the opener, including a double and a triple, then singled three times in Game Two.

As Musial came to the plate for the first time in the rubber game, the Brooklyn faithful began to murmur. A chant started to break out in parts of the crowd. "Here comes that man," it sounded like to *Post-Dispatch* writer Bob Broeg, who checked with the traveling secretary, Ward, to confirm it. Ward said it sounded to him more like "Here comes *the* man."

And when Broeg wrote it that way in the *Post-Dispatch* the next day, voilà! A nickname for the ages was born. "Not that man, but THE man," wrote Broeg. "And the nickname so aptly applied to a self-effacing player, one who lacks the color and cantankerous individuality of a Ted Williams, summarized the around-the-league regard for Musial, unquestionably THE man in the Redbirds' race to the wire against the Dodgers." His previous nickname, "the Donora Greyhound," was instantly forgotten. "Stash" was still preferred among intimates, however.

The sound of the Ebbets Field fans chanting for an opponent must have struck a chord within Durocher, for he had the Man walked intentionally on two of his four trips to the plate. Joe Hatten outpitched Brecheen, and Brooklyn ended the day 2½ games up on their rivals to the west.

The Cards went into a tailspin after that, losing six of nine. Clearly, Doc Weaver's patented "Triple-Double-Inverted Whammy," a goofy hand signal he used to "confound opponents since 1942," as he said, wasn't working its intended magic. Apparently, some of the Redbirds were having trouble with sign language. As the fireworks exploded over Sportsman's Park after a Fourth of July doubleheader split with the Cubs, St. Louis trailed Brooklyn by seven full games. It was a time-honored shibboleth in baseball that the leader on Independence Day would capture the pennant. Tradition and Leo Durocher were against St. Louis, and the combination was looking rather fearsome.

As if that wasn't bad enough news, St. Loo was struggling through a "hot dry summer," thanks to a major cut in production by local breweries. Scarce grains like hops and barley needed to be preserved for the starving masses facing famine in Europe, so the city recognized everywhere as "First in Brews" had to give its collective liver a break. "Millions will die unless we eat and drink less," Truman told the nation. Customers had camped out in the spring when the news was announced, to snap up the limited supply.

Those prescient few now turned to their cache to boost them through what was turning into a depressing summer on the Mississippi.

Chapter 22
"BULLSEYE!"

On June 9, Ted Williams made a lasting impression on his home park, and on at least one fan in attendance that Sunday. After helping beat Detroit in the first game of a doubleheader, Williams came up in the first inning of the nightcap with a man aboard. Fred Hutchinson, a burly man who once outwrestled a bear in spring training, tried to get cute, throwing Ted a changeup. "I saw it coming," Williams remembered with crystal clarity decades later. "I picked it up fast and I just whaled into it."

Despite a strong headwind, the ball shot out of the yard as though hurled from the big guns of a battleship. It flew well over the visitors' bullpen and far up the right field bleachers, landing on Seat 21, Row 37, Section 42. More accurately, it landed on the head of the occupant of Seat 21, Row 37, Section 42, a man named Joseph A. Boucher. Boucher lost the ball in the sun, and only reacquired it when it crashed through his fancy lid and ricocheted a few rows away.

Boucher was a construction engineer from Albany, New York, who loved the Sox and kept an apartment on Commonwealth Avenue for when his work brought him to Boston and gave him a chance to see his team. Thirty rows deep in the bleachers, a distance later measured by the team at 502 feet from home plate, he figured he was safe from getting conked by a batted ball. He was wrong.

"How far away must one sit to be safe in this park?" he complained to the *Globe* afterward. "I wish I would get hit by a home run," whispered a child who sat nearby. The paper ran a page-one photo the next day of Boucher holding his hat, a finger stuck through the hole. "Bullseye!" read the caption. Boston went on to win 11–6 and sweep the doubleheader.

Much later, the Sox would paint Seat 21, Row 37, Section 42 bright red, forever marking the spot of Ted's epic clout.

Williams has often been called the "greatest hitter who ever lived," a distinction that underlines his exceptional stats at the bat while nodding at the fact that he was an indifferent fielder, a clumsy base runner, and an exhausting teammate. He surely could rake, though, and that was all that mattered to him. In Bob Feller's deathless phrase, "trying to get a fastball by him was like trying to get a sunbeam by a rooster." Feller and Williams were close friends, two iconoclasts who recognized each other's prickly genius.

"Ted and I visited all the time," Rapid Robert remembered, "especially before ballgames in Fenway Park, where it was easy to meet between the clubhouse on the runway there under the grandstand." Williams thought Feller "the fastest and best pitcher I ever saw during my career." Warren Spahn wasn't so close with the Splinter, but would watch Ted watching him. "I mean, he studied 'em," Spahn said of hurlers. "He'd sit in that dugout with his hat pulled down over his face, looking out of the little holes in the top of his cap, blocking out everything else so he could focus just on the pitcher. That was his way of getting an idea if the guy threw a fastball, a curve, whatever. He was a great hitter with a keen eye."

His relations with the fans were far more contentious than they should have been, given his new war-induced attitude, not to mention his extreme success at the plate, especially at home, where he hit some thirty points higher over his career. But they failed to embrace their chilly, flawed superstar, and the lack of complete devotion set up a feedback loop, where Ted would go out of his way not to acknowledge or forgive the fans, despite the relative sweetness with which he'd begun the season. "I wanted to lift my cap to their applause," he admitted late in his career. "For some reason, I couldn't do it. And I knew it was wrong." He was a misunderstood genius—the fans thought him egotistical when Ted, by his own description later in life, carried a huge inferiority complex with him to the ballpark every day.

Williams seldom let his standing among the Hub's fan base affect his hitting, and thus far he had been dominating the American League. Cronin told the *Sporting News* that Ted was hitting the ball "as hard as anyone ever hit it. Yes, as hard as Babe Ruth." The rest of the Sox were matching the pace set by their slugger. Boston was an unstoppable offensive force through the season's first three months. The team scored 408 runs by the end of June; only two others even cracked 300. Bosox hitters were 1-2-3 in runs scored and RBIs, 1-2-4 in hits. Rudy York, the new Sox first baseman, alone powered 6 homers and 18 RBIs in June, ensuring a warm welcome from the Fenway faithful.

The team added another newcomer that summer. The offense's lone flaw was the lack of a pure leadoff hitter, so when the White Sox waived outfielder Wally Moses, the "other Sox" snapped him up. "Words can't express my happiness," Moses said about leaving the sad-sack Chisox for a team apparently racing to the pennant. "I'm glad to get my nose out of the mud." A bad shoulder kept Moses out of the service, but his brother wasn't so lucky. Harry Moses was a pilot in the Eighth Air Force, and he was interned in a German POW camp for twenty months after being shot down.

Moses was a gentle soul, one who seldom raised his voice, much less got into trouble on the field. But while still in Chicago, he had been thrown out of a game by umpire Red Jones. Wally could take some comfort in the fact that he was one of fourteen Chisox ejected. Jones warned a Chicago pitcher not to throw at Williams, and the Chisox dugout responded with catcalls. Jones ambled over and cleared out the lot of them. "Red, I've been in the big leagues

11 years," Moses pleaded. "I've never been thrown out of a game in my life. Honest to Pete, I never said a word to you on the bench. I was way over in the corner." Jones responded, "Wally, it's just like a raid on a whorehouse. The good go with the bad."

Boston led the Yankees by eight games after the Williams blast off Joseph Boucher's head, with an incredible 39–9 record. The New York press was suitably awed. "Cruel mothers are wont to scare little children by merely mentioning the Sox," wrote Arthur Daley in the *Times*. A few days later, seven hundred fans declared the race over and done with and applied for World Series tickets. Aghast at the presumption, the team refused them and banned the word "pennant" from Fenway Park until matters were clinched.

Meanwhile, the Sox ran ads in the Boston papers obliquely poking fun at the hucksterism going on in the Bronx under MacPhail's watch. "We Have Nothing To Sell But Baseball" was the tagline. Behind the scenes, however, Yawkey was huddling with his New York counterpart, brainstorming ways to keep their cash register ringing without cutting into profits or paying the players more.

The Yankees were on their second manager of the season, en route to three, a Steinbrenner-esque total that doomed the team to failure. Joe McCarthy had turned more and more to whiskey to get him through his hatred for MacPhail, and by late May, he had deteriorated badly, thanks to the team's mistake-strewn play and the sense that nothing he did would help the team against the machine from Boston. On May 23, the team boarded the *Yankee Mainliner* for a trip from Cleveland to Detroit. McCarthy was hitting the bottle hard and took out his frustration on a familiar target, pitcher Joe Page.

Page was a free-living, free-spending son of a Pennsylvania coal miner who inherited the old man's habit of spending whatever cash happened to find its way into his pocket as soon as possible. McCarthy would scream at Page that he was throwing his career down the toilet, a bit of hypocrisy given the fact McCarthy himself could often be found sipping at his omnipresent fifth of White Horse and plotting an exit from the Bronx.

On the flight to the Motor City, manager corralled player by slipping into the aisle seat next to Page and putting his leg up on the seat in front to lock him in, a maneuver that, given the Yanks' pioneering of regular flights on road trips, has to be considered another innovation by the Hall of Fame skipper.

McCarthy tapped Page on the arm. "You're going to sit and listen to what I have to say," McCarthy said. "What the devil's the matter with you?"

"Nothing," Page responded.

"When are you gonna settle down and start pitching? How long do you think you can get away with this?"

"Get away with what?" Page asked angrily. "I'm not trying to get away with anything. I'm doing the best I can. What do you want outta me?"

McCarthy began shouting so that he was audible over the plane's engines. The other players and the press, embarrassed, tried to act as if they weren't listening and nothing unusual was happening. "Who the hell do you think you're kidding?" McCarthy shouted, his Irish temper at the boiling point. "I'll tell you what I'm going to do. I'm going to send you back to Newark, and you can make four hundred dollars a month for all I care."

Page wasn't one to be shaken by that sort of threat. "That's okay with me," he said. "You wanna send me to Newark, send me to Newark. Maybe I'll be happier there."

Page's refusal to tremble at the hole card in any manager's deck—shaping up a bad apple by putting his job at risk—was the final straw. McCarthy stopped off at his hotel room for a brief respite, then flew home to Tonawanda, New York, and embarked on an epic bender. He managed to telephone MacPhail at some point the next day and resign. The Yankees publicly chalked it up to "hypertension."

Bill Dickey was named the player-manager, the first man other than McCarthy to lead the Yankees since 1931. The "Man Nobody Knows," so-called because of his bland personality, took over as top kick on May 28, which also happened to be the first night game ever played at Yankee Stadium. It was the pièce de résistance in MacPhail's agenda to boost attendance. Night ball had been banned during the war due to blackout conditions, but now that peacetime was here, the man who had brought artificial lights to the summer game was sure as hell going to bring night ball to the sport's grandest arena. The main grandstand featured six new light towers, with a total of 1,409 reflectors, all of a new design that MacPhail himself had overseen. Each reflector had a 1,500-watt lamp. The next brightest park, Forbes Field in Pittsburgh, had 864 reflectors.

It was a frigid night, cold and windy, the chill barely alleviated by the intense bright lights shining down from the rim of the Stadium. "Baseball's nocturnal trailblazer... overdid the thing a trifle," reported the *Times*. The intense wattage from the lights made the players feel like ants under a magnifying glass. It was as good an excuse as any for the 2–1 loss to the lowly Senators.

The Hall of Fame catcher-turned-manager also ended up running afoul of MacPhail. Dickey led the team to a respectable 57–48 record, and as the season waned, he wanted his future status made clear by the team. When Mac refused to commit to Dickey, he too quit, leaving coach Johnny Neun to finish out the final fourteen games of the depressing season in the Bronx. "I have no hard feelings about not managing," Dickey said on his way out the door. "I didn't enjoy it."

The Yankee Clipper wasn't enjoying much about his 1946 experience, either. Like McCarthy, the "New DiMaggio" went AWOL in late spring, thanks largely to another twist in his relationship with Dorothy Arnold. She had gone back to the man she was promenading with after the divorce, a wealthy stockbroker named George Schubert. The couple lived it up in a suite at the Waldorf while the

Clipper slept in stony solitude at the Edison Hotel, a relative flophouse. At least he had lodging, unlike so many others. The likable guy who went out of his way to please was replaced by the familiar surly, monotone Joe D. the New York press knew from before the war.

Joe's dourness only increased on July 7, the final day before the All-Star break. DiMaggio wrenched his knee sliding during a game in Philadelphia. He would miss about a month of action, which erased any hopes of a Yankees rally in the second half of the season. It wasn't like Joe was so dominant at the plate—when he went out, he was hitting just .271, albeit with 17 homers and 56 RBIs. He was named to the All-Star Game, of course—he would've had to have been lost at sea not to be named to the Midsummer Classic—but he couldn't play, and thus didn't make the trip to Boston.

No one else dreamed of missing it.

Chapter 23
ALL THINGS EEPHUS

IT WAS HARD not to laugh. The pitcher looked so goofy, the ball lobbed so high, up to twenty-five feet in the air. It didn't cross the plate so much as plop down on top of it. Umpires were as confused as batters. If the hitter dared swing, he was made to look foolish, often winding up on the seat of his pants.

Truett "Rip" Sewell may have been a behind-the-scenes force in torpedoing the nascent labor movement, but he had a clownish public persona that was defined by this mortar shell of a pitch. It was known as the "eephus" pitch, so named by teammate (and 71st Division Red Circler) Maurice Van Robays, who posited that "an eephus ain't nuthin' and neither is that pitch." Perhaps not, but it served Rip well enough to wrangle him an invite to baseball's best party.

The thirteenth All-Star Game was fittingly played at Fenway Park on July 9. Williams was the unofficial host. There had been no 1945 contest, due to wartime travel restrictions, and of course many of the stars had been away for two or three All-Star Games. Everyone missed the Midsummer Classic. Many of the players had not seen one another in years, and the sibilant whack of backs being slapped in joyous greeting filled the Olde Towne.

"I don't think I've ever seen a more festive occasion," remembered Phillies All-Star Frank McCormick, who was 4-F thanks to a back injury sustained when he attempted a one-and-a-half gainer into a hotel pool. "Guys who hadn't seen one another in years were crossing back and forth before the game to shake hands and visit. It was great."

A fan who was at the Fens for the game, Virginia Hanley, remembered the atmosphere to the *Melrose* (MA) *Mirror* in 1999:

> Everyone was in a relaxed, happy mood. We had won the war and most of our favorite players had come home safely. The men in the stands had fought in the same battles as the athletes and shared memories that they never spoke of to us "civilians." There was a strong feeling of togetherness in the crowd, both on and off the field.

The 1946 All-Star Game was special in many respects. One was the fact that, save for spring training, this was the first time Williams and Musial had ever been on the same field—at least on the mainland. The two great batsmen had missed each other in previous All-Star Games, with Musial not making the 1942 NL side and Williams being in the service when Stan made his first All-Star team the next year. But the two had competed in the Navy World Series in September 1945, six games held at Furlong Field in Hawaii for the pleasure of sailors and marines based there. Musial's NL stars got the best of Williams's AL crew, winning four of the six.

The All-Star Game at Fenway would be the first "real" showdown of the year between the Kid and the Man.

On the train to Boston for the game, Rip Sewell sat with Marty Marion and Terry Moore, and, perhaps feeling guilty over his role in smothering Murphy's union efforts in the crib, helped the Cardinals draw up a rudimentary pension plan, one that they hoped to unveil to the owners later that summer. Doc Weaver, the Cards trainer, was along for the ride too, and he helped with the details as well. Marion's back was so bad that Weaver was forced to room with his ailing shortstop on the road, and give him plenty of rubdowns and stretches. His proximity to Marion and his fondness for his charges got Weaver interested in helping them post-baseball as well, and so he got involved in Marion's pet project.

Rip was a longtime minor leaguer who appeared to end his career when he shot himself in the foot while hunting before the 1941 season. After recovering, he developed a lob delivery to augment his diminished fastball, and fattened up on weakened wartime opposition. He won seventeen, twenty-one, and twenty-one games from 1942–44, but his inclusion on the '46 All-Star team smacked of vaudeville. He was 5–5 at the break, was nursing an elbow injury, and was included mainly because NL manager Charlie Grimm needed another pitcher and it was thought Rip might elicit a few guffaws with the eephus.

Indeed, the game was a laugher. The American League had won eight of the twelve All-Star Games played to that point, and would dominate the rest of the '40s. True to form, the AL romped. Charlie "King Kong" Keller of the Yankees hit a two-run homer in the first off Claude Passeau, scoring Ted, who had walked. In the fourth, Kirby Higbe came in to face Williams. He threw a knuckleball that Ted walloped to dead center for a monstrous homer, one that had the crowd screaming for several minutes. Ol' Hig would forever maintain that the Splinter had "hit a pop up that the wind carried out of the yard." Williams singled in a run in the fifth as the AL extended to a 6–0 lead, and singled and scored in the seventh as well.

It was 9–0 in the eighth when Sewell came in to pitch. Grimm asked him to "throw that blooper pitch and see if you can wake up this crowd." Throwing a few eephi to go with a batting-practice fastball, Sewell gave up a run and let two men reach with two out. That brought Williams to the plate, and the remainder of the 34,906 who had bothered to stay to the end roused. The eephus was considered many things, including home-run proof. The Best Damn Hitter Anyone Ever Saw was about to test that theorem.

Williams didn't want any part of the circus and was shaking his head to say, "Don't do it." Sewell nodded right back—"Yes, I am." Sewell started right off with an eephus that Williams fouled off at the plate. Then a fastball that traveled about 80 mph tangled Ted up almost as badly, and he took it for strike two. Another eephus landed well wide of the dish.

The fourth pitch was what Sewell described as a "Sunday Super Dooper Blooper." "It was amazing how high Sewell threw it up in the air," Doerr recalled much later. "It came straight down on you." Williams had the pitch measured by now, though, and it looked more sumptuous than any meatball served up in the North End. He hopped forward a few steps to meet the arcing ball. In truth he stepped out of the batter's box, technically nullifying what came next, but no one gave a hoot.

That's because Williams sent the eephus hurtling over the right field wall and into the bullpen for a three-run homer. The screaming from the fans carried as far as the North Maine woods. Ted had parked the eephus! The un-homer-able pitch, homered. "I guess if anyone would hit it out, it would be Ted," said Doerr. "Don't you wish you could hit like that?" Williams asked Marion with a smile as he rounded the bases.

The final score was 12–0, Americans. Feller, Newhouser, and Jack Kramer of the Browns had combined for a three-hitter. The Senior Circuit was humiliated, and in the wake of the blowout, Breadon huddled with NL president Ford Frick for an emergency summit. The two discussed one of two options—going all-out to win, fan showcase be damned, or dropping out of the game altogether. Fortunately, cooler heads prevailed, and the exhibition nature of the contest went on until 2003, when it was decided that home-field advantage in the World Series would go to the league that won the All-Star Game.

After the break, the Sox swept the Tigers, then welcomed Cleveland to Fenway for a Sunday doubleheader on July 14. In the opener,

Boston fell behind 5–0 and 10–7 but came back to win 11–10. Williams hit 3 home runs, including a 3-run bomb in the bottom of the eighth to win it, to go with 8 RBIs, an exceptional week for most hitters.

Cleveland's manager, Lou Boudreau, was also its starting shortstop. He had had a pretty good game at the plate himself, hitting four doubles and a homer, setting a record for extra-base hits in a game. But he was best known for being a smart and slick fielder, one of the best gloves of the era. Boudreau was also a canny strategist, and he spent some time before the nightcap brainstorming some way of stopping Ted defensively. Short of putting five guys in the right field stands, there had to be a way of at least cooling him off.

Most teams took to walking Williams. He took a free pass more often in 1946 than anyone had in history to that point, except Babe Ruth in 1923. As Arch Ward put it, "Williams walks so much Joe Cronin has to slip carfare into Teddy's uniform pocket before every game."

But Boudreau had something more interesting in mind. He placed the left side of his infield, himself and third baseman Ken Keltner, on the right side, while also shifting the outfield around to right, "further to starboard than even Westbrook Pegler," wrote Red Smith. The "Williams Shift" was born. "On July 14, French-blooded Lou Boudreau, playing manager of the Cleveland Indians, celebrated a baseball Bastille Day by trying to guillotine the league-leading Red Sox's mighty Ted Williams," wrote *Life*.

It wasn't the first time a lefty slugger had seen such an alignment. Indeed, two other fellows named Williams—Ken and Cy—had seen shifts back in the early '20s. Ted smiled at the stratagem, and then pounded a double off the right field wall. He also walked twice in the game, another Sox win that put the team ahead by eleven full games in the AL race. He wasn't satisfied, however. "I wanted to hit a homer in the worst way so I could tell Boudreau, 'you put them in the right position all right, Lou, but you should have had taller men.'"

This iteration didn't get off to much of a start. But the Williams Shift had a curious effect on Ted. Other teams started employing it, and Williams steadfastly refused to bunt or slap balls to the gaping green in left for the easy hit. Hitting, of course, was his religion, and he was not about to change faiths because of some wacky defensive alignment. Changing course would just mess him up, he reasoned.

The shift mainly gave the Boston press another club with which to beat Ted for his supposed egocentricity. A team player would take the gift base for the good of the club. Williams clearly preferred to do what was best for Williams instead. His harshest critic, Dave "the Colonel" Egan, wrote in the *Boston Record* that the shift wasn't "a compliment to the hitting greatness of Williams. It is a sneer at his inability to hit successfully, except to one particular part of the lawn. It is a challenge, not to hit the ball where they are, but where they ain't, and he has been pitifully unable to cope with that challenge."

Boston swept the Browns in a doubleheader on July 21 to cap an 11–2 home stand. Williams hit .469 during the stretch, with 4 homers and 18 RBIs. If that was "pitifully unable to cope," then a competent Splinter would have truly destroyed the AL. As Boston prepared to head out on a long western swing, Ted was hitting .365 with 27 homers and 85 RBIs, leading the league in all three Triple Crown categories. His swing was locked in, a beautiful object to behold. The Sox were 65–25 at that point, 11½ games ahead of the Yankees. The Pinstripes had disappeared, and Detroit's hitting star, Hank Greenberg, was suffering through a horrendous season. The race was essentially over before August.

While Williams was dominating, Boston was hardly a one-man gang. DiMaggio was hitting .339. Doerr and York were 2–3 in the league in RBIs, Pesky and Doerr 2–3 in runs scored. Ferriss won his fifteenth game on July 21. Dobson and Hughson had won ten apiece. The team was a colossus, rolling to a pennant like Patton's Third Army.

Boston's generally laid-back (some would say stiff) fans noticed. The bandbox was filled to capacity every day. As would happen multiple times in the future, Fenway was proving itself too small to fulfill demand. "Fenway Park is just a surrey with a fringe on top, and seats approximately as many," wrote Egan. "The fact is that private enterprise, in this case represented by Tom Yawkey, was completely unprepared for this tremendous sports boom." Thousands of fans were turned away on a daily basis. "We had to turn away over 25 thousand on a dozen occasions," remembered Sox PR man Ed Doherty to Fred Lieb. "On several Sundays, and when Bob Feller pitched his two games against us, we had to stop people as far away as Kenmore Square if they didn't have tickets. There were as many people heading back for the subways an hour before the game as there were coming to the ball park."

Dommie had seen it coming. He spent a lot of time during the war hanging around an Australian port, thinking about getting back to baseball. To his way of thinking, he didn't belong to the Sox anymore—the war had made him a free agent, but Cronin—Yawkey's mouthpiece—came to see him after the surrender, "hopping mad" and wanting him to sign for $11,000. "That wasn't the figure I had in mind," DiMaggio said later. He worked Cro up to $16,000, and negotiated something even better—an attendance clause.

"I had it figured. I knew people wanted to see baseball. And we were going to be good." He got the team to pay him $500 for every 50,000 fans through the Fenway turnstiles past the 450,000 that had come out in 1945. The Sox drew 1,416,944 in '46, triple the year before and double the record. The Little Professor took in an extra nine grand thanks to his foresight.

During one of the Sox-Indians games at Fenway, the drama of the Williams Shift was interrupted by a moment of levity. A midget jumped out of the stands and ran onto the field, delighting the full house.

The new owner of the Cleveland Indians took in the scene with a mischievous smile on his face. *A midget—now he would be tough to strike out.* . . .

"I believe if baseball is dressed up a little bit, it's more fun for everybody," was the credo of Bill Veeck, American Original. Getting fans to come out to the park, and have fun while they were there, was his all-encompassing mission. The owner whose outside-the-box thinking made him a unique figure in the sport's history first bought into the majors in 1946. He'd fronted a ten-man group that paid $1,750,000 for the Tribe in late spring, and his syndicate included comedian Bob Hope, a Clevelander who looked forward to being an owner as "It'll give me my first chance to yell with impunity at the guys with the muscles."

Veeck's unusual path in baseball was cut by his father, William Veeck Sr., who was a sportswriter in Chicago. After slamming the Cubs routinely in his column, the owner of the team, William Wrigley, astoundingly gave Veeck the chance to put his money where his mouth was by hiring him to run the team as GM. That brought young Bill Jr. to the park every day, and it was he who conceived of the plan to grow ivy on the outfield walls.

Veeck started out on his own as a minor league owner with the Milwaukee Brewers. The Brew Crew was bankrupt when Veeck bought the team—on his first night in charge of the Brewers, all of twenty-two fans turned out for a home game. The Brewers under Veeck would become strong on the field, winning three American Association pennants in five years. Even better, they set records at the gate. Veeck greeted fans as they came into the park, sang in pregame serenades, and offered unusual prizes for lucky fans, like horses and pigeons. He had tightrope walkers and boogie-woogie bands perform before games. He held "Swing Shift" games that started at six a.m. so workers toiling nights and overtime in war factories could come out to the park.

In 1942 Veeck joined the marines. During the invasion of

Bougainville in the Solomons, a mortar recoiled irregularly and smashed Veeck's right leg. His foot was crushed, and multiple operations failed to save it. His marriage almost went too, but he sold the Brewers in an attempt to rescue it. He couldn't, but he did turn a sizable profit on the sale, enough to flip it (with the help of bank loans and a number of investors) into ownership of a big league team. Veeck was thirty-three. Almost certainly he was the last magnate who wasn't independently wealthy.

In 1946, the Indians were in the final year of playing the majority of their home games in League Park, on Cleveland's east side. The following season, Veeck would move the team full on into Municipal Stadium, the enormous "Mistake by the Lake" that would be the home of the Indians until the 1990s. League Park was squashed into a city block, and so had bizarre dimensions. The right field fence was only 290 feet away, for example, but was guarded by a 60-foot-high wall, almost twice as tall as Fenway's left field wall.

All of 8,526 were at the park on the June day when Veeck announced he was the new owner. He went straight there from the press conference. He mingled with fans, as was his habit, and an enormous ironworker jumped up and slapped him hard on the back. "This is the best damned thing that has ever happened to this town," the man told Veeck.

The hardhat had it right. Veeck still sported his jarhead crew cut, which accentuated his massive face and impish look. He refused to wear a tie, which ingratiated him with his working-class fans. Hobbling about, his right leg in a cast, covering every inch of the park on game day even though he got around on crutches, Veeck changed the culture of the Indians overnight. "Everyone agreed," he wrote in his classic memoir, *Veeck—As in Wreck,* "that the 'bush stuff' I had pulled in Milwaukee, like giving away livestock, would never go in Cleveland. So I gave away livestock in Cleveland, and the fans were delighted."

Indians games immediately went on the radio. The doors were

removed from Veeck's office, and he advertised his phone number, so fans could reach him day or night. He installed a full orchestra in the outfield, protected by chicken wire. He was the first to post NL results on the scoreboard of an AL park, figuring rightly that fans wanted to stay abreast of the entire majors.

"I'm a publicity hound," Veeck flatly told the press, and they loved him for the endless copy he offered. The Tribe, a going-nowhere club with only Boudreau and star hurler Bob Feller worthy of attention, were suddenly the talk of the town. Newspaper ads enticed Indians fans with slogans like "New Teepee For A Whooping Tribe" and "A New Band Will Beat The Drums." On August 2, Veeck staged a titanic fireworks display, with the sparklers forming a re-creation of planes dropping a huge bomb on a (presumably Japanese) battleship. The next day, Veeck wheeled out jugglers, drum majors, and a man who did a tricky bullwhip act, dodging players who were warming up even as he made like Indiana Jones. Word got around, and the following afternoon, with the Yankees in town for a doubleheader, an astonishing 75,595 paid to enter Municipal Stadium.

Not every gimmick worked out. Veeck hired Max Patkin, the "Clown Prince of Baseball," to goof around before games, which was fine, but then Veeck installed him as the first base coach. The league office cried foul. Veeck defied them, but when Ken Keltner was picked off first base at Yankee Stadium while Patkin made goofy faces, the experiment came to a screeching halt. Veeck hired another comic, Jackie Price, who liked to use a slingshot buried in his sleeve to "throw" a ball from home plate out over the wall. On his first two attempts at the trick, he beaned fans, who were hospitalized. The vaudeville hook came out to yank Price off the stage.

Like Paul Bunyan or Bill Brasky, tall tales of Veeck's exploits abound. Some of them are even true. Some are presumed true but probably aren't. For example, Veeck liked to talk about a movable screen in right field that he would have rolled in whenever a team with good lefty power hitters came to town. Likewise, Veeck is supposed to have signed a deal to buy the Philadelphia Phillies in 1942 and proposed to stock the team with Negro Leaguers, four years in advance of Jackie Robinson. But extensive research has uncovered no evidence that either story is true.

That November, Veeck would lose his damaged right foot to amputation, the thirty-sixth and final operation he would have on his war wound. He famously used his wooden leg as an ashtray while he chain-smoked through a thirty-four-year career as owner of the Indians, Browns, and White Sox.

In 1951, while in charge of the Browns, Veeck remembered what he had seen that afternoon back in '46. He employed a midget named Eddie Gaedel, wearing uniform number 1/8, to bat in a game against Detroit. Gaedel's 3'7" frame practically ensured a base on balls, which he drew, in his one and only plate appearance. Gaedel moved on to the Ringling Brothers Circus, while Veeck continued to dream up promotions on his way to the Hall of Fame. He would loudly proclaim his good fortune in life to anyone he met.

But when it came to luck, he had nothing on a farmhand down in Class B ball named Jack Lohrke.

Chapter 24
LUCKY

ON THE MORNING of June 24, the Spokane Indians of the Class
B Western International League were traveling by Washington Motor Coach at the start of a road trip. The first stop was Bremerton,
Washington, on the state's Pacific coast. Rain hissed down in small
torrents as the coach snaked through the Palouse. A couple of hours
into the trip, the bus stopped in Ellensburg for lunch, while the
driver, Glen Berg, zipped over to a nearby garage. He didn't like the
way the engine sounded, and the treacherous Cascade Range and
the Snoqualmie Pass were just ahead.

The major leagues continued playing right through the war, but the
same couldn't be said for many of the minor leagues. With more than
four thousand minor league players across the nation, of widely varying ages and abilities, going off to the service, only a handful managed
to keep playing. Anyone with any spark went right to the majors.

Major leaguers who saw combat were relatively thin on the
ground; not so, minor leaguers. With no reputation to protect them,
many minor leaguers found themselves in infantry units, aboard
warships, and flying bombing missions. Some wound up in horror,
like Jim Blackburn, a pitcher in the Cincinnati chain. Captured at
the Battle of the Bulge, he survived malnutrition and a sadistic guard
pulling his toenails out with a pair of pliers to return to baseball in
1946, briefly making the majors two years later.

Then there was Mickey Grasso, who replaced Dick Bouknight (the catcher who welcomed Jackie Robinson to white baseball by using racial epithets and humming balls close to his head) behind the plate for the Jersey City Giants. Grasso landed in North Africa in 1943 and was among the six thousand Americans taken prisoner by the Wehrmacht at a place called Hill 609. Flown to Europe, Grasso was imprisoned at Stalag Luft III in Furstenburg, Germany. He subsisted on bread and soup for months, dropping from a strapping 205 pounds to a sickly 145. But he still managed to play softball, and the Stalag had a sophisticated league, with American and National divisions and even a World Series pitting the champs of the two against one another.

Late in the war, the Russian army approached the camp, so the prisoners were marched in the opposite direction. Grasso and about ten others found themselves guarded by a group of senior citizens, as the able-bodied Germans had all been called away to fight the invaders. Grasso and his mates took the opportunity to run away into the forest. They were free, but now foraging in enemy territory. One of their group was a Jew who had escaped Germany years before. He spoke the local tongue, and talked them out of several dicey situations.

Grasso and the others walked all the way to the Elbe River, found a rowboat, and drifted toward a battle that was thundering across the river. They paddled to the American side and were met by the 35th Infantry Division, who told them that escape was foolishness—a few more weeks and they would have been liberated anyway. Grasso tried to eat the plates of food the soldiers gave him, but his stomach was so contracted he could only nibble on a chicken leg.

Less than a year later, he was behind the plate in Jersey City, and would get called up to the bigs for a cup of coffee at the end of '46.

Then there were those minor leaguers who paid the ultimate price. Joe Pinder, a pitcher with a "blinding fast ball," was killed at Omaha Beach. Hank Nowak would have been competing for a spot on the Cardinals staff, but he was killed in the Ardennes Forest during the Bulge. Another highly regarded Redbirds prospect, Luster Pruett, was shot to death in early 1945, as the Allies invaded Germany for the first time. Jimmie Trimble was a superstar prospect out of Washington DC, but his path to baseball glory was interrupted at Iwo Jima, when a Japanese soldier detonated a mine strapped to his body, killing himself and Trimble. Orioles farmhand Harry Imhoff was killed storming the beaches of Okinawa. Jerry Angelich pitched in the Pacific Coast League, and once took on Japanese legend Eiji Sawamura in an exhibition game. Angelich was killed defending Pearl Harbor on December 7, 1941.

According to research by the estimable Gary Bedingfield, 143 players with some minor league experience died in the war. That doesn't count Audrey Stewart, a member of all-black teams in West Virginia mill leagues who had volunteered for service despite being thirty-six years of age. Stewart was part of the 333rd Field Artillery Battalion, and he and ten others were captured in a farmhouse in Wereth, Belgium, during the Battle of the Bulge. Stewart and the others were marched into a field, tortured, and then executed. They would later be known as the "Wereth 11."

The Class B Western International League canceled play for three full years while the Pacific Northwest's finest young men went off to fight. Its first season back was 1946, and the play was ragged. The same was true across the minor leagues, which now numbered forty-two separate leagues, up from a dozen the year before. The White Sox alone operated seventeen teams; in 1945 they hadn't owned a single club.

The Spokane Indians were a mediocre group, even by the iffy standards of the WIL. They were in fifth place and headed nowhere special on the morning of June 24. The evening before, the Indians had played a doubleheader against Salem at their home park, Ferris Field in Spokane. The Indians rallied in the ninth in the nightcap to earn a split of the two games against Salem, the first-place club in the WIL.

In Ellensburg, the team ate hungrily, and quietly. The meal was interrupted by a state trooper who approached infielder Jack Lohrke with a message—report to San Diego with dispatch. The Padres, then a Pacific Coast League outfit, were recalling Lohrke to their team, a step up in class (more accurately, several steps up). The Indians' business manager had taken the call from San Diego and relayed the message to the police, asking them to find the bus and tell Lohrke.

Jack had a choice—continue to Bremerton and transfer there to a bus down the coast, or hitchhike back to Spokane and fly. He wanted to move on to his better gig as soon as possible, so he bid his teammates farewell over hamburgers and fries, grabbed his gear, and thumbed his way back east.

Had his teammates known much about Jack Lohrke, they might have thought twice about letting him walk away. In 1943, a troop train Lohrke was riding on crashed, killing three, with dozens seriously burned. Lohrke walked away without a scratch. He then went into combat in Europe, fighting with the 35th Infantry Division. Lohrke survived the Normandy landings and the Battle of the Bulge. On at least four occasions, the soldier standing or sitting next to Lohrke had been killed. Lohrke emerged from the war unhurt.

When he returned to the States, Lohrke was scheduled to fly to his home in Los Angeles from Camp Kilmer, New Jersey. Lohrke was bumped for "some VIP or something" from his transport flight at the last minute. He was angry and disappointed: "For one thing, I'd never been on a plane before." Luckily, he missed this one. En route to San Pedro, California, the transport crashed, killing everyone onboard.

Lohrke wasn't the only veteran on the Indians. Bob Paterson and Fred Martinez, two fine major league prospects, had seen combat. So had right-handed pitcher Milt Cadinha, 8–1 on the season, who had fought at Normandy and the Bulge, then been transferred to the Pacific, bound for Okinawa. Fortunately, he arrived after the hellish fighting on the island had ended, although he did make it just in time to be caught in a typhoon.

They all were lucky, but none so fortunate as Lohrke. That's because an hour after the third baseman began retracing his path back to Spokane, the Indians' team bus swerved to avoid a car that crossed the median on US 10 and plunged into the Snoqualmie Pass, a five-hundred-foot drop into a heavily wooded ravine. Nine of the players were killed, including Paterson, Martinez, and the team's best prospect, Vic Pacetti. Of the nine, all but Pacetti served in the war. Six others were injured, three critically. Berg, the bus driver, survived but spent four months in the hospital recovering from burns. Other teams lent players to the Indians, and the shell of the club finished out the 1946 season. Part of the proceeds from the major league All-Star Game was donated to the families of the perished.

"I guess it just wasn't my turn," Lohrke said afterward. "But how did the owner know we would stop in that town? And what if the call had come five minutes later?"

Jack Lohrke was indeed lucky. But he was plagued by survivor's guilt. "When you're the age I was back then," he told *Sports Illustrated* in 1994, "you haven't got a worry in the world. You're playing ball because you want to play—and they're giving you money to do it. And then . . . well, sometimes those names spring back at me.

"I'll tell you this: Nobody outside of baseball calls me Lucky Lohrke these days. I may have been lucky, but the name is Jack. Jack Lohrke."

Chapter 25

THE LEO BEAT

ON A SUNNY afternoon in early July at the Polo Grounds, Durocher was shooting the bull with reporters and Dodgers radioman Red Barber. The writers started talking fondly of Mel Ott, who they were watching give some batting tips to a Giants player; their comments got a derisive scoff from the Lip.

"C'mon, Leo, you have to admit he's a nice guy," Barber prodded.

"A nice guy?" Leo roared, loud enough for all five boroughs to hear. "I've been in baseball a long time. Do you know a nicer guy in the world than Mel Ott? He's a nice guy. In last place. Where am I? In first place. The nice guys are over there in last place, not in this dugout."

Frank Graham was there, and wrote up Durocher's rant in the *New York Journal-American* as "Nice guys finish last." As famous misquotations go, it's right up there with "Play it again, Sam" and "Just the facts, ma'am." But it is remembered today because it neatly encapsulated the win-at-all-costs ethos Durocher lived by.

Durocher's lippiness was considerably wind-aided by his presence in New York and its wolfishly competitive press corps. The typing class loved Durocher, who stood out from the genial but bland Ott and the cranky McCarthy like a peacock on the arctic ice. Bons mots were Leo's stock-in-trade, especially when telling the boys exactly how ultracompetitive he was:

"Show me a good loser in professional sports and I'll show you an idiot. Show me a sportsman and I'll show you a player I'm looking to trade."

"Win any way you can as long as you can get away with it."

"I want players that would put you in the cement mixer if they felt like it."

"I never posed as a choirboy. I was just a guy who wanted to win, and I would have taken your teeth to do it."

His battles with umpires were legendary, a stage for Leo to unleash his sharp wit. One time, an ump tried to intimidate him, growling in his grille, "I'll reach down and bite your head off." Durocher replied, "If you do you'll have more brains in your stomach than you've got in your head."

Another asked if the Lip had called him a "blind bat." "What, you can't hear, either?" was the swift response.

He was a drinking man, like most of his brethren, but unlike the hypocritical stance taken by most dugout leaders, Durocher wanted his players to bend their elbows. "You don't play this game on gingersnaps," he'd yell before buying a round for his guys. His casual attitude toward alcohol put Durocher on a collision course with his boss. Rickey was a strict teetotaler, a fact Leo discovered the year before. A pitcher named Tom Seats had been struggling with nerves, and Durocher started giving him nips of brandy for Dutch courage. Seats went on a winning streak, and Rickey asked Leo for an explanation for the turnaround. Durocher gave it to him straight, no chaser, upon which Rickey said, "He will never pitch for Brooklyn again," and cut Seats loose.

"Leo Durocher is a man with an infantile capacity for immediately making a bad situation worse," was one of Rickey's milder observations about his manager. Like so many others, the Brooklyn majordomo nurtured a fondness for the little battler, especially when he was driving an inferior team to the pinnacle of its collective ability, as he was now. "Put [Leo] in a corner," marveled Rickey, "and he's that same little kid from [Springfield] with the butt of a pool cue in his hand." But he knew Durocher was hanging out with a rough crowd, a group that included mobbed-up actor George Raft and actual wiseguys and gamblers like Bugsy Siegel, Ownie Madden, Memphis Engelberg, and Joe Adonis. Rickey strongly disapproved, and let Durocher know that hosting the gangsters in all-night card and dice games would get him in trouble eventually.

He didn't say anything about the ladies, but that would get him trouble, too.

They first met in 1944 at the Stork Club. She was there with a friend when Durocher walked in to wild applause. "Who is that?" she inquired. Told that it was the famous Leo Durocher of the Brooklyn Dodgers, she naively replied, "What's a Dodger?"

Laraine Day wasn't that innocent. She was a well-known actress by 1946, starring in eight of the ten *Dr. Kildare* films. When she met Leo again two years after that first encounter, she threw over her husband for him in a matter of weeks. Day was on a flight to Minneapolis that was delayed in Chicago, and Leo was stuck there too. He charmed her by taking Laraine and a friend to the Pump Room for dinner, and by casually greeting Joe Louis back at O'Hare. Just like that, Day was smitten. Women swooned for the slick manager all the time—Durocher was an accomplished swordsman, a rakish raconteur who kept a pad in Beverly Hills as well as Park Avenue, where his apartment looked more like an art dealer's place than a jock's.

For much of 1946, he squired around Edna Ryan, the Copa's number one showgirl, a long-legged blonde stunner from Long Island who "would have looked good in a burlap sack," according to Harold Parrott. She used to appear at the train station to tearfully wave goodbye to the team, then slip quietly into town on the next train to spend the evening with Leo. In spring training at Daytona, where there was a tremendous shortage of hotel rooms, Durocher found a way to sneak Edna in by having her bring her "sick mother" along with her. Jaws dropped when Mrs. Ryan turned up—at forty, every bit as gorgeous as her daughter.

Leo always kept a couple of other ladies on the side, including Nanette Fabray, a clever beauty who disapproved of Durocher's arguments with the umpires, and Kay Williams, a millionaire divorcée and the future Mrs. Clark Gable. There was always one or another at each road stop, and he was adept at keeping them from running into one another.

But this time, there was a hiccup. Edna was hanging out at Leo's place on Park and Sixtieth, while Leo was falling for Laraine. The ravishing showgirl was ambushed by the press, who brandished wire photos of Leo and Laraine canoodling in the Midwest while Edna cooled her heels in New York. "We were going to get married until...well, I met this other girl," was Leo's honest explanation. "Durocher Branded Love Thief" was the headline.

Leo was flying to Hollywood at every opportunity, using his pal Raft as a beard for his affair. Day had two adopted children, and they swiftly bonded with the animated Durocher. Not as swiftly as Day, perhaps, although she swore in her memoir that when Leo proposed to her, they had never been alone together. More likely, she fell for Durocher's savoir faire in the boudoir. Leo once explained his way with the ladies:

"Say you pick her up at seven o'clock. Grab her where it tickles at 7:05. No go? Tough, but hell it's early yet. There's still time to call another broad. You'd be surprised. Some damned famous broads say OK quick."

With charm like that, it's small wonder Day said yes when Leo asked her to marry him. They took a short jolt down to Juarez, Mexico, where Laraine got a quickie divorce and married Leo on the spot, not two months after they had met. Jorge Pasquel was not invited. Her kids would become Durochers, and she grew a new celebrity as the First Lady of Baseball, chucking aside her initial disinterest in the game to sit at every home game and bellow her support.

Today, the affair would be embarrassing. In 1946, it was scandalous, even though half the nation, it seemed, was splitting up. Reno, the traditional spot for quick splits, granted eleven thousand divorces in 1946, still the single-season record. Returning vets and the girls who married them just before they had marched overseas realized in droves that it wasn't true love that had brought them together. If it weren't for the huge number of new babies (five hundred thousand more births were recorded than in '45), there would likely have been even more divorces. Dr. Benjamin Spock reaped the benefit of the Baby Boom—his *The Common Sense Book of Baby and Child Care* was published that spring and went on to sell fifty million copies.

It wasn't the New York press, oft eager to don a righteous cloak if it drove newsstand sales, that led the moralist charge against Leo. It was political columnist and right-winger Westbrook Pegler who whipped up an anti-Leo frenzy. Pegler hated Leo and his louche life, and he lambasted Durocher day after day. When asked whether she knew about her paramour's rough-and-tumble life, Day said sarcastically, "If I didn't I got it from Westbrook Pegler." Pegler's stiff-necked take on the Day affair cost the Dodgers when he convinced the Catholic Youth Organization to withdraw sponsorship of the Knothole Gang, a Dodgers fan club aimed at kids. The CYO called Leo "a powerful force for undermining the moral and spiritual training of our young boys." That meant a lot of unsold tickets, and Rickey was incensed.

Most of the local press boys were more forgiving. They were a young group that rolled a couple dozen deep. Ordinarily, they were feisty and loved a good public hanging, but scribes like Dick Young of the *Daily News,* Bob Cooke of the *Herald Tribune,* and Herb Goren of the *New York Sun* preferred to rip the Lip over his baseball foibles, not his personal ones. They had plenty of material when it came to chronicling Leo's tantrums, which were legion. "I popped off on everything," Durocher admitted in his first memoir, *The Dodgers and Me.* He referred to the press as the "Assistant Manager's Association," and no one lived up to the title like Arch Murray of the *Post.*

"Tiger Arch," so-called for his Princeton degree, was a die-hard Dodgers fan first, unbiased chronicler last. He wouldn't change clothes if the team was on a winning streak, and traveling secretary Harold Parrott would put Murray on a low floor of the team hotel if things were going bad, lest he hurl himself off the balcony. Murray loved to send signals down to Durocher from the press box, giving him instructions on who should pitch and how best to position the defense.

The press was far harder on Rickey than on Durocher. His cheapness was their favorite subject, along with his sanctimony and his stretching of the truth to fit his needs. "The more he talks, the more we count the spoons," was a typical insult. Mainly, they preferred MacPhail, because he was great copy and shoveled them plenty of booze.

Jimmy Powers, aka the "Powerhouse," of the *Daily News* was Rickey's bête noire. He held Branch responsible for every setback, including the Cardinals' surge back into the race. The inciting incident of his season was the trade of displaced second baseman Billy Herman in June. Herman was popular and had a Hall of Fame career, mostly with the Cubs in the 1930s, but he was pushing thirty-five and had been supplanted by Stanky. So he was dealt to the Braves, a prison sentence traceable back to spring training, when Herman had demolished a Miami hotel room (a plasterer had to come in and dislodge the whiskey glasses embedded in the ceiling) and stuck Rickey with the $30 bill.

Powers went ballistic in print, returning to his moniker for Rickey, "El Cheapo," and writing, "One reader suggests that all fans get together and donate $20 bills upon entrance to the park . . . perhaps Rickey's desire for milking money out of his franchise will be satisfied, and he will pack his carpetbags and go away to another town and run his coolie payroll there."

Powers's vitriol could be dismissed as a lone vendetta, except for his main source within the Dodgers organization. Walter O'Malley was a minority owner and general counsel of the Dodgers at this point, and was steadily accumulating stock and power within the franchise. Mainly, he did this by running Rickey down at every opportunity. O'Malley liked his scotch and his Sunday baseball, and found many like-minded accomplices in the press, Powers especially. O'Malley would goof on Rickey's slovenly appearance, his miserly tactics, his wealth (Rickey was the sport's biggest earner when factoring in his cut of attendance and player sales), and his morals—O'Malley called him a "Psalm-singing fake." He liked to play "Pin the Tail on the Donkey" using a picture of Rickey, when he wasn't checking in on population figures in California, which had just passed the nine-million mark.

After Powers demolished Rickey in print for the umpteenth time, the naive team president turned to O'Malley for advice on whether he should sue for slander. No, was O'Malley's sly response, for "every newspaperman should hate you." So Rickey held off, and the calumny spread. Fans chanted "El Cheap-O" at games, and despite the surprisingly strong play of his team, he was relentlessly booed at Ebbets Field, to the point where his wife and family stopped going to games.

Such backbiting and agenda-driven reportage was seldom seen in the Dodgers radio booth. Red Barber was as evenhanded as a judge. Walter Barber, the "Old Redhead," got his start in broadcasting pushing a broom at the University of Florida. When a professor fell ill just before going on the air at the University Club, where Barber was a janitor, Red filled in. His debut behind the mike was thus reading a scholarly paper about "Certain Aspects of Bovine Obstetrics." At no point did he use the phrase "catbird seat," sadly.

MacPhail had snapped up Barber for Reds broadcasts in 1934, and when MacPhail moved to Brooklyn, he brought the play-by-play man with him. His country cadence and adherence to southern courtesy made him an unlikely icon in loud, pushy Brooklyn, but the marriage worked. His down-home catchphrases, like "They're tearin' up the pea patch!," "can of corn," and "walkin' in the tall cotton" are still legendary. He called the games in '46 with partner Connie Desmond, and as anyone who lived in the borough then will tell you, one could walk down the street and follow the action by radio, with all of Brooklyn seemingly tuned in to Red's call. He swiftly became a trusted part of the franchise, his reputation beyond reproach. Rickey told him about the plan to sign Robinson before he told anyone else in the organization.

Barber, broadcasting over WHN, was credited with making Brooklyn baseball popular with the ladies of the borough. Since the games were mostly on during the day, female listenership was high. Red took care to explain the rudimentary aspects of the game along with the nuances, and in so doing became a favorite of the distaff fans. "He is a ladies favorite," according to the *Saturday Evening Post* in 1942. "Before he came to Ebbets Field, the games resembled a For Men Only preview. But last year, 15,000 women stormed the gates for one game, and Brooklyn authorities claim the come-hither tones of Red are responsible."

Red didn't travel to road games to do live broadcasts until 1948, so in '46 he was still in the re-creation business, calling games by telegraph wire, and in some respects these were works of art as priceless as his live broadcasts. "We don't try to fake it," he explained to Red Smith that summer. "We have the telegraph sounder right in here near the microphone where it can be heard because we don't want to kid the listeners that this is anything but a telegraphed report."

Here's how it worked: A typist in a radio studio copied the wire report of the play-by-play sent by a stringer in some far-off press box. Red stood next to him at a robin's-egg blue lectern, where Barber kept his notes and elbows. Next to him was a stat man named John Paddock, cousin of the legendary sprinter Charley Paddock, who used a "Ready Reckoner," a book that had the calculations prefigured, to pass along batting averages and ERA on the fly. Paddock was a huge fan but willed himself to stay quiet and just gesture to Red. Barber read the report and ad-libbed from there.

For example, "Reiser up—bats left" popped across the wire. Red's description:

"And here's Pete Reiser. Hitting .283, 106 base hits. He's having a tough year, fighting that bad shoulder. Dickson will pitch very carefully to him. Reiser up, square stance, he's one of those square-built guys, not very tall. Strength is not necessarily dependent upon height. The Cards are playing this fellow a step in because of his speed...."

Or, some action would come in—"H. Walker up—bunt, foul...hit—Walker singled to right." Here was Red:

"Harry Walker, who's always nervous and pickin' at that cap of his, has to have it sittin' just right. He cuts at the first pitch and tries to bunt it, fouls it off. One strike. Melton working very deliberately, that's his custom, you know. Walker, with that two-toned bat of his—swings on it, bloops a single to right, turns first and stops as his brother Dixie fields the ball.... Walker and Musial takin' a lead off first and second. They both of them can run like scalded cats, you know."

The wire reports came in by Morse code, a language Red refused to learn, as he didn't want to know what was coming. "If you know in advance what's happening, you're no longer a broadcaster," he told Smith. "You're a dramatic artist."

That wasn't a description many threw at the Cardinals' best-known radio voice. Jay Hanna "Dizzy" Dean was even better known and beloved than Barber, at least in the Midwest, due in large part to his Hall of Fame career as the ace of the "Gashouse

Gang," the team that captured the 1934 World Series for St. Louis. His broadcast style was . . . unique. He was so down-homey that he made Barber appear like a Boston Brahmin. Unlike Red, however, he wasn't drippin' southern honey but Missouri mud, with diction and grammar that wouldn't have been out of place among Missourian Jesse James and his bushwhackers.

Typical constructions included "Musial ("Moo-sal") stands confidentially at the plate," "The runners held their respectable bases," and "Slaughter slud safe into second." A frequent sign-off was "Don't fail to miss tomorrow's game!" His grammar was so awful that midway through the season, a group of Missouri English teachers filed a complaint with the FCC complaining that Diz was destroying the language. It was a losing battle, for Dean, broadcasting over 1230 WIL, was wildly popular with Cards fans. "I know most of my fans are from my part of the world, the Ozarks," he explained. "They like it. A man's got to do that sort of thing in this business."

But this would be Dean's final year in the Cards' broadcast booth. At season's end, J. Roy Stockton, the talented and cranky elder statesman of the St. Louis press corps, brought a team party to a screeching thud by sarcastically toasting Breadon, aka "the man who made the close race possible" by selling players and being cheap. Jumping to the owner's defense was Harry Carey, who competed with Dean on 770 WEW (there was a third outlet that did Cards games as well, 1490 WTMV, but Breadon was working on a deal to consolidate all the games on a single rights holder).

When Carey finished brownnosing, he was greeted with death stares from Stockton, and warm thank-yous from Breadon, who promised, "I will never forget it." The following season, Breadon formalized a deal for a Cardinals radio network, one that soon would have KMOX and its massive signal as its flagship station. He chose Carey to be the main voice of those broadcasts, despite Dean's popularity and the sponsor he could bring with him, Falstaff Beer.

"I told you that I would never forget what you did," Breadon told Carey. "Well, consider this proof of that." Dean was out of a job, though he would soon be dropping his Ozark stylings on national audiences through Mutual Radio, and on television, which was just appearing over the horizon as an existential threat to radio in 1946.

Baseball's first televised game had been a collegiate affair in 1939. The NBC telecast of Princeton's 3–2 win at Columbia was simultaneously a technological breakthrough and a fuzzy, blurry mess. Still, the mere fact that pictures had successfully been transmitted from ballpark to set device meant that a professional game was next. The Yankees and Giants both passed on the honor, but when MacPhail was asked if the Dodgers would like to be a part of the first telecast, in August of 1939, he of course answered, "I'd love to." Barber interviewed Durocher on camera before the game, against Mac's old crew from Cincinnati, ironically. The screen was full of snow, the players indistinguishable and the ball invisible, as only one camera was used.

The efforts improved little during the war years, even as televised games steadily increased in frequency. NBC's pioneering director, Burke Crotty, returned from the service in late 1945 and by '46 was ready to implement improvements to the telecasts. The May 26 game between the Giants and Braves is an example. Crotty switched between a pair of cameras on the third base side, going to the batter after the pitcher released, and if the ball was hit, switching back as the other camera picked up the play. It wasn't perfect, but few were watching and experimentation was important.

Still, the critics were anxious for better viewing. *Variety* crushed NBC's 1946 efforts. "It's virtually impossible at the present developmental stage of video for a person watching the game from his home to get even a small share of the color and feeling that's made baseball the national pastime." Matters had improved by August, when NBC added a third camera to a Red Sox–Yankees game. *Variety* weighed in again, praising Crotty's direction, but slamming the man calling the action hard, saying he "evidently hasn't looked at many ball games," and was "only annoying."

Calling games was harder than it looked, according to the recipient of the abuse, Don Pardo, who would become famous for lending his dulcet tones to *Jeopardy!* and *Saturday Night Live,* among other exploits. "I thought I knew the game, until I got [to the Stadium]," he remembered decades later. "I didn't know enough to keep my mouth shut. I figured I had to keep talking. It seemed all right—what the hell did I know?"

Pardo was twenty-eight in 1946, a staff announcer at NBC assigned to *The Bill Stern Sports Review.* Stern was a well-known sportscaster famous for misidentifying players and finding outlandish methods for incorporating the correct one into the play he was calling. It was assumed Pardo knew sports, so he got sent to the three New York ballparks several times in 1946. Pardo had hurt his back playing high school basketball and was originally 4-F, but was reclassified and was about to be drafted when the war ended.

It was apparent that there were to be plenty of opportunities on television coming for Pardo and his colleagues. TV sets began to flood the market, coming in as cheaply as $130 ($1,500 or so nowadays). Dumont built a tremendous state-of-the-art studio in the Wanamaker Department Store, and linked New York and Washington by wire for the first time. Drama producers began testing Broadway-bound plays on TV instead of in out-of-town theaters. In short, as *Life* put it, "This year the infant industry began making noises that sounded adult." Plans were afoot to make the '46 World Series the first ever televised, but a deal couldn't be struck in time.

The industry was growing right in front of people's eyes, though they had to crane their necks to see the "steeplejacks" brave vertigo by climbing to the top of the Empire State Building to build a TV tower for WNBT. Entertainment shows began that summer, but like baseball telecasts, there were growing pains. The very first variety show, *Hour Glass,* aired Thursday nights at eight p.m. on NBC, theoretically inaugurating "Must See TV" and the historic run of programs the network has aired at that hour.

The Ed Sullivan Show, this wasn't. The musicians union threatened a strike unless live acts were banned, and a compromise led to enforced lip-synching by all singers appearing on the show. Mistress of Ceremonies Evelyn Eaton introduced the acts, which included Doodles Weaver's "rabbit act," standup comedy, theater-style one-act plays, and the dance team of Enrica and Novello, whose feet were cut out of the frame by inexperienced cameramen. Twenty thousand people tuned in on thirty-five hundred sets across New York City (by contrast, twenty million people listened to *The Edgar Bergen Show* each week), and the network received two fan letters. Both liked the show.

On July 13, the Dodgers played in Chicago, and a game was televised in Chicago on WBKB for the first time. Like other efforts, this effort was panned. A *Tribune* reviewer named Larry Wolters wrote, "Because of the considerable area of action in baseball this sport is much less satisfactory for telecasting than wrestling or boxing."

The Dodgers won that afternoon 4–3. But it was the sole victory for Durocher's crew in a nine-game stretch that threatened to undo their commanding lead. For at the same time, the Cardinals were emerging from their torpor.

Chapter 26

RED, WHITEY, AND "FOUR-SACK" DUSAK

IT WAS NEARLY nine o'clock in the morning, local time, when the atomic bomb went off. Code-named "Able," it was practically identical to the "Fat Man" that was dropped on Nagasaki eleven months earlier. On July 1, the device was dropped by a B-29 bomber called "Dave's Dream" and detonated over Bikini Atoll. "We found the only place untouched by war," said Bob Hope, "and blew the hell out of it."

The explosion was deafening, although the denizens of St. Louis were out of earshot. Still, something seemed to stir the Cardinals once July came. Maybe they were roused by another, less notable line from Durocher—"The Cubs are the team we've got to beat, not the Cardinals." The *Brooklyn Eagle* piled on, asking "Whatever Became of the Cardinals?" in a banner headline. Regardless of the sparking incident, once the Fourth of July passed, the Redbirds began to resemble the "old gray mare scenting the home feedbox," a phrase the *Post-Dispatch* directed squarely at its rural readership.

Musial was Musial, and Slaughter Slaughter, but otherwise, the first three months of the season had been marked by slumps (Marty Marion and Harry Walker weren't hitting), injury (Terry Moore was limping around on his bum knee), and poor pitching (Brecheen was 4–8, Lanier was gone, and most of the depth was in Boston on the "Cape Cod Cardinals").

It was a couple of kids that sparked the team. Red Schoendienst had proven himself valuable at several positions. As a rookie in 1945, he had filled in for Musial in left field while Stash was in the service. He began '46 at third to replace Kurowski, who had gotten hurt after a lengthy holdout. Then Marion went down for a brief spell, and Red took over at short. Finally, after Klein left for Mexico, the freckle-faced boy straight out of a Mark Twain novel took over at second, a position he held down as a regular for the next decade.

Al "Red" Schoendienst was from Germantown, Illinois, about forty miles across the Mississippi from St. Louis, and grew up worshipping the Gashouse Cards. His hair was strawberry, like the rest of the family, whose surname translates to "good service" in German. Clinton County was coal country, and the mines all had ball clubs wearing their jerseys. Red's dad, Joe, worked the mines, had been a good catcher in his day, and umpired the coal league games on Sundays. "Sunday was a big day for us," Red remembered. "Straight from the mines to the ball field." Red was more partial to fishing the nearby Kaskaskia River than playing ball, but he sensed he wasn't going to avoid a life underground in the mines by baiting hooks, so he played.

At sixteen, Red joined the Civilian Conservation Corps, a New Deal program that put the able-bodied to work building roads and houses across the Depression-hit country. He was mending a fence one day when a nail ricocheted off the wood and went straight into his left eye. At the marine hospital in St. Louis, he pleaded with doctors not to remove his eye, and they obliged, but his vision was severely reduced on that side thereafter. Hitting righty against right-handed pitchers was a problem, so he taught himself to switch-hit.

Undeterred, Red hitchhiked to a tryout with the Cardinals and was signed to a minor league contract. He tore up the bus leagues, hitting over .400 in 1943 and .373 in 1944 when he was called up for duty. His eye damage meant he wouldn't be a rifleman, so instead Red guarded Italian POWs at Pine Camp in upstate New York. While there, he built baseball fields and organized the prisoners into teams, teaching the soccer-mad prisoners the finer points of the National Pastime.

By the spring of '45, he was back with the Cards and swiftly became a fan favorite. Reporters called him "an itchy undershirt" for his ability to annoy opponents with his play. He was a solid hitter and an outstanding fielder, holding the record for fielding average in a season (.9934) for thirty years. Musial said Red had "the greatest pair of hands I've ever seen," and his ability to handle so many positions in the majors was a testament to that.

In the late '50s, Red was dealt to Milwaukee, where he mentored Hank Aaron on the finer points of the game. In 1958, his coaled upbringing came home to haunt him—he was diagnosed with tuberculosis and part of his lung was removed. It didn't slow Red much—he played for five seasons afterward. He coached and then managed the Cards for decades, leading the Redbirds to the World Series in 1967 and '68 and winning it the first time, and he was elected to the Hall of Fame in 1989. In all, he was with the Cardinals organization for fifty years. After that long in a Cards uniform, his nickname would be "Red" even if his hair was not.

If Schoendienst was a local favorite, Joe Garagiola was a hometown hero. He grew up in the Italian-flavored neighborhood of St. Louis called "The Hill," a lump on the Mississippi floodplain that loomed over the swank Forest Park area. Up on the Hill, narrow alleyways and crazy-quilt roads were the rule, a contrast from downtown's wide avenues and straightforward grid layout.

Joey grew up at 5446 Elizabeth Street. He was best buds with the kid and fellow catcher who lived at 5447 Elizabeth across the street, Larry Berra, later better known by his nickname, Yogi. They honed their talents at a vacant lot on the street that served as an incubator of athletic talent of all stripes. "We played all the time," Berra remembered to the *New York Times.* "We would go right after school and play until the 4:30 factory whistle. That's when our fathers got off work and we had to go home and open a can of beer. Then it was back outside to play." Joey's dad didn't know much about base-ball—he called runs "points"—and preferred soccer, as did many on the Hill.

Garagiola was big and fast and the best athlete in the neighbor-hood, dominating sandlot games that were a big deal on the Hill. By the time he was fourteen, the Cards were well aware of him, and the organization sent him to Springfield, Missouri, to work odd jobs with their Western Association farm team there. When he was legally able to sign at age sixteen, they got him for a mere $500. There was never any doubt Joe would sign with his favorite team.

The Cards took a long look at Berra too—and decided he would never be a major league regular.

Garagiola was called into the army in 1944 at age eighteen and made his way to the Philippines, where he played for the Manila Dodgers, a team fronted by Kirby Higbe. One day in Manila, Gara-giola was listening to an Armed Forces Radio vignette from the states that talked about a young catcher in the Cards system who was supposed to set the league on fire when he arrived. "And then, by God, the Paul Bunyan he was talking about turned out to be me!" he remembered.

A large part of the calculus behind selling off Walker Cooper was the team's conviction that Garagiola would be a star. He didn't get discharged until late spring of 1946, and made his way to the big club for the first time on May 26 in Cincy. He singled in his first game, wearing borrowed shoes from pitcher Ken Burkhart, as he had forgotten to pack his own spikes. Garagiola then added a clutch two-run pinch-hit single in his third game, a 12–11 win over Pitts-burgh.

He didn't hit too much for the season, finishing at .237 with three homers. Truth told, he never did pan out as a star, only hitting forty-two homers with 255 RBIs over nine years. But it was his youthful energy and steadiness behind the plate that helped rally the team. The wit and joie de vivre that ended up making Garagiola such a successful broadcaster after retirement loosened up an often-tight clubhouse, where the dominant personalities were either gruff or quiet. It was impossible to dislike Joey, and the crowds that came out to see him from the Hill helped boost the team's pocketbook as well.

Equally important to team morale was a clubhouse speech given by Kurowski in mid-June. After Musial had turned Jorge Pasquel down, the Mexicans had come hard after Kurowski, and with good reason. The third baseman had been outspoken about his feeling that he was underpaid, and had held out in a bitter dispute with Breadon for most of the spring. Upon his return, his bat had helped keep the team within shouting distance of the Dodgers.

Like Lanier, Kurowski, whose hair had turned shock white before he was a teenager, was a prime candidate to take Pasquel's cash. Instead, he told his assembled teammates that while Breadon may have been a tightwad, he believed in the sanctity of a contract. Whitey had signed to play ball in '46 in St. Louis, and he wasn't going to break that commitment. Coming from the flinty third baseman, who certainly was no front-office lackey (as Musial had been occasionally accused of being in whispers around the team), it meant something to the guys.

Kurowski may have been bitter about his paycheck, but he had overcome plenty to be a ballplayer in the first place. The sixth of ten children, Whitey grew up in the heart of Pennsylvania coal country, and his daddy lived his life in the mines of Reading (he grew up not far from Carl Furillo). At age seven, Whitey fell off a fence and onto some broken glass. The gash on his right arm turned infectious, and soon he had osteomyelitis, an infection that attacked the bone. Amputation was a possibility, but Whitey was lucky—he only needed four inches of his ulna removed. His deformed right arm was thus much shorter than his left.

There wasn't much room for sympathy among large Polish coal

families, and Whitey didn't ask for any. Instead, he played ball as if he had no handicap, insisting on playing third base because it had the longest throws to make. Unlike Ed Head or Max Lanier, he didn't train to change his throwing arm—he simply willed his weakened arm to catch up.

He had trouble reaching outside pitches, so he crowded the plate, taking the inevitable plunkings that followed. He was also a dead-pull hitter as a result of his shortened arm, which meant he sometimes saw shifts in the opposite direction of the ones aimed at stopping Williams. Second basemen would come over to the shortstop side of the bag when Whitey hit.

That didn't slow him much. His arm kept him out of the war, and Kurowski celebrated by becoming the best third baseman in the weakened circuit, averaging seventeen homers and posting an OPS of about .800 from 1943–45. But as if to disprove the calumny that he was only the best of a poor wartime lot, he hit .310 with 27 homers and 104 RBIs in 1947, his finest season as a pro.

But the player who perhaps best symbolized Redbird resiliency was Johnny Grodzicki. A top pitching prospect from Nanticoke, Pennsylvania (yet another kid to see hardball as an escape from the mills and the mines), Grodzicki pitched well in a trial in 1941. But five weeks after Pearl Harbor, he followed his two brothers into the army.

He transferred into the paratroopers, the 17th Airborne Division, and was dropped into France to relieve units defending the Meuse River sector in late 1944. From there, it was into the snowy Ardennes Forest to rescue the 28th Infantry Division, who had been overrun by German armored units during the Battle of the Bulge.

In March, the 17th took part in a massive drop over the Rhine and into Germany for the first time. On March 29, 1945, the 17th was moving eastward over the Issel Canal and toward Münster when it was hit by an incoming artillery barrage. Grodzicki caught shrapnel in his right hip and leg. His sciatic nerve was badly damaged, and the doctor at the field hospital thought Grodzicki's days of walking were over.

With the help of a cane, Grodzicki showed that walking wouldn't be an issue. He returned to Nanticoke for rehabilitation, but was itching to pitch again, despite the pain it caused. He worked out with the Cards in spring, and aided by daily treatments and hot towels, his leg didn't balk at the trauma of pushing off the mound. He wore a leg brace and got through four innings in a spring training game. Dyer would sooner cut off his own leg than cut Grodzicki. A roster spot was his for as long as he needed.

It was midsummer before Grodzicki was ready. He pitched for the first time on July 11, coming in to mop up during a 13–3 massacre at the hands of the Giants. The first batter he faced, Johnny Mize, launched a three-run homer. Welcome back to the majors, doughboy. He got the next two outs and took a seat, his amazing comeback complete.

Two days later, Grodzicki was on the mound again, in relief against the Giants once more. He was a little more awkward this time around, stumbling while fielding a bunt and getting charged with an error. He gave up two runs and three hits in two innings, as the Cards again lost. Grodzicki wouldn't get another chance to pitch until September. In a loss to Pittsburgh, Grodzicki was wild, walking four batters and surrendering two runs in an inning and a third.

The end was seemingly nigh, but Grodzicki kept working in the off-season, and in 1947 he was much more spry. He appeared in sixteen games that season, with a 5.40 ERA and mammoth respect from his teammates, and especially his manager. "Eddie loved his spirit and his stark refusal to accept defeat in his ambition to make the big time," said sportswriter Bill Corum of Dyer's belief in Grodzicki. Although Grodzicki's 1946 contributions were minimal, the Cards never replaced him on the roster.

★ ★ ★

The loss in Grodzicki's debut was one of the few in the 8–3 run that the Cards were on when Brooklyn came to Missouri for a four-game set on July 14. The Dodgers led by 4½ games, so even a split would be a satisfactory result from the series, which began with a Sunday doubleheader.

The opener was tied at three in the eighth, with starters Higbe and Beazley long since departed. Brooklyn reliever Rube Melton, a wild sort who led the league in walks and wild pitches in 1942, aimed rather than threw a fastball to Slaughter, and Country launched a two-run homer to win the game. He had knocked in four of the five Cardinals runs.

In the nightcap, Brooklyn scored a first-inning run when first baseman Ed Stevens doubled in Bob Ramazzotti, then held on to the 1–0 lead into the eighth. Vic Lombardi gave up hits but kept scurrying out of trouble. But then Musial tripled and came home on a Kurowski groundout, and the game went to extra innings. Dickson matched zeroes with Lombardi until the twelfth. The packed house of thirty-four thousand, having sat through five hours of baseball, was tense on their seat cushions. Even Mary Ott was quieter than usual.

Musial led off the twelfth. Before sending Lombardi out to the mound, Durocher made it perfectly plain that he wanted his pitcher to dump Musial on his ass with a brushback pitch or two. Lombardi didn't, and the Man whacked a homer to deep right to win it 2–1. Durocher was apoplectic in the clubhouse. "I'll never ask you to pitch tight to anybody again," he screamed at Lombardi, "because I can see you don't have the nerve to do it. You let them take the bread and butter right out of your mouth."

The Dodgers lead was down to 2½ games. Monday was "Red Schoendienst Day" at Sportsman's Park, an unusual fete for such an inexperienced player. A group from back home in Germantown, Illinois, gave him a shotgun as a gift, then Red helped shoot down the Dodgers with a pair of doubles and 3 RBIs. Musial continued to annihilate Brooklyn pitching with four hits, including his ninth triple and eighth homer of the year. Brooklyn starter Hugh Casey got exactly one man out before Durocher yanked him out by the scruff of his jersey.

But using five pitchers and sixteen position players in the 10–4 loss was the least of Durocher's headaches. In the third inning, Slaughter lined one to left that Reiser slid in to catch. Most witnesses felt he caught it, but umpire Al Barlick ruled Pete had trapped it. A run scored, and Leo went apeshit. He "barked and growled and circled Barlick like a contestant of a bull pit," reported the *Post-Dispatch.* "Leo waved his arms, kicked dust on Barlick's pretty blue pants, and all but rubbed noses with the guardian of baseball law in his protest."

After a three-minute brannigan, Leo was ejected, along with Reiser. Durocher was suspended five games and fined $150 by the National League. He skipped town that night, "flying to NYC on the QT"—St. Louis wasn't flashy enough for an idle Durocher, and the lovely Edna awaited back on Park Avenue, not yet having been tossed aside in favor of Laraine Day.

"Humpty Dumpty sat on a wall, and what happened to him is something that should be worrying the Brooklyn Dodgers today after three straight unsuccessful brushes with the Cardinals of Eddie Dyer," was the lede in the *Post-Dispatch,* and indeed, the "dazed" Dodgers needed some help from the King's Men. Or from Howie Pollet. The Cards' ace lefty's distinctively loud grunts were especially resounding on this afternoon. Pollet turned in a long, gutty effort. No official record exists, but Pollet estimated he threw two hundred pitches in the series finale on Tuesday. He hung in there and went the distance, but he gave up four runs and thirteen base runners.

St. Louis trailed 4–2 going in to the last of the ninth. Joe Hatten was pitching a gem. He had been knocked from the box in the first inning by the Cards back in May and made up for it with a complete game win in June, and now he was trying to do it again. But he nicked Marion with a pitch leading off the ninth, and pinch hitter Clyde Kluttz singled, bringing the winning run to the plate in the form of another pinch hitter—Erv Dusak.

Dusak was a hot prospect, considered by most to be better than Musial when both arrived in 1941. That page of the scouting report was quickly trashed, but Dusak was clearly being groomed to be the heir to Terry Moore's center field job. The Cardinals had a reputation for getting rid of guys a little early rather than a little late, and it was clear that was the plan for Moore. But Dusak hadn't impressed much with his chances thus far. Dusak had spent seventeen months in the South Pacific, playing ball on New Guinea and taking long swims to keep his fitness up, but it appeared that he had left some of his timing in the Bismarck Sea.

He dug in against Hatten, then squared to bunt, fouling it off. It happened again, and he was quickly down 0–2. Dusak scotched the sacrifice idea and launched the next pitch ten rows deep in the left field bleachers for a walk-off, three-run homer that sent Sportsman's Park into a frenzy, the Dodgers off the field in shock, and the Redbirds to within a half a game of first, the closest they had been to the penthouse in weeks.

An instant mythology blew up around the home run, the story being that Erv was given a new nickname as soon as he touched home plate—"Four-Sack Dusak." In truth, he had been given the moniker down in the Southeastern League, when Dusak starred for Mobile and a fan penned an epic poem in his honor that used the nickname. But now it was on everyone's lips.

Musial had hit .500 in the four-game sweep, with 2 homers, 2 triples, 3 RBIs, 5 runs scored, and a steal of home, along with playing error-free ball at a brand-new position. He pretty much cemented the NL MVP Award with the performance, especially with the New York press horde in town.

Philly came to town next, and Dyer was worried about a letdown, so he called a meeting and exhorted his guys at length about the import of keeping their momentum. Inspired, the Cards went out and lost 10–7. "Dyer is no William Jennings Bryan," wrote Broeg. But the Cards won the following four games to thrust themselves into first place.

Brooklyn had it worse. They took a desultory train trip to Cincinnati, getting to the hotel late at night. Roommates Higbe and Hugh Casey somehow neglected to lock the door of their suite (alcohol may have been involved), and a thief crept in and relieved the hurlers of $300 in cash and their paychecks, which they had received on the train. Even worse, the cat burglar swiped Higbe's social security card, so he was able to brazenly roll into a bank and cash both checks. Officials said the man spoke knowledgeably about other Dodgers when quizzed by excited employees.

For Harry the Hat, the postwar period that began by losing the ETO World Series was getting worse in 1946. During the tournament that culminated in the ETO Series, Walker hit third or cleanup, leaning in to try to pull the ball more often, looking for the power expected from his spot in the lineup. Back in St. Louis, he was hitting much lower in the order but still retained his wartime hitting style. It detracted from his natural ability to slap hits up the middle and the other way, skills that had gotten him to the majors. Unlike Musial, his wartime adjustments didn't enhance his hitting.

Of course, Walker was no Musial, but like Stash, who had overcome injury to achieve stardom, Walker kept getting shoved down only to rise again. He was nowhere near the prospect his older brother Dixie was coming out of Leeds, but he perfected what he called a "pushing and shoving kind of baseball," and the Cardinals prized grinders like him.

Harry and his wife, Dot, hadn't seen much of each other for a while now. Walker went straight from the army to Cards camp, and then was on the road quite often during the season. They clearly shared at least one night of fun, however, for Mrs. Walker was with child, and she bore her burden around St. Louis during the long, hot summer. In early August, Harry was in Cincinnati with the team, and Dot took their three-year-old, Terry Walker (named for Terry Moore), over to the home of Marty Marion in the Brentwood section of town. The Marions had a daughter nearly Terry's age, and both children had new tennis balls they were anxious to play with.

Dot was inside sewing with Mrs. Marion when Terry said he had to go outside and retrieve his ball from a neighbor boy, who had taken it. A few minutes later, the other child came to the door, frantic—young Terry had been hit by a car.

Dot raced to Terry as quickly as her seven-months-pregnant body could, finding him alive but badly injured. She delivered him to the hospital and sat in the waiting room, her maternity clothes covered in blood, while Terry underwent hours of surgery. His head and legs were in bad shape, but Terry pulled through—for the time being, at least.

Harry left the team and spent a couple of days with his family, but duty called, and he was back with the team in Chicago, the next stop on the road trip. By that point, the Cardinals and Dodgers were neck and neck. Durocher's return to the dugout revivified the Brooks, who won nine of eleven to close out July, including a vengeful win over Pollet at Ebbets Field.

With two months to play, there was nothing to separate the two teams. Both sides girded for a battle to the end.

Chapter 27
CPO FELLER

THIRTY-ONE THOUSAND fans packed Griffith Stadium in Washington DC on August 20, a sizable chunk of the 1,027,216 folks that would pass through the old barn's gates in 1946, twice as many as had been coming out in recent years, and a full quarter as many as had seen the Senators play in the entire decade of the 1930s.

Most of the crowd had been lured to the park on this Tuesday evening to see the game's best pitcher perform. Bob Feller was 21–8, en route to a 26–15 mark and a workhorse season in which he led the AL in starts, innings pitched, complete games, and shutouts.

Oh, and strikeouts. Of course, strikeouts. Because what Ted Williams was to hitting, Joe DiMaggio to graceful play, Stan Musial to class, "Rapid Robert" Feller was to throwing hard. It was his signature, his path to the bigs. And on this day in particular, it was going to be his moneymaker—or else.

Seems the smart guys in the military research lab had come up with a device to measure the speed of objects hurtling through the air, such as anti-tank missiles or artillery shells. Now that the war was over, it seemed only natural to deploy the "Lumiline Chronograph," as the instrument was called, on a weapon slightly less dangerous to enemy personnel—the Feller fastball.

A speed test had been arranged for that night in Griffith Stadium, with Feller whipping a few heaters at the machine before the game to put a scientific—nay, *military*—imprimatur on his velocity. Unfortunately, Clark Griffith, the owner of the Senators and the park and this sideshow, had neglected to inform Feller that there were to be two performances that day.

"It was like telling Fred Astaire he'd be doing his dance routines before the game," Feller said, "and the owner was going to make a lot of money from it and not give Astaire anything. You can imagine what Fred Astaire would have said about that. Well, I was saying the same thing."

"Rapid Robert" was not one to be trifled with when it came to cash. Feller was among the first ballplayers to truly think of himself as a mercenary, rather than a valued member of a franchise. He was loyal to the Indians, but only because they paid him. Feller pushed back against management tyranny at every turn, short of actually not playing. He also maximized income streams from every possible angle, most notably arranging barnstorming tours in the off-season (where he had tangled with Jackie Robinson). Red Smith called Feller's thirst for a buck "his customary search through the shrubbery for loose dimes," and this little extravaganza had the whiff of a quick payday.

So Feller refused to take part, staying under the stands until Griffith was forced to come down to him and negotiate. A few minutes later, Feller walked out to a loud ovation, $700 richer.

The Chronograph used photoelectric cells to clock whatever passed through the V-shaped opening on top of the device. It was mounted in front of the plate on wooden brackets, not unlike the method used to hang the first atomic devices off the ground in Los Alamos. It spent most of its time at the Aberdeen Ordnance proving ground over in Maryland, but had come into town with its army minders, along with Universal Newsreel cameras and dozens of press.

Feller took the mound, windmilled his arm a couple of times, then went into his easy, high-kicking delivery, humming one to catcher Frankie Hayes. The second pitch was the fastest the machine recorded, at 98.6 mph. However, since the machine measured the speed of the ball as it passed through its sensors, unlike modern radar guns that clock the ball as it leaves the pitcher's hand, it actually flew much harder. Some estimates put the fastball at 101–103 mph, others as high as 107.6 mph.

His fifth pitch missed the opening and slammed into the wooden support, splitting the wood and ending the test at a tidy $140 per throw. Apparently spent from the effort, Feller went out and lost 5–4 to the Sens.

Feller could be a gruff SOB with a loud opinion on most subjects, an abrasive personality who grew sharper edges as he aged and found little good to say about modern baseball and its players, whom he declared to be greedy, without apparent irony. Feller was also intensely patriotic, and his experience during the war colored his future perspective on those who were without national service.

Feller had volunteered for the navy on December 8, 1941. Later he was asked why he hadn't delayed his induction until he was called up. "The country is at war and we are losing," was his reply. That summed up the no-nonsense approach he had taken to life since coming off the farm in Van Meter, Iowa, to pitch in the big leagues at age seventeen. His very first start resulted in a fifteen-strikeout performance against the Browns, and he pitched a no-hitter on opening day, 1940. That fastball made him arguably the best hurler in the league, so he had good reason to stay in baseball until the war couldn't wait.

But not only did Feller join up straightaway, he also itched to escape Gene Tunney's physical training program, a cushy gig that would have allowed Feller to pitch instead of fight. So he went to naval gunnery school, and soon was placed aboard the battleship USS *Alabama*. For the first six months or so, duty was in the Atlantic, and light. "I was playing softball in Iceland in the spring," he remembered. But come 1943, the *Alabama* sailed to the South Pacific and went toe to toe with the Japanese Imperial Navy.

The battle wagon took part in several major campaigns, including the invasions of the Gilberts, Tarawa, Nauru, and the Marshalls, dubbed "Operation Flintlock." Truk, Tinian, Saipan, and Guam followed, and on to Palau, Ulithi, Yap, and the Philippines, including the legendary Battle of Leyte Gulf, where the *Alabama* was a picket defender for Admiral William "Bull" Halsey's flagship, the carrier USS *Enterprise.* "We have been to about every 'hellhole' on the face of the earth," Feller wrote Lew Fonseca, the promotions director of the AL. Feller's job was to direct antiaircraft fire, spotting planes, calculating their trajectory, and passing along fire solutions to the gunners. It was fast-moving duty, one not for the faint of heart or the slow of mind.

The navy offered Feller extended leave so he could pitch against the army in inter-service games, but he refused, citing his obligation to stay with his ship and its crew. So he was part of the Battle of the Philippine Sea, the fabled "Great Marianas Turkey Shoot," a massive Allied victory that decimated Japanese airpower for good. "It was the most exciting thirteen hours of my life," Feller wrote in his autobiography, *Now Pitching, Bob Feller.* "After that, the dangers of Yankee Stadium seemed trivial."

One afternoon off Saipan, he spotted someone who had fallen overboard drifting away to sea. Feller called in a rescue, and the sailor sought out the pitcher to thank him profusely. Feller wasn't so lucky on another occasion, when a crewman stopped by his berth to talk baseball, a regular occurrence on the *Alabama.* After the visit, the bluejacket went to dump some garbage overboard and was swept overboard by a rogue wave, never to be seen again. Feller was the last man to see him alive, and he later confessed that the incident haunted him for years.

In the latter stages of the war, the Japanese Army Air Force, crippled by the losses over the Marianas, began its kamikaze program. Battleships like *Alabama* were prime targets, and the Japanese hunted Feller's tub "like blind, maddened bulls." Feller would earn five campaign ribbons, six citations for gallantry, and eight battle stars, but the number that meant most to him was zero. That was how many times the *Alabama* was hit directly by Japanese torpedoes, bombs, or kamikaze planes, and how many crewmen were lost in two-plus years of combat.

He kept in shape on board by doing chin-ups, running around the deck, working a punching bag, and using a rowing machine. He never drank, and one time on shore leave in Scotland, he had eschewed a pub crawl in order to milk a local cow. In return, he was given several bottles of fresh milk, which he kept onboard and replenished at every opportunity.

Chief Petty Officer Feller did take a few opportunities to show off his pitching skills, including an outing against the crew of the battleship USS *Indiana* in a game on Majuro Atoll in the Marshalls in June of 1944. The affair was witnessed by *New Yorker* war reporter Eugene Kinkead. He watched Feller, decked out in "blue dungarees, a gray sweatshirt, a nondescript cap, and...plain black dress shoes," battle blistering heat and loud heckling from the *Indiana* crew, especially a Brooklyn boy yelling things like, "Oh yuh joik! Yuh couldn't beat Detroit and yuh can't beat us. Yuh stink."

The tiny field lay amid a palm grove. "A steady trade wind blew gusts of white coral dust over the infield," wrote Kinkead, "whose surface was notable principally for a number of large rocks. The recreational officer provided three sacks for bases, a piece of wood for home plate, a strip of chicken wire for a backup, and a chaplain for an umpire."

Feller wasn't especially sharp, but he managed to best the Indianans, despite the distraction of a shore party from another warship swinging at anchor at Majuro. They were hunting wild pigs in the jungle. "From time to time, we'd hear alarming scuffles and squeaks nearby," Kinkead remembered, "and then a quartet of sailors would emerge from the undergrowth, howling triumphantly and carrying a dead wild hog, each of them holding a leg."

Such practice, rough and raw though it may have been, helped Feller in the spring of 1945, when *Alabama* was taken off the line and Feller was transferred stateside, to Great Lakes Naval Station, a service-ball powerhouse. He pitched a no-hitter for GLNS on July 21 in front of ten thousand sailors. Feller was ready for the bigs again.

Meanwhile, Feller was getting reacquainted with his wife, Virginia Winther. They had married just before he went to sea, and had seen each other for all of five days in their two years of marriage. He was back in the majors by August and went 5–3 in nine late-season appearances with Cleveland.

In January of 1946, after a barnstorming tour of Latin America, during which he formed an opinion on an opponent named Robinson, Feller traveled to Tampa to set up a school for returning veterans to regain their baseball skills. He recruited several other major leaguers as instructors, and for once, there wasn't any pecuniary advantage involved. Feller made the camp gratis for anyone who could get there.

Feller didn't need much schooling to return to his prewar dominance. He hurled a three-hit, ten-strikeout shutout at the White Sox on opening day. Two weeks later, on April 30, the Indians were in Yankee Stadium, and Feller showed that he was indeed no longer terrorized by the House That Ruth Built. He went through his usual pregame routine, using a razor blade to shave down the calluses on his right thumb and ring finger, then picked up a ball to judge its weight. If it felt heavy, it was a bad omen, and this one felt a little fat.

So much for superstition. Rapid Robert pitched his second career no-hitter, a 1–0 gem that Cleveland won when Frankie Hayes (the same man who sat so Harry O'Neill could have his brief entry into the majors before meeting his fate at Iwo Jima) slugged a ninth-inning homer off Bill Bevens for the only run of the game. Feller had eleven strikeouts on 132 pitches. "He made Frank Merriwell look like a bum," said Joe McCarthy after the game. Feller's overhead stretch hid the ball from batters, and his long delivery saw his glove hand practically brush the hitter's cheek. He snapped his right arm forward "as though he were cracking a blacksnake whip," is how *Time* put it. The Yankees never stood a chance.

At one point, Snuffy Stirnweiss bunted, and Cleveland first-sacker Les Fleming let the ball roll through his legs. It was an error, but since the Stadium had no place on the scoreboard to inform the crowd of the scoring decision, the public-address announcer told the crowd that the play was scored an error. By the next day, MacPhail had a HIT/ERROR sign in place, the first of its kind.

A couple of weeks later, *The New Yorker* ran an article contrasting the no-hitter with Feller's impromptu game back at Majuro Atoll. "I don't doubt that this no-hit game," Kinkead wrote, "like the one he pitched before the war, will remain a long time in his memory, and I have a feeling that he won't soon forget, either, that game he pitched at Majuro in between."

Feller would go on to win 266 games, a number that clearly would have been over 300 had he not missed three full years and most of a fourth to war. He never regretted the time away from the game. "During a war like World War II," he said, "when we had all those men lose their lives, sports was very insignificant. I have no regrets. The only win I wanted was to win World War II. This country is what it is today because of our victory in that war." Or, as he told ESPN decades later, "I would never have been able to face anybody and talk about my baseball record if I hadn't spent time in the service."

One guy watching Feller closely was an Indians farmhand named Gene Bearden. Like Feller, Bearden was a fireballer who wound up in the navy fighting the Japanese. He wasn't as fortunate under fire, however. During the Battle of Kula Gulf in the Solomons on July 6, 1943, Bearden was blown off the second deck of the light cruiser

USS *Helena* by torpedoes, suffering a fractured skull and a ruined right knee. He was lucky in one respect—168 sailors had been killed aboard the *Helena,* but not Bearden.

He owed his life to an anonymous rescuer. "Someone pulled me out," he remembered after the war to the *Cleveland Plain Dealer.* "They told me later it was an officer. I don't know how he did it. The ship went down in seventeen minutes. All I know is that I came to in the water sometime later." The pitcher spent two days semi-conscious in a life raft until he was at last pulled from the sea and brought to a hospital ship.

Bearden got a plate in his head and a screw-in hinge in his knee, and went back to pitching. He won fifteen games with Oakland of the Pacific Coast League in 1946, and by 1948 he was in the World Series, shutting out Boston in Game Three en route to a championship.

The vicious fighting in the Pacific claimed only one major leaguer, the aforementioned Harry O'Neill. But there were several top players who lost their lives; they wore the colors of the Imperial Japanese military. Most notably, Dai Nippon's greatest pitcher went to war and didn't come back.

Eiji Sawamura was a star before Japan even had a formal baseball league. In 1934, at age seventeen, he pitched against a team of visiting Americans, an All-Star squad that included Babe Ruth, Lou Gehrig, Jimmie Foxx, and Charlie Gehringer. He struck out the Hall of Fame quartet in succession, and gave up just a single run in five innings. Onlookers swore his fastball reached 100 mph. Connie Mack was managing the squad, and tried to sign Sawamura up for the A's right away. But the shy teen was reluctant to leave home.

When the Japanese Baseball League began play in 1936, Sawamura was the star. Pitching for the Yomiuri Giants, the Tokyo-based team that are the Yankees of Japan, he hurled the league's first-ever no-hitter that September and posted a career record of 63–22 with a 1.74 ERA, despite losing two seasons to war, 1938 and 1939. Sawamura had been called to mandatory military service at age twenty, and in January 1938 was inducted into the army, the 33rd Regiment based in Tsu Mie Prefecture. He fought in China until April 1940, seeing little combat but little baseball as well. Discharged from the fighting across the East China Sea, Sawamura went back to the Giants and threw his third no-hitter of his career in July.

In 1941, Sawamura was called back up to the army and was sent to the Philippines, seeing considerable action as the Japanese chased General MacArthur from the archipelago and conquered the country. He earned a discharge in late 1942, and played what passed for Japanese wartime ball that year. Most of the other great stars, like Masaru Kageura, Masaki Yoshihara, Yukio Nishimura, and Miyoshi Nakagawa, were off at war—indeed, almost all were killed in action.

As the Allies closed in on the home islands, Sawamura, like all able-bodied men, was called back up for duty in the fall of 1944. He was on a troop-transport ship off the Ryukyu Islands, in the South China Sea, when the convoy was attacked by the USS *Sea Devil,* an American submarine. Two ships, the *Hawaii Maru* and the *Akigawa Maru,* were sunk. Sawamura was aboard one of the two (it is not known precisely which), and he disappeared beneath the waves forever.

The Japanese Baseball League would name its version of the Cy Young Award after Sawamura.

In another lifetime, Sawamura and his triple-digit fastball might have had the opportunity to play in America and chase the major league single-season strikeout record. In 1946, it was a man who had spent the previous few years fighting the Japanese who was in hot pursuit of Rube Waddell's mark of 347 whiffs.

With the Indians hopelessly behind the Sox, Feller (and Veeck) cast aside any thought of team play and single-mindedly chased the record. Feller was no doubt prodded by a promise of a $5,000 bonus from Wheaties if he could do it, and there was whispered talk of a cut of the extra box office he would generate. He began to pitch every fourth day, make relief appearances, and react angrily when he retired batters by methods other than the strikeout.

He was still dominant despite the extra work. On July 31 he took a no-hitter against Boston into the ninth inning, when Bobby Doerr broke it up. Feller won the game 4–1 for his twentieth win of the season. On August 9, Frankie Hayes, who had homered back in April to get Feller the win during his no-hitter in the Bronx, blooped a single off Feller in the seventh inning. Hayes had been traded to Chicago, and his hit was the only one the Chisox could muster. It was Feller's eighth one-hitter of his career, breaking the record held by Old Hoss Radbourn. On the thirteenth, he no-hit Detroit for six innings, but lost 1–0.

He reached three hundred Ks on September 8, and later a ten-strikeout game against the White Sox put him at 336. There was one series left in the season, at Briggs Stadium in Detroit. Two days after the start against Chicago, Boudreau put Feller in the game in the fifth inning, and let him go the rest of the way, even though an exhausted Rapid Robert was throwing lobs by the ninth. Detroit scored four times against him in the frame but fell just short, 9–8. More important, Feller struck out seven, leaving him at 343, five shy of the record.

Two days later, Feller was back on the hill for a showdown with the American League's other top pitcher, Hal Newhouser. New-houser was considered the antithesis of Feller—he had padded his stats during the war, winning the victories, ERA, and strikeout crowns in 1945, and the MVP Award in both '44 and '45. "Prince Hal" was 4-F because of a leaky valve in his heart. To his credit, he tried to join the service several times anyway, only to be rejected at every turn.

Newhouser spent the season disproving the cynics who felt he would struggle with the return of the servicemen. He won 26 games, with a 1.94 ERA and 275 strikeouts of his own, finishing second to Williams in the MVP race. The week before, he had two-hit the Indians in a ballyhooed showdown against Feller in Cleveland, a heavyweight fight that was awarded pitch-by-pitch coverage in the *Sporting News*. But Feller was better on this day, winning 4–1 to match Newhouser with twenty-six wins. In the sixth inning, he fanned Jimmy Bloodworth for strikeout number 348, besting Waddell and setting a new record that held until Sandy Koufax shattered the mark in 1965 with 382.

Chapter 28
THE JEWEL OF PIGTOWN

THE DODGERS LOST two of three to St. Louis at Ebbets Field in the first days of August. The third game of the set was a brutal loss, a 3–1 defeat at the hands of Brecheen and Pollet, making a rare relief appearance. Worse, Pete Reiser was back to his old bad habits. In the fifth inning, Kurowski lined a drive to left. Pete gave chase and appeared to make the grab, only to lose the ball when he slammed headfirst into the wall, "cracking it so hard that he was knocked unconscious," according to the *Times,* who reported that he was taken to Peck Memorial Hospital and diagnosed with a concussion.

It was just another day at the ballpark—and the infirmary—for the star-crossed Pistol Pete, who might have gone down with the greats of the game if only he could have stayed in one piece.

Durocher called him the best player he ever had, save for Willie Mays. And Leo thought Reiser faster than the Say Hey Kid. Unfortunately, he had no internal governor. Running into walls became his calling card, and it nearly became his cause of death on a couple of occasions. He once fractured his skull after colliding with a cement fence while chasing a Country Slaughter drive (but was able to throw the ball to the infield before collapsing). "My head felt like a hand grenade went off in there," he said afterward. Reiser was stretchered off the field eleven times in his career. He once had last rites administered to him at the ballpark after a particularly brutal meeting with an outfield barrier. Because of Reiser, Ebbets Field began padding the outfield fences in 1948, and the NL adopted mandatory warning tracks for all its parks.

He grew up in a tough section of St. Louis, to a poor family with an even dozen children. Reiser's father made $25 a week as a printer, and the Depression made a tough situation worse. Reiser adopted a swagger to keep life's troubles at bay. He earned his nickname by walking the neighborhood like Gary Cooper in *High Noon,* with toy pistols in his belt. He'd swipe his grandfather's old cavalry sword and chase his sisters around, "just to scare them." He ran with gangs like the Marcus Street Rats and the Sherman Street Creeps, but it was playing ball against his older brother Mike and his friends that made him truly tough. Pete spotted five years to his brother and crew but held his own on the diamond.

Soccer was his first love, and he was gifted. The sport was more popular in St. Louis than just about anywhere in the United States, and he figured he could win a scholarship to Notre Dame. He was even better at baseball, and that's where the money was. But he considered giving up the game when the Cards cut him early from a tryout camp when Reiser was fifteen.

Turns out, the Redbirds were just being coy. They knew all about the swift young stud who thought he belonged in the majors already. His attitude was key—he lived up to Harry the Hat Walker's maxim that "You've got to step out and take charge in this game or go back to the bushes. It's no pink tea out here." The Cards were hiding him from other teams, who watched Rickey's developmental moves like hawks. At fifteen, he was too young to sign but not too young to drive, so the team made him the "chauffeur" for head scout Charley Barrett at $50 per month. Actually, the legal driving age in Missouri was sixteen, so Barrett did most of the driving, but every now and then "on an open road he'd let me take the wheel," Pete recalled. They drove all over the South, checking out Cards farm teams and giving Reiser a crack to warm up with the minor leaguers.

Reiser may have had a veteran's mien on the field, but off it he was hopelessly green. He once picked up Barrett's tip from a lunch counter, thinking it had been accidentally left behind. "It was the first time I'd eaten in a restaurant," Reiser said.

His destined path to Sportsman's Park hit a sizable pothole in 1938. Baseball belatedly ruled that Rickey's minor league monopoly was against the best interests of the game, and Commissioner Kenesaw Mountain Landis ordered Pete and seventy-three other top prospects set free, for any club to sign. Rickey was aghast, but reacted with a cunning plan. He arranged for MacPhail, his old apprentice, to sign Reiser and then trade him back to St. Louis at some point, effectively stashing him away for the Cards.

Unfortunately, no one informed Durocher of this backroom handshake, and he fell hard for his new outfielder. One day in the spring of 1939, Reiser dumped a veteran shortstop named Billy Rogell on his keister breaking up a double play. "We don't play like that in spring training up here, you bush son of a bitch!" yelled Rogell. "I do," Pete responded, which was just what Durocher would have said.

He had taught himself to switch-hit in the summer of 1938 while in the minors, and dominated spring training in 1939. He was sure to make the club under normal circumstances, but because of the secret deal with Rickey, MacPhail sent him back down, which set off a tear-filled brawl between manager and owner. Leo retaliated by talking up Reiser to the press, so much so that it became impossible to simply hand him back to St. Louis for some no-names. Rickey balked at the new price, and since he could hardly go public with details of his devious and illegal plan, he was forced to let Reiser stay in Brooklyn.

Pete was a mainstay by 1941, leading the league in batting, runs, doubles, triples, and OPS—a spectacular season overshadowed by the historic campaigns put up by Williams and DiMaggio that summer, and by Dolph Camilli, his Brooklyn teammate who won the

NL MVP over Reiser. Pete also quickly established his reputation for knocking himself into next week, usually by running headlong into the outfield wall. He missed nearly forty games due to injury in his first two full seasons.

There was a positive side effect to the reckless play—Reiser was considered 4-F by the services. The navy rejected him, and the army was about to, until a zealous captain at his indoctrination center pulled his papers from the reject pile and sought Pete out. "What will you do if we let you go?" he asked. "Play ball," said the guileless Reiser.

The next sound Pete heard was the stamping of his orders to Fort Riley, Kansas.

On his second day at the base, he was sent on a fifty-mile forced march in subzero temperatures, and caught pneumonia. He was about to be discharged but a baseball-loving colonel intervened, keeping a now-well Reiser to build a team for the base. The colonel tore up his discharge papers right in his face. Years later, Reiser said he could still hear the tearing sound.

Loads of pro players passed through Fort Riley and played on Reiser's teams, including Harry Walker, Joe Garagiola, Alpha Brazle, and Murry Dickson. One day a black soldier came over to the field and asked to try out. A nearby officer told him he had to play for the camp Negro team, which didn't actually exist. Reiser long remembered the forlorn soldier walking away alone. "That was my first encounter with Jackie Robinson."

Most of the Riley players were sent to Europe, and combat, but Reiser was sent to Camp Lee in Virginia, where this time, his discharge was overturned by a general who wanted the best damn ball club in the armed forces. Reiser promptly slammed through a wooden fence chasing a fly ball, tumbling down a twenty-five-foot hill and into a ravine. Onlookers thought he was dead, but Reiser escaped with a dislocated shoulder. He might have been safer in combat.

In 1946 Reiser was making just nine grand, with a performance bonus that lifted him to $13,000. He easily achieved the standards required for the extra dough, despite reinjuring the same shoulder in May. Brooklyn trainer Doc (Harold) Wendler examined the wing, consulted *Gray's Anatomy* and the Hippocratic Oath, and told the *Herald Tribune,* "A few sunny afternoons will provide a cure." Flatbush must have been plagued by cloudy skies, for Pete's shoulder hurt all season, and he was forced to miss the All-Star Game because of it. "It wasn't as serious as the head injuries but it did more to end my career," he told writer Donald Honig. "The shoulder kept popping out of place, more bone chips developed, and there was constant pain in the arm and shoulder."

"Without Pete, the All-Star Game is a hoax," declared Jimmy Cannon. "He's the best player in the NL. Can you hear me good?" But, due to the injuries, that was no longer the case. In '46, it was his legs that provided the biggest threat. He would lead the league in steals with thirty-four, including seven steals of home. His patented move was to slide past the plate and flick the dish with his hand. Once in Chicago, he was called out on a steal attempt of home by ump George Magerkurth, who then admitted sotto voce, "God-damn did I blow that one. Sorry kid."

But Pete was already on the downward slope, and another close encounter with a cement wall in '47 accelerated his decline even further. "It had always been so easy for me, but now it was a struggle," he remembered. "The fun and pure joy of it were gone." He lasted a few more mediocre years and was out of the game by the early '50s, never having quite fulfilled that superstar potential. He made a lasting impression, however, on fences and fans alike. For example, every winter he was asked to visit the Missouri School for the Blind, and one day he asked the principal why they liked him so much. "Our children here have problems with walls," came the reply, "and we hear you do too. They figure you're one of them."

★ ★ ★

One day when Reiser had first come up to the bigs, he was out in right field when a female fan dropped him a note to take to Durocher. Figuring it was a liaison of some kind, Pete took the paper to Leo. Durocher read the scrawl, which related that pitcher Whitlow Wyatt was tiring and that Hugh Casey needed to get warmed up. Durocher dutifully made the change, Casey was bombed, and the Dodgers were forced to make a sizable comeback to win the game.

A furious Leo turned on Reiser in the clubhouse. "Don't you ever hand me notes from MacPhail as long as you play for me!" Reiser stammered out that the note wasn't from Mac, it was from a woman named Hilda. "Hilda??!!" Leo cried, and just walked away, for once at a loss for words.

Welcome to Ebbets Field, where the fans made pitching changes.

Few would have had the chutzpah to have a player hand deliver strategic advice to Leo Durocher, but Hilda Chester wasn't any ordinary booster. A pleasantly plump woman in a flower-print dress with a voice like an air raid siren, Hilda had been in love with the game since childhood. She wanted to be the first woman to play in the big leagues, but like most fans her athletic ability fell short, so she attached herself to the Dodgers like a barnacle. As a teen she hung around the offices of the *Brooklyn Chronicle,* sometimes glomming passes from the writers. She went to work as a peanut sacker at the park, transferring nuts from a fifty-pound sack to individual bags. It was a thankless job for non-pachyderms, but it got Hilda closer to the team.

A pair of heart attacks robbed her of her unique ability to bellow at the men in the arena, so she took to the implements—frying pans, pots, and, memorably, cowbells. She "could make more noise than four male hog callers" with her cowbells, and when she wasn't clanging away, she was waving her HILDA IS HERE! sign or leading fans in snake dances through the bleachers. Durocher had grown close to her by now, visiting in the hospital after her cardiac arrests and giving "Hilda wit da bell" a lifetime pass to the grandstand, which she eschewed in favor of the rowdier bleachers.

Howling Hilda repaid the favor during Leo's assault trial in April. She gave testimony that stretched credulity in saying the plaintiff had called her a "cocksucker," and "Leo came to my defense." Like Durocher, she managed to stay out of the clink and with her beloved Bums all summer.

For those fans for whom baseball wasn't enough, Hilda was just a slice of the unique entertainment options on hand at Ebbets Field, where Gladys Gooding, a St. Louis native and veteran of the RKO and Loews Theaters, entertained fans on the organ. "St. Louis Blues" was one of her favorites, along with "What a Difference a Day Makes," "Somebody Else Is Taking My Place," and "Give Me the Moon Over Brooklyn." One regular tune she played got the whole crowd singing, but visitors from elsewhere in the country wouldn't recognize the melody. It was a song called "Leave Us Go Root for the Dodgers, Rodgers," an ode to the fans of the borough written by Dan Parker, the sports editor of the *Daily Mirror.*

> *Murgatroyd Darcy, a broad from Canarsie*
> *Went 'round with a fellow named Rodge*
> *At dancing a rumba or jitterbug numbah*
> *You couldn't beat Rodge 'twas his dodge*
> *The pair danced together throughout the cold weather*
> *But when the trees blossomed again*
> *Miss Murgatroyd Darcy, the Belle of Canarsie*
> *To Rodgers would sing this refrain:*

> *Leave us go root for the Dodgers, Rodgers*
> *They're playing ball under the lights*
> *Let us cut out all the juke jernts, Rodgers*
> *Where we have been wastin' our nights*
> *Dancin' the shag or the rumba is silly*

When we could be rooting for Adolf Camilli
So leave us go root for the Dodgers
Them Dodgers is my gallant Knights.

The faithful would belt out every word.

Cramped and small, with hardly any foul territory, Ebbets Field was packed early on game day, with batting practice almost as important a spectator sport as the contest itself. There was no parking around the field (an issue that would cause O'Malley to force a move), so fans walked or trolleyed to the games. The nickname "Dodgers" came from fans having to dodge trolley cars on their way into the park. The narrow aisles and breezeways made Ebbets Field hard to leave as well; as a letter writer to the *New York Times* put it in 1938, "The home of the Dodgers is harder to get into than the Social Register and harder to get out of than Alcatraz."

The round park was a riot of color, with dozens of advertising boards competing for every inch of space on the outfield walls, interrupted only by a small hitters' background, a cooling dose of black amid the bright primary colors. Ebbets Field's outer hull was dominated by an art deco facade complete with gargoyles, semicircular windows, and medallions of baseballs encircling the diamond-shaped edifice. The famous rotunda featured a chandelier made of bats and balls. The ticket lines meshed with entrance queues, leading to a mishmash of humanity pushing toward a single goal—entrance to the world of the Dodgers.

Upon entering the park, fans were greeted with a unique smell, a pungent combination of beer, piss, mustard, grass, body odor, and even a hint of freshly baked bread, courtesy of the Bond Bread Bakery a couple of blocks down.

After the nose took its beating, the fans' ears were assaulted. The "Sym-Phony Band," a group of fans who sounded as if they had found their instruments on the way to the game and decided to jam, played mostly off-key tunes throughout the games. They serenaded the umps with "Three Blind Mice," and strikeout victims heard "The Worms Crawl In, The Worms Crawl Out," complete with crashing cymbals. Meanwhile, Tex Rickard, the public-address announcer, would intone malapropisms like "A little boy has been found lost," but everyone knew what he meant.

The fans themselves were mostly working class, and heavily representative of the borough's Italian, Irish, and Jewish admixture. In the scrappy Dodgers they saw themselves; struggling mightily but in the main unsuccessfully against the entitled fat wallets in their lives (represented by the Yankees). This wasn't the twee, artisan-food-crafting, stroller-pushing Brooklyn of today, but a waterfront city that still felt itself a separate entity from Manhattan. The Dodgers were part of the neighborhood fabric; if the players didn't actually play stickball, stoop ball, crack the top, coco-levio, Johnny on the pony, or red light–green light with the local kids, they encountered such games on the way to the ballpark. On a given day, celebrity pals of Durocher like Danny Kaye, Groucho Marx, or Perry Como could be spotted in the crowd. But perhaps the fan who best defined the borough's desperate strivings was a recently discharged army major who frequented Ebbets Field, "broadcasting" the games from the grandstand into his tape recorder, hoping to parlay his law degree into a career in sports, a Brownsville native who had changed his name from Cohen to Cosell.

Under the scoreboard in right-center field, a sign advertised Abe Stark's clothing store. Abe was a tailor who offered a free suit for anyone who hit the ad board on the fly. Atop the scoreboard, a Gillette ad invited customers to "Shave Electrically" (the fabled Schaefer Beer sign that doubled as an official scorer, the *H* or *E* lighting up according to the ruling on a play, wasn't there until 1948). The scoreboard was the centerpiece of the thirty-eight-foot-high wall that abutted Bedford Avenue.

Because of the bizarre street layout surrounding Ebbets Field (the park was built on the site of a festering garbage dump known as Pigtown, named in honor of the porcine inhabitants feasting on rotting fish and other aromatic cuisine), the wall was built at a crazy concave angle. It actually bent inward, so balls tended to carom at unpredictable angles, and Dodgers outfielders like Dixie and Furillo had to learn the baffling bounces. Ebbets was a paradise for hitters even before 1948, when the fences were moved in, but a nightmare for opposing players subject to catcalls from the fans, who were right on top of them. The center field fence had a gap at its bottom that allowed fans outside on the street to lie on their bellies and sneak a peek of the action, until a copper tapped his billy club on their feet, the signal to get up and move along.

One block west, at the Left Field Bar & Grill, fans gathered before and after games to dissect Durocher's ("Dee-ro-ture" in Brooklynese) gambits or pay off wagers or just hurl epithets at the Giants. An outlandish remark would earn the rejoinder, "What ya been smokin', bud, mario-wanna?" Other fans convened for suds and chatter at Seaford's Lobster House, or at the Subway Inn on Willoughby Street, or the lobby bar of the Hotel St. George.

The eccentricities of Brooklyn baseball were a major advantage for the Dodgers in 1946. They went 56–22 at home but were only two games over .500 away from their bandbox and adoring Dodgers Nation. Only one team would be able to go into the Ebbets Field cauldron and win more than they lost, and it just happened to be the red-clad squad that was locked in a pennant battle with the Bums.

Durocher had been operating at red-line speed for months, pushing, prodding, cajoling, bullying. "Leo will run a club just as he runs a game of poker," wrote Dan Daniel in describing the Durocher Method. "He will deadpan, he will exuberate, he will twit you, he will fool you." The two sides of Durocher's style were on display in mid-August. During a game against Philadelphia, Leo engaged in an epic rhubarb with umpire George Magerkurth, the man who admitted to Reiser he had botched a call on an attempted steal of home. Magerkurth ejected Leo and nearly tossed the entire Brooklyn dugout when they rallied to their manager's side. The Dodgers were swept by Philly in a doubleheader. The next day, Durocher responded with a maneuvering tour de force, using eighteen players to eke out a 3–2 win over the Giants. "It was like the bill in small-time vaudeville," Durocher would say of his oft-changing lineup.

One day later, August 14, Rickey revivified an old idea for squeezing nickels from fans. For a scheduled doubleheader with the Giants, the team split the games into a day-night format, with separate admissions for the two games. It was decidedly out of fashion in 1946, though in the teens several teams had tried to do it, only to find it quite unpopular with fans. Brooklynites grumbled, but more than fifty-seven thousand paid to get in over the two games, and the Dodgers rewarded the faithful with a sweep. "People will pay to see anything these days," a Philly cabdriver told Bob Broeg. "Crowds would come out just to watch them play marbles."

That truth was at the heart of Robert Murphy's efforts to unionize, but a few days later, the Pirates voted to drive the final stake in the American Baseball Guild by voting against Murphy's offer to represent the players wholesale in salary negotiations. Then they whipped Brooklyn, 10–0.

It was a fair representation of the players' mind-set. They wanted a better balance in their relationship with management. But they were willing to settle for pennies on the dollar, then go out and play their kid's game with an untroubled mind, not caring how close they were to truly collapsing the ramparts that held the owner's castle together.

Chapter 29

FIGHTING RETREAT

LARRY MACPHAIL WAS a man of contradictions, simultaneously a pioneer and a reactionary, a progressive and a conservative. He went to great lengths to push night baseball on the sport, then turned around and urged his fellow moguls not to schedule too many evening games. He brought cartoonish volume and cheesy attendance boosters to the dignified Yankees, while at the same time cementing the franchise's reputation for a bloodless corporate personality. Alcohol played a large role in his capriciousness, but the Yankees owner naturally tended toward the bipolar, even before hoisting his first highball.

So it was with the delicate subject of the color line. Had MacPhail still been in charge of the Dodgers, rather than the Yankees, he might well have been the one to sign a Negro. It was just the sort of controversial, landscape-altering move he favored. But when his biggest rival, Branch Rickey, did it instead, that soured Mac on the entire idea. Besides, the most important thing to him in 1946 was the program to woo great numbers of well-off fans to Yankee Stadium. Putting a black man in pinstripes would turn off a sizable number of those paying (and paying) customers. And all those black fans who would certainly come out in support of one of their own wouldn't be great for business, either. He had reached out to the swells for advertising and other means of corporate support, and when his new pals complained about the whirlwinds buffeting their businesses throughout 1946, MacPhail was swift to reassure them that, at Yankee Stadium if nowhere else, time stood still and all was as it had been. Had there been a few Negro business executives to woo, Mac's manner may have been totally different.

The triple-pronged assault on the closed shop the owners were running, personified by Robinson, Pasquel, and Murphy, battered the psyches of the moguls. When their grumbling turned to panic, MacPhail acted. Quietly, through the spring and early summer, he met several times with Breadon, Yawkey, Cubs owner Phil Wrigley, and the presidents of the two leagues, Ford Frick (NL) and William Harridge (AL). The "Steering Committee," as the cabal was called, then met officially in Boston on July 9 and 10, and then again a week later on the seventeenth and eighteenth, and three more times in early August.

The upshot of the meetings was that MacPhail, who among his other talents was a world-class assembler of facts and figures that he could marshal on behalf of whatever argument he was in at the moment, would put together a secret report on what the moguls were faced with, and make recommendations for courses of action.

The MacPhail Committee Report was exceptionally frank in its pessimistic outlook, a "damning document" in the words of historian Jules Tygiel. It condemned baseball's organizational structure: "Professional baseball has not attempted survey or analysis of its administration set-up for 35 years... without any material revision to meet changing conditions." It ridiculed the bickering that was pandemic among the owners when it came to making major decisions ("an acute situation representing almost total confusion"). It warned that unionization efforts would succeed if the next attempt began with minor leaguers, and not major leaguers who had more to lose.

The report conceded that the Reserve Clause was illegal bunk ("In the well-considered opinion of counsel for both major leagues, the present Reserve Clause could not be enforced in an equity court in a suit for specific performance, nor as the basis for a restraining order to prevent a player from playing elsewhere, or to prevent out-siders from inducing a player to breach his contract"), and that only intimidation and scare tactics could be used to dissuade players from jumping to Mexico or any other breakaway league. It acknowledged that baseball had been extremely fortunate that Jorge Pasquel's Liga was just broken down enough to not be a desirable destination for renegade players.

And the MacPhail Report recommended defending the color line at all cost, breaking out several spurious arguments for doing so. The race issue was being promulgated by publicity hounds who had no knowledge of baseball but were seeking to make political hay. Signing a handful of blacks was an empty gesture, as most Ne-gro Leaguers were ill-equipped for the majors. Lack of minor league experience crippled Negro League players. Negro League contracts must be honored. And so on.

The section of the report on race closed with a warning shot across Branch Rickey's bow. "There are many factors in this prob-lem and many difficulties which will have to be solved before any generally satisfactory solution can be worked out. The individual action of any one Club [read: Brooklyn] may exert tremendous pressures upon the whole structure of Professional Baseball, and could conceivably result in lessening the value of several major league franchises."

The real reason the owners wanted to keep baseball white wasn't racial but financial. They wanted to keep the rent money paid by Negro League teams flowing, and the white fans coming to the parks. No one save Rickey seemed to be able to conceptualize white fans wanting to pay to see electrifying players like Robinson in action, or the idea that black fans would make up for any whites who boycotted the park.

Given how inflammatory the report was, the Steering Commit-tee and its successors took great pains to keep its contents secret, asking the recipients to destroy their copies. The very existence of the report did not become public knowledge for five years, until a congressional committee accidentally uncovered a copy in 1951. The *Sporting News* ran excerpts that October, but as MacPhail was out of baseball and Robinson in, the revelation wasn't as explosive as it might have been.

Baseball put out the official report from the Steering Committee on August 27 at a full owner's meeting in New York, but it was a heavily redacted version of Mac's issuance, containing little about the color line and other controversial issues. This version had MacPhail proposing to adopt Negro League teams whole into the majors, "if and when they put their house in order," a meaningless bit of rhetoric aimed merely at heading integration off at the pass.

One matter not redacted from MacPhail's secret report was his slamming of baseball's outmoded organizational structure. Mac had threatened and cajoled his stubborn brethren into accepting a new executive council, made up of the commissioner, the league presidents, and a rotating duo of owners, who would rule on all manner of rules, regulations, and issues that would crop up.

Ensuring that the overdue changes wouldn't be too painful, and indeed would be implemented in such a manner that would leave the Lords of Baseball still firmly in charge, was Larry MacPhail's job. No one formally gave it to him, but he naturally took charge, and the other moguls let him run. It helps to remember that the owners of the era weren't exactly the "Malefactors of Great Wealth" whom Teddy Roosevelt battled. They were rich men, sure, but they had earned it the hard way, and kept it despite the best efforts of the Depression. Ownership of a ball club wasn't the license to print money it is today. There were no huge television contracts, no $9 beers, no stadia publicly funded on the backs of taxpayers. Most teams operated on small margins, with an outsized reliance on gate receipts, and they weren't happy with the idea of a shift to any type of "free agency," where players would force bidding wars for their services. As *Fortune* put it, "It is the express attitude of many owners . . . that the average big league ballplayer ought to be happy he's not back in Hoskins Corners driving a truck. (By the same logic Dorothy Lamour at option time should be grateful only that she is not running that elevator in Chicago.)" MacPhail foresaw the possibility of the Reserve Clause's demise and was eager to forestall it.

He pressed upon his fellow owners a radical idea. The players would be invited to a meeting, attended by representatives of each team, during which they would be granted a few inroads, some spoils that would get them off the owners' backs for a while. That, Mac reasoned, would give the players the illusion of controlling their destiny, and since they had already decided not to unionize (yet), the owners would look as though they were being magnanimous, while taking solace in the fact that the players were unlikely to demand anything truly groundbreaking.

Heck, Mac would even host the unprecedented meeting at Yankee Stadium. The owners set the discussions for a period starting in late July and extending through August, as the players' schedules permitted. They then hedged their bets by inviting only six player reps—three from each league (although each team had elected one or two).

Mac wasn't short for Machiavelli, but his plan had the devious brilliance of the prince. It isn't known if he suspected that the player reps tabbed to attend the meetings would be older, higher-salaried players, and thus ones with little to gain by fighting for the future, but that was the result. Dixie Walker represented Brooklyn, Billy Herman the Braves, Joe Kuhel the White Sox, Mel Harder was there for Cleveland, and coming upstairs from the Yankees clubhouse was Johnny Murphy. All were well over thirty. Twenty-nine-year-old Marty Marion, who was already active in trying to attain some new privileges for the rank and file, was the babe at the negotiating table.

"The invitation to participate is pap for noisy brats," thought Red Smith, and while most of the press lauded the owners for their largesse and forward-thinking, a handful saw through the charade.

John Lardner in *Newsweek* wrote, "It is one of those old-fashioned baseball coincidences that the owners did not get around to contemplating player's rights until the players began to hold clubhouse and hotel meetings in regards to same. The player has been a legal slave for better than a half century. In the middle of 1946, already, the magnates leap into battle in his behalf." He went on to liken the owners' promise of new benefits for the players to jailers promising an expansion of jail cells.

Perhaps, but to the players, this was significant progress, an opportunity to formally advance their platform while they, for once, held a card or two (even if they didn't realize they had aces full of kings). As Freddy Schmidt put it, "Because of the Mexicans the owners were scared. They had to give us something—not much, but something." The reps presented a dozen demands, including a pension plan, a minimum salary, severance pay, and spring training funds—essential planks of the American Baseball Guild, as it happened. Most notable, however, was what wasn't brought up—an abolition of the Reserve Clause. "It is interesting to us that the players recognize the absolute necessity of the Reserve Clause as the foundation of our system," MacPhail warbled to the press. Marion would later acknowledge that the players had been intimidated by years of witnessing "problem" players get discarded like old newspapers. MacPhail swiftly drew up an "agreement in principle." Commissioner Chandler, trying hard not to guffaw, called the demands "comparatively modest."

The owners granted a new minimum salary of $5,000, capped pay cuts at 25 percent, instituted medical benefits, ensured injured players they would be paid in full, began a league-wide pension fund, and agreed to pay $25 per week per player during spring training for expenses down south, the aforementioned "Murphy Money." The owners had been pushing for an expansion of the season to 168 games, but they agreed to table that idea for the foreseeable future.

As for the Basic Player Contract, it was rewritten after the 1946 season. Under the old system, the club held complete command—"The player will accept such salary rate as the club may fix, or else will not play baseball otherwise than for the club." Under the new contract, the teams could offer a new one-year contract at the previous season's salary, after which the player would ostensibly be free. However, the owners interpreted the language as being a perpetuating rollover clause, essentially locking players to a club, much as things had been. Without a Robert Murphy or any other legal minds on hand to protest this reading of the clause, the players quietly acquiesced.

Red Smith was angry that the gains were so puny. "The owners," he thundered in the *Herald Tribune,* "sought to forestall trouble by tossing the help a bone. They decided in advance how little they could offer and get by with. Then they called in the hired men and made a pretense of asking them what they wanted."

Given just how tenuous the moguls' position truly was, the fact that they had gotten away with their control intact at the relative cost of a few coins sprinkled into a park fountain was extraordinary. But the players walked away feeling they had won a large battle, if not the war. That wasn't a conflict they were looking to fight, anyway. For these veterans who were simply happy to be back playing ball again, going to the mattresses over working conditions was like the failed Operation Market Garden of 1944—a bridge too far.

Robert Murphy was outraged. "The player-management deal was cooked up to get rid of the guild," he told the *Harvard Crimson.* "It's the most barefaced attempt at a company union I have ever heard of. Eventually," he continued, "the new generation of intelligent, non-subservient players will...recognize that their greatest weapon is the strike, and will not hesitate to employ it if they must." He added sadly, "The players have been offered an apple, but could have had an orchard."

It would take Murphy's evolutionary descendant, Marvin Miller, to get the players their orchard. Miller negotiated his first contract as head of the Major League Baseball Players Association in 1968. He got the minimum salary raised from $6,000 (to where it had been raised in 1948) to $10,000. In other words, the magnates' canny maneuvering, led by MacPhail, to maintain control in '46 had bought them two decades and change of relative status quo—salaries still low, and the Reserve Clause still in place. Then, in 1975, Miller took the owners to court, where an arbitrator named Peter Seitz at last struck down the Reserve Clause, opening the door for proper free agency.

Chapter 30
HERE'S TO YOU, MRS. ROBINSON

ON JULY 25, 1946, a white farmer from Georgia named Loy Harrison paid $600 bail to get a black man named Roger Malcolm out of prison. Malcolm had been accused of stabbing a white neighbor of Harrison's, and at first the farmer refused to help when entreated by two of his other part-time employees on the farm, Roger's wife, Dorothy, and her brother, George Dorsey. But he changed his mind and went to the Walton County Jail, about halfway between Atlanta and Athens, to free Roger.

Harrison drove Malcolm, Dorothy, and Dorsey and his wife, Mae, back toward the farm, but via an unusual route, one that took the white driver and his four black occupants over the Moore's Ford Bridge. At the far end, a car blocked their path. A large group of white men, anywhere from a dozen to thirty, all armed, surrounded Harrison's car and hauled the Malcolms and the Dorseys out. George Dorsey, a recently returned veteran, realized what was about to happen and resisted, but was swiftly overcome.

The white mob shot the two black men and threw them in the Oconee River under the bridge. The two women were then shot in case they could identify any of the attackers.

Dorothy Malcolm was several months pregnant. Her unborn child was cut out of her body.

The FBI investigated briefly, found no one willing to talk about the killings, and dropped the case, which remains unsolved.

It was the last recorded mass lynching in US history, and the ninth of 1946. Additionally, a score or more black men and women had been rescued from mob justice at the last moment. President Truman, aware that more than 75 percent of the nation's black population still lived in the South, despite heavy wartime migration to the north and west, established a Committee on Civil Rights that recommended an end to housing segregation and federal punishment for lynchers.

The night after the events at Moore's Ford Bridge, Jackie Robinson and the Montreal Royals opened a series in Baltimore. Orioles fans had yet to reconcile the idea of a Negro ballplayer on the field with their heroes, and staged a pitch invasion in the first inning, forcing the teams to the clubhouse and delaying the game while police cleared the field. When order was restored, Robinson, his ears ringing with unending abuse from the stands, reacted by collecting three hits, including a two-run homer, and stealing home in a 10–9 Royals victory.

It was progress, more than could be achieved by a dozen presidential committees.

Horse racing's Triple Crown of 1946 was captured by Assault, the son of Bold Venture, who thundered from way back in the pack to overtake Natchez and win the Belmont Stakes, thrilling a huge crowd of New Yorkers who shivered through an unseasonably frigid June day. The pigeon-toed Robinson might have felt some kinship with Assault, the "Chocolate Champ with the deformed foot," who had overcome hardship to become a champion. But he had no time or energy to follow America's second-favorite sport. He did manage to watch boxing when he could, and enjoyed a mid-June reunion with former army acquaintance Joe Louis at the champ's training camp in Pompton Lakes, New Jersey, where Louis was readying for a rematch with Billy Conn. He posed for pictures wearing a single boxing glove, while the Brown Bomber held a baseball bat with languid grace; he appeared ready to bat cleanup for the Bronx Bombers at any moment.

Otherwise, the constant travails of pioneer life were wearing Robby down.

The local papers, the *Montreal Star* and the *Montreal Gazette,* were hardly anti-Robinson. But even as Jackie was taking the town by storm with his early success, they betrayed their true, if underlying, feelings by referring to Robinson as the "Coloured Comet," or "Dark Poison," or "Dark Danger," or simply "dark boy." By mid-summer, though, racial themes were no longer en vogue—Jackie had simply eliminated them through superb play. Instead of "Negro" or "black," he was referred to simply as "Robby."

"There doesn't seem to be anything he can't do," wrote Dink Carroll in the *Gazette,* and indeed, the hot rumor was that Rickey would call Robinson up to the big club to help them hold off the Cardinals. Hopper, by now an unabashed fan, told *Newsweek* that Robinson was "a player who must go to the majors." Royals GM Mel Jones was forced to reassure French Canada by telling the *Sporting News,* "He's passed the test here and he shouldn't have to go through that again in the big leagues this year."

Robinson continued to turn in extraordinary feats on the diamond, such as tagging and scoring from third on a pop-up behind second base, or keeping a rundown alive until nearly the entire opposing team was trying to tag him out. But overall, his sterling play began to fall off during the dog days of summer. Partially, he was hitting a rookie wall, unaccustomed as he was to playing such a long, and unremitting, schedule. He missed nearly three weeks in June with a calf injury. And the fact that the Royals played an extraordinary thirty-nine doubleheaders during the 1946 season surely didn't help. But it was the pressure that was his worst enemy.

"I haven't heard anything worse than you hear in college football," Robby insisted to Red Smith, but the truth was plain to see. "The stress continued to mount on Robinson," reported the *Sporting News.* He had trouble sleeping. He pecked at food. Rachel was having a difficult pregnancy, not helped by the shortages that afflicted Canada almost as much as the United States. She would get fevers that spiked as high as 105 degrees, and sulfa that helped reduce her temperature was hard to come by. But she was there for every home game, and provided Jackie some much needed domestic tranquility in the flat on Rue de Gaspé.

"Rachel's understanding love was a powerful antidote for the poison of being taunted by fans, sneered at by fellow players, and constantly mistreated because of my blackness," Jackie wrote in his autobiography, *I Never Had It Made*.

They met at UCLA, when Jackie was already an athletic star, and Rachel was just a freshman trying to find her way. The relatively few African-Americans on campus liked to hang out at Kerckhoff Hall, where the leader was a student named Ray Burkhart. Rachel met her future husband there, though she wasn't immediately attracted to him. "He was already a big man on campus," she remembers through the mists of time, "and when I saw him for the very first time, he was in a studied pose, with his hands on his hips. I thought he was arrogant because of it, and I hated arrogance."

But when they started talking, she discovered she had totally misjudged him. "I fell in love right away with his humility," she recalls. This being Los Angeles, the automobile played a part in their burgeoning relationship. "I found out where he parked his car," she recalls with a laugh, "and parked as close as I could every day." She was driving a beater she shared with her brother, one that barely made it to campus and back. Soon enough he was driving her around. They were together until Jackie's death in 1972. It was one of the great American love stories of the twentieth century.

"I always felt that I was meant to stand beside this great man, not behind him," she says today. "And he wanted me there. I supported him, I listened to him, I watched him compete. I worried about him, especially when all those beanballs were thrown his way." But there was never any judgment, any recrimination. If this was her husband's destiny, Rachel would be right there too.

But even with the extraordinary spousal support, Jackie's play continued to suffer. His errorless streak ended at fifty-seven games with a pair of flubs. He started to slump at the plate. Jittery, exhausted, and frustrated, Robinson finally paid a secret visit to a Montreal physician, who told Robby he was on the verge of a nervous breakdown. The doc wanted Robinson to sit and rest for a while, maybe a full month.

It wouldn't have been an unreasonable request, given what he had endured to that point, and the fact that Montreal had long since clinched the top spot in the standings. But Robby could not *not* play. He was leading the league in batting average, for one thing, and worried that fans would interpret his sitting out as a sign that he was merely trying to protect his numbers. And of course, he didn't want to give the bastards the satisfaction. Most powerful was his competitive nature. Robinson reframed his exhaustion as an athletic challenge. He took off exactly one day, taking the opportunity to go on a picnic with Rachel. Then he returned to the lineup.

Two weeks before the season ended, Jackie was back in Baltimore, the scene of so much racial animus. Early in the day, the *Sporting News* reported that several Montreal scribes rated Robinson as the best Royals second-sacker of all time. He celebrated by stealing home in another win over the Orioles, and this time, his dash and daring was rewarded with a standing ovation from the crowd, their hate at last broken by admiration.

"After that, I started to relax," he later wrote. If he could turn Baltimore's crowd to his side, anything was possible. He just might make it through this trying season. He captured the batting title, and prepared for the playoffs.

On the final day of the International League's regular season, the US Armed Forces Commander in Europe, General Joseph T. McNarney, was quoted as saying Negro leadership qualities were "below the standards required for the efficient performance of certain types of combat duties."

Clearly, there were still some hearts and minds to capture.

Chapter 31

THE AUTUMN OF THEIR DISCONTENT

BOSTON CRUISED THROUGH August, going 21–11 during the dog days, and maintained a double-digit lead in games. On September 5, the Sox won their eighth straight, a 1–0 shutout from Jim Bagby. Bagby had a harelip, and was difficult to understand when he spoke, so he made up for it by cursing every third word or so. He once reamed out Ted Williams for not hustling after a ball hit down the line. "For Christ sake, go after that fucking ball," he bellowed.

"I'll tell you what, Bagby," Williams yelled back. "When you pitch, I won't play."

"Is that a promise?" Bagby replied. "If you don't play, I might win a fucking ballgame." Everyone within earshot understood every word.

Boston led the league by an astounding 16½ games after Bagby's gem, and were one win away from taking the pennant. The team cleaned out DC-area liquor stores of their champagne stock in preparation for the clinching celebration during a series with the Senators. But then they slumped and lost six straight games, leaving the bubbly flat and the team surly.

Perhaps they were worried about events overseas. The phrase "Cold War" wouldn't be commonly used until the following spring, but the tense standoff with the Communists began in earnest in the fall of '46. Two unarmed American cargo planes were shot down over Yugoslavia, with five killed and seven more taken prisoner, initiating an uneasy showdown with Marshal Tito. The Soviets left troops in Iran far beyond their promised pullout date, precipitating a crisis. A drunk Russian soldier in the American sector of Berlin nearly caused an international incident when he stood in the street and refused to let a streetcar pass. US soldiers shot him in the foot when he fled. Truman had been forced to fire his commerce secretary, Henry Wallace, after Wallace wrote a letter advising unilateral disarmament and appeasement of the Russians. On Wallace's way out of the White House, Truman called him a "rat bastard."

The Russians didn't have the bomb—yet—but the just-dawned Atomic Age clouded minds and jangled nerves across the country. Those inclined to forget were jolted back to reality by John Hersey's monumental report on the destruction of Hiroshima in the pages of *The New Yorker,* published on August 31. So one nuclear weapons control exponent tried to enlist the barbers of Pennsylvania to talk atoms instead of baseball. "You must admit, barbers reach a good cross-section of people," said Lillian Watford to *Life.* "You know how they are always talking in their shops about baseball and so on. They might profitably be talking about the implications of atomic energy instead."

Across the globe, conflict raged, and the likelihood that the United States would be drawn back into war someplace seemed to grow each day. Hindus and Muslims butchered one another in India. The Chinese civil war grew more heated, while famine swept the land ("Starving Chinese Eat Bark" was a typical report from the Middle Kingdom). Partisan bands raged across the Balkan countries, continuing a centuries-old ethnic war that had been given temporary legitimacy by World War II. The British vainly attempted to fend off freedom fighters/terrorists in Palestine, as the group known as Irgun, led by future Israel prime minister Menachem Begin, bombed the King David Hotel in Jerusalem, killing ninety-one people.

The *Washington Post* ran a cartoon that captured the mood that

September. Entitled "The Beautiful Post-War World," the image showed figures representing the United States and Russia, Labor and Management, Muslims and Hindus, and Truman and Congress, all with arms folded and backs turned to one another.

The postwar world had been beautiful for the Red Sox until now, but the losing continued from DC up to Philly. Boston lost a pair of games in the Liberty City. The winning pitcher of the second game for the A's was a Canadian right-hander named Phil Marchildon. He was Connie Mack's best pitcher before the war, and was slowly regaining that status after it.

He was fortunate to be playing at all.

After winning seventeen games for a Philly squad that won only fifty-five games all season in 1942, Marchildon joined the Royal Canadian Air Force, posing with another star athlete, Boston Bruins stalwart Roy Conacher, during the induction ceremony. Marchildon was offered a chance for easy duty as a fitness instructor in the Toronto area, where he was from, but he passed. "I figured I might as well go in all the way," he remembered in his memoir, *Ace*.

Marchildon was made a tail gunner and flew in the rear of a Halifax bomber, the multiuse, heavy-duty British plane overshadowed by its contemporary, the Lancaster. His war boiled down to counting missions—reach thirty, and he'd rotate back home, out of danger.

In the back of the Halifax, Marchildon was tucked into a crawlspace seventy feet from the cockpit. Even though Marchildon was an unimposing 5'10", 170 pounds, there was barely room for his parachute. Inside his snug bubble, he kept watchful eye for the telltale glint of silver that presaged a German fighter, or for the evil black puffs of flak that burst without warning around his turret. "On every mission I was tense as I scanned the skies looking for fighters who would attack at a moment's notice," he remembered years later. "There was no time to relax once you were over enemy territory."

After D-day, as his mission count climbed toward and then past twenty, the close calls mounted. Once, over Caen, France, shrapnel from antiaircraft bursts riddled his plane, scarcely missing an engine. The crew coaxed the damaged bomber back across the Channel.

Occasionally, some light moments broke the tension. One day an English friend brought Marchildon in as a ringer in a game of "American rounders" against some Yanks from a nearby base. The flyboys were swaggering about, confident in their ability to handle some Brits in their National Pastime. Then Marchildon took the mound, and one by one, the Americans went from waving to their English girlfriends to waving meekly at Marchildon's fastballs and curves. "Jeez, are they all this good?" one muttered. Finally, they were let in on the joke and deluged Marchildon with autograph requests.

By mid-August 1944, Marchildon and his crew of seven had reached twenty-five missions. In his memoir, Marchildon compared the vibe around the base to a team whose pitcher is throwing a no-hitter. No one spoke of the few remaining missions, for fear of jinxing them.

Just before 9:30 p.m. on August 17, 1944, Marchildon took off on mission number twenty-six. It was to be a "gardening expedition," Bomber Command slang for mine-dropping, to the entrance of the harbor at Kiel, close to the Danish border. Six Group, Marchildon's command, were considered experts at "dropping vegetables," and were thus flying over the Baltic Sea, far from the main thrust of the bombing over the city of Kiel. Marchildon's plane was fifty miles from the city, over water, when a German fighter appeared from nowhere, far from any action. Marchildon never saw him until the bullets shredded the wing.

Protocol called for Marchildon to don his chute, then try to help other crewmen with theirs, but his turret was far too small for him to maneuver the chute over his shoulders, and the plane had only a few seconds of airtime before it plummeted into the Baltic. So

Marchildon pushed himself free of the turret, got the chute on, and leapt out a hole in the airframe.

He fell from seventeen thousand feet. The wind immediately blew off his boots and hat. It was pitch-black, just before one a.m., and he had no idea if he was coming down over land or sea. Drifting through the Stygian blackness, he thought back to movies he had seen growing up. The unlucky ones forced to bail out on celluloid always seemed to control descent by pulling on the strings of the chute, so he tried it. His velocity increased so rapidly that it "scared the hell out of me," and he quickly let go.

Without warning, Marchildon splashed into the water. He worked his harness and heavy electrical pants off, so they wouldn't pull him under. It was summertime, so hypothermia wasn't an immediate worry, but the current was against him, pulling him further from shore.

He heard a shout. It was another crewman, the navigator, George Gill. He was the only other man to escape the stricken plane. The two joined up, but there wasn't much of a plan to be formed. They were at the mercy of the sea, and whoever happened to be on it.

After several hours, Marchildon and Gill began to resign themselves to facing the inevitable. They would be lost at sea. Just then, a light flashed on the horizon. It was a boat, coming straight for them. It could well have been a German patrol boat, but it mattered little to the fliers.

As it happened, the boat was a Danish fishing vessel, and the crew pulled the two men aboard. Amazingly, they had seen the plane go down and were cruising about looking for survivors. Even more unlikely, they claimed to be members of the resistance, and they outlined in broken but understandable English a plan to smuggle Marchildon and Gill to neutral Sweden.

Unfortunately, the plot lasted only until the boat returned to the dock. A squad of German soldiers was waiting there for transport, and they challenged the fishermen about their shivering new friends. The Danes had little choice but to tell the soldiers the truth, at least their version of it—these were Allied fliers, and they were planning to turn them in all along!

Marchildon and Gill were split up, and the A's pitcher was sent to a POW camp in Sagan, southeast of Berlin, in an area that is now Poland. It was the infamous Stalag Luft III, only six months before the site of "the great escape" on March 24, 1944. Years later, Steve McQueen and Charles Bronson would dramatize the event, when seventy-six prisoners escaped through an enormous tunnel they had painstakingly dug under the wires. Only three made it to safety in England—fifty were executed upon recapture.

By the time Marchildon reached the camp, such desperate lunges for freedom were pointless. The Allies were homing in on the Third Reich from east and west, and the smart play was simply to ride things out until liberation. Ten thousand Allied airmen were imprisoned at the camp. Marchildon was POW number 7741.

Stalag Luft III was set in a black forest with ugly, scrawny fir trees. There was a main wire enclosing the camp, then a second a hundred meters farther into the forest. The area in between the two was a no-man's-land, and anyone who encroached would be immediately shot. It was bleak terrain, and as the calendar turned closer to 1945, frigid as well. The *Kriegies* (short for *Kriegsgefangenen,* the German word for prisoners of war) traded with the guards, cigarettes for radio parts, and built ham sets that kept them abreast of the Allied advance.

The large majority of the *Kriegies* were Americans, so there was plenty of baseball and softball playing at Stalag Luft III. There were formal leagues in the warmer months, but by the time Marchildon arrived, ball games were mostly played just to kill time and prevent muscle atrophy. There were more severe risks than strained hamstrings. One day, Marchildon was playing softball when a ball got away and rolled under the wire. The nearest *Kriegie* yelled out to the guard on duty, *"nicht schiessen, posten!"* ("sentry, don't shoot!"), and was waved in. As he bent to pick up the ball, the guard, a particularly sadistic one hated by the prisoners, shot dead the *Kriegie* he had invited into the no-man's-land.

In late January, the entire camp was told to pack whatever possessions prisoners could carry—they were going to be marched northwest, away from advancing Russian forces. Snow was piled several feet deep in the forest, and fell in intense bursts. Marchildon, who knew from winter weather, built a sleigh to carry his food and extra clothing. That proved prescient. Many of his fellow prisoners staggered through the drifts under the weight of their goods and were forced to throw away vital provisions, or collapsed from the effort and were left behind.

There were destinations in mind for the men of Stalag Luft III, but they were usually deemed unsafe for the Nazis to venture before the forced march arrived. So the tramp just kept going. For three months the men marched, eventually covering hundreds of miles of snow-covered Silesia. Men died in myriad ways. Sometimes, an American dive-bomber would appear from the clouds and strafe the column, unwittingly killing friendly prisoners. They were pounded by stray artillery, attacked by wolves in the forest, shot or clubbed to death by the guards for the smallest of offenses. Many died of disease, or exposure, or simply exhaustion. They were all acutely aware that the war was near an end. To see so many die so pointlessly weighed heavily on the *Kriegies.*

Those who survived learned to love the sight of rural farmhouses, where they could barter smokes for food, beer, and baths. One woman offered soap to Marchildon. It was a dirty hunk, obviously several years old. Marchildon gave her a fresh bar he had received in a Red Cross package. The woman deeply inhaled its aroma and nearly fainted with pleasure.

By spring, Marchildon was on his last legs. He had dysentery and had lost thirty pounds. The forced march had mercifully stopped, and the pitcher was camping in an abandoned farmhouse, barely able to muster the energy to rise. Then, on May 2, someone noticed that the guards had simply disappeared. That got Marchildon to his feet. There was movement in the nearby trees. It was a British artillery unit. Liberation was finally at hand.

All the German guards were captured. Marchildon and some other softball players pointed out the scowling guard that had shot the *Kriegie* in no-man's-land. He was promptly marched out in a nearby field and executed.

Marchildon returned to Canada to recuperate and put on some weight. It was difficult to adjust. On his first night home, he was unable to sleep in his bed, choosing the ground instead. The quiet and tranquility of a nation untouched by war unnerved him. Sudden sounds sent him jumping in shock. There were so many people around he couldn't focus on any one of them.

Salvation came from baseball. Connie Mack phoned him up and asked him to return to the A's. The two had an uneasy relationship, based, unsurprisingly, on the idea that Mack, the owner/operator of the team, never paid Marchildon what the player felt was a fair salary. But the pitcher went back to what he did best. Mack had a point when he told Marchildon, "Even if you don't pitch this season, it will do you good to be back with your teammates." He didn't mention that he had already scheduled a "Phil Marchildon Night" at Shibe Park and needed the man himself on hand to boost attendance.

Even as he welcomed the normalcy of being with the guys, Marchildon was slow to adjust to his old life. His hands shook, and he couldn't shake a feeling of dread that something terrible was about to happen, like a friendly airplane screaming out of the sun to fire on him. A reporter who chatted with him wrote, "Yesterday as I sat beside him on the A's bench he brushed his hands over his forehead, pulled at his fingernails, scratched his chin, rubbed his eyes, constantly shifted from one leg to another, squirmed in his seat and stopped and started conversations." Phil admitted to him, "I was on my way to the ballpark and suddenly something gripped my nerves. I wanted to pick up a brick and toss it through a window." Marchildon was clearly, in retrospect, suffering from a form of post-traumatic stress disorder. But PTSD and other forms of combat fatigue were little understood at the time.

His teammates didn't help much. They were always asking him to relive the night he was shot down. Once, fellow hurler Bobo Newsom asked Marchildon the date he was sent into the Baltic. When told it was August 17, 1944, Newsom replied, "Right, Connie Mack Night in Philadelphia. The night the Yankees shot me down." The brash Bobo, who once offered his autograph to President Roosevelt, was a particular source of irritation, and Marchildon had to threaten to shut him up by force to end the barbs.

Marchildon wasn't actually scheduled to pitch on "Phil Marchildon Night," August 17, 1945, one year to the day after he was shot down. He was just supposed to make a speech and wave to the crowd. But Newsom, that night's starter, got sick, so Marchildon took the ball. He was rusty and still not back to full health, and it showed. He pitched two innings, giving up four hits, four walks, and two runs. The stats weren't great, but Marchildon was encouraged by one thing—his arm felt surprisingly good. Once he got the kinks out, he felt, he would be okay.

Fast-forward to spring training, 1946. True to form, Mack underpaid his war hero and past ace. "I want Marchildon to show me he is the same pitcher he was before the war," Mack told the press. Understandable in context, perhaps, but it further embittered Marchildon. Mack finally agreed to pay $7,500, with a promise of another $1,000 in June if Marchildon pitched well enough to earn it.

Two days after signing, Marchildon was accidentally sliced open by a teammate, a crazy busher from the Deep South who liked to play with knives. The gash on his hand didn't heal until May, when he finally made his debut. He pitched well, lost some tough ones, started 0–5, and was 4–7 at the All-Star break, when his wife, Irene, gave birth to their first child. After a two-hit victory over Chicago in July, Mack gave him his bonus.

★ ★ ★

The win over Boston evened his record at 13–13 on the year. After the victory, Marchildon said he thought the Sox seemed "listless."

Indeed, Boston had saved its worst for last. The celebratory champagne was being carried across half the American League, from Washington to Philly to Detroit to Cleveland, without being cracked open. There was no thought of an epic collapse (they still led the AL by fourteen games), but the wait at the precipice was getting on the nerves of everyone in Boston.

Williams was getting on people's nerves himself. Throughout his career, he would often wear down toward the end of the season due to illness. Even as a kid in San Diego, late-summer fevers plagued him, though he never did figure out why. Now he spent many a ball game in a fog, from either a head cold or the medication he took to treat it. "He practically had pneumonia, he was so sick," remembers Bobby Doerr. "He was real run down." "I'm tired physically," Williams admitted to the press late in the season. "I'm on the go all the time and I wish it were all over."

Meanwhile, his Triple Crown hopes had dissipated like a sneeze in the air. Once the leader in all three categories, he fell behind Mickey Vernon of the Senators in the batting chase, and Hank Greenberg, Detroit's slugging star in the twilight of his fabled career, in home runs and RBIs.

Greenberg had suffered through a miserable 1946. He had been the first major league star to be called up for service, way back in 1940. He was honorably discharged on December 5, 1941. Two days later, he was back in the military, volunteering (the first major leaguer to do so after Pearl Harbor) for the Army Air Corps. "We are in trouble," he told the *Sporting News,* "and there is only one thing for me to do—return to the service. This doubtless means I am finished with baseball and it would be silly for me to say I do not leave it without a pang. But all of us are confronted with a terrible task—the defense of our country and the fight for our lives."

He saw duty in the China-Burma-India theater, scouting terrain for potential B-29 bases. One day, as the bombers were taking off for a mission to Japan, one of the planes faltered. Greenberg remembered later, "The pilot saw he wasn't going to clear the runway, tried to throttle down, but the plane went over on its nose at the end of the field. Father Stack, our padre, and myself raced over to the burning plane to see if we could help rescue anyone. As we were running, there was a blast when the gas tanks blew and we were only about 30 yards away when a bomb went off. It knocked us right into a drainage ditch alongside the rice paddies while pieces of metal floated down out of the air."

Greenberg was stunned and couldn't talk or hear for a couple of days, but otherwise he wasn't hurt. "The miraculous part of it all was that the entire crew escaped," Greenberg continued. "Some of them were pretty well banged up but no one was killed. That was an occasion, I can assure you, when I didn't wonder whether or not I'd be able to return to baseball. I was quite satisfied just to be alive."

He came home in mid-'45 and proved he was far from "finished with baseball." Greenberg walloped a homer "on a line as flat as old beer," in Red Smith's phrase, during his first game back, and hit a grand slam to clinch the pennant. Hebrew Hank then slugged a memorable three-run shot to win Game Two of the World Series, as the Tigers bested Chicago in seven.

But for most of the summer of '46, he was considered washed-up at age thirty-five, his 28 homers, 88 RBIs, and .268 batting average through August far below his standard numbers. Then a fellow Tiger, an even older one named Roger "Doc" Cramer, who at forty was fortunately still extremely juvenile, slipped into the Sox clubhouse one afternoon at Fenway and stole one of Ted's bats. Cramer presented it to Greenberg, and Hank duly, in his words, "embarked on his annual fall salary drive" with the new lumber.

He smashed a dozen homers in three weeks with Splinter's splinter, until it shattered one day. Undaunted, Hank hit 5 more with his own previously uninspiring ash, to give him 16 for the month of September and 44 in all, good for best in the league. His 39 RBIs during the exceptional month gave him that title as well. Grantland Rice opined, "Greenberg's surge is one of baseball's greatest achievements." When the season ended, he gave Williams a fresh bat as a thank-you.

Ted wasn't too happy about the whole thing. He suspected, as did some others, that Greenberg and Vernon were getting grooved pitches in an effort to deny Williams the Triple Crown. As Austin Lake wrote, "Rival athletes gradually grew sour at Ted for his aloof swagger and chill hauteur toward his fellow craftsmen." Pitchers, in the Williams worldview, were dubious characters who lacked morals. He could easily envision some of those snakes not coming high and hard at the popular Greenie so they could stick it to The Kid.

Williams hit but .272 in August, and his power evaporated in September, hitting just 4 homers with 9 RBIs all month. The cumulative effect of the swoon was to once and for all undo all the talk of post-service maturity that was the common theme of ink spilled Williams's way early in the season. Prewar style feuding with the press was again commonplace for the man who once grumbled, "Pour hot water over a sportswriter and you get instant shit." One day he unloaded on his ghostwriter for the *Globe,* Hy Hurwitz. "I get tired of looking at a little squirt like you," he grumbled. Hurwitz retorted, "That makes us even, for I get tired of looking at a big galoot like you." The fans were turning on Ted once more as well, a twist Jimmy Cannon found insincere. "Ted's harangues have offended the people of Boston," he wrote, "who believe a guy should take their abuse with a counterfeit humility and cower before their scorn."

Williams's worst moment came after an A's outfielder and Czechoslovakian immigrant named Elmer Valo robbed Ted of a home run by going over the low Fenway fence in right field to spear a screaming line drive. Valo landed awkwardly on the railing, and crumpled to the ground in agony. Williams savagely kicked first base in anger and screamed expletives on his way back to the dugout, indifferent to Valo's plight even as he was stretchered off the field. The Boston fans booed him loudly, and the press gave him a good beating.

Even the glad tidings of finally wrapping up the AL flag didn't lift tensions—if anything, they were exacerbated by an incident that night. On September 13 in Cleveland, the Indians put on the shift when Williams came to bat in the first inning. Contrary to his usual method, the Splinter lined a rocket the other way, to deep left-center. Left fielder "Fat Pat" Seerey was way over toward center, and Williams cruised around the bags long before the portly outfielder could run it down. It was the only inside-the-park homer of Ted's career. Hughson made it stand up with a three-hit shutout, and the 1–0 win at long last put the Sox in the World Series. After the game Williams laughed, "Someone said 'is that the easiest homer you ever hit?' And I said 'hell no, it was the hardest. I had to run.'"

Mayor James Curley ordered firehouses across Boston to sound gongs, sirens, and bells for fifteen full seconds to celebrate the victory. The champagne at last flowed in the Sox clubhouse. Harold Kaese, whose *Saturday Evening Post* piece had slammed Cronin and the Sox back in the spring, now magnanimously sent Cronin a telegram that read, "Congratulations to a champ who made me a chump." Indeed, Cronin had done an excellent job skippering the Sox to a runaway pennant, especially given the pressure he was under in spring training.

Yawkey was traveling with the team on the epic road trip and was staying with them at Cleveland's Statler Hotel. He decided to throw a party for the boys that night. However, relations between the press and the Sox had deteriorated to the point where Yawkey feared a scene might break out when the hard stuff started to flow, so he arranged for a separate, press-only bash elsewhere in the hotel.

Naturally, the writers took this as the worst insult of all. They were being treated as lepers incapable of social graces, "scullery maids" in the words of Al Hirshberg. And when the irascible Huck Finnegan of the *Boston American* inconveniently got into the same elevator as Cronin on the way to their respective parties, the result was a swearing match between floors. Then Lake sought out Yawkey after a few belts and engaged in a shouting fight with the owner. After this fateful evening, the press really took it to Williams, Cronin, and Yawkey at every opportunity. Ironically, the Splinter wasn't even there for the fireworks. He had blown off the festivities, supposedly to visit a wounded war vet at a local VA hospital, though that was never confirmed. His absence caused a sensation, of course. *What kind of teammate misses a pennant celebration?* wondered the press.

Ted was temporarily cheered a few days later, when two thousand fans from Gardner, Massachusetts, the center of furniture building in the United States at the time, descended en masse on Fenway to present Williams with the world's largest chair. It weighed 750 pounds, and a photo of the Splinter in his oversized throne ran in papers across the country.

But on September 26, an off day before the final three games of the season, Williams was driving with Doris to an exhibition game when his car slid out of control on a wet highway and skidded head-on into another vehicle. No one was hurt, but both cars were totaled. Williams got his car replaced for free, while the other unfortunate in the accident was ridiculed in the press for committing the ultimate Boston crime—he had never heard of Williams before the Splinter slammed into his automobile.

The scary incident put a capper on a dreadful month. *What next?* Ted must have thought. Unfortunately, he would find out soon enough. If Williams thought the bad tidings were over, he was quite wrong.

Chapter 32
VICTOIRE

LEO DUROCHER PUT up a mighty ruckus, as was his wont, alternately threatening to quit and to punch someone's lights out, but all his hootin' and hollerin' couldn't persuade Rickey to call Robinson up to the Dodgers in time for the pennant race, though he might have provided the difference in the tight battle.

Instead, Jackie stayed with Montreal for its biggest games of the season. The top four teams in the International League held a playoff. With a 100–54 record, and an eighteen-game margin in the standings, the Royals were seeded first. In the opening round, Montreal led Newark three games to two, but trailed 4–3 in the last of the ninth in Game Six. Royals first baseman Les Burge appeared to take strike three, but it was called a ball. On the next pitch, Burge homered to tie the game. Three Newark players and manager George Selkirk were ejected after reacting hysterically to the call.

But it got worse for the Bears. The next batter singled, and Herman Franks doubled off the scoreboard. The runner scored on a close play, despite the efforts of Newark catcher Larry Berra. Berra went berserk, and teammates had to restrain him from killing the ump, Art Gore. Gore had to be escorted from the park so the Bears couldn't rip him limb from limb.

In the IL finals, Montreal pummeled Syracuse in five games to win the Governor's Cup. That left the "Little World Series," a duel for top honors in triple-A baseball that pitted the Royals against the champs of the American Association, the Louisville Colonels. Best known for Thoroughbred racing, Louisville was also a rabid baseball town, with fans of both races, including Cassius Clay Sr., whose four-year-old son would add another sport to the city's profile as an adult.

Unfortunately, the races seldom commingled. Louisville adhered to a hard-core segregationist policy. The Colonels ownership, mindful of their white fan base and its attitude, set a strict quota on the number of black fans allowed into Parkway Field. Hundreds of black fans were turned away from the gates for the first three games, all of which were played in Louisville to save money on travel expenses. Many of them had traveled great distances to see one of their own take on the whites.

Robinson was in a "deep funk" in the days before the Series. He had played well but not spectacularly in the IL playoffs. Now he faced his first true exposure to southern mores since spring training. Louisville infielder Al Brancato recalled, "He didn't even have a place to stay. There were no hotels that would take him, so they didn't even know whether or not they were even going to play."

Montreal did, and in the face of "some of the worst vituperation I had yet experienced," courtesy of the Louisville fans, Jackie crumbled. He went 0–5 in the opener, the first time all season he had done so, and the Royals lost 7–5. "Everything he did, they booed him," said Colonels pitcher Otey Clark. "I remember our pitcher, Jim Wilson, knocked him down, and the fans cheered."

The worse Robinson played, the more vicious the crowd got. "A torrent of mass hatred burst from the stands with virtually every move I made," Jackie recalled. Typical badinage from the stands:

"Hey black boy, go on back to Canada and stay there!"

"Yeah, and take all your nigger-loving friends with you!"

Robinson was hitless again in Game Two and committed an error, but the Royals pitching dominated in a 3–0 victory to tie the Series. But the Colonels crushed Montreal 15–6 in Game Three, to retake the series lead. The season was threatening to come apart. After months of brilliant play, Robinson and the Royals were bowing to hate and anger at the worst possible time.

But on October 2, the Series shifted to Montreal, and everything else shifted as well. Robinson returned to a city livid over the way he had been treated in Louisville. The Colonels players bore the brunt of their anger, getting booed vociferously every time they emerged from their dugout. "I didn't approve of this kind of retaliation," said Robinson in his 1972 autobiography, "but I felt a jubilant sense of gratitude for the way Canadians expressed their feelings."

Gratitude was one thing, scoring runs another. On a freezing night, Montreal was being shut down by Otey Clark. Down 4–0 and then 5–2, the Royals were in danger of being put on the brink. But Robinson doubled in the eighth and scored to make it 5–3. In the ninth, Clark gave up a pair of runs to tie the game. "It was my most embarrassing moment in baseball," Clark said fifty years later.

In the tenth, Jackie came up with a man on second. He looped a curveball into center field for a hit that knocked in the game-winning run. Fans flooded the field in celebration, and Robinson couldn't get back to the clubhouse for nearly half an hour, such was the adulation.

Thursday, October 3, wasn't nearly as cold as the day before, and Montreal celebrated by getting off to a fast start. Jackie doubled and scored to give his side the lead. He tripled and scored in the seventh, and bunted for a hit to score Campanis in the eighth. Montreal won 5–3, and was within a game of the LWS title.

Over nineteen thousand fans packed Delorimier Stadium for Game Six. Curt "Coonskin" Davis got the ball for Montreal. The ancient (he had turned forty-three a month before) hurler had won 158 games in the majors (mostly with the Cardinals), and pitched in two All-Star Games and the 1941 World Series, but he would say that this game meant more to him than any he had ever pitched. Ol' Coonskin pitched the game of his life that chilly afternoon of

October 4. He held Louisville to three hits and no runs. Robinson singled, stole second, and scored the game's first run—as it turned out, the only one Davis would need. Montreal added an insurance run to give them a 2–0 win and the Little World Series championship. After the horrid start in Louisville, Robinson wound up hitting .400 for the Series.

A massive throng swarmed the field after the final out. Jackie weaved his way through the crowd and made it to the locker room. A wedge of police tried to clear the park, but no one wanted to leave. As Sam Maltin reported in the *Pittsburgh Courier,* "They refused to move and sang *Il a gagné ses épaulettes* ['He won his bars'] and 'We want Robinson.' It was a mob ready to riot." Hopper and Davis came out and were carried around the field, but the throng wasn't satisfied—they wanted to show their love for Jackie.

A group of ushers went to the clubhouse to tell Robinson "some fans were waiting to see him." Jackie went back out to the field, where thousands slapped his back, hugged him, and kissed his cheek. Jackie, tears streaming down his face, tried to disengage himself, but the crowd would not be denied.

After the hero's treatment, Robinson was finally released to shower and dress. He had little time to linger—he had a train to catch. Robinson was off to Detroit to begin a month-long barnstorming tour. He had signed up his fellow black farmhands in the Dodgers chain, Roy Campanella and Don Newcombe, along with Negro League stars Larry Doby and Buck Leonard, by guaranteeing them $5,000 apiece (the tour would prove disappointing at the gate, and Robinson would have to dip into his signing bonus to make good on the promise of five grand to his fellow stars).

With less than an hour to get to the train, Robinson threw on his clothes and made to leave. According to Maltin, "he had a tough time packing his gear as people came trooping in to wish him luck. They all said they wanted him back." Clay Hopper stopped him at the door and shook his hand. "You've been a great ballplayer and a fine gentleman," said the manager who once questioned Robinson's very humanity. "It's been wonderful having you on the team."

Buoyed, Robinson opened the clubhouse door, only to have his heart sink. Thousands of fans remained—if anything, the crowd had grown. There was nothing to do except plunge through and hope for the best. Calling upon his days as a football star at UCLA, Robinson juked, jived, and shoved his way to the street, where he took off at a sprint. The crowd ran after him. Just then, a car hired by Rachel, who was already at the station and feared her husband might be late, screeched up and rescued Robinson.

As the car took off down the street, hundreds of fans trailed in its wake. It was the last Montreal would see of Jackie Robinson, and everyone knew it. He had given them an eternal season, and the fans wanted it to last just a few moments longer. Maltin famously captured the irony in the *Pittsburgh Courier:* "It was probably the only day in history that a black man ran from a white mob with love instead of lynching on its mind."

Chapter 33
THE STRETCH RUN

EVEN AFTER MONTREAL'S triumph, Rickey and the Dodgers stuck to their guns—no Jackie Robinson in Brooklyn until 1947. He had been through enough for one season, and the team wanted him to recharge for the coming test the following spring. Brooklyn had sputtered through a 16–13 August, but come autumn, Durocher cracked the managerial whip once more, rendering moot the argument over Robinson's promotion to the big club. In September, Brooklyn won nine of its first ten games. Perhaps the credit should go to Stanky, who on August 31 got into a brawl with Goody Rosen of the Giants and was ejected. Not much roused the Durocher Dodgers like a good brannigan. True to form, seven different Brooklyn pitchers won games during the stretch, and Reiser, fresh out of the hospital from a bout with pleurisy, ran the Giants silly by stealing three bases, including home for the seventh time, in an 11–3 rout.

Arthur Daley was overcome by Reiser's play, and he was effusive (and unknowingly prescient about a certain Montreal Royal and soon-to-be Dodger) in the *Times.* "The mercury-footed outfielder has had a moral relapse and gone larcenous once more, stealing bases by the gross lots. He creates such an undercurrent of excitement in the stands whenever he moves onto the base paths that the opposing team immediately gets a mass case of the jitters. He's the only man in the game who can upset the opposition entirely by doing no more than standing a few feet off base, a quizzical, mischievous grin on his face."

Leo took the credit, but the strong play may also have come from Rickey's promise of a new car to each man if they won the pennant. Rickey's generosity spurred the club to pool some cash and get a nice gift for their boss. They bought him a boat, and wanted to present it to him publicly before a game. But Rickey had stopped attending due to the treatment he was getting from the fans. So the players lured him to Ebbets Field by telling him Durocher and Furillo were brawling in the clubhouse. Rickey enjoyed playing peacemaker, so he hustled down to the park, only to be surprised by the boat. When he came out on the field, he was booed vociferously.

The Brooks would need every victory, for St. Louis went 9–2 over the same ten-day period.

On the eleventh, the Dodgers and Reds hooked up at Ebbets Field for a ridiculous nineteen-inning scoreless tie, the longest in major league history. Johnny Vander Meer, he of the back-to-back no-hitters back in '38, pitched fifteen blank frames. By the time he finally gave way, "Brooklyn bats were as heavy as crowbars." Dixie Walker threw a runner out at the plate in the top of the nineteenth, and even heard some boos from the home fans, who were exasperated by the lack of runs. Four Brooklyn hurlers went into the gloaming before the game was finally called, four hours and forty minutes after the first pitch.

It was hardly the way Durocher wanted to prep for the final series of the regular season against St. Louis, who came to town the following day. A listless group of exhausted Dodgers was in no condition to put up a fight in the series opener, and they lost 10–2, Garagiola's three-run homer off Higbe in the first inning sending all non-diehards (as if there were any) fleeing Ebbets Field within half an hour. That put the Cards up by 2½ games, and hope was leaking out of the borough. The overachievers seemed to have hit their ceiling.

But Brooklyn bounced back strong the next afternoon, thanks to a clubhouse meeting before the game conducted at top volume by the inimitable Leo the Lip. The Dodgers responded to the expletive-laden pep talk with four in the first off Red Munger, who had at last returned from the service. Munger trudged to the showers, knocked from the box in the very first inning. Suddenly, the strains of reveille and artillery fire wouldn't have sounded so bad to him.

The Cards fought to within 4–3 by the ninth inning. Musial then tripled. Kurowski lifted a fly to center, and Musial, thinking third base coach Mike Gonzalez was yelling, "Go, go!" broke for the plate. But he was screaming, "No, no!" and Furillo unleashed his cannon arm to throw out Musial and save the game. Ol' Hig, driven from the box the day before, relieved with 2⅔ hitless innings. When asked afterward if he should think more about tomorrow, and not risk burning out his players, Durocher sneered, "Tomorrow!? Tomorrow it might rain!"

He was platooning Howie Schultz and Ed Stevens at first, Furillo and Whitman in center, Bruce Edwards and Ferrell Anderson behind the plate, choosing daily between three different third basemen, and tossing in whatever pitcher seemed to strike his fancy at that moment. There were only four regulars in the lineup—Stanky, Reese, Dixie, and, when healthy, Reiser. Leo was getting mileage out of every man on the roster.

So Durocher's stratagem for the rubber game of this enormous series wasn't a complete shock. Leo started Ralph Branca, who was back in good graces after the salary dispute back in the spring. Branca had also gotten on Durocher's shit list by refusing to pitch batting practice. But the Dodgers pitching staff was spread thin, so all was forgiven for the former NYU star.

Sort of forgiven, anyway. Durocher planned to use Branca for a single batter, then switch to lefty Lombardi, mainly just to screw with the Cards' heads. But Branca retired Schoendienst on two pitches, and then Walker and Musial went out softly as well, so Leo, ever the hunch player, stuck with his big righty. "Being angry, I guess it pumped me up," remembered Branca. "The adrenaline got to flowing, cause in the first inning I got them out on five pitches. I walked in, and Durocher said, 'Keep throwing like that, kid. We're going to keep you in.'"

Branca went on to hurl a three-hit shutout, a 5–0 win that brought the Dodgers back to a virtual tie for the lead. "His assorted curves caught corners as if magnetized," wrote the *Post-Dispatch.* "After that, I believed in myself," Branca recalled. "That was the tempering of Ralph Branca." Meanwhile, the thirty-three thousand fans at Ebbets Field put the Dodgers over the 1.5 million mark on the season, setting a new NL record.

"Not even Hitchcock could improve upon this race," wrote Broeg, and the next day brought a scene that could have come straight from the fabled director's twisted imagination. The Cubs were in Brooklyn for a doubleheader and won the first game in ten innings. The second game lasted half that, for Ebbets Field was invaded by a pestilential horde of gnats in the fifth inning. "The unusual spectacle of thousands of persons frantically slapping scorecards and newspapers puzzled the denizens of the press box," Roscoe McGowen admitted in the *Times,* until the little biters descended on them too. The game was called, and umpire Beans Reardon told the press, tongue firmly in cheek, that "anyone who thinks the game was called for any reason but darkness is bugs." Since the Cubs had batted five times, the game was official, and Brooklyn was awarded a 2–0 win.

Up in Boston, the Cards kept pace. Williams, Cronin, and several other Sox watched as Musial lasered five hits around Braves Field as the Redbirds won the next day. "Every one of the hits left Musial's bat with the velocity of .30 caliber bullets projected from a Garand M-1 rifle," Broeg wrote, as if auditioning for *Stars and Stripes.*

Stan and the rest of the players couldn't help but notice that later that night, Joe Louis defended his heavyweight title for the twenty-third time, knocking tomato can Tami "the Bronx Barkeep" Mauriello out in just two minutes and nine seconds of work, for which Joe was paid $103,611. Between that figure and the new attendance records, the wiser of the ballplayers would have realized then that the owners had pulled a fast one and were getting an incredible bargain for the players' services.

But they were ballplayers first, so they put aside their financial calculations in favor of the pennant chase. Brooklyn was agog over the race, which stayed tighter than Rickey's wallet for the last couple of weeks. On the steps of Borough Hall, the Rev. Benney S. C. Benson knelt and intoned: "Oh Lord, their chances don't look so good right now, but everyone is praying for the Bums to win. We ask you not to give…St. Louis any better break than you give us." Meanwhile, a new young couple took their honeymoon at Ebbets Field during a key stretch. A Dodgers fan named Raphael Skopp, on death row in Massachusetts for armed robbery and homicide, spent his final hours listening intently to a September game. The criminals went the other way with the Redbirds. While the Cards were beating the Cubs 1–0 at Wrigley Field, with Brecheen pitching a shutout and knocking in the game's only run, thieves were making off with several gloves left behind in the St. Louis clubhouse.

Two days earlier, the Cards had come to Chicago to open the series. Waiting for Slaughter was a process server. His estranged wife, Josephine, was filing for divorce. Enos accepted the papers while in the dugout runway taking practice swings, waiting to hit. He almost missed his at bat dealing with the server. His teammates, knowing Slaughter could have drummed up an injury to miss the trip and avoid the Illinois court, "made him virtually their hero," according to the *Boston Globe.* He was giving new meaning to the phrase "taking one for the team."

Everyone, it seemed, was doing likewise. Pee Wee Reese had a deep gash on his leg that required seventeen stitches, but he didn't miss an inning. Reiser was a mess, typically, playing despite the bum shoulder and a badly sprained ankle that caused him to miss several games in September. Meanwhile, Howie Pollet continued to take the ball despite a shoulder injury that sent waves of pain down his back and neck. He went 3–3 with a 3.96 ERA in September, not bad considering his injury but a far cry from the 10–4, 1.33 he put up in July and August before he felt that first stab of agony.

St. Louis returned home from its long road trip on the *Illinois Central,* putting both the Dodgers and the Cardinals on home ground for the final week. "Cards Reach Fork in Road, Need Knife to Butter World Series Bread" read a somewhat baffling *Post-Dispatch* headline upon the team's return. The *Brooklyn Eagle* set its own feelings to verse:

> *If Lippy kicks the flag away*
> *And hands it to the Birds*
> *He won't have much to say*
> *Except ten thousand words.*

Leo was left speechless by the results of the twenty-fifth. Leading Philly 9–6 in the ninth, his team came unglued and coughed up five runs and the game. Durocher used a record eight pitchers to try to save the day, to no avail. Meanwhile, Sportsman's Park rocked as Musial tied a game against the Reds with a ninth-inning hit off the nasty Johnny Vander Meer, and Dusak played hero again by knocking "a fastball that now is the souvenir of a sure-fingered fan who was sitting halfway up in the bleachers just under the hot dog stand." The full house went crazy. A New York writer covering the game said, "For the first time I've got the feeling I'm in Brooklyn." The attendance figure at Sportsman's Park went over the one million mark, leading J. Roy Stockton to write, "No longer can the magnates weep in their beer pleading they are struggling along in a small population center and therefore cannot afford to pay big salaries...the players all know there is gold in them there strong boxes, and the boys will want some of it—plenty of it."

The Cards led Brooklyn by a game. But then Pollet and Dickson were rocked on consecutive days, and the Dodgers brought the race back to equipoise. But it was a Pyrrhic victory. Reiser, now also hobbling with a bad hamstring, had told Leo he could "play but not run" against the Phillies. He reached on a fielder's choice in the first inning. Inexplicably, Leo flashed him the steal sign. Reiser therefore took a long lead, and when pitcher Charley Schanz threw over, Pete jammed his ankle awkwardly sliding back in to first. As his star screamed in pain, Durocher rushed out, ashen, yelling, "Get up, you're all right!" But he wasn't. The bone was sticking through the skin. Reiser had a broken ankle and was done for the season. Durocher, casting about for someone to blame other than himself, settled on the Ebbets Field groundskeeper, saying, "The rocklike ground grabbed his spikes."

The race went to the final weekend tied. As Hollywood unions picketing studios brawled with hired strikebreakers and a car ran over a striker, Roy Rogers (star of no fewer than eight pictures in 1946) was far from the strife, watching his beloved Cardinals from a box seat at Sportsman's Park. The Redbirds beat the Cubs 4–1 behind Brecheen's brilliant pitching. It was the Cat's fourth victory of the month, combined with a 1.69 ERA. Brooklyn responded with three in the first off Johnny Sain, Boston's twenty-game winner, and won 7–4. The race was tied after 153 of the 154 games scheduled.

Sunday, September 29, was gloomy in St. Louis, and since a rainout would not be replayed, the pennant could have been decided with one team listening on the radio and not competing, a scenario that seems outlandish today. Fortunately, the wet stuff stayed away. So did the offense for the two front-running clubs. Mort Cooper, a former Cardinals pitcher, was the ironic hurler for the Braves against the Dodgers, and he did his old club a favor by shutting out the Brooks on four hits (President Truman sent Cooper a congratulatory telegram for his effort). St. Louis led Chicago 2–1 after five innings, but Munger gave up five runs to the Cubbies. "Back to the Army with ya!" yelled a fan as Munger left the game. Back at a downcast Ebbets Field, "Everybody and their Aunt Kate lifted their dragging chins" as the score was posted on the out-of-town scoreboard late in the Dodgers game.

The Cards lost 8–3, and for the first time in major league history, two teams were tied with no games left. They were both 96–58. "The ding-dong battle ended in a blanket finish Sunday and wound up even-Stephen," according to the *Post-Dispatch*.

The unprecedented situation would require something brand-new in the sport's long history. A three-game playoff between Brooklyn and St. Louis would decide the 1946 NL pennant and give one team a berth in the Fall Classic. "There's a World Series every year," noted Red Smith, "but there's never been a clambake like this."

Chapter 34
THE FIRST PLAYOFF

THE PUBLICITY DIRECTOR of the National League, Charlie Segar, flipped the coin. Down a scratchy telephone line to the Cardinals' office on Dodier Street, Sam Breadon called heads, and lost. Thus the choice was Durocher's. Leo looked over at Ford Frick, the league president, whose feet were up on the massive oak desk in his office, and announced his decision. The first-ever playoff series would begin in St. Louis. The Lip wanted to have the potential deciding game played at home, so he agreed to head to Missouri for the opener, then host Games Two and Three, should a third be necessary.

Unfortunately for the Dodgers, Durocher wasn't factoring in the marathon train journey west. In retrospect, he should have raced to Rickey and traveling secretary Harold Parrott and demanded that the team charter an airplane. But the Dodgers hadn't flown all season, and they weren't about to start now, on the eve of the biggest games of the year.

Game day dawned with good news from Germany. Twelve Nazis who were on trial in Nuremberg had their fates decided not far from Soldier's Field. They were sentenced to death, the appointment with the hangman set for two weeks hence. The condemned men appealed to face the firing squad instead, but were rebuffed. Three others, including Rudolf Hess, got life in Spandau Prison. Albert Speer was given twenty years, Admiral Karl Dönitz, the German naval commander named to succeed Hitler after the Führer killed himself, ten.

Back in St. Louis, writers filled out MVP ballots. Musial was the obvious winner. But the Man was in no mood for self-congratulation. He was too busy sweating the coming best-of-three series. Stash thought this new playoff setup carried far more pressure than did the Fall Classic. After all, as he pointed out, "Once you're in the Series, win or lose, you're in the money." The loser of this tiebreaker wouldn't get an extra dime.

Durocher chose Branca as his starter for the opener, still impressed by the big righty's late-season charge. "It'll be Branca and we'll win," the skipper swaggeringly told the press mob on the train west. Brooklyn, despite the limp to the finish, seemed, to the press at least, to be playing with the house's bankroll. The *Times* reported that the Dodgers "breeze[d] into town with their characteristic jauntiness... from their general mien one could easily imagine they had achieved their objective by winning their last twenty in a row."

The Cards, by contrast, looked far more wooden, at least to the amateur psychologists at the Paper of Record. The Redbirds "appeared extraordinarily subdued if not downright discouraged." Certainly Pollet was trending downward; he had been shelled in his previous two outings, and his shoulder injury, which by now had led to a further oblique strain, was affecting his play. Whether or not to start him in this most crucial contest was a question that gripped the city and the manager.

Dyer may have thought of Pollet as a son, but with less than two hours before the first pitch, the time for familial grace notes was over. The skipper turned harshly on the little left-hander.

"Your back either hurts or it doesn't," snapped Dyer, a hush falling over the clubhouse. "There's too much at stake and besides, I'm not going to risk your future on one ball game. So give me a straight answer, not 'I'll try.'"

"Eddie, I'm going," replied Pollet.

The box office took a beating due to the lack of advance sale. A frosty evening kept to a handful the overnighters who lined up for tickets. The ones who showed up lit bonfires to ward off the chill. Many were allowed to seek solace in their cars while keeping a place in line. But the cold front moved through quickly. Tuesday, the first of October, was swathed in brilliant warm sunshine, around seventy-five degrees, a perfect afternoon for baseball. Scalpers were selling $1.75 tickets for $1, and only 26,012, about 8,000 shy of capacity, turned up. So as Dyer and Durocher posed for photos, the stands were only two-thirds full. Leo muttered through his smile, "You ain't gotta chance, Eddie."

"I know, Leo," Dyer laughed back. "Your ghostwriter said that two weeks ago."

No one wrote that Durocher had blown the pennant by burying Branca for months, though Ralph sure felt that way. "If they had pitched me, you know we would have won at least one more game than we did," he said years later. Now Durocher tried to make up for past sins by starting his moody right-hander in the opener.

Five years later, Branca would surrender one of the most famous (or infamous, depending on your rooting sensibilities) home runs in baseball history, Bobby Thomson's "Shot Heard 'Round the World" in the 1951 playoff. That, combined with a 1–2 record in the World Series, would saddle Branca with a reputation of being poor in the clutch. That stigma really started with this game, though it's a bit unfair. The Cards loaded the bases against him in the first inning. Garagiola then blooped one off the end of his bat that didn't even reach the outfield grass but fell safely, enough to score Moore with the game's first run. Branca escaped without further damage.

One of Leo's first basemen, Howie "Stretch" Schultz, tied it by swatting the first pitch of the third inning into the left field seats, but the Cards reestablished control in the bottom of the frame. A groundout scored one run, and the Hat brought in another with a chopped single over Branca's head, which made it 3–1 and ended his afternoon. "They really didn't hit the ball hard," Branca recalled years later. "It was just a bunch of nub hits."

Meanwhile, Pollet was once again "poison to the Brooks." He winced with every delivery, and each batter appeared certain to be his last. As Sid Keener wrote in the *St. Louis Star-Times,* "The fog was gone from his fastball and it came up to the plate, hanging and big. Pollet grimaced with agony every time a 3–2 pitch came up and he had to lay it in there with his body behind it. No one could believe he could go nine innings, but he did." Reiser, itching to mimic Pollet and play while hurt, but unable to do so with his leg in a cast, grew too uncomfortable in the dugout and repaired to the trainer's room as the Dodgers, clearly affected by the long train trip, wallowed fruitlessly for two-thirds of the game.

Finally, in the seventh, the logy Dodgers threatened. Two men were on with one out when Schultz came up again. The 6'7" slice of tall timber sometimes called "Steeple" came through again, rapping a single down the right field line. One run scored, but Slaughter screamed over, cut the ball off, and gunned it to third. Bruce Edwards was out by twenty-five feet, ending the threat. In the bottom half of the frame, Musial tripled and scored to restore the two-run lead. In the eighth, the Cards flashed another bit of defensive wizardry, as Marion, using a brand-new, bright-yellow glove, speared a Furillo liner just above his shoe tops with two on and two out. He called it afterward "the hardest ball I've had hit at me in a long time." And in the ninth, a gasping Pollet was rescued by Walker, who ran down Reese's "lusty drive" into left center, and the Cards held on for a 4–2 win. Pollet had allowed eleven base runners, but gutted his way to a memorable victory.

The Dodgers and Durocher dressed "with ornate slowness" in their clubhouse, baffled that they had lost. Several admitted that the long trip west had sapped them of energy, and wondered why they hadn't flown. Durocher mustered enough juice to race out of the shower, naked but for flip-flops, to order the press out of the clubhouse. "This is a real big story," mused one writer on the wrong side of the door. "Leo Durocher not talking should be the lede in every newspaper in the country."

One Dodger available for comment was clubhouse "boy" Johnny Griffiths, a middle-aged man with a gift for making mystifying Berra-style proclamations long before Yogi arrived on the major league scene. Johnny's take on the game—"The Cards didn't look so good today, except for the score."

Pollet certainly didn't look good afterward. He resembled a "feeble old man" as Doc Weaver ripped the tape away from his rib cage and back. Dyer yelled out, "The Cokes are on me, boys!" (Durocher, he was not), but the Cards barely cracked a smile in the locker room, aware of the challenge that still lay ahead. As the First Fan, President Truman, said to *Newsweek,* "I'd feel better if the last two games weren't in Brooklyn."

Dyer decided it would be prudent to keep the baseball gods on his side. He rummaged through a packed-up trunk to pull out the pencil that he'd used to make out that day's lineup card. The superstitious manager wanted to ensure that he would use it again for Game Two.

The Cardinals' train back to New York made excellent time, pulling in after just twenty hours. The *Dodger Special,* on the other hand, was delayed. It arrived at 4:45 p.m., just under twenty-three hours from the time it crossed the mighty Mississip', headed east. No fans were on hand to greet the team at Penn Station—they were busy elsewhere. While the players were sleeping off the journey at home or in hotels, several thousand fans camped overnight along Montague Street for the right to buy unreserved seats for Game Two of the playoff series. More than twenty thousand fans had lined up three days before to buy the reserved seats, despite a cold downpour. The first man to arrive on line offered the night watchman $25 to allow him to sleep in the vestibule of the Dodgers' offices, but he was rebuffed. A special detail of police from the nearby Bergen Street precinct was called in to keep order. "We could sell this game out on out-of-town sales alone," remarked one Dodgers executive in awe. The fans who showed up and braved the elements were taken care of, but not the ones who sent in telegrammed requests.

The foul weather, the violent tendrils of a hurricane making its way north, extended up the Atlantic coast and was a primary cause of yet another deadly air crash, this one in Newfoundland. Thirty-nine army wives flying a charter across the ocean to visit their husbands perished when the plane flew straight into a hillside. Rickey and Breadon no doubt read the news and congratulated themselves, cynically, on not hiring planes for the playoff.

The weather leading up to Game Two was frightful, but as in St. Louis, the baseball gods conjured perfect conditions for the action. Thursday, October 3, was sunny and warm, with the game-time temperature at 65 degrees. Dyer's men had gained confidence from the win back home—the team only packed one day's worth of clothes, assuming they would finish Brooklyn off. The scoreboard operator disagreed. The display announced to incoming fans that St. Louis would be playing at Ebbets Field "Thursday and Friday."

Some 31,437 fans managed to cram into the ballpark's every cranny. Over four hundred of them were active servicemen, who got in free with their uniforms. Scalpers charged $25 for $1.75 seats, but the fish had to buy a seat for Game Three as well, making the total cost of admission $50. There was no shortage of ticket swapping anyway. The *Post-Dispatch* thought, "You couldn't have traded the Brooklyn Bridge (with a sirloin steak thrown in) for a ticket." The arena was festive, as a World Series air pervaded, minus the bunting on the fences. Dizzy Dean sported a ten-gallon hat for the occasion, looking as out of place in Flatbush as one possibly could. Brooklyn Borough President John Cashmore (a born politician with that name) appealed to local businesses to allow employees to listen to the game during the workday.

Murry Dickson and Joe Hatten took the ball for St. Louis and

Brooklyn, respectively. It was a matchup of established vet against nervy rookie, as well as righty versus lefty and army versus navy. Hatten had mostly lived up to his promise, with a 14–11 record and a 2.84 ERA that was eighth-best in the NL. But he was wild, walking 110 and leading the league by plunking 7 batters. Dickson, by contrast, was the model of control, with but 56 walks allowed. The right-hander, 15–6 on the season, preferred to confound hitters and have them dribble harmless grounders than to pump away with heat that was difficult to contain.

The home team scored first, but it was St. Louis that soon imposed its will. Dickson backed his own effort with a second-inning triple that gave the Cards a 2–1 lead. In the fifth, Musial lashed a line drive down the right field line for a two-out double. In the stands, Arthur Daley of the *Times* overheard a nearby fan mutter, "That Musial kin really powder them hits...the bum." Daley wrote, "He almost made it sound tender."

Durocher decided to intentionally walk Kurowski so his lefty, Hatten, could pitch to the left-swinging Slaughter. The move backfired in the Lip's mug. Slaughter slashed a triple to the right-center-field fence, making it 4–1. "It made me very happy when they passed Kurowski to get to him," Dyer later said, giggling. Dusak singled home Country, driving Hatten from the game and beginning a parade of relief pitchers. Up in the broadcast booth, Dizzy Dean was feeling his oats, calling Brooklyn an "up and coming little town" and, in the ultimate case of the pot calling the kettle black, goofing on the way the locals spoke.

St. Louis piled on three insurance runs and led 8–1 entering the last of the ninth. Dickson had been dominant, not allowing a hit since the very first inning, and just two overall through eight. Large sections of the crowd emptied, giving up on their beloved Bums before the last out was made.

Back in St. Louis, Breadon was listening to the game on a portable radio that was a seventieth birthday gift. Several friends and associates were with him, and the mood was loose. As the ninth inning began, Breadon pulled a celebratory bottle of Japanese scotch from his desk, but a friend restrained him before he could pour. "Let's wait until this thing is over," he counseled.

It turned out to be wise advice. Augie Galan led off with a double, the first Brooklyn hit in roughly two and a half hours. Then, a blizzard of bad news for Dickson—a triple, a single, a wild pitch, and a walk to Reese that had Dyer sprinting to the mound to pull his starter. Two were in and two were on, and there was but one out. Ebbets Field, silent just moments before, was now bubbling with noise at the possibility of an epic comeback.

Dyer turned to Brecheen to put the Cards in the Fall Classic. No sooner had Dyer sat back down in the dugout than Edwards bounced a single to left, scoring a run to make it 8–4. The next batter, Cookie Lavagetto, walked to load the bases. Incredibly, the tying run was coming to the plate with only one out.

The entire borough seemed to levitate with noise and anticipation as Stanky strolled up. On deck, batting for Whitman, was Schultz, the hero of the opener and a towering Jeff to Stanky's Mutt. As Brecheen noted afterward, "Stanky had the smallest strike zone in the league, and Schultz had the biggest." Back in St. Louis, "[Breadon's] office was now heavy with nervous fear."

The Brat was clearly looking for his specialty, the walk. He barely moved his bat as Brecheen fired in pitches. Stanky worked the count to full. Then the Cat went with a curve, and Stanky watched it go by for a called strike three. The volcanic noise stilled momentarily. There were two down.

Now the "Leaning Tower of Flatbush" came up. He had homered two days before, and all of Brooklyn was praying for one big swing. "I don't know if the stands could have stood up if he hit one," said Reese. Dyer came out to the mound and told Brecheen to relax. "Forget about a home run. Just get the ball in there." Annoyed at the clichéd advice, the Cat waved him away.

Brecheen put the first pitch in there, as told, and Schultz whacked it down the left field line. It landed in a cloud of dirt...just foul. An inch to the right, and three runs would have scored.

The count went to 3–2 once more. This time, Brecheen threw a screwball, something he knew Schultz wasn't expecting. "I almost fell down swinging at it," said Schultz. He missed the pitch by about a foot, and St. Louis had made it to the World Series.

Fans filed out of Ebbets Field, crushed. Some yelled, "Yes, you're bums, you bums." One approached the celebrating Cardinals with his fists balled, ready to tangle with the whole team, but midseason acquisition Clyde Kluttz endeared himself to his mates by knocking the man down. Another fan dashed in and yanked Slaughter's cap from his head. A squad of four cops chased the man and returned the lid to Country.

Back in St. Louis, the town went nuts. Hundreds of people listening to a radio loudspeaker in front of a liquor store on Washington Avenue danced in the street, stopping traffic. Confetti and wastebaskets were dumped from office buildings. Baggage men wearing broad grins broke the news to travelers at Union Station. Fans eager for World Series tickets started to gather at Sportsman's Park within half an hour of the pennant being won.

Back in Brooklyn, the Cards celebration was somewhat muted by the frigid showers in the visiting clubhouse. Slaughter came out shivering. "You go and make history with everything you do, and then they give you ice water to take a shower in." Garagiola ran up and down the lockers, stark naked, yelling, "There will be no joy in Flatbush tonight!" Dyer pointed out to reporters who had been praising Brooklyn for its gumption that "no one club has the monopoly on courage." The press boys grumbled in reply. They had preferred a Brooklyn win, thus saving them the long schlep west for the Series. Few gave either side a shot against the mighty Red Sox, but at least a Brooklyn–Boston Series would leave more time for carousing. Leo Ward disagreed—on the bulletin board, under

The nonpareil St. Louis Cardinals slugger Stan "the Man" Musial. Before a 1946 series in Brooklyn, he was known as "the Donora Greyhound" or simply "Stash." Dodgers fans chanted, "Here comes the Man," at Musial, and a nickname for the ages was born. (Transcendental Graphics / theruckerarchive.com)

Harry "the Hat" (R) and Dixie Walker (L), the only brother combination to each win a batting title. Dixie's hitting tips would pull Harry out of a slump just in time for October heroics. (National Baseball Hall of Fame Library, Cooperstown, New York)

Bob Feller, in the midst of no-hitting the New York Yankees on April 30, 1946, at Yankee Stadium. Feller would break the major league single-season strikeout record later that summer. (Transcendental Graphics / theruckerarchive.com)

American Baseball Guild director Robert Murphy outside the Pittsburgh clubhouse on June 7, 1946. Inside, the Pirates voted not to strike, dealing a deathblow to Murphy's unionizing attempts. (AP)

Jack "Lucky" Lohrke (seen here in the early 1950s), who survived World War II and several other close calls, including leaving his minor league squad moments before the team bus crashed, killing nine players. (National Baseball Hall of Fame Library, Cooperstown, New York)

Leo Durocher heads for the clubhouse after his Dodgers fell to the Cardinals in the first-ever playoff series. Little did Leo realize he had just finished his last full season managing Brooklyn. (AP/Corbis)

The MVPs of 1946, Ted Williams and Stan Musial, share a laugh. Unfortunately, neither star would have a good World Series at the plate. (AP)

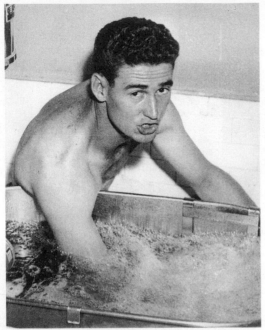

Ted Williams treats his injured elbow after being hit by a pitch in an exhibition game before the 1946 World Series. While Ted claimed otherwise, many felt the injury affected his performance against St. Louis. (AP)

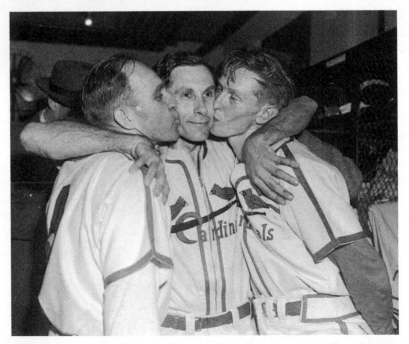

Harry "the Cat" Brecheen receives some love from teammates Enos "Country" Slaughter (L) and Red Schoendienst (R) after beating Boston in Game Six of the 1946 World Series. (Bettmann/Corbis)

The decisive moment of 1946: "Slaughter's Mad Dash" from first base ends with Enos sliding across home, easily beating Johnny Pesky's late and off-target throw. It was the winning run in Game Seven of the World Series, which St. Louis won 4–3. (Transcendental Graphics / theruckerarchive.com)

Ted Williams was disconsolate after losing the '46 Series, the only postseason appearance the "Splendid Splinter" made in his long and brilliant career. Next to Ted is pitcher Mickey Harris, who lost two games in the Series. (AP)

The Cardinals celebrate their title. #1—Whitey Kurowski, #9—Enos Slaughter, #4—Marty Marion, #6—Stan Musial. (Transcendental Graphics / theruckerarchive.com)

the details of the train trip back to St. Louis, the traveling secretary wrote, "Next Victim—Boston!"

Across the hall, Rickey was first to the losing clubhouse, but found himself shoved aside before he could get in. "Just a minute, Pop, stand back!" A burly man with an angry sneer rushed past, followed by a dapper gent with slick-backed hair and movie-star looks. It *was* a movie star—George Raft, Durocher's buddy, with his bodyguard, Killer Gray.

Soon, other friends of Durocher filled his office. The Lip, squeezed out, sat smoking on a trunk outside. He rubbed his face with the palm of his hand, and quietly told reporters, "In my book, the Dodgers did a better job finishing second than the other club did winning. In spring training I looked at this club and couldn't see it above fourth place." Nearby, a box of lovely thirty-eight-page World Series programs the Dodgers had printed up in case they had won sat unused. "I'll probably be here until I die," he told reporters who asked him about his taking the Yankees job.

Durocher had worked wonders. His masterful season pulling the strings of his blue-clad marionettes had taken a merely above-average squad to the brink of a pennant. The Manager of the Year Award didn't exist until 1983, but if it were voted upon in 1946, Durocher would have won in a landslide. As he walked slowly out of the park and onto Bedford Avenue, Killer Gray up ahead to clear out the riff-raff, the Lip could temper his disappointment with pride in the job he had done.

Certainly, few would have believed that he had just managed his last full season in Brooklyn.

Chapter 35
SPLINTERED

TED WILLIAMS LAY in a crumpled heap at home plate, his face contorted in pain. He had just been beaned by Washington Senators lefty Mickey Haefner, and his right elbow was already swelling up. Bobby Doerr, standing down at first base, was horror-struck. The small crowd at Fenway was dead silent. Their collective dreams of a championship season had just turned into an apparent nightmare.

Worst of all, this was a game that should never have been played.

The Sox finished the regular season with a 104–50 mark, the most wins by the franchise since 1912 and a record that hasn't been matched by the team since. Williams was voted the AL Most Valuable Player in a trot, despite falling short of the Triple Crown. It was the first time he had won the award, having lost out to Yankee Joes DiMaggio and Gordon in 1941 and '42, despite hitting .406 one year and winning the Triple Crown the next. His final stat line read thusly—a .342 batting average, 38 homers, 123 RBIs, and a staggering 156 walks. That put his on-base percentage at .497, meaning Ted reached base nearly every other time he came to the plate. His OPS was an off-the-charts 1.164, the third highest of his storied career. His wins-above-replacement player rating, or WAR, was 10.7, the highest of his career. In other words, a team that sported an average player in left field instead of Ted would win eleven fewer games. To appreciate just how incredible Williams was in 1946, consider that Musial's WAR was only 8.4, and Ted's figure was twice that of

Bobby Doerr (5.3), himself an All-Star having an outstanding year. The year Williams hit .406, 1941, his WAR was 10.1.

Williams had considerable help in the Boston lineup. Pesky led the league in hits with 208, batting .335. Doerr and York knocked in 119 and 118 runs, respectively. Along with Dom DiMaggio and pitchers Hughson and Ferriss, the Sox had an astounding seven players in the top thirteen of the MVP voting. As a team, Boston led the AL in runs, hits, batting average, on-base percentage, and slugging percentage. The Sox also committed the fewest errors of any team. Ferriss finished with 25 wins, Tex 20, and the staff compiled a 3.38 ERA, an excellent showing in such a hitter-friendly park as Fenway.

Boston was the gambler's choice against any team from the NL by a wide margin, but the fact that the Senior Circuit was taking so long to decide a pennant winner wrong-footed the team. The age-old sports argument of rest versus rustiness came into play, as the Sox looked at nearly a week of waiting before the Series got under way. "It certainly hasn't helped my disposition to have things drawn out so long," Williams admitted.

Where others saw difficulty, Yawkey and the front office saw a profit opportunity. They announced that a best-of-three series of exhibition games would be staged at Fenway, pitting Boston against an All-Star squad made up of the best the AL had to offer.

Exhibition games were commonplace in the prewar era, and the tradition carried into 1946. Owners used them to gin up extra income and interest, raise money for charity, and wring some more ball out of the players, at little or no cost to the team. In-season exhibition games generally gave players who saw little playing time a chance to play, and the better players, like Williams, sometimes got a bonus for dressing up and taking some no-pressure whacks.

So Joe DiMaggio came up from New York, managing to lose his uniform along the way. He took the field wearing Boston red, a development that led many to speculate on how he would look donning that uniform full-time, should he be dealt for Williams in the coming winter. Newhouser, Greenberg, Eddie Lopat, Dizzy Trout—nearly twenty top players, including Phil Marchildon, came to an icy Boston for the games. They were issued rooms at the Kenmore Hotel.

Cronin liked the idea that his team would get to face some competition instead of lying idle during the NL playoff. The press wasn't wild about it, slamming the games as typical behavior for the "money-mad magnates." As it happened, the exhibitions were a bust at the gate, drawing only a couple of thousand diehards in the chill. The Sox won two of the three games, a Pyrrhic victory if there ever was one.

That's because the plan blew up in Yawkey's face in the third inning of the first game. He was rewarded for his efforts with the sight of his talismanic star writhing in pain. Haefner had tried to throw a sweeping curve, but was unable to grip the ball properly in the frigid air. "My hands were so cold I just couldn't break it," he lamented. Williams was helped from the field, his arm hanging limp at his side. Cronin was white as a sheet. Yawkey looked as if he were about to vomit.

The team doctor, Ralph McCarthy, examined the elbow, and assured Ted that nothing was broken. Just to be sure, however, the two men rushed up the street to McCarthy's office for X-rays, which confirmed the doc's diagnosis. "It should be as good as ever unless unforeseen complications develop," he told the press, while noticeably refusing to speculate about Ted's prospects for the World Series. Williams spent the rest of the afternoon in the Sox whirlpool, the lump on his elbow growing to the size of an egg.

It was the worst-case scenario for the Sox: the club superstar injured on the cusp of the Series during meaningless, and unnecessary, exhibition play. Cronin took the opportunity for some spin, saying the incident was cause for rethinking the playoff system, ignoring the elephant in the room—he had backed the exhibition plan, and now was reaping the whirlwind.

The day wasn't a complete disaster for Boston, thanks to an unlikely source. Earl Johnson, unhittable in April and May, was no longer a reliable pitcher out of the bullpen, in the main because of a family near-tragedy. Early in the summer, he had been called home to Seattle suddenly, as his wife was near death. Johnson gave her no less than six blood transfusions, and she pulled through, but the stress, both physical and mental, wearied him badly. His numbers cratered, and Boston blew leads in several games as a result. But there was another reason, and Hank Greenberg was kind enough to let Johnson in on it—the hurler was tipping off his pitches. Hank felt comfortable revealing the tell, now that Johnson would be facing National Leaguers in the Series.

Useful news as that was, the Hub was completely focused on Ted's damaged ulnar joint. Williams woke up the next morning "in agony," according to Doris, and sitting around a hotel room with nothing to do didn't help matters. Finally, the couple decided to go for a walk and some shopping. Naturally, they were spotted, and the press derided Ted for having the unmitigated gall to walk around when he should have been resting his arm.

The man just couldn't win.

Chapter 36
THE WORLD SERIES

ROBERT KIST OF Clayton, Missouri, was the first to arrive on line. He got to Grand Avenue outside Sportsman's Park around two o'clock in the afternoon of Thursday, October 3, eager to be among those purchasing unreserved tickets for the opening two games of the World Series. Sales of the tickets would begin the following morning.

When the time came to buy his allotted pair of ducats for the first two games, roughly eleven thousand fans were behind Kist, in a mob steadily growing beyond restraint. Several score of police attempted a semblance of crowd control, but they were overwhelmed. Kist bought his seats, but couldn't get out of the crowd that was pressing forward. He was borne aloft by a sea of humanity. The Cardinals' ticket sellers promptly closed the windows, and after ten minutes, order was restored—only to devolve into chaos once the windows reopened.

One woman was so overcome by the scene that she fainted—but the crush was so great, she couldn't fall down, a fact that may have saved her life. After several minutes she was extricated from the crowd and sent to the hospital for observation. A fan named Louis Menendez unwisely wore a Red Sox cap. He was clobbered over the head with a brick and robbed.

It got worse ninety minutes later, when the available tickets were gone and the windows abruptly slammed shut. Several thousand fans were unfulfilled, and let the team know it. Boos rang out along Grand Avenue and adjoining Dodier Street. "We've been here all night!" fans yelled. "As far as I'm concerned, the Cards can go scrub a duck," one shouted. "I wouldn't go see them now on a bet!" Several fights broke out, but the sheer weight of the crowd prevented larger destruction.

It had been two long years since the all–St. Louis World Series of 1944, and to say the city was eager to have the Fall Classic back in town was an understatement.

The Series opener was scheduled for Sunday, October 6, and perhaps it was due to the Sabbath, or more likely the wave of negative reaction for the team's handling of the ticket sales, but the line for unreserved game-day seats was far more orderly. Art Felsch, the self-proclaimed "Number One Baseball Fan," was first in line, having arrived the night before from Milwaukee with his trusty packing box to use as a seat. Felsch was thus the first on line for unreserved seats for the eighteenth straight World Series. In stark contrast to the playoff game six days earlier, tickets were scarce. A *Star-Times* reporter wrote that he saw ushers selling tickets, and newsboys hustling game programs—with tickets tucked inside—for $20 a pop. One lucky fan got tickets by writing AL president Harridge a request. She was Grace Goodhue Coolidge, the former First Lady of the United States.

A "holiday air" settled over downtown as game time (1:30 p.m. CST) approached. Hotels were mobbed, in particular the Chase and the Jefferson, respectively the official baseball executive and press hotels. Streets were jammed with fans, players, buskers, and touts attempting to steer the mob into local eateries and saloons. Most retail stores were closed on Sundays, but the signs on the windows told a familiar story. Shortages were legion, of men's business shirts, of lingerie and underwear, of toilet paper, of butter and milk.

The worst shortage, and the one most on the mind of carnivores across the country, was the continued lack of meat. "The U.S. was frustrated and meat-mad," reported *Life*. Truman had been forced to end price controls on beef, and "a reckless group of selfish men," in his words, conspired to hold back millions of cattle and hogs to drive up demand. Truman's enemies in Congress egged them on—many cattlemen were Republican contributors, and the end of price controls and a hungry populace was good for GOP hopes in the coming midterm elections, bound to be a "beefsteak election," in Speaker of the House Sam Rayburn's construction.

In New York, the shortage was so dire restaurant owners began shuttering their doors. One was desperate enough to hurl himself off the Brooklyn Bridge. The city demanded Truman nationalize the stockyards of the Midwest and end the "meat famine." The black market thrived as prices were driven up to nearly $25 per pound of prime beef. Exacerbating the situation was a report from Nuremberg, where Rudolf Hess, Hitler's deputy führer, complained that he was getting too much beef in jail and would prefer some lighter fare, especially some prunes.

The press gang headquartered at the Jefferson Hotel had dined on sirloin while covering the Series throughout the war, but now, in peacetime, with matters never better in their profession otherwise, they had to suffice with chicken or (horrors!) fish. Something was definitely wrong in America when folks couldn't enjoy a steak during the Fall Classic.

The Sox came to town eager to put the debacle of the exhibition series behind them, and made for the Chase Hotel, only to find that there were few rooms at the inn, thanks to the playoff delay. So the Sox piled wholesale into rooms meant for two. "Fists had been flung, distemper abounded . . . and some of the Sox slept six to a room," wrote Davis J. Walsh of the International News Service. Yawkey and Cronin came from New York, where they had watched the playoff series, and were on a train that broke down several times, at last arriving at Union Station hours behind the team. The Sox pored over scouting reports furnished by the Dodgers. They were constantly reminded that no Bosox team had ever lost a World Series—they were unbeaten in five trips. "Don't let us down!" read the front-page headline in the *Globe.* In many baseball quarters, it was considered unthinkable that Boston would ever lose a World Series—and certainly not this one.

Confidence may have reigned among the Sox players and coaches, but Williams was an island of despair unto himself. His elbow hurt ("See my red splotch?" he would say to reporters who asked him about it), probably far worse than he let on. His head cold refused to go away, and he downed drugs in the clubhouse—he was "stuffed with antibiotics," Doerr remembered decades later. His downturn at the plate had left him doubting his wondrous talents. Grantland Rice wrote, "After several visits with Ted I can only see a bewildered and baffled young fellow who is over-trying, over-anxious, and wondering what it is all about."

Worse than the physical ailments was the mental torture, especially now that rumors abounded that he would be traded after the season, for DiMaggio, for Newhouser, for a bag of balls and a used fungo—it depended on who was writing with what "reliable source." The papers practically needed to add extra sections to accommodate all the trade talk.

All Williams could say about the matter was, "I have kind of a hunch I won't be with the team next year. I've heard nothing, that's just what I pick up from what I read. After all, I probably would be the last one to know about it." There was talk Ted had made a couple of $100 bets that he would be in a different city come spring. So long as it wasn't New York, he could live with it. "I just don't want to play there," he often said. He preferred to quit, or play in Mexico, than to suit up for MacPhail in pinstripes.

Fueling the bonfire were Yawkey's lukewarm non-denial denials when asked directly about his star. By the time the Series traveled to Boston, the owner would be forced to state outright that Williams would be back in 1947, if only to untangle the coils that had wrapped around his star slugger's mind. For his part, Cronin thought the rumors were part of an elaborate "National League scheme" to throw the Sox off stride.

Yawkey was no doubt angered over the public negotiating Williams was engaged in over his coming salary. He was making $50,000 and had been telling the press that figure should rise to at least $75,000, "or the waters of the Charles will be seared from the heat," as one writer described Ted's state of mind. A recent article in *Collier's* on Ted had stirred the Hub too, especially a quote from Williams about Yawkey's supposed lack of empathy for his boys. "Three years in the war and never a letter from [the Sox]," groused Williams to *Collier's*. "Never one to Dom or Johnny Pesky or any of the fellows. Just wait till they want to sign me next year." It was a criticism that went against the run of play, given Yawkey was far more loyal than most owners, often to his ruin. The fact that Ted had been going through a slump while unloading to reporters about his contract stuck in Yawkey's craw.

At least Williams wouldn't have to worry about the Boudreau Shift in the Series, according to Dyer, who insisted, "We plan to play Williams straight up."

Sportsman's Park, the "somewhat dilapidated but none the less [*sic*] historical arena," according to the *Times,* was a miasma of sound and color. There wasn't an inch to be had for a little personal space. Fans clung to walls to peer onto the field, others perched on railings, while the stands were packed four and five deep at each seat. Many who bought standing-room-only tickets were backed so far from the field by the crush they were marooned up against the refreshment stands in the outfield, left without a view of the field.

Tragically, a sixty-two-year-old man chasing a batting practice foul was caught in a pileup for the ball and died of a broken neck. Another, a forty-three-year-old, suffered a fatal heart attack before the game got under way.

There was a decided frontier feel to the crowd. Many wore ten-gallon hats, and many more clanged cowbells, reminders of the Cardinals' appeal to the wide swath of the Midwest and Southwest that was far from the regular migrations of the big-city baseball traveling circus.

Frank Miller's local twenty-five-piece group entertained the crowd with its big-band jazz before the game. At one point, a batting practice fly ball was hit toward the ensemble. An agile musician caught the ball in his French horn.

Perhaps the most colorful character in the rickety grandstand was a seventy-seven-year-old bricklayer from Oxford, Georgia, named Harry Thobe. He wore a white-linen suit, a straw boater, and carried a red parasol, a curious costume for a man who claimed to be "crashing my 18th straight World Series." Thobe liked to say he was the "only bricklayer with diamond teeth," a setting he showed off to anyone who asked.

Veterans who hadn't been to the park since before the war were startled to find pretty girls in slacks walking the aisles selling candy and smokes, rather than young boys in caps. Most found it a welcome change. One thing remained unchanged—the pervasiveness of gambling. Fans still bet on virtually every movement on the field, from whether a pitch would be a ball or a strike, to the number of errors in a given inning, to how many runs the losing team would score. Reporters with deadlines complained that it was difficult to find an unused phone to call in stories, as they were all in use by fans placing bets.

The Game One pitching matchup offered a stark contrast in Texan physiques—strapping Tex Hughson for Boston, puny Howie Pollet for St. Louis. It seemed metaphoric for the Series, the atom smashers from the AL tangling with a scrawny but scrappy bunch from the NL. Indeed, the muscular Sox were heavily favored in the betting odds. St. Louis gambling commissioner Jimmy Carroll, the town's official bookie, put it at 20–7 for the visitors. Those were the longest odds of any team in Series history, save the 1914 Boston Braves, the "Miracle Braves" who won it all despite being a 4–1 underdog. John Drebinger summed up the feelings of most of the country when he wrote, "Stop Musial for a day, and either Slaughter or Kurowski, and you've got the Cardinals pretty well bottled up."

But he also tacked a hedge onto his prediction of Sox in five: "This having been a season wherein nothing appeared too fantastic or incredible to happen, it could be that one more upset lurks around the corner as a rousing climax."

Happy Chandler threw out the ceremonial first pitch, and the Series got under way even as the cheers for the commissioner were still rolling. Hughson hadn't found out that he was starting until he showed up at the park and found a ball under his glove, the standard Sox method of informing pitchers they were toeing the slab. The short notice didn't faze Tex, as he easily retired Musial in his first Series at bat. Pollet started strong too, and neither team got a base runner in the first inning.

In the top of the second, Williams, looking sharp in the Sox's new gray road uniforms, came up for his first appearance, which featured two jolts—a chorus of boos, which would rain down on him during every at bat in St. Louis, and the Cards fielders pulled around toward right in a "Dyer Shift." So the rookie manager had been engaging in some psychic warfare by insisting he wouldn't shift his defense for Williams (a less-charitable explanation was that Dyer was lying through his teeth). Rattled, the Splinter bounded one right into the shift, where Schoendienst grabbed it in short right field and threw him out.

While the crowd was still razzing Williams for his mulishness, the Sox drew first blood. York was hit by a pitch, Doerr walked, and Pinky Higgins lobbed a single to center to put Boston on the board. Higgins had been trying to bunt, and was pulling his bat back when he accidentally connected to drive in the first run of the Fall Classic.

It stayed 1–0 for several tense innings. In the fourth, Slaughter scythed a rocket to deep center. An inside-the-park home run looked possible, but Gonzalez threw up the stop sign, and Country held up with a triple, where he ended up stranded. Slaughter trotted out to his position in right field, shaking his head over Gonzalez's conservative approach.

In the sixth, Williams came up again to a shower of boos. "He gives me the heebie-jeebies every time I look at him," said one fan. On the first pitch, Pollet fooled him so badly "Thumping Theodore" lost control of his bat, which went flying directly over the scalp of Yawkey, who was sitting in temporary box seats at field level. If ever there was a Freudian slip of a bat, this was it. Angry at the laughter from the crowd, Ted proceeded to knock a rope into center for his first hit of the Series, staring at the fans on his way to first. But he too advanced no further, as Pollet squirmed free from trouble.

The Cards tied the game in the bottom of the inning when Musial doubled home Schoendienst. Then they loaded the bases looking for more, but Hughson struck out Garagiola with a "squirt of kickapoo joyjuice," Red Smith's frontier euphemism for a blazing fastball, and the game moved to the seventh tied at one.

The Cards stranded two runners in the seventh, and Terry Moore threw DiMaggio out at second in the top of the eighth to snuff a threat. The play was doubly inglorious for Little Dommie, who managed to rip a large hole in his pants sliding futilely into second.

In the bottom of the eighth, the Cards got a two-out lucky break. Kurowski singled, and Garagiola fell behind 0–2 before stabbing an indifferent fly ball to center. Ordinarily, DiMaggio would have stuck it in his pocket, but he lost the ball in the thick haze that had begun to settle over the field, and it clonked off his arm, falling for a double. "The rusted girders of old Sportsman's Park fairly shook," reported the *Times*. Kurowski made for home, and Garagiola for third. DiMaggio recovered and threw to Pesky, who checked the situation and pumped home, then threw to third to nail Garagiola, a beat before Kurowski touched the plate, apparently saving the run.

But third base umpire Charlie Berry was waving his arms. He called Higgins for interference on Kurowski as the Card rounded third base. Later he said, "Higgins just about put a wrestling hold on Kurowski." Grantland Rice called it a "Doc Blanchard block." The Sox argued for a bit, but after the game all admitted that the call had been correct. The run counted, and the home team led 2–1. When Doerr whiffed to start the Sox ninth, St. Louis was two outs from victory.

Then the baseball gods offset the Cards' good fortune with some for Boston. Higgins grounded one to Marion at short. While "Slats" was Marion's best-known nickname, or maybe "the Octopus," regulars at Sportsman's Park called him "the Groundskeeper," for his finicky habit of picking up pebbles in the dirt around him, real or imaginary. Mostly they were real, as the horrible playing surface in St. Louis was well known throughout baseball. Boston players called it the "Rock Pile" or the "Granite Quarry." "They had infields on those Pacific islands that were better'n this," Pesky complained. DiMaggio had noted the day before that it was a lightning-fast surface, and shook his head at how it might affect play. "Any improvement made here has to be for the better—it can't get worse," thought one writer.

Marion was as adept at handling the minefield as anyone, which is why it was such a shock when Higgins's harmless grounder took a bad hop and caromed right between the Groundskeeper's legs and into the outfield. Marion was further angered when he caught broadcaster Arch McDonald calling it an "easy play" on the radio the Cards had turned on in their dugout.

Rip Russell pinch hit and singled a pinch runner, Don Gutteridge, to third. Dyer stuck with Pollet, and was rewarded when the lefty struck out catcher Roy Partee for the second out. But Tommy

McBride came up and bounced a seeing-eye single between short and third to tie the game at two. "An inch either way and either Marion or Kurowski would have gobbled it up," wrote Jerry Nason in the *Globe.*

In the ninth, Earl Johnson relieved Hughson and showed that Greenberg's tips had been spot-on. His "puzzling slants" set the Cards down in order, and the game went to extra innings. Pollet came back out, despite the fact that nine innings of work had further damaged his injured shoulder and back. He was in such agony that teammates later said he had been digging his fingernails into his palm to deal with the pain. With one out in the tenth, Williams popped out meekly, which brought a roar from the crowd. Up next was a man who years before would have aroused great passion on the western frontier—the Indian brave, Rudy York.

York had hit well at Sportsman's Park all season, slugging .578 and knocking in twenty-three runs against Browns pitchers, triple the number of any other road venue. "St. Louis must be part of the reservation," wrote Harold Kaese. But Pollet had baffled him with slow stuff all game, snarling York "like a kitten in yarn." Now, though, the lumbering first-sacker swatted a 2–0 pitch well over the left field wall and into the refreshment-stand area, aka Blake Harper's Frankfurter and Peanut Emporium, where it was caught by a veteran named Phil Waterman with one hand, the other holding a beer at the time. Waterman had played some ball at Fort Knox with one Joe Garagiola, and was rooting all-out for his Cards. Thus he was "sore" that his catch didn't retire York. "This is a souvenir I could have gotten along without," he said.

The Bostons spilled out of their dugout in celebration. Pollet winced visibly on the mound, dropping into a pained squat. St. Louis was now down 3–2. But fate seemed on their side to the end. Schoendienst led off the tenth by bouncing one to Pesky, who booted it. "The Sox were jittery as new brides all day," thought the *Globe.* Red was sacrificed to second, and Musial and Slaughter were next in the order. The crowd, sensing doom for Boston, made a terrific din.

But Johnson, the "Earl of Emergency," was equal to it. He was a closer before the term meant anything to baseball fans. He had made twenty-four relief appearances during the season, finishing fourteen games. And he put this game away, toying with the best hitters in the National League. Pitching as always with a broad grin, Johnson got Musial, a "poisonous hitter," in the eye of the *Globe,* to ground easily to second, and Slaughter to pop a weak fly to right, and the noise in Sportsman's Park came to an abrupt halt. Boston had won 3–2 and taken a 1–0 lead in the Series. "They need to promote the Earl to Duke," yelped Williams.

York was nearly stampeded by the press corps after the game, backing away from the throng with his hands up "the way people do when a big dog jumps up at them with their friendly paws," thought Jimmy Cannon. All wanted to know what pitch it was that York had deposited beyond the grandstand. But no one agreed. York said, "I just shut my eyes and swung," before dubiously claiming it was a fastball. Pollet said it was a curve, Cronin a scroogie. In the *Star-Times,* Oscar Fraley summed up the confusion. "Sherlock Holmes, Charlie Chan, nor the local homicide squad never tackled a problem such as this one."

Cronin sucked on a cold Coke and bragged on Johnson. "That boy from the Belgian Bulge looked pretty good out there, didn't he? That Johnson's not bad for a boy who had 190 straight days of combat service." The Sox chanted "Three more to go!" in the tiny visitors' clubhouse, one "built for half their number." The raucous celebration was "something new for this fighting ball club from staid Boston," thought Arthur Daley.

It was a much more somber scene across the hall. Dyer was unusually frustrated, actually pushing a reporter away from him. Kurowski angrily fired his glove into his locker and "cussed for a solid minute," but otherwise the Cards were silent, aware they had let a winnable game slip through their grasp, mainly because of a bad bounce. They had been one strike away, and "may never get that close again," Grantland Rice remarked. It was a "game to sire nightmares" in the words of J. Roy Stockton. The *Times* had a more optimistic take, calling the game "a thrilling struggle that was ample reward to fans for the trouble they experienced in purchasing tickets."

Meanwhile, up on the Hill, locals told each other that Garagiola had won the game, it was just that "the other guys lost it." It was as sound an explanation for what had happened as any.

Baseball dominated discussions around breakfast tables and luncheonette counters across St. Louis, but everywhere else the news from Nuremberg was on everyone's lips. According to the wife of Germany's secretary of state under Hitler, Otto Meissner, Der Führer had fathered a child with the wife of Joseph Goebbels! The introduction of scandal into such a sober story riveted the nation for a couple of days. Magda Goebbels, known as something of a Nazi Party socialite, had supposedly had an affair with Hitler in 1934 while at a Baltic Sea resort. The resulting love child, named Helmuth, closely resembled Hitler, and Frau Meissner's newly released testimony claimed that the dictator favored him. Helmuth had committed suicide along with his familial, if not biological, father as the Russians advanced on Berlin.

Meanwhile, the highest-profile Nazi to be sentenced to death in Nuremberg, Hermann Goering, broke down weeping in his cell as photos of his wife and children were removed in preparation for his date with the hangman. Major Frederick Teich, of Newington, Connecticut, the commander of the internal security detachment at the prison, assured the press that suicide precautions were "so good they cannot be improved."

Much of St. Louis was equally despondent after the Cards threw away Game One, but the team itself got over it quickly. Red Smith got to the heart of it by writing, "tempered in the longest, hottest pennant race that ever was, the laborers in Sam Breadon's scabrous yard have had plenty of occasion to manhandle adversity in the past."

Another capacity crowd of 35,815 enjoyed brilliant afternoon sunshine at Sportsman's Park as Game Two got under way. The Cards were in a must-win situation, unable to fall down 0–2 and go to Boston with any realistic hope of returning to the Midwest still alive in the Series. So with his back against the wall, Dyer turned to the Cat, Harry Brecheen, to oppose Mickey Harris.

A stiff breeze was blowing, straight in from center field, and the pitchers took advantage, throwing strikes secure in the knowledge that hard-hit flies would likely stay in the park. Neither team threatened until the third, when Del Rice led off with a double off Harris. Rice was the Cat's preferred catcher, feeling more comfortable throwing to him than to Garagiola. Rice was an outstanding athlete, and probably better at basketball than baseball—he played with the Rochester Royals in the National Basketball League (the forerunner to the NBA, which would begin play for the first time a few weeks later) in the off-season. Ironically, he was 4-F because of a physical disqualification, thanks to bad knees from his days playing college football.

Now Rice took a small lead off second as Brecheen stepped in. The pitcher was no threat with the bat—he'd hit .183 during the season, with 6 measly RBIs. But now he "pickled one" to right, scoring Rice with the game's first run. The crowd erupted at the unexpected largesse. One unlucky fan, who had been filming the proceedings with his rudimentary movie camera, was so startled by the sudden explosion of noise that he dropped his camera, ruining his film.

As updates of the game were announced regularly over the PA system at St. Louis police headquarters, the Cards struck again in the fifth. Rice started the bonfire again with a base hit, and Higgins kicked Brecheen's easy grounder to third. Then the Sportsman's

Park infield decided to even things out from the day before. Moore's bounder to second "suddenly elected to avoid Doerr as if he were a typhoid carrier." The bad-bounce single scored Rice, and Musial brought in the inning's second unearned run with a groundout.

That made it 3–0, and that was more than enough for Brecheen. He cruised to a four-hit shutout, tossing screwball after screwball at the hapless Bostons. "His screwball wasn't a strikeout pitch, but it was an out pitch," Schmidt explained decades later. "He'd keep it down and get one ground ball after another." The Series was tied at one.

"Brecheen had the ball doing just what he wanted," lamented Williams, who had been unable to get the ball out of the infield. "I hate to admit it, but it was beautiful to watch." Not so lovely was the sight of Williams bashing into the shift time and again, like a football team determined to run the ball against an eight-man line. Ted just wouldn't call an audible. "I know that those wide-open spaces in left loom invitingly, but with that short right field fence, the percentages are still in my favor for hitting to right," he explained chattily after Game Two. Cronin was less upbeat. "I've talked myself blue in the face" to get him to hit to left, he complained. "As soon as he steps to the plate all he can see is the challenge that the set-up presents to his hitting ability."

Perhaps there was more to the slump than the shift. Years later, Bobby Doerr would lament that the umpiring had thrown off Williams and the other Sox. "I always felt, ever since that Series, that umpires become pitcher's umpires during the World Series," said writer Clif Keane. "Brecheen would throw inside and Williams would back away and during the season those were balls but during the World Series they became strikes." Indeed, Williams had taken six called strikes in the first two games. For a hitter of his renowned eyesight and plate judgment, that was an unusually high number. Brecheen and Pollet had gotten consistently ahead of the Splinter, and any hitter, no matter how immortal, is less effective down in the count.

Despite the fact that the sun had disappeared behind threatening clouds, happy fans milled on the field long after the final out, reluctant to leave. Ushers prevented them from cutting across the diamond to the Grand Avenue exit, in an attempt to head off damage to the field, which was a classic case of shutting the barn door long after the horse had escaped.

The Sox wanted to get on a chartered plane and get back to Boston as soon as possible, but the weather turned for the worse as they dressed. Before long, sheets of rain poured down, and the flight plans were canceled. Traveling secretary Tom Dowd was forced to feverishly change plans from air to rail at the last moment, leaving the team to make a desultory trek to Union Station for the long train trip back east. As they traveled through western Massachusetts, their tired eyes could look out the window and see Sox fans making obscene gestures at the passing train. A sheet draped across the outside of an envelope factory near Springfield held a succinct message for the Scarlet Hose—RED SOX, YOU SMELL.

Imagine the reaction if the Sox hadn't won the opener.

Chapter 37
THE SERIES COMES TO THE HUB

THE BALL ROLLED to a halt on the infield dirt near third base. No one was within fifty feet of it. A more perfect stratagem to achieve a base hit against this particular Cardinals defensive alignment couldn't have been devised. The only surprise was the identity of the man who had dinked his way on base. He stood down at first, laughing in spite of himself.

Ted Williams had bunted. He had finally foiled the shift.

The packed, sellout crowd of 34,500 were astonished, waiting for several pregnant seconds before letting loose with a standing ovation. At last, Williams had used common sense and hit one where they ain't. The way he was going, the only question anyone had was "What took so long?"

The moment would be summed up in the next day's *Globe,* which used Pearl Harbor–sized headlines to scream, "TED BUNTS!"

The return of the Fall Classic to Boston had apparently been a tonic to Ted's warped noodle.

Certainly, the populace of the "Athens of America" was at a fever pitch for Games Three through Five of the Series, all of which would be played at Fenway Park. "Not since Paul Revere aroused the countryside 180 [actually 171] years ago has this [city] found itself stirred to such a high pitch of excitement," reported the *Times.*

World Series tickets had gone on sale on September 10, and the volume of applications mailed to Fenway would have sunk a Boston whaler. Some five hundred thousand hopeful fans sent in their paperwork, for only sixty-six thousand available tickets over the three games. Those postmarked after 12:30 a.m. simply didn't have a shot. Tickets were thus "harder to come by than a southern accent on the Commons." The line for eighty-five hundred game-day tickets wound down Lansdowne Street in an arctic chill, several tens of thousands strong. The first man on line was the wonderfully named Grover Cleveland Gilmore. The Back Bay resident sat for thirty-four hours in his candy-striped chaise lounge to snag the precious pasteboard.

Unfortunately, the ordeal tuckered Gilmore out to the point that he fell fast asleep in the third inning of Game Three. Even the roar that accompanied the Williams bunt couldn't rouse him. According to his wife, the shouts merely caused him to mumble, "Just wanna see Ted hit one more time, he's sure to park one...," before resuming his snoring. The missus dragged him home, where he slept straight through Game Four as well.

The hope of seeing some October baseball had been a salve for many fans otherwise buffeted by the ill winds of the day. One shutout Boston booster was so disappointed that he sent Dyer a lucky penny that had been in his family since 1826 and vowed to root against the Sox. The *Times* reported that "big business men" unable to find tickets had been bombarding the Fenway catering firm with requests to be vendors for the Series. "Even executives" were clamoring to fling peanuts and hawk beer if it meant a glimpse of the action.

The shift to Boston gave the national press a chance to take its full measure of the local fan base. The writers, especially the New Yorkers who dominated the faction with a national forum, came away with an odd admixture of praise and condescension that is jarring to the modern fan, accustomed as he is to the top-volume shriek of Red Sox Nation.

The general ethos was summed up as neither Brooklyn fanaticism nor the bland sophistication of a Yankees fan but a dull middling of the two extremes. "[The Boston baseball fan] takes his pennant winning in a moderate manner that sets him apart from other fans," thought the *New York Times Magazine*. But at the same time, "Outsiders will be surprised to learn that the Red Sox fan does not wear a tuxedo when occupying a box seat." With the outsized success of this team, though, matters were on the uptick. "Only occasionally now does one come across the traditional Boston fan who shouts "Yippee!" in a thin and timid voice, and then only after looking around carefully to see that he is heard by no one who knows him."

Reverse elitism soaked through the coverage, as the working-class reporters poked fun at the Brahmin swells suddenly discovering hardball. According to the *St. Louis Star-Times*, "even on elite Chestnut Hill, where lawn tennis and tea drinking are customarily the favorite sports," the Sox were the talk of the Olde Towne. Another out-of-town reporter insisted he overheard a conversation between a couple of young chaps with crew cuts. "How do you think the big game will turn out?" asked one. "We have a splendid club," responded his chum. "I would say we shall defeat Princeton by at least six points."

This of course was nonsense, as anyone who had the misfortune of sitting near Mrs. Lolly Hopkins could attest. A Hub version of Hilda Chester or Mary Ott, "Megaphone Lolly" traveled from Providence to Beantown for every game (the Braves, too), a devotion that cost her roughly $1,000 per season (nearly $12,000 in today's cash, not factoring in the exponential increase in ticket prices). She sat in Section 14, right behind the home dugout, and unloaded on players, umps, even writers up in the press box, with a salty monologue that was further seasoned by the amplifier that occasioned her nickname.

There were other inimitable Fenway faithful, including the fellow who hauled an ancient ship bell into games and rang it during rallies; the Sun Bums, denizens of the right field bleachers who stripped to their underwear on hot days; a band dressed in British redcoats that scratched out tunes; and a screechy regular who taunted the opposition with a voice that "sounds like a stick being drawn along a picket fence." During the regular season, one heckler got on a Cleveland player named George Case so remorselessly that Case sprinted from his position in left field into the stands to attack his insulter.

The Sox were New England's team, of course, drawing crowds from several states, which made for a far more diverse group than the assemblage at Ebbets Field. As the *Times Magazine* noted, a typical fan had "to his left a farmer from Maine, the girl to his right a debutante, the man in front of him a GI with a wooden leg, and the gent behind him apparently is a Groton master, the way he keeps imploring the Red Sox, 'come on fellows, do win this game if you possibly can!'"

Older fans would insist that this bunch wasn't nearly the measure of the 1912 or 1916 Bostons ("Kid, if you think Williams is hot stuff, you shoulda seen Tris Speaker"), but overall they were pleased that Yawkey had at last assembled a group worthy of their standards. After all, for a long period between the wars, the best this drowsy franchise could muster were crowds that came to cheer the opposition.

The fixation of the Boston press on Williams also amused and baffled the out-of-town writers. "[Boston's Williams Complex] is worth a journey there to behold it, provided you do not mind the risk of being three to five days late in hearing about the declaration of the third world war or the first rocket flight to the planet Neptune," wrote John Lardner in *Newsweek*. Bill Corum wrote in the *New York Journal-American,* "Yessir, [the press] killed the fatted calf for poor Ted and then batted him about the head with the bones. What happened with the meat, as with all meat, is an OPA secret."

Williams sold papers, plain and simple, and thus was alternately treated as a piñata or a pearl, depending on the needs of the day.

Sometimes, the press couldn't make up its mind. An alert reader perusing the *Globe* that morning would find a note determining that "Ted is low" on page 35, only to flip to page 37 and discover the counterdiagnosis—"Williams Happy."

Currently, of course, the "Knights of the Keyboard," as Ted called the Boston press corps, had their knives out for the underperforming Splinter. "Gents who couldn't hit one of those toy balloons in the park with two tennis racquets are volubly explaining infallible ways to which poor Ted can cope with the shift," noted Corum. Before Game Three, Williams waved away reporters who asked in a thousand different ways about the state of his elbow and his mindset. He preferred to talk about a pair of sick friends who were on his mind, one back in Palos Verdes, California, the other in Peoria, Illinois.

The furor over Williams was handily obscuring the fact that his fellow MVP, Musial, had been a damp squib in the first two games as well, with just 1 hit and 1 RBI in 9 trips to the plate. The less-numerous Mound City press, exemplified by the genteel Bob Broeg, weren't as bloodthirsty as their Boston compatriots, and Musial was far too winning a personality to be the target of backlash after two poor games.

Still, the Man was bothered by the troubling start. Two years earlier, he had played well in the Streetcar Series against the Browns, topping .300 and slugging over .500. But that was at the height, or more appropriately the depths, of wartime baseball. The competition wasn't much better than what he had faced playing ball for the navy in 1945. In 1942 and 1943, Musial had been mediocre in the Fall Classic. In those two Series, plus the first two games of this one, covering a dozen games, he was only hitting .222, with 3 RBIs and no homers.

So he was eager to do something to shake himself from the doldrums, and that was obvious from the first inning of Game Three. Batting on a cold but sunny afternoon, as advertising balloons floated above the scene, Musial walked with two outs and stole second, putting him in scoring position for Slaughter. But Musial was interested only in a solo act. Boo Ferriss was Boston's starter, and as he looked to the plate, the former "Donora Greyhound" took off for third, only to be easily thrown out when the pitcher calmly stepped off the rubber. It was a long, humbling trot back to the dugout after that, the Fenway fans proving their vocal capabilities were at least comparable to those in Brooklyn.

The Sox compounded Musial's misery in the bottom of the frame. Pesky singled off Cards moundsman Dickson with one out, overcoming a bout of the jitters that he admitted was plaguing him. "It didn't help to have well-wishers telling me about it all the time," he laughed. He moved to second on a grounder. Williams was intentionally walked, a sign of utmost respect given his struggles. That brought up York, and the hero of Game One provided the home folks with an encore, pulverizing a "let-up curve" from Dickson over the word "Shadow" in the Gem Blades ad board ("Avoid Five O'Clock Shadow") on the tall wall in left for a three-run homer.

"I didn't want to walk him," Dickson explained after the game, "and I thought he'd be looking for a fastball, so I threw him a curve that didn't fool him a bit." For his part, York called it a "dry spitter." "It was a bad pitch, that's all," Dyer said ruefully. "I love Indians," Ferriss said of his Cherokee catcher after the game.

Dickson's early struggles might have been traced to the fact that his warm-up pitches were interrupted by photographers who kept running between him and the plate. Prevented from properly stretching out his arm in the chilly air, Dickson was still trying to loosen up during the first inning. "That was my own fault," he admitted. "I could have gone to the bullpen while we were batting. Maybe I should have knocked over a couple of those photographers."

The three runs were more than enough for Boo, who dominated the Cards as thoroughly as Brecheen had held the Sox down the game before. The final was 4–0, and the only time a Cardinal got past second base was with two outs in the ninth, when Musial finally got a hold of one and tripled to deep center. But Ferriss struck out Slaughter (strike three was pitch number 107), and the game was done. True to his habit, Boo grabbed the ball as a keepsake, and gave it to his mother, who was sitting behind first base. He was now 14–0 on the season at the Fens. The Sox had restored order and led two games to one.

All talk in the happy Boston clubhouse, and in the papers the following day, was of Williams's capitulation back in the third inning. As Red Smith wrote in the *Herald Tribune,* "The Kid's bunt was bigger than York's home run. 34,500 witnesses gave off the same quaint animal cries that must have been heard at the bonfires of witches in Salem when Williams, whose mission in life is to hit baseballs across Suffolk County, pushed a small, safe roller past third base." Drebinger added, "Boston's pet and number one problem child had made a monkey out of a very unorthodox defense and the home folks were happy." The only one silent on the subject was Williams himself. "It's not my day, it's Ferris and York's," he said, and left quickly.

Dyer had even less to say. He trudged into the clubhouse, muttered "Munger" when asked about the starter for Game Four, and went straight to his office, not to reappear.

Williams was bunting, and Dyer was blowing off reporters. Only three games had been played, and the Series was already one for the books.

The Sox win on Wednesday only catalyzed the already simmering passions in Boston. A melee erupted on the game-day ticket line Thursday morning, fans brawling with police who desperately tried to restore order. Not enough windows had been opened to serve the demand, and as a result, a large number of the 125-man security detail was injured in the brannigan. Police Commissioner Thomas

Sullivan was so upset that he canceled the detail for Game Five the next day.

It may well have been that the fighting fans were upset over all the ordinary, day-to-day goods they still couldn't acquire. In addition to meat, everyday items such as eggs, cheese, coffee, milk, sugar, and toilet paper were almost impossible to find. A truck strike in the city had even caused a shortage of baby food. A story in the *Globe* told of housewives fistfighting over goods in stores across the city.

The 175 friends and family of Cronin's in from California to watch the Fenway portion of the Series put their food-gathering troubles on hold for a few days while partaking in hotel fare. The Sox manager was chesty before Game Four. "The show's over after tomorrow's game, boys," he assured reporters. Many of them took notes while fighting sleep. The press headquarters, the Copley Hotel, had been overbooked thanks to the playoff delay. "You had to be Harry S. Truman or Dizzy Dean to get a room without a gun," wrote one St. Louis reporter. "Here's a tip to the out-of-town visitor," wrote Jerome Sullivan. "Bring a full field pack complete with pup tent, blankets, and bedding roll with you. There is no room in Boston hotels, period. Bring some K-rations as well, for there is no meat in town, either."

Dozens of newsmen were forced to sleep in the lobby, which was constantly packed with "suave notables of film and other worlds," including the underworld, as a "queer assortment of rough looking characters talked Series odds" long into the night. All over the city, strange bedfellows were formed as people packed into hotel rooms, echoing the national housing shortage. Durocher was staying with three NL umpires, "which shows you how tough it is to get a room in this town," according to the *Atlanta Journal*. The Kenmore said it would have no problem accommodating Hank Greenberg in a ballroom. "What he needs is a seven-foot bed, and we have one," the night manager told the *Globe*.

The Cards were at the Kenmore too, where the worst they had

to deal with was an invasion of bobby-soxers in the lobby, screaming for autographs and hounding bellboys. To escape, several players took in "Captains Courageous" at the Orpheum Theatre.

A common theme in both hotels and among fans across the nation was the performance of the Mutual Network radio announcers, in particular the genial but bland lead broadcaster, Arch McDonald. McDonald called Washington Senators games during the season and was best known for saying, "They cut down the old pine tree!" after Senators wins. McDonald was one of the first voices of New York baseball, broadcasting Yankees and Giants home games in 1939 after MacPhail brought Barber to Brooklyn. Arch had dubbed Joe DiMaggio the "Yankee Clipper," but otherwise proved too cliché-ridden and low-key for the big city. He was known as "Master of the Pause" for his habit of calling a pitch, and simply staying silent until the next one. He played better in DC, where a slower style was more appreciated.

Arch and his Series partners, Red Sox broadcaster Jimmy Britt and columnist Corum, were called dull, drab, and severely lacking in enlivening detail. *Variety* panned the national broadcasts as "terrible." "Britt sounded pedantic and stilted and at times seemed to be talking about some game he remembered seeing during spring training," opined the entertainment mag, continuing, "A Broadway wag accused McDonald of trying to muscle in on Ralph Slater's racket—you know, the hypnotist who defies you to stay awake."

St. Louis fans were especially vexed, accustomed as they were to the captivating likes of Dizzy and Harry Carey. The *East Side Journal* wrote that McDonald "broadcast a game with the same lack of animation with which the treasurer of a Morticians Association might read his annual report." Much of the blame went to the sponsor, Gillette, and its Detroit ad agency, Maxon, which had selected the trio, notably leaving the Ozark-accented and English-challenged Dean out of the booth. The razor company pushed the blame onto Chandler, while stealthily trying to recoup the $175,000 it was paying as title sponsor. Thousands of fans wrote angry letters and telegrams to Gillette, including one critic who set his complaints to verse:

> Our razor blades are keen
> The sharpest ever honed
> Broadcasts! They have been
> The dullest ever droned

Williams, himself hoping to regain his usual razorlike keenness, spent much of batting practice lining ropes to left, apparently having found religion. He ducked into the clubhouse as the Cards meandered onto the field, many of them aiming their bats at the sky like shotguns, mocking Williams's penchant for coming to Fenway in the early mornings to shoot the birds that congregated in the grandstand.

The Cardinals may have been down two games to one, and the sharps put long odds on a comeback, but they remained confident in the clubhouse. The feeling may have been uncorked by a pregame stem-winder from Dyer, who uncharacteristically lit into the team for playing "listless, stupid ball." Red Barrett loudly told anyone listening that Hughson had no chance of beating the Cards on three days' rest. The numbers backed him up. Tex was 8–1 on the season with four or more days off, but a pedestrian 12–10 when given just three days to reenergize his wing.

The team also remained faithful to Munger, even though he was still trying to regain the strength and stamina on the hill he had displayed before the service. Few could forget the sizzling stuff he had displayed in 1944, when he had gone 11–3 with a 1.34 ERA, and with Pollet still questionable with his injury, there was little second-guessing of Dyer's choice of starters, even if Munger had been unimpressive in his ten appearances since returning from Germany. The big redhead walked out to the mound with a "wad of eatin' terbacker bulging in his right cheek" and went to work.

It was another frigid afternoon in New England, "a topcoat as necessary as a scorecard." Luminaries including George Raft, Toots Shor, Joe Louis, and Joe DiMaggio were in the crowd, emerging from several layers of warm clothes to sign autographs. Robert Murphy was spotted before the game, headed away from the Fens, as though the players' "pancaking" of his union plans had turned him off the game. Kurowski brought his four-year-old boy onto the field, swaddled in a huge coat. Whitey introduced his son to umpire Al Barlick, and his kid refused to shake Barlick's hand.

The chill didn't seem to bother Big Red, as he disposed of the Sox lineup the first time through without a hit. By the time Moses got Boston's first knock in the third, the Cards were ahead 6–0. A "Modern Boston Massacre," in the eyes of the *Globe,* was under way.

Barrett and the others who questioned bringing Hughson back on three days' rest were spot-on. It was apparent that Tex's fastball lacked zip when Slaughter turned on a second-inning heater and sent it four hundred or so feet into the right field stands, a shot that "imperiled the occupants" of the seats there. It was the first Cards run in fourteen innings. Slaughter, true to his nature, sprinted all the way around the bases, "as though Governor [Maurice] Tobin would veto the hit before he got home." Two more scored on a hit by Harry the Hat and a Pesky error, a portentous chain of events, as it happened.

The third inning undid Hughson, as the "run-starved Redbirds tore into him like a pack of hungry wolves." He surrendered a single to Schoendienst, threw away a sacrifice bunt attempt by Moore, and left a fat curve hanging for Musial to poke off the giant wall for two runs. That was it for Tex—five runs allowed, and an early shower. He hurled his glove into the dugout wall with more force than he had any of his fastballs. "Poor Tex," muttered Rowena Hughson, his wife, in the stands. During the pitching change, Williams slumped miserably against the left field scoreboard.

The game was as good as over. The "Blokes in the Red Blazers" pummeled six different pitchers for twenty hits. Cronin was forced to "juggle his pitchers as fast as Leo Durocher." The ninth inning was a twenty-minute-long debacle for the home team, as the Cards scored four runs on five hits and two Boston errors, mercifully leaving the bases loaded. About a third of the 35,645 that had jammed the park remained to see Munger finish off the 12–3 rout. Slaughter, Kurowski, and Garagiola all had four hits (tying the Series record), Marion three, and every starter at least one. The Series was tied at two, or as the inimitable Diz put it, "tighter than a ranch hand on Saturday night."

The press was astounded that the Cards, who oddly, despite the presence of strong hitters throughout the lineup, were casually dismissed as a banjo team reliant on defense, could so thoroughly destroy an excellent hurler such as Hughson. "You might as well say Babe Ruth was famous for all those defensive home runs," wrote one astonished onlooker. Inevitable comparisons were made to the Battle of Bunker Hill and other slugging outbursts by the Colonial Army. About the only positive the *Globe* could find in the day's events was that none of the Sox wives had worn the same hat as she had to Game Three.

Fans back in St. Louis celebrated the win, and some got an extra treat. A meat truck overturned downtown, and the locals descended on the spilled beef like piranhas. Meanwhile, Yawkey's horrid day was completed when he returned home to learn that the hotel room of his sister, Mrs. Emma Auerbacker of Louisville, Kentucky, had been burgled. She lost $2,700 in diamonds and emeralds.

Friday, October 11, was Eddie Dyer's forty-sixth birthday, and it was only appropriate that he turned to his favorite son, Howie Pollet, to help make it a happy one. Pollet was on the field early, stretching his shoulder and back, hoping to make it through one more big game. But his body didn't have any miracles in it. "Pollet asked me to tell Dyer that his back was killing him," recalled Schmidt. "I did, but Eddie didn't want to listen to me."

The infirm Pollet wouldn't have to worry about one key element of the Boston attack. Doerr had been forced to leave Game Four late in the afternoon after suffering a migraine brought on by looking into the sun, and he would be unavailable for Game Five. His replacement at second base was Don Gutteridge, whom the Cards knew well. Gutteridge had been a Redbird early in his career, and spent the war years with the Browns, including the '44 team that tangled with the Cards in the "Streetcar Series." He had been in Toledo as a player-manager for much of 1946, but the Sox begged him to come aboard midseason as bench depth, and here he was, back in the World Series.

Gutteridge celebrated his good fortune by leading off matters for the Sox with a base hit off Pollet. "Eddie's Boy" clearly wasn't right. He had gutted his way through two solid postseason starts, but this time, he lasted a mere ten pitches. Pesky singled after Gutteridge, and Pollet grasped his side in agony. With one out, Williams lined a single to right over the shift to knock in his first (and only) run of the Series. Dyer came to get Pollet after that.

Alpha Brazle limited the damage for a while, but the Cardinals had trouble with Joe Dobson. The burly righty, called "Burrhead" for his curly shock of hair, had lost his left thumb and part of a forefinger to a boyhood accident involving a dynamite cap and some juvenile hijinks. He spent his war service at Camp Wheeler in Georgia, pitching steadily, so he was in good shape for the '46 season. His wife was the secret hero of this day. Against the odds, she had managed to find a restaurant that served steak and surprised Joe with a reservation the night before the game. "There hasn't been any meat in our house since the boys made their last western trip," she told reporters.

The protein gave some zip to Dobson's "atom ball," a sharply breaking curve that he used as his out pitch. "It exploded like 'Operation Crossroads' [the code name for the Bikini nuclear tests]," he said with a touch of crass. After an unearned run due to a Pesky error in the second, Dobson and his nuclear device handcuffed the Redbirds the rest of the way.

Gutteridge singled again in the bottom of the second, barely scoring Partee, giving the Sox a 2–1 lead. Garagiola argued the call bitterly, claiming he had blocked the plate—and showed the ump a cleat mark in his arm as proof, to no avail. In the fifth, the Sox threatened again. Pesky singled again, and stole second. DiMaggio walked, bringing Williams to the plate.

Behind the dish, Garagiola chatted up his new pal. "I always thought he was stuck up," Joe admitted later, but after joshing with Ted over the course of five games, he had changed his mind. Williams had a habit of filling in the cleat holes others had left in the batter's box, and Garagiola yelped, "I do the same thing!" After that, the two were fast friends. "The original dream of boyhood is big and clean in him and untouched by the sickness of greed that is gripping the world," Jimmy Cannon wrote of Garagiola that morning, and he spent most of the Series sporting a broad grin, astonished at his Providence. "I saw Chico Marx the other day," he gushed after Game Four, "and I was looking for George Raft all game, but didn't see him." "He's walkin' on air," said his roommate, Slaughter. "He's the happiest boy in the world." It didn't hurt that his admirers on the Hill had just gotten him a new car.

But he wasn't some overawed yokel—the kid belonged on the big stage, as shown by his four hits in Game Four. Now, with two on and nobody out, he showed more mettle by calling for a high fastball from Brazle, anticipating a double steal. Sure enough, the play was on. Williams struck out on a ball near his eyes, and Garagiola hummed one to third to nail Pesky, a rousing strike-'em-out, throw-'em-out double play.

But cunning wasn't enough for the Cards on this icy afternoon. Leon Culberson, the third right fielder Boston used in the Series, homered to make it 3–1, and in the seventh, the Sox busted it open. Dommie started the rally with a double. In a clear signal of Williams's weakness, Brazle pitched to him and struck him out again, then intentionally walked York. Pinky Higgins doubled to foil the strategy, and later in the inning Marion let a sharp grounder carom off him for a two-run error to make it 6–1.

Harry the Hat pulled a pair of cosmetic runs back with his fifth hit of the Series in the ninth inning, but Dobson finished off St. Louis for the complete game victory, 6–3. The Sox now led 3–2 in the Series, and celebrated in the clubhouse as though they had won it all. After all, the teams had alternated winning each game, so logic dictated Boston would win Game Seven, at worst. Dobson, overcome with emotion, was too teary to speak with reporters.

Down the hall, Dyer concentrated on the positives, mentioning Walker's continued strong play and his team's resilience. As Marion said, "You can't name a single game we haven't won when we absolutely had to. We can do it again." But all eyes were on the corner of the room, where the indispensable heart of the Cardinals was writhing in pain as Doc Weaver examined him.

Slaughter had been hit on the elbow by a pitch in the fifth inning. It wasn't an "atom ball" but a good, old-fashioned ninety-five-mile-an-hour heater from the strapping Dobson. Country hadn't reacted when nailed, in true country hardball fashion, and in a show of defiance stole second on the next pitch. But the pain forced him from the game a couple of innings later. The elbow had swollen alarmingly since. Now both teams had a star slugger with a lame appendage.

The Cardinals trained it back to Missouri on the *Pennsylvania Special,* which needed a hospital car to minister to the various damaged players. Slaughter wore "one of them electric jackets pitchers wore in those days but it didn't do me no good." The heavy covering over his arm and shoulders made Enos sweat as if "he'd just climbed out of a kettle." Moore was limping badly on his damaged knee, which had the consistency of polenta. Only a "special 'dope' ointment," as the press called it, applied by Doc Weaver before every game, allowed him to play. Marion's back was so stiff that after the season he would forgo his usual winter job at a printing firm in town and retreat to his home in Richburg, South Carolina, to rest it. Pollet, Rice, Grodzicki—the infirm outnumbered the healthy on the Redbird roster. "There's gloom aboard this special train," reported the *Star-Times.*

The casualty count nearly worsened when the *Special* collided with a stalled auto that straddled the tracks in El Dorado, Ohio, about thirty miles from Dayton. "I tried to start it but I couldn't so I jumped out just before it was hit," said the driver, Gene Alger. His car was demolished, but a trailer full of corn he was towing was undamaged—"not an ear was lost," according to reports.

The Sox flew back west, save for eight players who preferred the train, including Doerr, who didn't want the pressurized air to inflame his migraines. Despite the two games of resistance from the Cards, the Boston team remained a "wisecracking, swaggering crew that cockily predicted a speedy end to the Series," according to the United Press. "Don't worry about any seventh game," Cronin, who turned forty on Saturday's off day, assured all who listened. "There won't be one." If Cro's braggadocio was spot-on, Boston would have its first championship since 1918.

Chapter 38
CAT SCRATCH FEVER

THE *PENNSYLVANIA SPECIAL* backed into Union Station. Slaughter, still sweating heavily, was off the train seconds after it stopped, pushing through the thousand or so fans who greeted the team so he could race to St. John's Hospital for X-rays. They were negative, but he remained unable to wiggle his fingers. "My whole hand's dead," he admitted to Jimmy Cannon. Early reports off the train en route to St. Louis put Slaughter as being out for the remainder of the Series, and even Robert Hyland, the team doctor who had procured the music for the team the night Musial took over at first base, concurred.

But Doc Weaver wasn't so sure. He spent the Saturday off day wrapping Slaughter's wing in towels soaked in hot saltwater, and lugged a portable electric heater to Slaughter's room at the Chase, where Country "baked out" the elbow. While contrary to modern training thought, which prefers ice, the heat treatment had the effect of reducing the swelling to the point Enos felt he could give Game Six a go.

The placebo effect shouldn't be discounted. The simple fact was that Slaughter was determined to play, and no doctor was going to dissuade him. Hyland had told him in no uncertain terms that playing was an enormous risk. "You have such a bad hemorrhage that if you get it in the elbow again I may have to amputate your arm," the "famous surgeon" (as the *Times* referred to him) told his patient.

"I guess I'll have to take that gamble—the fellers need me," he told Hyland. "No matter what you say, I'm playin'."

The off day was like Super Bowl week, where the combination of hundreds of reporters and no game made for some brief illusory scandals. Several Red Sox, including Ferriss, York, and Culberson, took in the St. Louis Zoo in Forest Park, where the *Post-Dispatch*'s W. J. McGoogan encountered them complaining about the meager shares they would be getting due to the small size of Fenway and Sportsman's Parks. The players then spent the next twenty-four hours or so insisting there was no place they'd rather be than playing for a championship.

Grover Cleveland Gilmore, the fan who had passed out cold after waiting two days on the ticket line at Fenway, had become a press sensation, and the *Globe* did its part, picking up the tab for Gilmore to fly to St. Louis. Gilmore required special fortitude to get there, as he had never flown before. Originally booked on American Airlines, the flight was canceled due to "traffic conditions." Eastern, Trans World, Northeast—all came up empty. Desperate, he was about to cancel when United got him on a flight west. "I felt a little shaky," he admitted, but he felt better during a photo op with his namesake, Grover Cleveland Alexander, the Hall of Fame pitcher.

In more poignant news, Harry Walker learned that he had a new daughter. Carole Walker was born back in Leeds, Alabama. After the huge scare when his son, Terry, was hit by the car, Walker was eager to get down south as soon as possible to be with his injured boy. At the same time, he was certain he would play a big role in the de-nouement of the Series, especially now that a flaw in his stance had been ironed out. It was Dixie who had seen it when the Dodgers played the Cards in September, when Harry was slumping badly. "You're lunging and taking your eye off the ball," big bro counseled, despite the pennant race. "Try pulling your feet together. It won't seem natural at first, but it works." Sure enough, the Hat started to hit, just in time for the postseason.

Housing, or lack of it, dominated the off-day talk, as it had throughout the year in all walks of life. The playoff delay meant the Series now collided head-on with a Missouri medical examiner convention and state PTA conferences, which took up most of the available hotel space. Folks already ensconced in their rooms refused to vacate for incoming baseball fans, with the result that a great number slept in cots in hotel dining rooms, or on park benches, or not at all.

That was certainly the case in the area surrounding Sportsman's Park, where once again the ticket lines took over. "Early [Sunday] morning, Sullivan [Street] near Grand [Avenue] looked like a bivouac, with a dozen fires blazing along the ball park wall," reported the *Post-Dispatch*. "Fans waiting for tickets stood around the fires, heads wrapped in blankets," to ward off the chill, down below freezing.

A crowd of 35,678 got into the ramshackle old park for Game Six, creating a roar that began about an hour before first pitch and never let up. The chill had once again been burned off by an Indian-summer sun, and the warmed crowd let loose with a fusillade of noise, including a police siren that sounded regularly in the right field corner. The cacophony went on despite the absence of Mary Ott, the leather-lunged fan, who was sick and frustratingly unable to attend the season's final home stand.

Fans were asked not to bring boxes, stools, or chairs inside, as they had in the first two games. And a "one fan per step" in the aisles policy was strictly enforced. The throng strained to hear Benjamin Rader, whose band was fresh off a well-received appearance at the signature St. Louis event of the season, the Veiled Prophet Ball, play "To Each His Own," and other tunes before the game.

Down in the clubhouses, a drama was unfolding that for some players was every bit as important as the game to follow. The small Series pool, from which shares would be paid out to each player, was originally meant to be augmented by the money Gillette paid baseball for the radio rights to the Series. Instead, that cash was now ticketed for the nascent pension fund, and several Boston players were pissed about it. Marty Marion, the driving force behind the plan, spent several minutes in the enemy clubhouse trying to change the minds of the holdouts, while Pinky Higgins gave an impassioned speech on behalf of players who had already retired from the game. The browbeating worked—the Sox voted unanimously before the game in favor of the plan. On his way out to the field for the game, Marion gave Happy Chandler a thumbs-up—a new pension system was ready to go.

Brecheen was the obvious starter for St. Louis. Hughson seemed the equally likely starter for the Sox, but Cronin mysteriously went with Harris, announcing that he wanted to save Hughson for Game Seven if things went south. Considering Ferriss was ready to go for Boston the next day, it seemed a curious stratagem—holding back the staff's second-best hurler in case the ace needed bailing out. Cronin's gamble to start Dobson and rest his top two in Game Five had paid dividends, thanks to his "Celtic ancestry." In the words of Arthur Daley, "He consulted with Leprechauns." Now, he was playing his hunch once more.

To Dyer, it was defeatist thinking he would never have countenanced. He gleefully accepted Cronin's largesse, saying, "We got to Harris once and we can get to him again." It was another way to give his team the psychic edge. *See?* he could tell his team. *They still think so little of you guys in the opposing dugout that they're sure any of their pitchers can beat you!* "These Cardinals are not a Gashouse Gang," noticed Harold Kaese. "Eddie Dyer had made them a team of psychologists. They beat your brains out with a plush-covered window weight, instead of a hammer."

But it was the Cat who struggled at first. Boston loaded the bases in the first inning, and Dyer had Red Munger warming up as York strolled to the plate with one out. But Brecheen got him to hit into a double play, and Munger sat down.

A sacrifice fly from Moore got the Cards on the board first. Later in the third inning, Musial came up with two out and a man at second. He bounced one to deep short, and legged out an infield hit. "You'd swear he was just a .210 hitter happy to have a slim chance to get on," thought the *Post-Dispatch,* commenting on the way the usually staid Musial pumped his fist upon beating the throw. Kurowski followed with an RBI single to make it 2–0 Cards.

Slaughter received a tremendous ovation when he first ran onto the field, and got an even larger salute now as he dug in to face Harris. Up in the stands, Dr. Hyland held his breath. "I said to my neighbor, 'there is a boy diving himself out of baseball,'" he said later. Country, whose attitude was summed up with a pregame "to hell with my right arm!" gunned the first pitch he saw back up the middle to score Musial and chase Harris from the game (Enos would aggravate the cursed arm again on a pickoff, and need more X-rays after the game). Cronin glumly went to replace Harris with Hughson, wondering what would have happened had the tall Texan started the contest, especially after Hughson shut out the Birds on two hits over the next four innings. Harris went berserk in the Boston clubhouse, slamming his glove on his locker over and over and kicking his civilian clothes to the floor.

The choice of starter would haunt Cronin well after the Series. As the *Times* put it, "There is nothing sadder in baseball than the hunch that goes astray." Daley went back to the Irish well for his commentary: "The Leprechauns...gave him a bad steer this time. Perhaps Joe feels—the meat shortage being as acute as it is—that a bad steer is better than no steer at all."

For his part, Brecheen was once again mystifying the Sox lineup, conducting a master class in changing speeds and eye level. No less an authority than Harry's wife, Vera, had pointed out to Broeg that Brecheen had faced most of the Boston hitters in the minors and knew how to attack them. Williams, who hadn't hit a ball out of any park since September 11, agreed with Mrs. Brecheen. "They certainly know how to pitch to me, cause I'm getting what I'm not expecting." Ted managed his fifth hit of the Series, another single, in the ninth with Boston down 4–1, but York hit into another double play to end the game. "Cronin should send his regulars to the zoo, lure them into cages, and replace them with orang-outangs [*sic*] who can hit," suggested Kaese.

Dyer's first words to the Cat in the happy Cards' clubhouse were "I wish you were twins." Brecheen had been masterful once more, giving up only three hits over the final seven innings. "The Red Sox have some fine hitters when you give them what they want," he said, as a 78 of "Woodchoppers Ball" had the happy squad dancing around the room. "But I didn't do that." Photographers made Slaughter and Schoendienst kiss the Cat over and over again for the cameras. "He doesn't get this many from his wife," cracked Country, happy to hear the X-rays were negative once more. For his part, Williams's ghostwriter Hy Hurwitz used some grisly feline flavor in "Ted's" column. "The Cat not only skinned us again, but he feasted on our flesh and scratched on our bones."

The Cat was so effective he overcame a major faux pas from Cards' PA announcer Charley Jones. As Brecheen warmed up for the ninth, he heard Jones tell fans that tickets for Game Seven would be available for sale the following day. The St. Louis dugout, aware that Jones had just spit at the baseball gods, were apoplectic. "We were ready to shoot that guy," recalled Munger. But superstition was no match for the Cat's stuff.

The season, appropriately and to the consternation of many writers, would last as long as possible and be decided by an all-or-nothing Game Seven. The World Series was "in the laps of the Gods," as the *Times* put it, and the immortals had been capricious indeed through six games.

Chapter 39
THE MAD DASH

THE SERIES TOOK Monday, October 14, off, so the Cardinals would have a full day to sell tickets for Game Seven. The late notice combined with the beginning of the workweek to prevent mass hysteria, but the expected thousands lined up for the chance to witness the deciding game. Anything was likely to happen Tuesday afternoon. As Daley had written in the *Times,* "This has been such an astonishing and incredible show that no one would raise an eyebrow if the Mississippi River suddenly changed its course and carried Sportsman's Park out to sea—not a bad idea at that."

Cardinals fans jamming the streets passed around rumors. A story that Louis B. Mayer of MGM Studios fame wanted to buy the Cardinals and move them to Los Angeles had spread like wildfire during the Series. Breadon had to announce that he had no intention of selling. Of more immediate concern was that Slaughter supposedly was out after aggravating his injury. Country spent most of the day with his elbow wrapped tight, and he missed the light workout the Cards held around noon. But short of a fresh bullet wound, there was no chance Slaughter was going to miss Game Seven. "The weak fall by the wayside, the strong shall carry on," he said, laughing, while stretched out on the clubhouse rubbing table.

Another worried word passed around the streets of downtown St. Louis was that Williams had found his groove in batting practice and was smashing homers left and right. In fact, Ted was busy getting tips from Tex Hughson, of all hitting experts, who called the Splinter over after a session in the cage and advised him to correct part of his stance. Ted told reporters that he had received a letter from a fan calling the Dyer Shift "a crime" and that "It's up to you to make crime pay." "That's what I'm trying to do tomorrow," he said, laughing. The Cards' manager was also hearing it from fans complaining about his "gangster tactics" that were "bound to upset the poor fellow" (meaning Williams). Dyer didn't signal any inclination to change his strategy due to hate mail.

After the workouts, the players mostly hit the cinema to avoid thinking about the game the next day. *The Big Sleep* ("Bogie and Bacall, together again! Terrific again!") had just been released and was a popular choice among baseball people looking to kill time. *The Best Years of Their Lives,* the big hit of the year that captured elements of the nation's difficult postwar homecoming, was no longer in theaters, so other popular choices were *Nobody Lives Forever* with John Garfield at the Ambassador or Ava Gardner in *The Killers* at the Fox. The Cardinals were probably less partial to Danny Kaye as *The Kid from Brooklyn* and to *Mr. Ace,* which starred Leo Durocher's buddy George Raft.

Judgment at Nuremberg was still fifteen years from being made, but the events that made up its final reel were unfolding in Germany even as the teams got ready for Game Seven.

The condemned Nazis in Major Teich's secure military prison in Nuremberg spent their final hours supping on a traditional German meal of potato salad, sausage, cold cuts, black bread, and tea. Most read Bibles, except Hermann Goering, who paged through Theodor Fontane's novel *Effi Briest.*

The creator of the Luftwaffe knew he didn't require help from above. He had assistance on the ground. A nineteen-year-old guard named Herbert Lee Stivers had befriended Goering during the long months of trial. "Goering was a very pleasant guy," Stivers told the

Los Angeles Times in 2005, when he at last came forward with his story, one that unlocked a mystery that had confounded historians for six decades. "He spoke pretty good English. We'd talked about sports, ball-games. He was a flier and we talked about Lindbergh." As Stivers walked Goering to and from the courtrooms in the Palace of Justice, he never thought that his prisoner would contemplate suicide. "He was always in a good frame of mind."

Outside the prison, Stivers had met a beautiful, dark-haired local girl. Seeking to impress her, he gave her an autograph of his imprisoned charge. The girl, apparently named Mona, introduced Stivers to a pair of her friends, named Erich and Mathias. They asked Stivers to pass Goering notes hidden in a fountain pen. Seeing no harm, he agreed. A few days later, after the death sentence had been announced, they asked Stivers to smuggle in some "medicine." Stivers agreed, saying he would bring the empty pen to Mona the following day. He never saw her or the men again.

Stivers had unwittingly brought Goering a capsule of potassium cyanide, which Goering crunched down on early in the morning of October 15, hours before he was set to meet the hangman. He lay down on his cot, began twitching, and died almost instantly.

The American guards were dumbfounded. Goering's person and cell had been searched almost daily. A guard examined everything ever handed to him, including food, and a blue-helmeted MP was never more than three feet away. The light burned twenty-four hours a day in his cell, and he was not allowed to sleep with his face to the wall, turned away from the guard outside. His hands had to remain above his covers while he slept. Yet despite the claims that "suicide was impossible" at the prison, there was Goering, barefoot in a blue pajama top and black silk bottoms, dead on his bed, having cheated Allied justice.

He was the only one. The other Nazis were manacled and marched into the prison gymnasium, where three gallows had been erected. Von Ribbentrop, a man who once compared Jews to crop pests that should be eradicated similarly, was the first man hanged, shortly after one a.m. local time, or six p.m. St. Louis time. He shouted, "God save Germany! My last wish is that Germany rediscover her unity and that an alliance be made between East and West and that peace reign on Earth!" as the trapdoor swung open. No photos or movies were allowed to capture the hangings. Reporters watched through binoculars from an attic opening seventy-five yards away. It took seventy minutes to hang all ten prisoners, as many fell with not enough force to break their necks. One, General Wilhelm Keitel, took a full twenty-four minutes to strangle to death.

As Robert Conot, the author of *Justice at Nuremberg* (upon which the movie was based), wrote, "It was a grim, pitiless scene. But for those who had sat through the horrors and tortures of the trial, who had learned of men dangled from butcher hooks, of women mutilated and children jammed into gas chambers, of mankind subjected to degradation, destruction, and terror, the scene conjured a vision of stark, almost biblical justice."

Harry Brecheen was too sick to chew over how Goering had managed to kill himself. He showed up at Sportsman's Park on the morning of Tuesday, October 15, feeling god-awful. He had been surrounded by the press after Game Six, and by the time he finally got to shower, all the hot water was gone. Chilled, he found his immune system was riven by a virus. "I had a fever and a cold and my head was about to bust open," he said. At least he wasn't going to have to pitch, since he had gone nine innings two days before. The Cat "filled up on aspirin," bundled up despite the warm weather, and plopped on the bench.

Murry Dickson would be the man to carry the hopes of St. Louis, the greater Cardinals Nation, and the entire National League on his slender right arm. Thanks to the extra off day, Ferriss would get the ball after a long six-day layoff. Sadly, no one thought to pose the two starters together for a photo. As Dickson only rose to Ferriss's shoulder, the photog would have had to back up considerably to frame them.

It was another glorious day, with a brilliant autumn sun slanting through fleecy white clouds. Temperatures soared into the mid-'70s. Undaunted, many women in the crowd of 36,143 wore fur coats, as befit such an august occasion. The official attendance reflected the ticket sales, but there sure appeared to be many more than that number in the house. Ramps were jammed tight, concession stands blocked. Few had decent standing-room vantages. Most offered just a sliver of the outfield green for a view. Fans eluded the rule barring chairs and boxes by piling seat cushions four and five high and standing on them in the aisles. The stands were packed so tight some writers needed a full half hour to climb the stairs to the press box. One sweat-covered man complained that "they must have sold four tickets for every seat."

Back in Boston, thousands jammed the Common to listen to the game broadcast over public-address speakers at the Parkman Bandstand, and many thousands more filled the Hatch Memorial Shell down by the Charles River, where the Boston Pops usually drew the crowds. Vendors sold refreshments to the masses, mostly cold drinks, as the afternoon was unseasonably warm in Beantown. Fans who had braved the chilly games at Fenway cursed their luck.

Breadon had used the off day to order his minions to scour the countryside for meat and booze for the press boys, and so the writers had a sumptuous feast for lunch. It was so nice, Breadon and Yawkey ate there as well. Given the sky-high costs of the fare, one reporter estimated the Cards owner had spent about twenty grand (over $200,000 today) on the huge spread, a stunning display of largesse from the tight-fisted owner.

The usual array of baseball royalty was there, including Chandler, Frick, Harridge, and Rickey, along with retired greats like Rogers Hornsby, Tris Speaker, Arky Vaughn, and Ol' Pete, Grover Cleveland Alexander, the Cards hero of 1926. Military brass was represented by several top officers, along with Jimmy Doolittle, the Missouri boy who had galvanized a shocked nation with his raid on Tokyo shortly after Pearl Harbor. Given St. Louis's status as baseball's western frontier, an appropriate whiskered face in the crowd was the star of many Hollywood oaters, Gabby Hayes.

Rader's band entertained early arrivals once again, and at 1:15 sounded "Take Me Out to the Ballgame." At 1:28, the orchestra whipped through a tight national anthem, and precisely at 1:30, Dickson let loose the first pitch of the game.

Seeking to avoid a repeat of his previous start in Game Four, when photographers prevented him from a proper warm-up, Dickson had ushers ring the mound as he loosened up this time. It didn't help. The first two batters, Moses and Pesky, lined singles, and DiMaggio knocked a run home with a sacrifice fly. Williams came up with a man on first and a chance to really get his team off to a flying start, and he laced one to center. It had extra bases written all over it, but ancient, ailing Terry Moore rewrote the play, running down the liner, "his knee knocking like an old crankshaft," gloving the ball in the deepest part of the park. Williams trotted grim-faced back to the dugout, getting a sympathetic pat on the back from first base coach Del Baker en route.

Ted made up for his failure at the plate with a rare bit of hustle and dash in the field. Schoendienst led off the game for the Cards with a base hit that curled away from Williams. Thinking double all the way, and realizing who was in left field, Red tore for second. But Williams got to the ball with alacrity and gunned Schoendienst down. Red's shame mounted when Musial doubled down the left field line. The Man was stranded when Slaughter, shaking out his injured arm after every pitch, struck out.

Harry the Hat got his team even in the second inning, lashing a line drive that Williams caught but scoring Kurowski on a sacrifice fly. People inexplicably tossed dollar bills from the upper deck after the run, enriching the lucky fans below. Ferriss was pumping in sharp curves that required catcher Hal Wagner to squat well to the side of the plate, and he got out of the inning. The score was one-all, and stayed that way until the fifth.

The question was which pitcher would make the next mistake, and it appeared to be Dickson. Pinky Higgins launched a "Mastodonic clout" to center. Moore once again gave limping chase. The *Post-Dispatch* judged he was running "at the speed of Whirl-away," a testament to Moore's ability to block out pain. At the last second, after a fifty-yard gallop, the captain reached out backhanded to snare the fly as he slammed hard into the wall. The crowd was orgiastic in reply to their battered hero's nimbleness with the leather.

Walker led off the bottom of the fifth with yet another base hit, and was sacrificed to second. Then Ferriss, whose brother Bill had gotten a friend to watch his gas station back in Shaw, Mississippi, so he could drive to Missouri and see the game, made the mistake. He threw a curve to Dickson, perhaps not realizing the good-hitting pitcher had batted .277 on the season. Dickson had his "pants in the grandstand," Boo said, but the fooled Dickson still managed to loop one down the left field line that fell for a double, scoring Walker easily. Back-to-back singles by Schoendienst and Moore scored a third run, driving Boo out of the game with a suddenness that surprised everyone. Cronin went to Dobson, who navigated the Musial-Slaughter-Kurowski minefield without giving up any more runs. It was a key dousing of a significant brushfire, but the Sox trailed 3–1 nevertheless.

Williams flied out once more with a man on in the sixth, slamming his bat down in disgust. The game proceeded quickly, tensely, to the eighth. Dickson had cruised for seven innings, allowing just three hits, baffling the Crimson Hose with his usual wide array of pitches. But some managerial maneuvering by Cronin pumped a bit of life into his team. Cro pulled one colorfully named pinch hitter, Rip Russell, from his bench to hit for Wagner, and he led off the eighth with a single. Another pinch hitter, the even more memorably monikered Catfish Metkovich, hit for Dobson, and he pulled one down the left field line for a double, with Russell stopping at third. Just like that, the tying runs were in scoring position.

Dyer was pacing back and forth, wondering about making a move of his own. Dickson was primed to fall, and Dyer was inclined to lift him. But exactly who would face the top of the Sox lineup was the question. Dyer only trusted two men in this spot. One, Howie Pollet, was too infirm to play. The other, Harry Brecheen, not only had hurled nine innings in Game Six but also had been coughing and shivering for the past few hours.

Dyer ambled down to where Brecheen sat miserably in the corner of the bench, and asked him how he felt. The question hung in the air. There was no noise in the Cards dugout.

"My arm feels okay, at least," said the Cat. And with that, he rose with a bit of a wobble, grabbed his glove, and went out to try to bring a championship to his team.

The next batter was Wally Moses, who later said he was "astounded" to see Brecheen come in. The surprise was enough of an edge for Brecheen, who struck out Moses with a curveball in the dirt. The Cat was relying purely on guile at this point, and that wasn't enough with Pesky at the plate. The Sox shortstop guessed at a screwball and tattooed one right at Slaughter. Ten feet in either direction, and Pesky might have gotten both runners home. Instead, Country barely had to move for it. At third base, Russell, remembering the throw that nailed York earlier in the Series, didn't test Slaughter's arm, damaged though it was.

That brought the Little Professor, DiMaggio, to the dish. He adjusted his glasses and focused his laser-beam stare at the Cat. In a guessing game, few were equipped to defeat Dommie. He looked screwball away and rapped the first pitch off the right field fence on one hop, scoring both runners to tie the game at three. A stunned hush descended over Sportsman's Park, the only noise happy shouts from the Boston dugout.

It was a great moment for the oft-overshadowed little brother of the Clipper in the Bronx. It might have been the singular moment of his career. But it came with a catch. DiMaggio was thinking triple from the time the ball leapt off his bat, but as he dug hard, he came up lame and had to hobble into second. It was what the press called at the time a "charley horse," a medically meaningless phrase that disguised the painful true injury, a torn hamstring. It took a full twenty minutes to stretcher Dommie off the field, and the St. Louis crowd gave him a nice ovation as he left. Leon Culberson went in to run for him.

And that brought Williams up with a chance to undo all the negative karma from the game, the Series, the last month, the kerfuffle over his enlistment, his relationship with the press and the city of Boston—every damn thing. A hit here, six outs by the Sox pitching staff, and Ted would be forever remembered as the hero of the '46 Series, regardless of what had transpired earlier. Indeed, his injury and struggle at the plate would be spun as something he had majestically overcome when it mattered most, adding to his legend. It was the biggest single at bat of his career, both to that point and in retrospect.

On the first pitch, Williams fouled one right into Garagiola's bare hand, smashing his index finger severely enough that the catcher had to come out, replaced by Rice. The delay of several more minutes stretched the tension taut. Ted couldn't help but think about what Brecheen might throw him with one strike, and try to stay a step ahead. He effectively iced himself.

Brecheen came in with a fastball, and Williams, looking for the screwball that was Brecheen's out pitch, was jammed. He popped one to Schoendienst on the infield grass. There was no classic Terrible Ted outburst after this failure, no cursing, no busting lights in the dugout runway. He was numb.

Still, Dommie's clutch hit had pulled the Sox from the brink of defeat, and now the pressure was on the Cards to respond. Boston made three changes before the bottom of the eighth. With Wagner pinch hit for, Roy Partee went in to catch. Culberson took over in center field for the lamed DiMaggio. And the new pitcher was...

Bob Klinger?

The by-the-book move was to bring in the relief specialist and southpaw, Earl Johnson, to face the lefty Slaughter, who was leading off the inning. Instead, Cronin went with Klinger, US Navy 1944–45, a right-hander who had pitched with the Fifth Fleet team in the Pacific. Now, just over nine months after his discharge, Klinger stared in at the redoubtable Country, who carried his bat to the plate with his pain-free arm. Coincidentally, Klinger had faced Slaughter in Country's first major league game, way back in '38. Enos got a knock off him that day.

A "near non-entity," Klinger had gone but 3–2 on the season (albeit with a 2.37 ERA) in just twenty-eight appearances. Worse, his son had contracted polio in September, and Klinger hadn't pitched in a real game in nearly a month, not since September 19, when he didn't retire a single St. Louis Brown he had faced, right there at Sportsman's Park. It had been exactly thirty-four days since he last got an out. Now here he was, taking the mound on the road in the late stages of a tied Game Seven of the World Series.

Sure enough, Country ripped a single up the middle, and the Sportsman's Park throng roared. But Klinger, to his credit, quieted the instant second-guessers who were calling for Johnson in the press box, retiring Kurowski and Rice with little trouble. That brought another dangerous lefty to the plate—Harry Walker. Cronin still refused to play the percentages, and stuck with his right-hander. Walker had been getting the business from the Sox bench all Series. "The boys think Dixie's younger brother is something of a show-boat," the *Globe* explained, and the catcalls doubled in intensity as Walker strode to the plate.

It had been a frustrating season for Walker, one in which he hit merely .237 with three homers, but he had stroked six hits in the

Series thus far. He was making up for his failure to deliver in the ETO Championship back in Nuremberg, a series that seemed like a lifetime ago. In fact, little more than a year had passed, but much had changed. The stakes were a bit higher, but to Walker, the situation wasn't much different—it was a big moment in a big game, and he had vowed to come through. He pulled at his cap edgily, ten, twenty times, then stepped in.

Just at this crucial juncture, one massive Cardinals fan was forced to leave his radio. President Truman was listening in the Oval Office with some Missouri cronies when he was reminded that the annual visit from the Supreme Court was nigh. He dashed up to the residence to change into formal attire, only to discover later that his guests had arrived in business casual. Meanwhile Dommie sat on the bench, leg extended and covered in ice bags, and tried via hand signals to move Culberson over toward left. He did move a bit, but not enough for DiMaggio's liking.

Down at first, Slaughter looked into the Cards dugout, expecting and getting the steal sign from Dyer. For the man who believed running was everything in baseball, the man who had once been admonished by Dyer for not sprinting in from the outfield, this situation was a no-brainer. Country would be off for second with dispatch.

He was off on the first pitch, but Walker fouled it away. The next two pitches were well out of the strike zone, Klinger giving the catcher, Partee, a chance at throwing Slaughter out. But Country had outguessed the battery, and stayed put. The count was now 2–1, a good hitter's count. Hat on, hat off...

Dyer signaled for a hit-and-run play. Slaughter bolted. Klinger, pitching from the stretch, critically failed to pause after taking the sign, allowing Country to get a walking start without fear of a pick-off. Pesky, the shortstop, went to cover second base. The pitch was a good one, a sharp breaking ball that Walker didn't get much wood on. But he managed to lob a "dying seagull," in his words, out into left-center.

Now came one of the most fabled, dramatic, and controversial moments in baseball history.

Playing center for Boston wasn't the fast, slick-fielding Dominic Paul DiMaggio, who was considered an even better defensive player than his brother. Culberson, an average gloveman, was out there. He had no chance to catch the ball, despite Dommie's efforts to move him over. He raced about fifteen paces to his right, cut in front of Williams, who had more ground to cover, and got the ball on a hop.

Of all the critical elements to this oft-dissected play, that bounce is usually ignored, but it played a large role in what unfolded. The horrendous surface of Sportsman's Park was very much on Culberson's mind. He was a little psyched out by the idea of the ball taking a weird hop and getting past him, in which case Slaughter would surely score the go-ahead run. "He was a little too cautious," Bobby Doerr remembered long after. "I don't blame him—that ballpark was terrible. They put in a new turf for the Series, and in practice a ball went right under the grass. I actually had to reach under the grass to get the ball, that's how poorly the field was kept. Certainly the outfield wasn't smooth during game seven."

So Culberson took a safe arc toward the ball, retreating more than he should have. The difference was hardly noticeable to the fans and press above, but the hurtling Slaughter picked up the delay at a sub-atomic level and made the decision then and there to try to score. And, of course, the mere presence of Culberson rather than DiMaggio, who had thrown out three runners in the Series, was reason enough to weigh a dash for it all.

The ill-fated Culberson bobbled the ball slightly as he tried to glove it. Pesky now changed direction (he had been lunging toward second base as Slaughter broke, remember) and raced out to grab the relay throw. Slaughter was still two long steps from third base as Culberson reached the ball. He whirled and casually tossed a lol-lipop to Pesky. The center fielder was convinced the runners would hold at first and third, and there wasn't much he could do about either. Pesky recalled that Culberson "kind of lofted the ball." Pesky took the throw, his back to the plate. Country had just stepped on third base and... *holy moly!* ... was not stopping.

Slaughter had had the whole play in front of him. Had Walker's hit been to right-center, Country might have been forced to check up a little and make sure the play was developing as he anticipated. He surely would have relied on his third base coach, Mike Gonzalez, for help.

Instead, Slaughter got to third and picked up speed. Gonzalez was frantically waving for him to stop, but Slaughter knew there would be no repercussions for ignoring Gonzalez. "It was a suicide run," remembered Schmidt, who saw it all unfold from the Cardinals bullpen. "He went right by Mike Gonzalez, who was signaling for him to stop." (Some papers reported that Gonzalez actually was signaling Slaughter home—"Gonzalez flapped the come-in sign like an excited mother hen," went one recap—proving only that the boys in the press box were caught unaware by Slaughter's gambit too.) Gonzalez had held up Slaughter at third earlier in the Series, and Country had gone to Dyer to ensure that the next time he thought he could score he could disregard his third base coach. "Traveling like the western wind," Slaughter cut the base hard and sprinted home. Gonzalez desperately backpedaled to get out of the way as Country sprinted right past him.

Pesky turned, looked toward third, took an instant to locate Slaughter barreling homeward, and threw to the plate. That moment of hesitation has gone down in baseball history as a colossal blunder, a flub that kept the Sox from winning the Series, an extension (or, more precisely, the first real bitter taste) of "The Curse of the Bambino." In reality, Pesky reacted about as well as could be expected, given he was caught off guard, like everyone else.

By the time Pesky got the ball, realized what was happening, and threw home, only a missile of a throw was going to get Slaughter. It wasn't. The *Star-Times* described the toss—"Pesky lobbed it with a peculiar gentleness as though he finished the apple and this was the core he was flinging away, the lightness of it making it impossible to travel fast."

Partee's parents had driven all the way from California to see their son play, so at least two members of the crowd were hoping for a play at the plate. As the catcher remembered the play years later, "Pesky took a little hop—a skip—and he threw the ball to me, but it was so high. He didn't have a real strong arm like [utility infielder Eddie] Pellagrini. If Pellagrini had been playing shortstop he'd be out by ten feet."

Unfortunately for the Partee family, Pellagrini wasn't even on the Series roster. Pesky's throw sailed well up the third base line. The catcher was well in front of the plate when he fielded it, "as though he had started toward Pesky in order to take the ball away from him." Country actually slowed before sliding in safely, mainly to avoid colliding with the next hitter, Marion, who was a few feet in front of home on the third base line and surprised to look up and see Slaughter bearing down on him. He pointed down to instruct Country to slide, a moot gesture—Slaughter could have scored standing up with ease.

Sportsman's Park went berserk. Fans threw programs, scorecards, hot dog wrappers, hats—whatever they could get their hands on. The crowd noise had gone through several distinct notes—a huge roar as Walker's hit touched down safely; a downshift that swiftly turned into a shocked clamor as Enos barreled around third; an urging bellow as he chugged home; and now an eardrum-shattering detonation as the Cards went ahead. It was now 4–3, and who could believe it had just happened?

The question has reverberated down through generations. *Did Pesky blow it?* A careful examination of the game film reveals, well, just about anything the viewer wishes to see, like most frame-by-frame parsing of videotape. Pesky certainly doesn't come straight home, and there is a brief but noticeable double clutch. But it's also apparent that the die had been cast by that point. In retrospect, the play was over as soon as Culberson threw the ball to Pesky, rather than coming straight home.

The forces that have sought to alleviate Pesky from blame tend to point an accusatory finger at the press for pinning it all on the shortstop with its usual lazy pack mentality. Certainly, lines like "Pesky stood as though mesmerized by Slaughter's impertinence" and "Pesky plucked the ball from his glove and held it in his bare hand...an unexplainable disinterest seemed to tamper with his reasoning and he placed the ball back in the hollow of his greasy leather" (both from St. Louis writers) gave an impression that Pesky had screwed the pooch, and unfairly so. The concept that these writers, and others, embellished the delay thanks to a penchant for dramatic overstatement and the groupthink of the press box is fair.

However, it should be noted that radioman Arch McDonald thought Pesky had "hesitated" right away as he called the action. It is also fair to argue that any time a shortstop takes a relay throw as a runner is only just touching third base, as Pesky had, he should be able to gun down or force that runner to turn back. Cronin thought the instant it took for Pesky's eyes to adjust to the shadows surrounding home plate in the late afternoon sun was the decisive factor.

Some fault certainly lies with Pesky's teammates. Williams and Doerr in particular should have been able to make the oblivious Pesky aware that the ball needed to head for the plate. "If Doerr...had hollered 'come home with the ball,' I think he could have thrown me out by 8 or 10 feet," Slaughter said afterward. Doerr recalls that he did just that, and that Ted was yelling "home! home!" as well, but that the freight train roar of the crowd prevented Pesky from getting the message. Years later, the other shortstop in the game, Marion, absolved his opposite number for that very reason. "I can't blame Pesky at all," he said.

Instead of seeking to place goat horns, the better bet is simply to acknowledge the verve and élan Slaughter displayed. "Running bent over as though he were on an invisible bicycle," the balding hustler scammed Pesky, even as he was making an amazingly athletic play. Given the fact that the team doctor had strongly encouraged him not to even dress for the game, and the throbbing pain continued to drum away at his focus, Slaughter's gumption is even more astounding. His Mad Dash is rightfully still mentioned among the most dramatic and memorable moments in World Series history.

There is another, slighter controversy attached to the play, less important save for sentimentalists and the man who got the hit that allowed Country to score. While baseball lore and fans of the phrase "Slaughter scored from first on a single" cling to the idea that Walker indeed slapped a mere base hit, the play was scored a double right away, despite some disagreement in the pressroom. "Gentlemen," scolded Bob Broeg, "you have taken all the romance out of a great play." Dutifully, his and the all the other accounts in the next day's papers refer to the hit as a double.

Again, to the film—upon reexamination, it is rather apparent that the play was truly a single, with Walker advancing a base on the throw. No one could tell that to the Hat, however. He spent the rest of his days reminding people that he had doubled in Slaughter—*Just ask the official scorer!*

Perhaps the best way to conceptualize Slaughter's Mad Dash is to put oneself in the mind-set of a fan that afternoon, one of either the lucky thousands in the park or the millions listening on radio. Exhausted by years of war, the expected benefits of peacetime had largely been denied this fan. The prospect of more war loomed. Everyday goods that should have been in abundance were either impossible to find or cost a fortune. He or she had been forced to descend to bribery or the black market to house, feed, clothe, and clean the family. In all likelihood, this fan had struggled to find a decent place to live, had either walked out on his job or been affected by others walking out on theirs, or had seen his cost of living skyrocket, and quite possibly all three. St. Louis fans had also spent the last few months living under the specter of a polio outbreak that claimed hundreds of lives.

It may have been small recompense, but the thrilling baseball season had offset the pummeling this fan suffered almost every day in 1946. The game was constant, the excitement and thrills it provided powerful enough to put a smile on his or her face even though tomorrow promised another excruciating battle on any of a dozen fronts. And now, on the final day of an amazing season, the tension had risen to unbelievable heights. Fans huddled nervously around radios in office buildings and country drugstores, in schools and luncheonettes and public spaces across America.

Then one man, whose very name evoked God and country and war, had taken matters into his own hands, seized upon a calculated risk, and saw it pay off in spades. He had ignored tradition and conventional wisdom, cast off advice and resistance from outside forces, and changed history with one moment of valor and gusto.

Fans across the country had a strong, unified reaction: How we long to do the same! And much of the story of the coming two decades, during which *Pax Americana* reigned supreme, was that of people undertaking Mad Dashes of their own.

The Cards now led 4–3, but the inning wasn't over. After an intentional walk to Marion, Cronin belatedly lifted Klinger from the game. Johnson at last loped to the mound, his omnipresent smile rather out of place at the moment. Dyer let Brecheen hit with two on and two out after Slaughter scored, signaling to all that he was ready to live or die with the Cat. The pitcher rolled out, then readied to take the mound for the ninth inning. It was up to Brecheen to bring the Redbirds the title.

But nothing was coming easily for the ailing Brecheen. York led off with a single to left. Doerr then eschewed a sacrifice and blooped a hit into short left, just past a lunging Marion, and Boston had two on with nobody out. The crowd shifted nervously in their seats. To lose now, after Slaughter's dash, would be doubly devastating. A couple of Boston runs here would relegate Country's heroism to the dustbin of history.

It was dead quiet in the park as the Cards gathered at the mound to discuss strategy. The infielders agreed that they would go hard after Doerr at second if they had a shot—the potential go-ahead run was critical. Sure enough, Higgins bunted right to a hard-charging Kurowski, who gunned it with his deformed right arm to second to force Doerr.

The weak-hitting Partee came up with runners at the corners. "He hadn't given me any trouble," crowed Brecheen afterward. A squeeze play or a fly ball would have tied the game, but Partee could only manage to pop a foul wide of first. Musial had a long run to glove it, and made a sizzling throw home just in case the pinch-runner for York, Paul Campbell, had any crazy ideas of tagging up. Now there were two out.

The pitcher's spot was next, and Cronin sent Tommy McBride up to pinch hit. Brecheen tossed him a "good screwball," and McBride rolled it to second. "I hit a low liner right by Brecheen's left knee," McBride remembered more than fifty years later, exaggerating the pace of the ball a touch. "I thought I had a hit." Schoendienst didn't field it cleanly. The ball rolled up his arm, forcing premature roars of victory to gag in horrified throats. But the second-sacker and lifelong Cards fan recovered nimbly and flipped it to Marion at second for the force, and the game was over. "Red goes down as the first man to engineer the final out of the World Series by snaring the ball with his armpit," wrote Vernon Tietjen.

At precisely 3:47, the first postwar World Series champion, the St. Louis Cardinals, was officially crowned.

Chapter 40
AFTERMATH

SPORTSMAN'S PARK EXPLODED with release, the tension of the Series erupting in a bellow that caused the Mississippi to ripple. The seat cushions that fans had used as stepladders now came flying onto the field in the hundreds. Fans descended onto the playing field, covering every inch. A dozen tried to dig up home plate, while a lone guard fended them off. Brecheen was carried off the field by his teammates, fighting the mob at every step. He was soon "hauled down like goalposts," in Red Smith's description. The Cat "escaped injury at the hands of the crowd only by miracle." A pair of fans sportingly patted Cronin on the back as he trudged forlornly to the clubhouse, gazing intently at his shoe tops.

The excitement was too much for Ol' Pete. Alexander suffered a heart attack as he tried to leave the game. He was taken not to the hospital but to his room at the Broadview Hotel in East St. Louis, where he recuperated. He lived another four years before dying in 1950.

Wild celebrations broke out across St. Louis. Fans threw confetti, bills of lading, and toilet paper out of buildings across town. A paper snowstorm enveloped grinning pedestrians. "Parts of Olive and Washington [Streets] were soon ankle deep in paper," according to the *Post-Dispatch*. Boys in woolen underwear garnished with green streamers ran through the streets. Car horns honked without pause, and drivers put hastily handwritten signs in their windshields—CARDS WASHED BOSTON'S SOX and CARDS HAD A BOSTON TEA PARTY were examples of the wit on display.

The celebration continued long into the evening, as bars and nightclubs were jammed while people danced in the streets. "A mild October night felt like New Year's Eve," reported the *Star-Times.* There were "countless St. Louis hangovers" the next day. "Those aren't blues they're singing in St. Louis tonight," the *Globe* pointed out.

The scene inside the winning clubhouse was almost as wild. "Soft drinks were forgotten" amid a celebration that "almost beggars description," according to the *Times.* Beer flowed in immense quantities, and the players poured it over each other's heads. There was no champagne. Red Barrett yelled for some, and Dyer yelled back, "I'll buy it, boy, I'll buy it!" Dyer, who was still in full uniform thirty minutes after the game ended, quickly went hoarse from shouting. His hair was mussed, his uniform askew, and a large vein throbbed noticeably in his neck. He hugged Breadon tightly. "And we'll win it again next year!" the owner promised, less than an hour after winning this year.

When asked about his pitching star, Dyer said, "I figured I could get two good innings from him." Brecheen could barely speak, overcome by emotion and exhaustion. He stammered out, "Who got the [game] ball?" and Marion came over to present it to the Cat. "I was saving it for you," said Slats with a smile.

Eddie Dyer Jr., sixteen, pushed his way through the crowd to embrace his old man. Both started to cry. Eddie Jr. had begged his father's permission to miss school that day, assuming (correctly) this "probably will be the only Series you will ever be in." The manager made sure to credit Doc Weaver, who "saved Slaughter, Moore, and Pollet for me."

Writer James B. Dawson was knocked over three times by giddy ballplayers, then wrote, "It was risking life and limb to be there." The room shook as a partition collapsed. Ford Frick was carried around on victorious shoulders, while his AL counterpart, William Harridge, was "elbowed and jostled," apparently the cost of being on the losing side.

Harry the Hat was busy assuring people that the official scorers got it right—he deserved a double. "My regular season average was only a decoy!" he yelled with a broad smile. "Them Sox pitchers kept thinking 'here's a guy who can't hit nothin'.'" Walker had finished the Series with a .412 batting average, and a 1.053 OPS, along with 6 RBIs, none bigger than the last one. More important, he made good on the promise to himself made a year earlier, on a makeshift diamond in Nuremberg. This time, he had come through in the World Series. Nearby, Musial laughed as though he had been the one to hit .412 (Stash managed to hit just .222).

Slaughter was surrounded at his locker, his right arm encased in bandages, uniform top off, mostly bald pate gleaming from suds. He downplayed his dash, the "electrifying spurt that doubtless will linger for many years," as the *Post-Dispatch* called it. "I just had to run, that's all," said Country with his best down-home humility. "To me it was just a routine play." He professed ignorance as to what Gonzalez was signaling to him—and that it was a moot point. He was coming home from the moment the hit landed safely and Culberson took that safe angle to the ball. He chalked up his speed on the base paths to Billy Southworth, "who taught me to run on my toes."

The press gang wanted to hear from the day's starter, Dickson, but he couldn't be found. Turned out he was so furious at being taken out that he left the park and drove around in his car, listening to the final innings on the radio. After the final out, he tried to return to the clubhouse to celebrate, but the chaos on the streets prevented him from getting anywhere close.

Sixty feet away, in stark contrast, the Red Sox clubhouse was funereal. They could hear the Cards whooping it up next door. It had been a crushing loss. A team that seemed so superior had been outhustled, outplayed, and outwitted. "What happened to Klinger, to

Cronin, and to the Red Sox *en famille,* was something not fitting to wish upon a hound dog," wrote one reporter. It had been a major upset, one that set Jimmy Carroll back a reported $45,000 (over half a million bucks today) in gambling losses. As Daley wrote in the *Times,* "The red-faced gambling fraternity either is paying off in sheer embarrassment or else heading over the nearest fences, suitcases in hand, taking it on the lam." One local fan had a different challenge. Losing a bet on the Sox, he was forced to push a potato with his nose two city blocks. It took him forty minutes.

Williams, catatonic, sat in front of his locker, unable to speak. He had been a complete bust in the Series, managing just five hits in twenty-five at bats, all singles, with but a mere RBI. He at last rose, silently handed his Series check to the clubhouse boy, Johnny Orlando, went to the shower, and wept openly for several long minutes. He stayed in the clubhouse, poleaxed, long after his teammates had dressed and boarded the bus that would take them to the train bound for home.

Ferriss, the starting pitcher, was likewise desolate. "Those were good pitches they hit," he said sadly. "I just don't understand it." Cronin was besieged with questions asking why he used Klinger when he did, for which there was no good answer—Cro thought Klinger would come through, and he hadn't.

In the championship cauldron, a team's weakness is invariably, often ruthlessly, exposed. Dating back to the *Saturday Evening Post* article in the spring, Cronin's competence in the dugout had been the Achilles' heel Sox fans worried about. While he'd had a mostly triumphant 1946 season, there were still concerns—his inability to boost the club late in the year and to get Williams to stop ramming his head into the shift, and his use of the pitching staff. Sure enough, when the games mattered the absolute most, Cronin had gone wobbly with pitching decisions and been unable to rouse his signature player from the Cardinals' mind games. Inevitably, it seemed, the lone flaw in this magnificent team had been its undoing.

Happy Chandler dropped by to pay his respects, patting several players on the back. He stopped to whisper in the ear of the miserable Williams.

"God love you, Ted," he said.

"I never missed so many balls in my life," responded the Splinter.

Pesky quietly, stoically, took the blame for the loss. "If I was alert, I would have had him. When I finally woke up and saw him running for home, I couldn't have gotten him with a .22." A little later he said, "I'm the goat. I gave Slaughter at least six strides with the delay." A couple of weeks later he was still at it, telling Grantland Rice, "Slaughter simply outsmarted me—that's all there is to it." These comments cemented Pesky's "holding the ball" gaffe in baseball lore, making him a goat on par with Bill Buckner and Mike Torrez in Red Sox history. They were unnecessary, but no one, not Culberson, nor Williams, nor Cronin, spoke up and shifted culpability away from the shortstop. So the blame vacuum was filled completely by Pesky. As he put it many years later, "There are still people today who think I'm a piece of shit."

He did speak for the team when he summed up the Series loss. "It's a sad thing when you think you should have won and you don't." He paused for a long minute, deciding whether to say more. "It doesn't make any difference now. The hell with it."

Roughly a thousand fans gathered outside the clubhouse gate. They showered Cards players with cheers and kisses as they emerged. Musial pushed through and hopped in a waiting car that sped him to the airport. Like Robinson after the Little World Series, the Man had more baseball to play. He was joining Bob Feller's barnstorming tour in Los Angeles, and there was a game the next afternoon. Unsurprisingly, perhaps, he went 0–4.

Most had dispersed by the time Williams finally dressed and made his way out of the clubhouse. A small group of remaining Cardinals fans jeered him—"Where's Superman?" they yelled. The bus brought the team to Union Station, and Williams trudged alone to the train. A reporter for the International News Service captured the melancholy scene:

> It was 2 hours and 48 minutes after the last out of the last game of the 1946 World Series, and into Union Station at St. Louis came an outsized gent with glazed-in hate in his eye and the elaborately careless tread of a man who walks alone. Glancing neither right nor left, he stalked up the ramp to his Pullman, seated himself at the window and gazed glumly at the banal scene without. His name was Ted Williams, and only three months ago, at the All-Star Game, he had been the delighted and united chant of the press pavilion and the toast of a nation's fans.
>
> Less than two minutes later came a motley array, straggling along without interest or apparent destination, as might a broken-down old theatrical troupe, or the forlorn remnants of the historic retreat from Moscow. But naturally that wasn't Napoleon in front shambling along with head down and eyes lowered. It was Joe Cronin.

Williams let his emotions flow in the train car, crying again as fans looked on awkwardly outside the window just a few feet away. Their natural urge to taunt was offset by the naked anguish they were witnessing.

The endless train journey back to Boston was about as chipper as the one that had brought Franklin Roosevelt's body from Warm Springs, Georgia, to Washington eighteen months before. Williams got control of himself and killed time chatting with Doerr and reading books on his favorite subjects, including one Cronin had given him, *To Hell With Fishing* by Harold Tucker Webster. Teammates awkwardly tried to cheer Ted by talking about other stars who had flubbed in the Series. Meanwhile, Cronin and Huck Finnegan got into it again, with Cro threatening the writer with a bread knife.

News of the gut-wrenching loss had stunned the Towne that was so confident of victory just days before. Theaters interrupted matinee shows to break the news of the loss. A switchboard operator answered calls "Hello—the Sox lost 4–3." A traffic policeman appraised of the final score distractedly waved two right-angled lanes of cars forward at once, causing a jam up in the intersection. Not everyone was upset. Claire Brown, a secretary at CIO headquarters on Tremont Street, said, "I'm glad the Series is over. I've heard nothing but Sox and the Series from my boyfriend for the last couple of weeks. Gets a little boring." Aboard the USS *Walton* at the Charlestown Naval Base, a navy CPO from St. Louis ironically named Walker sweated out the final innings. "I was a nervous wreck," he admitted. "The night's on him," said one of his mates after the Cards had won.

The Red Sox disembarked at South Station, "still wearing those 'we didn't know it was loaded' expressions," according to United Press. Three hundred fans awaited the team. Cronin had gotten off near his home in Newtonville, Massachusetts, so he was spared any second-guessing on the platform. Williams detrained and was whisked away by a policeman friend.

There was to have been a public reception for the Sox at Copley Square emceed by Mayor James Curley. It was canceled at the players' request.

Epilogue

HARRY WALKER DIDN'T even stick around for the party in St. Louis. As soon as Game Seven ended, he piled into his car and drove south to see his new daughter and injured son. He drove through the night, and crossed into Alabama early the next morning. A highway patrolman pulled him over, as Walker was considerably exceeding the speed limit in his haste.

"Buddy, I've been gone for seven months," Walker said, and told the officer why he was in such a hurry.

"Man, get on home," said the cop, and Walker was back on his way to Leeds.

It was a happy homecoming for the Hat, who spent the off-season running the family hardware store with his brother. "Not many people talked baseball with me that winter," he remembered later. "It was a little surprising, to be honest." Early in 1947, Walker got into a salary dispute (what else?) with Breadon and found himself traded to Philadelphia. It turned out to be a blessing. Shibe Park was tailor-made for his stroke, and Walker switched to a heavier bat that kept him from trying to pull too much. He wound up leading the NL in hitting in '47 with a .363 average. Coupled with Dixie's batting title in 1944, the Walkers became the only brother combo to each win a batting title.

Walker went on to have a solid managing career. His logorrhea and baseball acumen were memorably captured in Jim Bouton's groundbreaking diary of life in baseball, *Ball Four.* The Hat managed the Astros and Bouton in 1969, and is portrayed as a man who gives nonstop advice to his players—and is always proven correct. At one point, Bouton admires a blazer with a family crest Walker is wearing. "Contrary to rumor," Bouton writes, "the crest is not an open mouth on a field of wild verbiage."

Walker wasn't tarnished with the same stain of racism that is usually applied to his brother Dixie, who is remembered as having protested Robinson's presence on the 1947 Dodgers, forcing Rickey to trade him (the truth is more subtle than that). But Harry, too, betrayed his Alabama roots on several occasions, and had troubled relations with black players throughout his playing and managing career.

Like his country, Walker was slow to let go of old prejudices. Even the finest of men, ones who had sacrificed and fought for freedom to defeat fascism, had to be dragged into a rapidly changing era. Harry Walker, and many more like him of the so-called Greatest Generation, was a man of nuance and contrast. These men had fought for their country and come home to find it (and themselves) irrevocably changed. Each dealt with it with varying degrees of acceptance.

Away from the game, Walker's life was laced with tragedy—young Terry never fully recovered from his injuries, and he died from a staph infection in 1948, not yet six years old.

The other half of the Mad Dash duo, Country Slaughter, had a difficult off-season. His injuries left him so battered he thought he might be finished with the game. "My elbow is still hemorrhaging, and I have two broken ribs," he told a reporter later that winter. Worse, his divorce threatened to leave him destitute. "Enos is just a country boy on a country income," said his lawyer during the proceedings. "He has slim hopes of ever playing again." The lawyer said all Country had to live on was his slight farm income back in Roxboro and his World Series share, which, thanks to the small capacity of Fenway and Sportsman's Parks, was the lowest in decades.

Of course, Slaughter would play again—for thirteen more years, in fact. He won two more championships with the Yankees at the end of his career, and was elected to the Hall of Fame in 1985. Three more marriages, for a lifetime total of five, qualified Country for a far different enshrinement.

Joe Garagiola had a happy World Series winning night, as the Hill toasted its favorite son until dawn. The following day, the hungover and exhausted catcher went to Sportsman's Park to gather up his gear. He loaded his car, then went inside to say farewell to a few team employees. Unfortunately, Garagiola neglected to lock up. By the time he returned to his auto, all his equipment had been stolen.

As an omen for the future of Garagiola and the Cardinals, it served its dark purpose. Joey never did live up to his promise, lasting only eight largely mediocre seasons with four different teams. "I thought I was modeling uniforms for the National League," he said of his itinerant career. It was the kind of wit that made Garagiola a better TV personality than ballplayer, and he would become a longtime analyst for NBC, along with doing guest-host duty on the *Today* and *Tonight* shows.

Marty "Slats" Marion went on to manage the Cards in 1951, only to be replaced by, of all people, Eddie Stanky. He ran the Stadium Club at Busch Stadium for nearly two decades, like so many of his teammates remaining forever close to the franchise. He never did make the Hall of Fame, a fact that incenses Stan Musial and Red Schoendienst, who stumped for their fellow infield partner for years, unsuccessfully (Red was voted in by the Veterans Committee in 1989). Harry "the Cat" Brecheen pitched effectively for several more seasons, as did his buddy Howie Pollet, and Murry Dickson too, though Dickson would later be accused, without much convincing evidence, of being an inveterate doctor of the ball. "I don't use anything but 'woofle dust,'" he claimed, which hardly quieted his critics. Dickson made up for the two years he lost to the army by pitching until 1959, when he finally hung it up at age forty-two.

The wrenching adjustment from a wartime footing to a peacetime one got smoother after the '46 season was over. Dickson was one of millions of soldiers who eased back into civilian lives, a great many of them helped mightily by the GI Bill. A crash program to create more housing got people off the streets and into homes of their own. The newly elected Republican majority in Congress passed the Taft-Hartley Act, known as the "slave-labor bill" in union circles for its draconian measures aimed at blunting the power of organized labor. For better or worse, the paralyzing strikes of '46 vaporized, not to be repeated. Shortages eased, wages rose, and the Depression never returned. The Cold War waxed and waned, but never exploded into an atomic exchange.

Baseball benefited from the era of peace and posterity, embarking on a decade of interest and grandeur unmatched in the sport's history. The era between 1947 and '57 remains distinct, albeit in the main because of the preeminence of the New York teams; it may have been the "Golden Age" in the Big Apple but not so much in Chicago, Philly, or Boston.

One major part of the sport's appeal during the late 1940s and 1950s was, to hear many from within and without baseball tell it retrospectively, the lack of player movement, by which is meant the absence of free agency as was ushered in by arbitrator Peter Seitz in 1975, when he declared pitchers Andy Messerschmidt and Dave McNally free to sign with any team, at last killing off the Reserve Clause. Those who extol the greatness of this time talk about the true loyalty between player, franchise, and city that were built up, leading to a bond impossible to replicate in modern baseball, when the player who spends the entirety of his career in a single uniform is rare (of course, the Golden Era ended when the Dodgers and Giants shattered that bond by moving to richer pastures in California, a form of free agency available to the owners of those teams).

While the fact that Joe DiMaggio and Ted Williams and Stan Musial, among many others, played their entire careers in one city was laudable to some extent, it is a rather meaningless construct. Few would doubt that free agency, and the resulting interest in the annual guessing game over where top stars will sign, has been a net positive for the sport, and the progress in simple freedoms and employment rights the players have won is self-evident.

What those who hark back to the greatness of the postwar game are really referring to is the money players made; more accurately, the ratio of average player salaries to that of the average fan. Aside from the game's few highly paid superstars, your typical ballplayer in the '40s and '50s made about, and often less, what the middle-class rooter in the grandstand made, and often had to work a second off-season job to achieve that. Today, of course, the difference in tax brackets is a chasm, with the fan finding little to no common ground with even the most marginal of players.

The fact that baseball managed to enact its own version of a Taft-Hartley Act, with the full cooperation of the players, no less, is what gets celebrated in the sepia-toned longings for a return to this period. Indeed, when the era is invoked, the players are invariably called "the Boys." In no other epoch of baseball is there such a juvenilizing of the men who played the sport. None considered Ty Cobb or Babe Ruth or Dizzy Dean "boys," nor Reggie Jackson or Dick Allen or George Brett, nor Dwight Gooden, Ken Griffey Jr., or Mike Trout. But the postwar players willfully acceded to far less than they had coming to them, and their reward was to live on in a nostalgic halo, worshipped forever by fans who thought they too would play the game for peanuts, if only they could.

The Golden Age that was at hand was in many ways a sunset hue, the fading light of a time when fans could see themselves in the ballplayers they cheered.

There was a group of players who missed out on the glory, however. The Mexican jumpers were banned from returning to the majors, and though the Liga was listing badly in 1947, most of them played on, having little option. By 1948, however, nearly all had jumped back to the country that had barred them from playing ball, despite the fact that they had no jobs.

Max Lanier had a plan, though. The southpaw pitcher got the band together by forming a team that included fellow former Cards Lou Klein and Fred Martin, plus jumpers Sal Maglie, Harry Feldman, George Hausmann, and Danny Gardella, and took them barnstorming, hoping to earn $1,000–$1,500 per game. Unfortunately, almost every team of worth refused to play them, for fear of being banned by Organized Baseball for consorting with known felons, so to speak. Lanier's team wasn't even allowed to play in any park used for major or minor league games. So their 81–0 record was amassed against third-rate collectives on remote, often shoddy diamonds. And financially, the team was ruined by the lack of notable competition. Lanier lost about $8,000, though he made some of it back by selling the bus the team used to transit the countryside, looking for games.

Gardella was about the only player to enjoy the experience, crooning songs aboard the bus to rapturous reviews from his fellow outcasts. The good feelings wouldn't last, however, once Gardella sued baseball for compensation and reinstatement. He won a loud victory in early 1949 when a federal appellate court in New York called the Reserve Clause "an enterprise holding men in peonage." Justice Jerome Frank sent a chill through the moguls who ran the game when he opined, "Only the totalitarian minded will believe that [salary] excuses virtual slavery." The appellate court recommended a jury trial, one that would not only adjudicate Gardella's case, but test the Reserve Clause, as well as baseball's long-held exemption from antitrust laws. "I'm helping to end a baseball evil," Gardella, who was reduced to a $36-a-week job as a hospital orderly, told reporters.

While some players, notably Jackie Robinson, backed Gardella, most remained unable to bring themselves to break the shackles that bound them. In a disturbing irony, it was the Mexican jumpers who worked hardest to undermine Gardella. Mickey Owen, who was bankrupt and desperately selling off farms and livestock he had acquired with his Mexican bonus money, met with Commissioner Chandler in early '49 and was given assurances of a quid pro quo—Owen and the other jumpers would be reinstated if they could get Gardella to back off. Owen got eleven of his former Liga playmates to sign a "reinstatement petition," and they presented it to the singing former Giant. He refused to drop the case.

Branch Rickey was loud in his opposition to Gardella. Just a few years earlier, he had broken from his fellow moguls to integrate the game; now he turned company man, saying any who opposed the Reserve Clause had "avowed Communist tendencies" and "deeply resent the continuance of our National Pastime." Chandler vowed to fight the case all the way to the Supreme Court but in June attacked on a different front, reinstating the jumpers after all. He was counting on Gardella to return to the game and forget his day in court. Lanier, Klein, and Martin returned to the Cardinals. Owen had been supplanted behind the plate at Ebbets Field by Roy Campanella, so he went to the Cubs. None had much impact after their sojourns down south.

But Gardella refused to fold. Even as his trial began in September, and Chandler was deposed in open court, and a settlement seemed imminent, Gardella wanted to keep fighting. "It was baseball which was so wrong—so undemocratic for an institution that was supposed to represent American freedom and democracy," he said. His attorney, who was in for half of any settlement amount, pushed him to take baseball's offer of $60,000. "If you sue someone for something, why should money appease you?" Gardella asked. "It is like Judas taking money and saying, 'I'm being bought off.'" But for all his talk, the player finally caved at the endlessly repeated urgings of owners, Chandler, and his own attorney. Gardella took the $30,000, agreed to never again sue baseball or discuss the Reserve Clause, signed with St. Louis, got one at bat, and was released unceremoniously. Chandler told reporters after the settlement, "I'm so relieved. If I were a drinking man I'd get drunk."

From his home in Bel Air, Maryland, Larry MacPhail no doubt raised a glass for him.

Leo Durocher was suspended for the 1947 season by Happy Chandler, a harsh punishment for assorted misdemeanors that included consorting with Raft and his underworld pals, allegedly rigging a craps game that took an active player for a sizable amount of cash, staining the sport with his affair with Laraine Day, and, most damaging, feuding with Larry MacPhail. Chandler called them the "accumulation of unpleasant incidents" in announcing the suspension; the press, stunned, fell on the side of Jimmy Cannon, who likened the yearlong ouster to a man "getting the electric chair for running a red light."

So Jackie Robinson was managed by Burt Shotton rather than Leo in his rookie season. A genteel sort, the polar opposite of the combative Durocher, Shotton gave a lone demand upon accepting the job—that he not have to wear a uniform. Robinson won the inaugural Rookie of the Year Award, the Dodgers set attendance records, and the team won the pennant, losing the World Series to the Yankees in seven wondrous, memorable games. It's hard to imagine Durocher improving on that, though watching him coexist with Robinson on a day-to-day basis would have been fascinating. The press horde missed out.

Durocher returned in 1948, but he was damaged goods. Ironically, the friction with MacPhail drove a final wedge between Leo and Branch Rickey, and in July of '48, Durocher negotiated a jump across the river to the hated New York Giants (replacing the "nice guy" himself, Mel Ott), a spit in the face of loyal Brooklyn fans and a traitorous move whose impact is hard to comprehend in this modern day of regular team movement. But true to Leo's tenacious nature, he thrived in the face of controversy, winning a couple of pennants (including the memorable 1951 playoff, a crushing blow to Brooklyn made even more painful by Durocher's presence in the opposing dugout) and the 1954 crown in Harlem, and managed until the mid-1970s. He was inducted into the Hall of Fame in 1994.

The "other" manager in the historic race of 1946, Eddie Dyer, didn't last as long, getting fired in 1950 after a fifth-place finish, returning to Texas and the oil business for good. He remains one of only four managers to win the World Series in his rookie season at the helm.

He is less remembered for a moment from the following season, when Jackie Robinson paid his first visit to St. Louis. There was widespread talk of the Cards refusing to take the field against a black man, and legitimate rumors of violence from the stands. "I had serious misgivings about what was going to happen in St. Louis," Robinson wrote later. "Then a wonderful thing happened. When I walked out onto the field, Dyer got up from the bench and shook my hand. He welcomed me to St. Louis and the big leagues. I'll never forget some of the things he said in that quiet moment. It lifted some of the load from my shoulders." As with Lou Rochelli and George Shuba, Dyer's matter-of-fact tolerance has been lost to history in favor of Pee Wee Reese's moment of acceptance of Jackie. There are no statues of Shuba shaking Robinson's hand, or Dyer huddling with Jackie in front of thousands of Cards fans spitting venom.

"Singing" Sam Breadon sold the Cards after the 1947 season, and died eighteen months later. The team then entered a long fallow period that was difficult to comprehend for their fans, who were quite used to regular pennants and championships by this point. Ironically, it was in large part because of those fans, in particular the ones management thought would react badly to black players wearing Cardinal red, that the franchise declined.

Missouri was a hotbed for secessionist firebrands and bushwhacking thugs during the Civil War, and the descendants of pro-slavery fighters made up a sizable portion of the Cardinals' fan base. Their attitude toward blacks hadn't mellowed much. So while Robinson and Don Newcombe and Roy Campanella were sparking the Dodgers, and Willie Mays and Monte Irvin were starring for the Giants, and Hank Aaron, Roberto Clemente, and Frank Robinson were becoming Hall of Famers, the Cardinals remained pale. They didn't integrate until 1954, and it wasn't until the team underwent a complete turnabout and embraced black stars like Bob Gibson, Lou Brock, and Curt Flood in the 1960s that the franchise returned to its assumed place in baseball's penthouse.

The perceived, fair or otherwise, intolerance toward black players on the part of St. Louis fans raises an interesting counter-factual—what if Branch Rickey had remained in charge of the Cardinals and not gone to Brooklyn? Does he integrate the game along the banks of the Mississippi? Does someone else do it in Brooklyn? Does it even happen until the next generation, when civil rights took on a moral imperative? Fortunately, destiny brought circumstance and personality together at the right time and, perhaps more important, in the right place.

Jackie Robinson had seemingly passed every test required for entrance into the major leagues. He had dominated at Montreal on a championship team. He had withstood all manner of taunts, slights, and enemy actions on the field and off. He had grown as a person in the cauldron of being the first black man in pro ball.

But that wasn't enough. With the handwriting on the wall, in early January 1947, baseball's owners called another secret meeting in New York. There was but one item on the agenda—Jackie Robinson, and whether he should be allowed to play in Brooklyn during the upcoming season.

There wasn't much debate. Branch Rickey stood up at the meeting's outset and said flat out that he intended to promote Robinson to the majors. He was met with stony silence. Then the other stand-patters, from MacPhail, Yawkey, and Breadon to owners of lesser stature, like Bob Carpenter of the Phillies, Powel Crosley of the Reds, and Walter Briggs of the Tigers, all stood and announced their opposition. Horace Stoneham, the owner of the Giants, said that fans would burn down the Polo Grounds the first time Robinson came to play. Undeterred, Rickey called for a secret ballot. The vote was 15–1 against, with Rickey the lone yea. Even Bill Veeck, who would integrate the American League by signing Larry Doby a couple of months into the 1947 season, voted no.

The vote was an unfortunate way for MacPhail to begin his final year in baseball (Sam Breadon, too). His position of respect in 1946 was undone by cascading other embarrassments, most of them brought about by drink. The Yankees won the 1947 pennant and World Series, but MacPhail destroyed both celebration parties by attacking others in an alcoholic rage, including fellow owner Dan Topping. The day after this catastrophe, MacPhail sold his stake in the team to Topping and stepped away from the game he had done so much to transform and, in his shortsighted way, try to protect.

His outrageous conduct overshadowed his achievements in the short and medium term. MacPhail should have been a first-ballot Hall of Famer for his impact on the sport, but instead it would be a quarter-century after his eligibility before his name was called at last in 1978. Sadly, Mac had passed three years earlier. But this man of firsts achieved another when his (now late) son, Lee, who had followed in Dad's footsteps and become a baseball executive, was enshrined in 1998. Larry and Lee are the Hall's lone father-son combo.

While the owners congratulated themselves on seemingly deterring the threat to their restricted club, Rickey outflanked them. He traveled to Kentucky to call upon a sympathetic ear—Commissioner Chandler. Ironically, Chandler had only gotten baseball's top job at the insistence of Larry MacPhail. Installing Chandler, whom MacPhail figured he could control with ease (and usually did, as proven during the Mexican League crisis and the Durocher flap), was one of MacPhail's first moves after returning to baseball after the war ended.

But now the Commish defied his benefactor. Chandler was happy to let Jackie become a Dodger, telling Rickey, "I'm going to meet my maker someday, and if He asks me why I didn't let this boy play and I have to say it's because he's black, that might not be a satisfactory answer."

But Chandler worried about MacPhail's reaction and feared that he would be overstepping his bounds if he unilaterally allowed Robinson to play. So he informed Rickey that there was no bylaw or language specifically preventing a black man from playing. As with the Reserve Clause, it was not something that would ever stand up to a legal challenge. Therefore, should Robinson's contract pass through his office, there would be no reason for Chandler to deny it. Robinson would be granted access in a backhanded manner. The owners could raise a stink, but Chandler was willing to risk that they were too craven to declare their racist stance publicly, given the legal and PR ramifications that could come of denying Robinson's entry into the game. On that note, he was correct.

So it came to pass that Jackie Robinson officially broke Major League Baseball's color line on April 13, 1947. He became Brooklyn's first baseman, despite all that work on improving his pivot on the double-play ball the spring before. Ed Stevens was collateral damage, sent to Montreal with the promise of a recall by Rickey, who told Stevens he was trying to deal second-sacker Eddie Stanky and would then move Robby to his more natural position. Stevens had a trying year with the Royals, taunted across the International League for "letting a nigger take his job." After the season, it was Stevens, not Stanky, who was dealt.

Stevens may have been wronged, but it was baseball fans who should have felt more aggrieved. By Robinson's second week on the diamond, it was readily apparent that baseball was much better for having black players involved. Those who had heard the legends of Josh

Gibson, Cool Papa Bell, and Oscar Charleston could only wonder at how much richer the majors would have been for their presence. In that context, the war and its accidental advancement of civil rights proved a boon to the game. Not so the Negro Leagues, ironically, which fell by the wayside after the color line was broken, their raison d'étre now gone with Robinson, and soon Larry Doby, Monte Irvin, Satchel Paige, and many others moving over to "white folks' ball."

Robinson starred for the Dodgers for several seasons, winning the MVP in 1949 and the World Series (at long last) with Brooklyn in 1955. But his career and potential for managing afterward was cut off by the onset of diabetes. He quit the game after the '56 season, with an executive position at Chock full o'Nuts coffee in his hip pocket. He suffered in retirement, the insulin injections doing little to slow the ravaging of his once-perfect physique. He was elected to the Hall of Fame on the first ballot in 1962, a temporary salve to an all-too-brief post-baseball life that was marked by a (later repudiated) turn to backing the Republican Party and anger over the sport's sloth at hiring black managers and executives. He passed in 1972, at which point he was nearly blind from the diabetes. He was a mere fifty-three years old, the same age Babe Ruth was when he too died far too soon.

Thousands of mourners attended the funeral service at Riverside Church in New York. Reverend Jesse Jackson gave the eulogy. But for all the words spilled over Robinson, his impact, his courage, and his legacy, it was a respectful nod from Leo Durocher that best captured his on-field persona, and was how Jackie insisted he be judged. "You want a guy that comes to play," quoth the Lip to Roger Kahn in his classic *The Boys of Summer.* "This guy didn't just come to play. He come to beat you. He come to stuff the goddamn bat right up your ass."

His widow, Rachel, has lived on, sustaining the Jackie Robinson Foundation in New York with her extraordinary energy and intelligence, even at age ninety. She puts in three days a week at the

Foundation. "Work has always been essential for me," she said one afternoon in her office, which is lined with photos of her husband. She lost Jackie, along with her mother and her son, Jackie Jr., in a short period between 1971 and 1973. The grief was overwhelming, but the Foundation has allowed her to concentrate on "something alive, so I could move forward, not look back. Gradually it became less painful." The Foundation provides full four-year scholarships for disadvantaged students of color, some 1,400 as of 2012.

Rachel continues to work on another project—raising money for a Jackie Robinson Museum, ostensibly to be built adjacent to the Foundation's offices in Tribeca. But she is some $20 million short of the funding needed for construction. Perhaps this can be spun as a positive—that Robinson's pioneering efforts have been so well documented and recognized in recent years, including the permanent retiring of his number 42 across the entire sport, that a museum is somewhat redundant at this stage. But surely one is worthwhile, if only to ensure that future generations are kept aware of what Jackie Robinson meant to baseball and the country.

The Red Sox would suffer even more than St. Louis at the hand of racial intolerance. Infamously the last team to integrate, in 1959, the Bosox spent decades tilting at the AL windmill zealously defended by the Yankees. In the immediate aftermath of the loss to the Cardinals, there was disappointment (fans and press alike referred to the team as the "Red Flops" all winter) and shock. After all, for the first time ever, Boston had lost in the Series. Grantland Rice summed up the feeling around baseball—"Boston's World Series fortress, unconquered for 43 years, has fallen at last." It made Pesky's stammer and Williams's flameout that much harder to understand, and Slaughter's dash that much more of an event.

But then the Sox found new and ever more excruciating ways to lose big games and big series, and Pesky's "blunder" took on greater and greater import as the seasons passed without a championship.

Fifty-eight more empty years would go by until the Sox finally lifted the World Series trophy, an unfathomable spell for the Olde Towne Team. Certainly, one can't overlook the historic failure of the team to sign black players, even after the Sox color line was at last broken, as a component of the franchise's historical heartache.

A couple of days after the Series, in his ghostwritten column, Ted Williams "joked" about the defeat. "I knew it would be a whale of a game . . . but I didn't think we'd be the ones wailing." At another point he drolly observed his newfound fear of cats (or, more accurately, Cat Brecheens). "I'm glad it's all over. Now I can go hunting and fishing. But there's one thing I'll steer clear of. It will be wildcats in the fields and catfish in the streams. Brother, keep those cats away from my path and away from my peepers."

The column's wordplay, courtesy of Hy Hurwitz, glossed over the devastation the Splinter felt over the loss and his role as goat. Had Williams known then that this was to be his lone chance at October glory, he might have been a candidate for electroshock therapy, a common treatment for depressives in the 1940s. As it was, decades later, when asked if he had any regrets from his career, he mentioned not the years he missed to war but the 1946 World Series.

Williams's defenders pointed out that his injured elbow had robbed the Kid of his beautiful stroke. "You can't pin the horns on somebody who is physically unable to do something, and Ted just wasn't able to physically hit the ball consistently," wrote Whitney Martin of the Associated Press. Others, most notably Colonel Egan in the *Boston Record,* were less charitable. Egan never forgave Ted for his '46 flop, and referred to him as "the inventor of the automatic choke" every time Williams came up short thereafter.

Not even Egan could deny the full greatness of Ted's career, however. Williams was inducted into the Hall of Fame in 1966. Still, as if to remind him of his contretemps with the press over his career, twenty voters decided Ted wasn't worthy of immortality, at least on the first ballot.

While Williams's failure in the '46 Series was the standout flop, Musial had hardly been better. The Man did outhit the Kid .222 to .200, drove in four runs to Ted's one, and could at least point out that five of his six hits went for extra bases. And he had the good sense to flee town immediately, going off on the barnstorming tour organized by Bob Feller the day after Game Seven. One of his opponents on the tour was Jackie Robinson. Musial had a similar opinion to Feller's—that the first Negro in baseball wouldn't accomplish much in the major leagues. "He didn't impress me too much when I saw him in '46," Musial told interviewer William Marshall in 1978. "He wasn't graceful . . . and he had a short choppy swing [and] it didn't look like he had a good arm. I figured the guy wouldn't do well in the big leagues," Musial finished with a laugh.

Musial, like many great players before and since, struggled on the Series stage. In four appearances in the Classic, 1942–44 and '46, Musial hit .256 with a single homer and just 8 RBIs. But much of that lack of production was obscured by the war and the fact that the Cards won three of those four World Series. Had Boston been victorious, Musial's legacy might well be different. Instead, he is regarded as the greatest, and most beloved, player in Redbirds history. Three years after Williams was elected to Cooperstown, Stan the Man followed him into the Hall of Fame, both entering in their first year of eligibility.

The two greats will always be linked by the 1946 Series. In the great sweep of history, Williams is unilaterally remembered as the greater player, and he was certainly the better hitter—although not by as much as one would assume. Stan, on the other hand, was the better fielder (at two positions), better base runner, better hustler, better teammate, and better person. That was the contemporary judgment as well—that Williams, for all his artistic brilliance at the plate, was touched out by Musial due to the Cardinal's all-around qualities.

But history hasn't been quite as kind to Musial as it has to Williams. As the value of all those bases on balls began to be better understood in the 1980s and '90s, Williams's de facto stock soared. Meanwhile, Ted's gruff exterior and inability to domesticate was transmogrified into a necessary adjunct of being baseball's Marlboro Man, his loner instincts and no-nonsense mien a throwback to the frontier persona America has long idolized, if not identified with. Williams's failure to tip his cap to applauding fans too became a symbol of his fealty to a little-known code understood only by *ubermenschen,* especially after John Updike immortalized Ted's homer in the final at bat of his final game in 1960, and his subsequent ignoring of an adulatory Fenway crowd. "Gods," Updike wrote in his classic piece in *The New Yorker,* "do not answer letters."

In *his* final at bat, on September 29, 1963, at Sportsman's Park, Musial singled in a run against Cincinnati, rapping a knock past a lunging rookie second baseman for the Reds named Pete Rose. Unfortunately for Musial's legacy among the sporting intelligentsia, John Updike was elsewhere.

But it was the latter-day deification of the soldiers who fought and won World War II that gave Williams his final propulsion past Musial, even though neither man actually saw combat in the conflict. Ted's service in Korea, replete with actual missions and heroic photos of the superstar in the cockpit of his fighter jet, became conflated with his necessary and exemplary, if less heroic, work during World War II. Regardless, having reached the top of the pyramid in not one but two of the manliest pursuits possible (three if you count his excellence with the rod and tied fly), Williams cemented his status as an American hero. Musial? Well, he was a great ballplayer, sure, and a helluva nice guy, but what did he do during the war? Run a water taxi at Pearl Harbor? Williams was Chuck Yeager; by contrast, Musial merely Chuck Taylor.

Both sluggers would meet with sad declines. Williams died in 2002, after which his soulless corpse became the subject of a tug-of-war between his son John Henry, who wanted his body frozen cryogenically until science could kick-start him back to life, and his daughter Bobby-Jo Ferrell, who wanted the body cremated. John Henry, who himself died of leukemia in 2004, won, and Ted's body was stored at a facility in Scottsdale, Arizona, where, according to a tell-all book by a former employee, his decapitated head was swatted around in a grotesque bit of batting practice by technicians at the frigid plant.

Musial passed away on January 19, 2013. He had been spared ghoulish indignities, but toward the end of his life he suffered his own living nightmare. After decades of goodwill ambassadorship, the Man began to slip into dementia and advanced Alzheimer's disease in the late 2000s. He had moments of cognition, and was able to receive the Presidential Medal of Freedom from President Barack Obama in early 2011, but for the most part he was unaware of his surroundings and, sadly, his own standing within the game and the franchise with which he is so closely identified.

With the expected Fall Classic storyline of the Man vs. the Kid, a slugging showdown between the Most Valuable Players of 1946 not panning out (these things tend to happen in sports), the small difference between the teams over seven games was chalked up to the brilliant pitching of Brecheen and his cohorts, along with the fact that Joe Cronin's managerial acumen had been lacking. The Series had been an "Instant Classic" in today's vernacular, with Slaughter's Mad Dash immediately taking its place in the rarefied air of great World Series moments.

The '46 Series became a defining moment in baseball history in another way. The tight competition and breathless ending captured the imagination of a new postwar generation of fans, who would mark the Series as the seminal moment in their baseball fandom. The great Mickey Mantle remembered in his memoir, *All My Octobers,* that the '46 Series, and the heroics of fellow Oklahoman Harry Brecheen, sparked his love for the game. A future Mantle teammate on the Yankees, Ralph Terry, also from Oklahoma, recalled, "We used to listen to the Cardinal games on radio when I was a kid, and the 1946 World Series when the Cardinals beat the Red Sox got me hooked on baseball."

Fans as diverse as baseball historian Hal Smith, a nine-year-old in Florida who escaped into baseball to ease the pain of his parents' divorce, to this author's own father, a ten-year-old boy in Westfield, New Jersey, got their start loving the game by listening to Slaughter's Mad Dash. The incredible twists and turns of the season and the Series, coming so soon after the end of the war and the subpar baseball on display, galvanized the next wave of fans. They would infuse the coming decade with an outsized interest and significance that catapulted the era from being just another time when baseball was popular to being a special and beloved epoch.

On April 21, 2012, the Red Sox staged a 100th birthday celebration for Fenway Park, which, unlike Ebbets Field and Sportsman's Park and even Yankee Stadium, remains erect and pretty much the same as it was in 1946. The high point of the gala was the introduction of 213 former Sox players, culminating with the double-play duo from the 1946 team, Johnny Pesky and Bobby Doerr. The crowd roared as the ninety-two-year-old Pesky and the ninety-three-year-old Doerr were wheeled out to their old positions.

Less than four months later, Pesky passed away. As of this writing, only Boo Ferriss and Doerr remain from that memorable team that was the first Sox side to lose a World Series. At his home in Texas, Ed Stevens kept a large photo of the '46 Dodgers on his wall, one by one crossing out the names of each teammate as they departed this mortal coil. When Ed died in July of 2012, there were only three names not crossed out—Ralph Branca, sparingly used catcher Mike Sandlock, and pitcher Jean-Pierre Roy, who appeared in but three games. Of the 1946 Cardinals, Schoendienst, Garagiola, and Bill Endicott, who appeared in just a pair of games, remain with us. Freddy Schmidt, whose recollections livened up this narrative, passed away in November 2012.

Eight men, all of them pushing or already past ninety years old. Writ small, this is the same story of the attrition of the citizen soldiers who fought World War II. The Department of Veteran Affairs has estimated that one thousand World War II vets die each day. Eyewitnesses to Slaughter's Mad Dash and the Battle of Midway and the Eephus Pitch and D-day and Jackie Robinson's Debut and the Liberation of Dachau are disappearing rapidly. The tides of history are lapping at the top of the seawall, soon to flood over this extraordinary era in the annals of our country. When the last of these men and women have passed, our collective loss will be considerable.

But, as Cicero wrote, "The life of the dead is placed in the memory of the living." This book aims to be a part of that remembrance.

Acknowledgments

Once again I have relied upon the excellent ambience and the thumbprint cookies (especially the raspberry) at Dancing Goats Coffee Bar in Decatur, Georgia, to help in the writing of this book. My great thanks to the staffers there. Thanks too to the folks at the Decatur Public Library and the Atlanta Public Library, where I also wrote a fair amount, in addition to conducting research.

I spent a fair amount of time in other libraries as well. The fine folks in the Microforms Section at the New York Public Library were critical, as always. The central branch of the St. Louis Public Library was closed for renovations when I visited late in 2011, so I was relegated to the Compton branch. This turned out to be quite a stroke of fortune, as the staff there were very friendly and knowledgeable about the collections temporarily stored there. Frank Absher also helped me out from the Mound City, as did Paula Hogan and Jennifer Jackson with the St. Louis Cardinals, and the people at the Missouri History Museum Library and Research Center. The staff at the Boston Public Library not only answered all my questions but talked me into getting a library card, even though I live about a thousand miles away.

Sara Abdmishani Price, the collection coordinator at the Louie B. Nunn Center for Oral History at the University of Kentucky, was extremely helpful, especially when she pulled my bacon out of the fire after I misplaced several key files. Thanks, Sara, and "Go Yankees!"

Several historians in the United States Marine Corps aided my efforts, including Dr. Charles Neimeyer and especially Annette Amerman. Thanks too to my old TV producer pal Brian Natwick, now at the Military Channel, for helping point the way. And Dave Gallagher at WartimePress.com helped uncover some priceless information.

I spent another fun week in the A. Bartlett Giamatti Research Center at the National Baseball Hall of Fame and Museum in Cooperstown, New York. Unlike my last journey to the heart of baseball in midwinter, the sun was out and the snow stayed away. Thanks to the staff there, led by Tim Wiles and assisted by Freddy Berowski, along with archivist Claudette Scrafford and photo guru John Horne. At Georgia State University, archivist Kevin Scott Fleming dug up answers to all my questions with alacrity.

I received tremendous help from Japan from the wise and wonderful Robert Whiting, author of *You Gotta Have Wa* and the recognized master of knowledge concerning Japanese baseball. Miwako Atarashi at the Japanese Baseball Hall of Fame and Museum answered all my questions and put up with my horrible attempts at her language. Many thanks, Miwako-chan.

Several other writers contributed kind words, support, and guidance. Michael MacCambridge, Mike Vaccaro, Jeff Pearlman, Thomas Mullen, Inman Majors, James Andrew Miller, and especially Jonathan Eig—thank you all, and I'm looking forward to your next books. Also thanks to Jason Stallman, Connor Ennis, and Jay Schreiber at the *New York Times,* Brent Cunningham at the *Columbia Journalism Review,* and all my editors and fellow wordsmiths who have helped make me a better writer along the way, in particular Bryan Curtis.

One of the more pleasant aspects of researching this book was spending time with the players who were around for the 1946 season (sadly, just a handful remain who are alive and able to talk). Bobby Doerr, Boo Ferriss, Eddie Robinson, the late Freddy Schmidt, George Shuba, the late Ed Stevens, Virgil Trucks—thank you, gentlemen. Also thanks to the recollections of fans who passed along their memories from that time, including Hal Smith, Arnold Hano, Mike Dooley, Howard Alley, and especially William Jucksch, and all the men of the 71st Red Circlers. To the late Stan Musial and Johnny Pesky, and the others who were willing in spirit but not in health, thanks to you too.

It seems extraordinary that the Jackie Robinson story seems so distant to so many people, when his widow, Rachel, is still alive and so vibrant. I spent a very special afternoon in her company at the Jackie Robinson Foundation in New York City. While she is ninety years young, and still as beautiful as a California sunset, Rachel shouldn't be taken for granted. Her direct link to one of the greatest and most important athletes in American history is precious for historians and fans alike. Hopefully posterity will give Rachel her due as the all-important woman alongside the man.

Once again, John Parsley at Little, Brown embraced this book when it was just a kernel of an idea and helped shape it into an actual narrative. His sound judgment and advice are in every nook and cranny of this book, be it through the pen or a softly spoken word in my ear when I needed it the most. John's assistants, William Boggess and Malin von Euler-Hogan, gave important support. Karen Landry provided a hawklike pair of eyes in production editing, and her passions for baseball and proper syntax helped me avoid looking foolish, as did copyeditor Suzie Walker, who also gave the manuscript a once-over. Thanks as well to Heather Fain, Theresa Giacopasi, Anna Balasi, and Elizabeth Garriga for their efforts. Enormous thanks go to Michael Pietsch for the stroke of brilliance in conjuring the title of this book. And, as always, thanks to Reagan Arthur for all of her support. May she be baffled by my tweets for many moons to come.

I'm proud to have once again relied on the services and oft-crucial advice of my redoubtable agent, Farley Chase of Chase Literary Agency, and even prouder to call him my friend. Cheers to you and the CLA, good sir. Thanks too to "our" cousin, Ben Wolf, and his family, to Corey and Carol Surett and the whole extended family, and especially to Mark Sternman, my oldest friend and interactive baseball research engine, who again contributed to this work in manners too numerous to elucidate.

Most of all, I wish to express my gratitude to my family. My mother, Judith Weintraub, for instilling the love of books and reading at such a young age; my "two dads," Arthur Weintraub and Peter Gibbs, whom I took care of in the dedication; my brother, Mark, the true writing talent in the family, his wife, Laura, and their kids, Kayleigh, Jack, and Ryan, whom I love as my own; and most especially to my beloved wife, Lorie Burnett, my best friend and editor, without whom none of this would be possible, and my children, Phoebe and Marty, young enough to wonder and utilize that crazy energy but old enough to recognize "Daddy's book!" when they see it. Here's another one for you two to point to with pride.

Notes

Introduction

MacPhail was inconvenienced by the strikes that defined 1946 early on—in January he tried to make a long-distance phone call, only to be stymied by a telephone operators' strike. He marched down to his local telephone office and tore up the place. Mac was fined $50 for his redecoration efforts.

Other estimates of strike figures put the number of workers who walked off the job at 4.6 million, with 116 million workdays lost.

American soldiers began shouting for demobilization while the ink on Japan's documents of surrender was still wet. Troops being sent to the Pacific stretched signs over their transport trains that read WE'RE BEING SOLD DOWN THE RIVER WHILE CONGRESS VACATIONS. On September 15, 1945, the commander of the 95th Division, General Henry Lewis Twaddle, addressed his soldiers on the necessity of their being sent for occupation duty. "The boos from the soldiers were so prolonged and frequent that it took [General Twaddle] 40 minutes to deliver a 15 minute speech," according to the *Washington Post*. Thirty-five hundred soldiers on Guam began a hunger strike to protest their continued service. Thousands of servicemen marched down the Champs-Élysées to rally in front of the US Embassy, shouting "Get us home!" Congress had little choice but to bow to such pressure abroad and from the families of soldiers at home.

The Maginot Line was named for French Minister of War André Maginot and was a series of garrisons and fortresses along the French border with Germany. It was believed to be impregnable, but the German army simply bypassed it and conquered France in a matter of weeks.

DiMaggio wouldn't get a raise until 1948, when his salary increased to $70,000. The next year he became the first player to sign for $100,000.

Phil Rizzuto on the postwar shortages: "You couldn't get stockings, you couldn't get girdles. [His wife] Cora didn't need a girdle, I'll tell you that. She's pretty well built."

Hillerich & Bradsby, whose factories in Louisville had been reconfigured to pump out a million or so M1 carbines during the war, reverted to its original product—baseball bats.

Chapter 1: The "Mature Ted Williams"

During World War II, spring training sites were determined by the head of the Office of Defense Transportation, Joseph Eastman, who drew a line at the Ohio and Potomac Rivers to create west and south borders for spring travel. Commissioner Landis signed off, thus creating the Landis–Eastman Line. Only the St. Louis clubs stayed put. Brooklyn moved from Havana to Bear Mountain, New York, while the Cubbies went from Phil Wrigley's private California island to French Lick, Indiana, the vacation town better known today as the hometown of Larry Bird.

Williams is known for having remarkable eyesight that allowed him to excel in two pursuits best avoided by the astigmatic: hitting and flying. Recent studies by ophthalmologists using Landolt rings (circles with a gap that the subject picks out) have determined that the average visual acuity of baseball players is 20–13. Williams was thought to have 20–10 or better vision.

Later in his career, Williams would add a second ghostwriter. The joke went that he platooned them—one for lefties and one for righties.

The song about Dom DiMaggio was a parody of Les Brown's "Joltin' Joe DiMaggio." The full lyrics:

> *Who hits the ball and makes it go?*
> *Dominic DiMaggio.*
> *Who runs the bases fast, not slow?*
> *Dominic DiMaggio.*
> *Who's better than his brother Joe?*
> *Dominic DiMaggio.*
> *But when it comes to gettin' dough,*
> *They give it all to brother Joe.*

Of the ballplaying DiMaggios, it was said that Joe had the best bat, Dom had the best arm, and Vince had the best voice (he was an aspiring opera singer).

The most interesting inter-DiMaggio on-field drama probably came in 1949, when Dom embarked on a thirty-four-game hitting streak. He was still nearly a month away from his brother's record, but Joe decisively eliminated the threat by making a diving grab to end Dommie's streak.

Joe Cronin hit pinch home runs in both ends of a doubleheader on June 17, 1943, one of only two players in history to do so.

The closest equivalent to Tex Hughson's oddball vernacular might be Boomhauer from the Fox television show *King of the Hill*.

The 1945 Red Sox finished 71–83–3, 17½ games back in a distant seventh place.

Boston trained in several places during the war, including the Tufts University campus in Medford, Massachusetts; Baltimore, Maryland; and Pleasantville, New Jersey.

The Malmedy Massacre took place on December 17, 1944. The Sixth Panzer SS Army was being spearheaded by tank units under Obersturmbannführer (roughly equivalent to Lt. Colonel) Joachim Peiper. After seizing a small fuel depot near the larger Stavelot fuel dump, Peiper ordered one hundred twenty captured soldiers to be marched into a field. SS machine guns opened up. Eighty-four men were killed, as the rest ran into the nearby forest. There remains much controversy and confusion over the event—Peiper denied ordering the massacre, although his unit went on to kill many more POWs during the desperate attempt to break out of the Ardennes Forest (a congressional inquiry put the number at 362). Peiper was tried in Dachau in May and June of 1946. He was originally given a death sentence but that was commuted. He was released in 1956 and assassinated in 1974 by what was thought to be former French Resistance fighters earning some long payback.

Clem Dreisewerd actually has a unique place in baseball history. After a decade of being shuffled around the minor league system of the New York Giants, he wrote to Commissioner Kenesaw Mountain Landis complaining about his treatment by the big club. Convinced that Clem had suffered enough, Judge Landis granted him free agency on New Year's Day, 1938.

Chapter 2: The Fallen

On August 7–9, 1944, several months after Elmer Gedeon lost his life, the 394th Bomb Group took part in a series of missions over St.-Lô, France, destroying all four rail bridges into the city and several other heavily defended targets. For its work, the group won the Distinguished Unit Citation. One pilot, Captain Darrell Lindsay, won the Medal of Honor for pressing home an attack and safely ejecting his crew despite the fact his right engine was on fire. The medal was awarded posthumously—Lindsay went down with his Marauder.

The V-1 rocket was also known as the "Doodlebug." They killed some twenty-three thousand civilians in Britain before the launch sites were overrun.

The B-25 bomber that Gedeon crashed was known as the "Mitchell," in honor of Billy Mitchell, the champion of air power in the 1920s.

Gedeon was an excellent football player for the Michigan Wolverines, in addition to being a terrific baseball player, but it was in track that he truly excelled. His specialty was the high hurdles, which at the time had events encompassing 120 and 70 yards. Gedeon was the Big Ten champ at both distances.

The famous photo of the marines hoisting the flag over Mount Suribachi was taken by Joe Rosenthal of the AP on February 23, 1945. It was actually the second flag raising of the day. The first involved a smaller flag, and the camera that snapped its raising was destroyed in a firefight. Rosenthal took his Pulitzer Prize–winning shot later that day, when a group of six marines hoisted a larger flag. Only three of the six left the island alive. Later, a controversy erupted over Rosenthal's supposed staging of the shot. In reality, he had posed a group shot of the men, and when he asked if he had posed it, answered, "Sure." This was later confused into Rosenthal admitting he had posed the flag-raising shot, which he adamantly denied doing, and there is no proof that he did.

The "Turkey Knob" was a bizarrely shaped rock formation near Iwo's highest point. Beyond it lay a natural bowl known as the "Amphitheater." The fight to capture this area of the island was so determined and deadly it was called the "Meat Grinder" by the marines.

Sixty-eight hundred Americans died in the invasion of Iwo Jima, with roughly twenty-six thousand overall casualties. Of the twenty-two thousand Japanese on the island when the first Yank waded ashore, all but 216 were killed or reported as missing and presumed dead.

Chapter 3: Kidnapping the Kaiser and Other Adventures

Thanks to Hitler's monstrosity, the hatred engendered by Kaiser Wilhelm in the United States during the First World War is largely forgotten. But he was regularly referred to as "The World's Greatest Criminal" in cartoons and editorials, and crowds chanted "Down with the Kaiser" at games and other gatherings. In Britain, he was even more despised. David Lloyd George won the Prime Ministry based on a "Hang the Kaiser" campaign.

MacPhail kept the Kaiser's ashtray in his office for his entire career.

MacPhail served under Colonel Luke Lea in France, in an artillery regiment that fought with noted valor in Saint-Mihiel and the Argonne. Lea was the ranking officer in charge of the irregulars who stormed the kaiser's billet, a one-term senator from Tennessee, and the founder of the *Nashville Tennessean* newspaper.

It was MacPhail who insisted Redland Park be renamed Crosley Field in honor of its new owner.

The first night game in baseball history was played on May 24, 1935. It was a gala affair. There were bands, fireworks, speeches, and then a countdown to the flipping of the switch that would turn on the lights. Via a special conduit, Franklin Delano Roosevelt did the honors from the White House. After twenty minutes or so, the field was illuminated enough to play ball, and the Reds beat the Phillies 2–1.

Branch Rickey Jr. would later tell his father that his job under MacPhail was all title and no power.

Durocher would estimate conservatively that MacPhail fired him twenty-seven times between 1939 and 1942. A typical exchange came after the Dodgers won the 1941 pennant while on the road. Mac rushed to the 125th Street platform to climb aboard the returning train and celebrate with the team. But Leo had ordered the train not to stop, lest some players get off to party in Harlem. So MacPhail stood there as the train roared past him, mussing his red hair. He fired Durocher for the offense in the midst of the victory party that evening but then reconsidered in time for the World Series.

A cynic would note that MacPhail's urge to join the service at such an advanced age came on the heels of Brooklyn blowing a 10½ game lead and the pennant to St. Louis in 1942.

While the $3 million sale price for the Yankees was considered a steal for a franchise *Fortune* called "as much of a national institution as the Metropolitan Opera or the *Emporia Gazette*," it was also the highest bid received, by a considerable margin, and in addition the only bid with any actual money put down at the time of the sale.

DiMaggio reportedly demanded combat duty in 1943, embarrassed by the ease of his wartime lifestyle. But that could well be the imagination of a worshipful press.

DiMaggio didn't always homer while playing in Hawaii. The great baseball writer Arnold Hano remembers seeing DiMag strike out while Hano was on his way to combat duty in the Pacific.

The Yankees trained in New Jersey during the war, first in Asbury Park in 1943, then in Atlantic City the next two seasons.

It would be hard for baseball fans of the 1930s and 1940s to believe that soon another man named Joe McCarthy would come along and eclipse the fame of the manager, but . . .

Chapter 4: Reunited Redbirds

The Cardinals trained in Cairo, Illinois, from 1943–45.

Both the Cardinals and Yankees used Waterfront Park for spring training. The Yankees also drilled extensively at nearby Crescent Lake Park.

Slaughter's hemorrhoid operation wasn't talked about in the press as such, as contemporary mores prevented discussion of such a delicate region. It was a far cry from the 1980 World Series, when George Brett's hemorrhoid condition dominated the media coverage.

Beazley was part of an ugly incident in 1942. He argued with a black train porter, who cursed the pitcher. Beazley hurled his travel bag at the porter, who pulled a knife and slashed Beazley's right thumb. He pitched the next day regardless.

Dickson's nonchalance about his time in combat may have stemmed from an experience in American Legion ball. In 1933, Dickson was pitching for the Leavenworth team at the Kansas State Prison in Lansing. A convict named Wilbur Underhill, the "Tri-State Terror," led a gang that commandeered the game and took the teams and the warden hostage in an escape attempt. But a company of guards appeared with tommy guns and convinced the prisoners to surrender.

Dickson was wise to refuse the job as General Patton's driver. Shortly after the war, Patton was killed in a jeep accident. In fairness, some conspiracy theories hold that Patton was actually murdered and the accident was staged.

Dickson was granted a furlough from the army to pitch in the 1943 World Series, thus becoming one of only two active members of the armed forces to ever appear in a Fall Classic. Fred Thomas of the 1918 Red Sox played in the Series while on leave from the navy.

Dickson may have been small, but he was durable. He made more than forty starts in each season between 1946 and 1954, and pitched until 1959.

Brecheen may have been "the Cat" to the baseball public, but to Eddie Dyer, he was "the Weasel," a far less domesticated moniker.

Chapter 5: From Hitler to Hardball

It's important to note that while US and British forces fought heroically, the Germans were truly defeated by the Russians on the eastern front. If the Allies were ranked hockey-style, the Red Army would be the number one star of the ETO.

Ewell Blackwell's best season was '47, when he won sixteen straight decisions, led the NL in wins, strikeouts, and complete games, and came within two outs of back-to-back no-hitters. He no-hit the Braves on June 18, 1947, then went into the ninth against Brooklyn five days later without giving up a hit, until Eddie Stanky singled.

Ewart Walker went 25–31 with a 3.52 ERA between 1909 and 1912 while pitching for the Senators.

Walker was able to tug on his hat so often at the plate because batting helmets were yet to be used. Larry MacPhail was the man who invented the batting helmet while in Brooklyn after seeing Pee Wee Reese and Dixie Walker, Harry's brother, get beaned. Still, it didn't catch on right away, and both players took balls to their unprotected heads even after they had helmets designed for them.

Nahem's father, a well-to-do import-exporter, drowned when the *Vestris,* a British steamship, sank off Virginia in November 1928.

Nahem's Communist affiliations would plague him after he left baseball. The only job in New York he could find, despite his education and high profile, was unloading banana boats on the East River. He was forced to move to California, where after many years he found work with the oil company Chevron.

Nahem's nephew, an outfielder named Al Silvera, cracked the major leagues in the mid-1950s for a cup of coffee with Cincinnati.

"Ducks" were so-called because they were designated as DUKW's by General Motors, who built them. It is not an acronym—rather, the *D* designates a vehicle designed in 1942, the *U* stands for "Utility," the *K* indicates front-wheel drive, and the *W* indicates powered rear axles.

Leon Day pitched in a record seven Negro League All-Star Games (often referred to as East-West All-Star Games). He struck out fourteen men in one All-Star Game and once fanned nineteen in a game in Puerto Rico. Monte Irvin called Day the equal of Satchel Paige and Bob Gibson.

The ETO World Series was merely a springboard for Day's 1946 season with Newark. He pitched a no-hitter on opening day against the Philadelphia Stars, led the league in wins and strikeouts, batted .469, and helped pitch the Eagles to the Negro League World Series title over ETO World Series teammate Willard Brown and the Kansas City Monarchs.

Day was one of the handful of Negro League stars to be inducted into the Hall of Fame while he was still alive, though he was in a hospital bed, stricken with complications from diabetes, when the call finally came in March 1995. Leon died five days later. "I think that's what he was waiting for," said his sister Ida May Bolden. Leon's wife, Geraldine, tearfully spoke on his behalf at the induction ceremony in Cooperstown that summer.

Willard Brown was elected to the Hall of Fame in 2006. Brown played a couple of seasons in the early 1940s in Mexico, earning the nickname "Esa Hombre" ("That Man"), which makes him sort of the Stan Musial of the South.

Brown's inaugural major league homer is somewhat well known for what happened afterward. Brown had borrowed the bat he used from teammate Stan Heath. Heath then shattered the bat against the clubhouse wall rather than use it again, an act that has acquired a racist tinge over the years. However, there is little evidence backing this take. Heath was known to be very superstitious, and he didn't like the idea that Brown had "used up one of the bat's home runs," according to team traveling secretary Charlie DeWitt. Indeed, Brown singled Heath out for going out of his way to make Brown and Negro teammate Hank Thompson feel welcome.

The Fédération Française de Baseball was the brainchild of a Parisian sportswriter named Georges Bruni. He wrote a prospectus, which read in part, "It is very difficult to become a good player after the age of twenty because of our total ignorance of a rather important action known as 'throwing the ball,' an athletic gesture not practiced in other sports. Certain players may have an inclination to throw with both arms."

In the south of France, lefty batters were mistakenly taught to run to third after hits. After many mid-base collisions, the tutors called Bruni at Paris HQ for clarification of the rules.

A reserve on the 71st Red Circlers was a player named Jim Gladd, who was a minor leaguer in the Giants system. He returned to the team's top farm club in Jersey City and was there for Jackie Robinson's professional debut in April 1946.

Chapter 6: The Dodgers Take Daytona

The Dodgers trained in Bear Mountain, New York, during the war. In 1943, one onlooker to their drills was Madame Chiang Kai-Shek, who was en route to the White House for secret meetings with President Roosevelt.

Truman of course would defeat Dewey in the presidential election of 1948.

Pee Wee Reese's father, like Durocher's, worked for the railroads. Reese's père was a detective.

George Raft was on the downslope as an actor in 1946. Part of his fall came from reportedly turning down roles in *Casablanca, The Maltese Falcon,* and *High Sierra,* all gratefully accepted by Humphrey Bogart.

Dick Young, it should be noted, didn't exactly have a sterling reputation as a humanitarian himself, especially as he aged.

The fictional Dick Whitman/Don Draper played high school football, not baseball, and certainly wasn't a war hero, though he's a helluva ad man.

Carl Furillo's career would end with a brush against the Reserve Clause. In 1960, the L.A. Dodgers wanted to send Furillo to the minors for what the team termed "temporary roster problems." After fifteen seasons in the majors, Furillo refused a demotion to the bus leagues and was released. He sued the Dodgers, and gave testimony to a congressional committee formed to determine whether the Reserve Clause was legal. Furillo was successful in court, winning damages, but Congress didn't touch the Reserve Clause, and Furillo found himself blackballed from baseball. Even the expansion 1962 Mets, desperate for any ties to the old Dodgers, refused to touch Furillo.

Chapter 7: "The Right Man for This Test"

The original Pacific Coast Conference included UCLA, USC, Oregon, Oregon State, Washington, Washington State, Stanford, Cal, Montana, and Idaho.

Jerry Robinson, Jackie's father, ran off with another woman.

The Robinson home at 121 Pepper Street in Pasadena no longer stands, but there is a bronze plaque on the sidewalk where it used to be.

Jackie wasn't the only great athlete in the family. Older brother Mack took silver in the 1936 Olympics 200-meter dash, just behind a pretty fair runner named Jesse Owens. Robinson returned to a Pasadena that cared little for his Olympic achievement ("The only time I was noticed was when somebody asked me during an assembly at school if I'd race against a horse," he once said) and was reduced to sweeping the streets in his Team USA warm-up jacket. He had a remote connection to baseball, working as an usher at Dodger Stadium, and found his calling as a truant officer for Pasadena schools. A relief of his head stands next to one of his brother's across the street from Pasadena City Hall, a belated recognition of the city's most famous athletic offspring.

Rickey hedged his bets in some quarters of the press after signing Robinson, telling reporters that Jackie was only being signed to Montreal because he was "too old for Class B." This was make-believe, as the plan all along was for Robinson to play in Montreal.

Dixie Walker would famously run afoul of Robinson in the spring of 1947, which ended up in the Dodgers trading away the "Peepul's Cherce." During Jackie's first spring with the team, reporters were naturally curious to hear what the southerner thought about the Negro newcomer. But there was nothing to write about. Walker was secure in the knowledge that Robinson would be far away in Montreal when the season began. "As long as he's not on the Dodgers, I'm not worried," was Dixie's lone comment on the matter.

Bob Feller's impressions of Robinson were formed during barnstorming tours, when Jackie hit Feller with relative ease. It should be noted that the off-season tours were a major source of added income for Feller, and the breaking of the color line directly affected his bottom line. So Feller had a fiduciary incentive to knock Robinson, feeble as the effort was.

Robinson's press nickname while with the Honolulu Bears was the "Century Express," in honor of the $100 per game he received to play. The team was awful, winning only two games in 1941. Robinson played quarterback as well as halfback, and returned punts. He sprained an ankle early in the season and was hampered throughout the campaign. Only 550 fans attended his last game in the islands, a 19–13 loss to the Healanis.

Jackie was still at sea aboard the *Lurline* when Pearl Harbor was attacked. The windows were immediately painted black, and the passengers ordered to don lifejackets. Robinson reportedly refused to wear his.

Robinson applied to Officers Candidate School early on, but his application, along with those of many other blacks, was lost in the bureaucracy for three months. Joe Louis then was transferred to Fort Riley for a short stay. The blacks at the base told him about the delay, and after a couple of well-placed phone calls, Robinson and several other blacks were allowed into the program. Jackie graduated in January 1943 as a second lieutenant.

Robinson's signing by Rickey remains controversial in the context of the Negro Leagues. Rickey refused to compensate the Monarchs for stealing their gate attraction, secure in the knowledge that there would be little in the way of legal action. After all, the Negro Leagues could hardly sue to keep a black man *out* of the major leagues. "Rickey raped us," said Effa Manley, the owner of the Newark Eagles, with characteristic bluntness. "He had us over a barrel, and he knew it." By contrast, the New York Giants paid Manley for the rights to sign Monte Irvin, as did Bill Veeck and the Indians for Irvin's teammate in Newark, Larry Doby.

Irvin had the audacity to ask for a percentage of his sale price, $5,000, which got him nothing except bad press.

Chapter 8: Reality Check

Daytona, already more enlightened racially thanks to Mary McLeod Bethune, began dismantling Jim Crow in the wake of Robinson's training camp. In 1948, the city's well-known Peabody Auditorium would be desegregated, and the famous beach itself would follow suit in 1955.

Sanford, Florida, would return to the civil rights foreground in early 2012, when an unarmed black teenager named Trayvon Martin was shot to death by a neighborhood watchman, mainly because he felt the hooded sweatshirt Martin was wearing looked suspicious.

On October 12, 1945, two weeks before Robinson's signing with Montreal, a black man named Jesse James Payne was accused of raping a white girl, kidnapped from jail, and lynched in Madison, Florida.

Paul Derringer carried two nicknames—"Oom Paul," for his size (6'3" and well over two hundred pounds), and "Dude," for his nattiness. He was said to change clothes five times a day. Derringer won 223 games with the Cards and Reds, but was best known for duking it out with just about anyone, including a conventioneer in a New York hotel. Worst was the occasion when he underwent surgery and, upon coming to, coldcocked the nurse standing over him.

Chapter 9: The Most Interesting Man in the World

The player Danny Gardella scared witless from the balcony of the hotel was fellow Giant-turned-Mexican jumper Nap Reyes.

The fabled toreador Manolete was renowned in Spain and Mexico for his preternatural ability to stand nearly stock-still and yet manage to evade the onrushing bull. But his luck in the ring ran out a little over a year after Danny Gardella saw him at dinner. He was gored in August 1947 in a ring in Andalusia. Generalissimo Franco ordered three days of national mourning out of respect for Manolete's greatness.

Sal "the Barber" Maglie owed his future success in the majors to his days in Mexico. Through endless practice he discovered a curveball he could make snap even in the altitude. By the time he was pitching at sea level in New York for the Giants, his curve was the most fearsome in the league. Maglie also learned the finer points of pitching from his manager, former Cincinnati Reds great Dolf Luque.

Alejandro Carrasquel was the uncle of the better-known Chico Carrasquel, the shortstop from Venezuela who played for four different AL teams in the 1950s.

Even with Vern Stephens back in the fold, the Browns would finish 66–88–2, in seventh place, a full thirty-eight games behind Boston.

Tommy Henrich was at the plate in Game Four of the 1941 Series when Owen missed the third strike from Hugh Casey. Two were out and no one on in the ninth, and the Dodgers led 4–3. After Henrich reached on the passed ball, Joe DiMaggio singled, and King Kong Keller blasted a two-run double to right. After a walk, Joe Gordon hit another two-run double, and the Yankees won 7–4 to take a 3–1 lead in the Series. The next day, the *Brooklyn Eagle* ran a headline with the enduring phrase, "Wait Till Next Year."

Ironically, Owen had set an NL record for handling 476 chances without an error in 1941.

Phil Rizzuto recovered from his malaria-stricken 1946 season, regained his stamina, and won the 1950 MVP Award.

Chapter 10: Opening Day

Truman joins Herbert Hoover and Ronald Reagan as presidents who may have been natural left-handers, but were taught at an early age to use their right hand. In recent years, four holders of the top job, including Gerald Ford, George H. W. Bush, Bill Clinton, and Barack Obama, are southpaws.

Mel Ott is one of baseball's more underrated superstars. Along with his 511 homers, he hit .304 for his career, with a .947 OPS. Between 1937 and 1966, Ott was the all-time leader in home runs in the NL, until Willie Mays passed him en route to 660. The year 1946 saw the first season since 1928 that Ott did not lead the Giants in homers. Of Mel Ott's 511 home runs, 323 were hit at the Polo Grounds. That is the record for most round-trippers hit at any single park.

Ott's home run total, astounding as it was, may have been severely handicapped by the NL baseball, which in the decade before the war was far less tightly wound and much less springy than its AL counterpart. In the span 1931–41, the AL averaged about 20 percent more dingers than the NL per year, and one year, there were 40 percent more. Starting in 1946, baseball adopted a more uniform specification for its baseballs, and the stark power contrast fell away.

The best hitter in the NL annually receives the Mel Ott Award, a testament to his brilliance at the plate.

Unfortunately, Ott wasn't nearly as stellar a manager. His career record was 464–530, and the Giants finished no higher than third on his watch.

Dorothy Lamour was one of World War II's most popular pinup girls, along with Betty Grable, Rita Hayworth, and Lana Turner. She was also a critical figure in the war bond tours that raised considerable money for the war effort. She is considered responsible for some $21 million in war bonds sales.

Trygve Lie was the first Secretary-General of the United Nations. The world body met from March until August of '46 at Hunter College on Park Avenue in New York City while a more permanent building was being erected along the East River.

Chapter 11: Jackie's Debut

The fact that Robinson's first official game in Organized Baseball took place in Jersey City is commemorated by a bronze statue at the PATH Station in Journal Square.

The McAlpin Hotel is now a condo complex called the Herald Towers.

Wendell Willkie wrote *One World* after he traveled the globe in 1941, after being easily beaten by FDR in the 1940 presidential election. Roosevelt brought the defeated Willkie into his cabinet in a political maneuver, but when *One World,* in which he urged America to adopt a "world government," was published, the president dumped Willkie. The book was a major success, but Willkie never held political office.

Baz O'Meara is legendary in Canada for being the man who bestowed the nickname "the Rocket" on the great Montreal Canadiens forward Maurice Richard.

Mickey Grasso would become Jersey City's regular catcher in 1946, playing eighty-seven games, but wasn't yet on the Little Giants on April 18.

In left field for Jersey City, however, was someone who would become quite famous in baseball annals, if not quite as fabled as Jackie Robinson—Bobby Thomson.

Robinson's declaration that "God has been good to us today" after the opener against Jersey City ironically calls to mind Confederate general Stonewall Jackson's words after the Battle of Antietam—"God has been good to us this day."

Chapter 12: Trial by Fury

Head's new son was named Rickey, in honor of Head's boss.

Head is part of the "All Body Parts Team," which also consists of Rollie Fingers, Barry Foote, Elroy Face, Dave Brain, Ricky Bones, and Harry Cheek.

Fluoroscopy is similar to X-ray technology, except that physicians use it to gain real-time looks at moving images from inside the body, rather than static ones.

Famous members of Murder, Incorporated included Albert "The Mad Hatter" Anastasia, Abe "Kid Twist" Reles, and of course, Bugsy Siegel and Meyer Lansky. The trials that broke the murder-for-hire syndicate mostly took place in the early 1940s.

Durocher was probably unable to stand a fair trial in Brooklyn—he was far too popular in the borough. An example—he once slugged a Giants player named Zeke Bonura during a brawl, and was fined $25 for it. The Ebbets Field faithful not only took up a collection and paid the fine for Leo, but the plan was to change it into pennies and and throw it on the field so league officials would have to pick them up. Cooler heads prevailed, however, and the fine was paid the conventional way.

If Slaughter's hustle sounds familiar, it's because the man later synonymous with all-out effort, Pete Rose, was inspired by Country. "I used to watch the Reds games on television," said Charley Hustle in 1963. "One day, the Reds were playing the Cardinals. Slaughter drew a walk and ran hard to first base. I decided right then and there that was what I was going to do as long as I played ball."

Slaughter himself got a less-lethal dose of the rabbit fever that killed his father, laying him up for weeks.

Chapter 13: Those Splendid Sox

The man who mixed the color scheme for the "Green Monster" was a veteran of Normandy and Purple Heart-winner named Emil Disario. He worked for the misleadingly named California Pain Company and experimented with various hues until settling on the green that still covers the left field wall. His daughter, Christine, claims credit for suggesting the nickname "Green Monster." Disario died days before Fenway Park's centennial celebration in 2012.

For many years the John Fitzgerald Expressway, part of Interstate 93, was an elevated road that passed through Boston. It was held up by green-colored girders and was known as "Boston's Other Green Monster." It moved underground during the (endless) construction project known as the "Big Dig."

Pesky hit only seventeen homers in his long career, so they are not difficult to isolate.

Pesky's Pole is 302 feet down the right field line at Fenway, at least according to the number stenciled on the wall. However, aerial photography has shown the pole to be only 295 feet from home.

Bobby Doerr's sister Dorothy was a heck of a ballplayer as well, playing on an all-girls team that "beat all the boys teams," according to Bobby.

The WAVES were a volunteer unit of women serving in the navy: "Women Accepted for Volunteer Emergency Service." They were actually in the service and held rank, although the word "emergency" meant that the enlistment only was good through the war—once it ended, the women returned to civilian life. The army version of a distaff service, the Women's Army Corps (WAC) began as an auxiliary adjunct and not a part of the army itself (it was originally WAAC, Women's Army Auxiliary Corps). In 1943, the army brought the ladies into the fold.

Eddie Pellagrini would be traded in 1947, part of a package that brought Vern Stephens, erstwhile Mexican Leaguer, to Boston.

Chapter 14: Baseball for the One Percent

The Congressional Medal of Honor winner who threw out the initial postwar first pitch at Yankee Stadium was Hulon Whittington of Jamaica, New York. His citation for the Medal of Honor reads as follows:

> For conspicuous gallantry and intrepidity at the risk of life above and beyond the call of duty. On the night of 29 July 1944, near Grimesnil, France, during an enemy armored attack, Sgt. Whittington, a squad leader, assumed command of his platoon when the platoon leader and platoon sergeant became missing in action. He reorganized the defense and, under fire, courageously crawled between gun positions to check the actions of his men. When the advancing enemy attempted to penetrate a roadblock, Sgt. Whittington, completely disregarding intense

enemy action, mounted a tank and by shouting through the turret, directed it into position to fire pointblank at the leading Mark V German tank. The destruction of this vehicle blocked all movement of the remaining enemy column consisting of over 100 vehicles of a Panzer unit. The blocked vehicles were then destroyed by handgrenades, bazooka, tank, and artillery fire and large numbers of enemy personnel were wiped out by a bold and resolute bayonet charge inspired by Sgt. Whittington. When the medical aid man had become a casualty, Sgt. Whittington personally administered first aid to his wounded men. The dynamic leadership, the inspiring example, and the dauntless courage of Sgt. Whittington, above and beyond the call of duty, are in keeping with the highest traditions of the military service.

Here was the breathless ad copy for the Yankees' home opener that ran in many of the local papers on the morning of April 19:

> Baseball experts are saying the 1946 Yankees pack the greatest wallop of any team in either major league. Come out to the Stadium opener today and see the team which broke all Spring Training attendance records!

Henry Kaiser was best known in 1946 for transforming shipbuilding during the war, thanks to his decision to weld instead of rivet the steel hulls together. Later Kaiser would become an automobile, aluminum, and steel magnate. Today he is a household name thanks to Kaiser Permanente, the first-ever health-maintenance organization, which he began in 1945.

Tiny Bonham was well known for exercising with an iron ball the size of a baseball. He used it to make the real thing feel light, in the manner of a hitter swinging two bats in the on-deck circle. Mariano Rivera, the Yankees immortal closer, uses a similar device.

Chapter 15: Casualties

Pteromerhanophobia is the scientific term for the fear of flying.

The C-54 United Mainliner the Yankees used to fly from city to city declined rapidly, and there were several near-crashes in 1947. A team insurrection was narrowly headed off by manager Bucky Harris and Joe DiMaggio, who in essence told his teammates to suck it up.

Shepard is not to be confused with Pete Gray, the one-armed outfielder who played for the St. Louis Browns in 1945 and came to symbolize the "anything goes" level of play during the war years.

Shepard was reunited with Dr. Loidl, who saved his life in Germany, thanks to an Englishman named Jamie Brundell. Brundell had met Dr. Loidl while on vacation in Hungary in 1992. The German had asked if Brundell could help him find the identity of the American he had saved back in 1944. After a few phone calls, Brundell contacted Shepard, and a meeting in Vienna was arranged. Shepard and Loidl went to the farmhouse where the two encountered each other during the war. When Loidl put his arm around Shepard, the former player thought, "By God, those are the same arms that pulled me out of the cockpit," according to an interview he gave the *Los Angeles Times.* "It was a very strange feeling, and I really broke down." The reunification was captured by *This Week in Baseball,* which aired a segment on Shepard's story.

Catfish Metkovich (real name: George) never lived down the injury that gave him his nickname. Casey Stengel never let him forget it, bellowing in his presence, "We got a first baseman who gets attacked by a catfish!" Metkovich had some Stengel-esque moments of his own. Once, during a trying day in the field at first base, he yelled at the nearby umpire, "Don't just stand there—get a glove and give me a hand!"

Soon after Spahn returned from the service, his stuff was being talked about across the National League. One Philadelphia writer transcribed a conversation he overheard between Phillies manager Ben Chapman, Phils outfielder Del Ennis, and Giants first baseman Johnny Mize:

> **Chapman:** "Spahn has one of the greatest overhand curves I've ever seen."
> **Ennis:** "Never mind the curve. What I have to watch for is the change of pace he throws. I swing at it before it is halfway to the plate."
> **Mize:** "The curve and change of pace are all right, but it's that fastball. It does tricks as it reaches the plate."

Spahn teamed with fellow pitcher Johnny Sain to form a fabled pitching duo in Boston. Their lack of help on the staff was the impetus for the phrase "Spahn and Sain and pray for rain," a rhyme first credited to Gerry Hern of the *Boston Post.* There was more to it than just the one line:

> *First we'll use Spahn, then we'll use Sain*
> *Then an off day, followed by rain*
> *Back will come Spahn, followed by Sain*
> *And followed, we hope, by two days of rain.*

One wounded player who didn't make it back until 1947 was Lou Brissie. Fighting with the 88th Infantry Division (the "Blue Devils") near Florence, Italy, Corporal Brissie was severely wounded on December 7, 1944, three years to the day after Pearl Harbor. A 170mm German artillery shell exploded near him, breaking both his feet and his left tibia and shinbone, and riddling his shoulder, hands, and legs with shrapnel. Brissie doggedly fought off doctors who wanted to amputate his leg, shouting, "I'm a ballplayer! You've got to find another way!"

Brissie at last found a doctor to operate rather than amputate, and his long journey back to baseball began. A metal plate was inserted in his leg, and he was apparently the first patient in the Mediterranean Theater to be administered penicillin. Connie Mack, the same A's majordomo who brought Phil Marchildon back to the game, assured Brissie he would get a crack in Philadelphia. Brissie was outstanding in the low minors in 1947 and was given his promised crack at the majors on September 28, 1947. It was Babe Ruth Day at Yankee Stadium. Brissie lost to the Bombers 5–3 but was solid enough to warrant a look in 1948. He was given the honor of starting on opening day, a doubleheader in Boston. The other A's starter that day was Marchildon. Brissie won fourteen games in 1948, and sixteen more in 1949, despite pitching in pain on every occasion.

Chapter 16: Montreal

Eddie Robinson, a longtime major league player and executive, was a Baltimore Oriole in 1946—he won the International League MVP Award over Jackie, who needless to say was no relation. Eddie didn't remember any untoward treatment of Jackie in Baltimore, but conceded "that was only on the field."

When asked in 2012 what she and Jackie were talking about on that first plane trip to Montreal back in 1946, unsurprisingly Rachel Robinson didn't remember.

Delorimier Stadium is one word, while Rue *de Lorimier* is two words.

A plaque now commemorates the Robinsons' home in the Villeray District of Montreal.

Robinson biographer Jules Tygiel believes Rickey purposefully stacked the 1946 Royals with his best prospects to ease pressure on Jackie. Six Royals made the International League All-Star team. Still, there is no evidence Rickey did anything but advance players through the Dodgers chain as he ordinarily would.

Chapter 17: The Brat

Though few remember it today, the Cubs and Dodgers were bitter enemies through the 1930s and '40s. Fights between the teams, while not usually rising to the violence of the '46 brannigans, were commonplace. Once, in the early '40s, Cubs pitchers knocked down an incredible fifteen straight Brooklyn hitters.

Babe Herman was dealt to Boston on June 15, 1946.

While the Walker brothers in some respects lived out an extraordinary dream, they also both suffered the unspeakable tragedy of losing a child.

Chapter 18: Paralysis

During the railroad strike, the Browns "rained out" their game with the Indians and Bob Feller because they wanted the gate from the resulting doubleheader. Had the Cards not made it to Cincy in time to play, the Reds would have taken the forfeit, preferring the win to the gate. It was up to the home team.

One of Max Lanier's sons, Hal, played ten years in the majors, mostly in San Francisco. Hal was later Manager of the Year in Houston in 1986.

Lanier lost almost the entirety of his $30,000 bonus investing in a restaurant, Max Lanier's Diamond Club in St. Petersburg.

Murry Dickson's first start didn't come until June 20, when he bested Philly in his initial outing, going all the way in a 9–1 win. He wouldn't lose a start until late July, and finished 15–6.

Lanier was cut off from any pension plan thanks to jumping to Mexico, and lived out his days subsisting on Social Security.

Lanier got back to the majors, pitching in the early 1950s for Bill Veeck in St. Louis. This was a dreadful franchise. In '53 the team lost eight straight when Veeck decided to hold a champagne-drenched pennant party to loosen up the guys. "We went out the next day, all nice and loose," recalled Lanier, "and lost our ninth straight."

Chapter 19: *Finito*

Larry MacPhail hired Ruth to be a coach on the Dodgers, mostly as a PR move. But the Babe took it as a prelude to managing the club. When his old enemy Durocher was hired instead, Ruth was especially anguished.

Mexico's version of Pearl Harbor came in May 1942, when German U-boats sunk a pair of crude oil transports, *Faja de Oro* and *Potrero del Llano*. Mexico declared war on June 1. Mexican pilots fought bravely during the liberation of the Philippines, among other action her countrymen saw. But Mexico's main contribution to the war effort came from the roughly three hundred thousand of her citizens who crossed the border to work in US factories churning out matériel.

Estimates of the average Mexican League player salaries don't factor in the large bonuses the Pasquels paid.

The eight teams in La Liga included the Mexico City Diablos Rojos, the Vera Cruz Azules, the Puebla Ángeles, the San Luis Potosi Tuneros, the Monterrey Industriales, the Nuevo Laredo Tecolotes, the Tampico Alijadores, and the Torreon Algodoneros.

Ray Dandridge was one of the very few Negro stars to live somewhat large in Mexico. He earned a salary of $9,000, lived in a six-room apartment, rent free, and had both a maid and a tutor for his children, who came gratis, thanks to Señor Pasquel. Still, given his excellence and what the American jumpers were getting, Dandridge was underpaid.

In one incident, Pasquel offered $1,000 to any player in the league who threw a no-hitter. But when a hurler named Adrián Zabala appeared to accomplish the feat, Pasquel ordered an error ruled a hit and didn't pay Zabala.

Chapter 20: Strike Out

The man Ty Cobb beat up in the stands had no hands. When informed of that fact, Cobb yelled, "I don't care if he has no feet!"

The replacement team the Tigers used after the Ty Cobb sympathy strike lost 24–2 to Connie Mack's Philadelphia A's. Mack played most of his starters for the full nine innings.

The American Federation of Labor merged with the Congress of International Organizations in 1955.

Jimmy Brown was a solid leadoff hitter for the Cardinals before the war, finishing sixth in the MVP voting in 1939. He joined the Army Air Force in 1943 and played baseball for the 4th Ferrying Group Globetrotters. He was released by the Pirates after the 1946 season and went into coaching.

Sewell did pitch the day before the proposed strike, on June 6, the original strike date. So that is probably where the confusion lay when he talked about his brief speech in the Pittsburgh clubhouse to William Marshall for the Chandler Oral History Project in 1979. Brooklyn was the opponent, and the Dodgers scored nine runs in the fifth to saddle Sewell with a 13–8 loss.

Sewell expounded on his antiunion stance to William Marshall—"Unions are where they belong like coal mines and truck driving and people that can't help themselves, but in the sports it's a competitive competition, and if everybody is going to be created the same way, give them all twenty thousand dollars a year and say, 'Go out and play.' There's no incentive for a fella to go on up and be a top hero, like Musial and Slaughter, Ruth, Gehrig, Foxx. These great ball players, there's no incentive to go any farther. If you going to have a union just go to the Soviet Union and then pay them all the same thing."

The history of players, especially star players, speaking out against abolishment of the Reserve Clause is a long one. Ty Cobb himself lamented those who played only for the money and not for the love of the game, as he had, way back at the turn of the century. In the 1960s, when Curt Flood challenged the Reserve Clause in court, Willie Mays and Carl Yastrzemski campaigned against him, and Joe Garagiola testified against him. Henry Aaron signed a three-year, $200,000 contract in 1971, then said free agency would "destroy" baseball.

The lack of a standardized schedule, which left owners free to move individual games around at the last moment to maximize profits, was a major complaint of the players, but one that wouldn't be addressed right away.

Bing Crosby, a minority member of the syndicate that bought the Pirates from Benswanger, would often shower in the Pittsburgh clubhouse. He would sing as he did, giving free shows to the players.

Chapter 21: Here Comes "The Man"

Dick Sisler fizzled as a wunderkind in St. Louis, but he managed to earn a place in baseball history as a Philadelphia Phillie in 1950. He hit a three-run, opposite-field home run in the tenth inning of a game at Ebbets Field to win the "Whiz Kid" Phils the pennant. The dramatic blow was overshadowed historically when Bobby Thomson hit his "Shot Heard 'Round the World" the very next season.

Musial played at Donora High School with Buddy Griffey, the father of future player Ken Griffey and the grandfather of future Hall of Famer Ken Griffey Jr.

In 1948, the worst recorded air pollution accident in US history took place in Donora. Twenty died and hundreds were seriously affected by fluoride leaks from the Donora Zinc Works, owned by US Steel. The "Donora Death Fog" spawned numerous lawsuits and calls for legislation to protect the public from industry's fouling of the air.

The failure of the Cardinals to bring up Musial earlier in 1941 cannot be blamed on "starting his arbitration clock," which is a huge factor in such decisions today. Teams often delay bringing up prospects to the big club in order to put off the date the player is eligible for arbitration of his salary, which happens after three years of service. Obviously, this was not part of the calculus in Musial's day.

Musial finished his career with 475 home runs and 1,951 RBIs.

The stat that perhaps best defines Musial is that he played in 3,026 games as a major leaguer and was never ejected once.

Another—Musial struck out three times in a game only once in his twenty-two years in the game. It happened during that final season, 1963, on July 28 against the Cubs at Wrigley Field. The Chicago faithful probably disbelieved their eyes, as Stan had hit .317 with 67 homers and 286 RBIs against the Cubs in his career.

The automatic pinspotter was invented by Fred Schmidt (not to be confused with Cards pitcher Freddy Schmidt), who brought it to American Machine and Foundry, better known as AMF. Brunswick had been dominating the bowling industry until it rejected Schmidt's patent. AMF surpassed Brunswick as a result.

Musial's love of bowling had a bitter moment when he was sued by his partner in Red Bird Lanes—Joe Garagiola. The suit alleged that Musial's son Dick was being paid $750 a month without Garagiola's knowledge. It was settled with undisclosed terms, but the two players had a bitter falling out over the suit, to the point that Musial refused to throw out the first pitch of Game Four of the 2006 World Series when he discovered Garagiola was on hand to catch it. He tossed out the pitch for Game Five instead.

The Cardinals' official address was at 3623 Dodier; the Browns were at 2911 North Grand, around the corner.

Chris von der Ahe was a character deserving his own book. He combined elements of Larry MacPhail and Bill Veeck, turning Browns games into public spectacles. He would have his players gather in full uniform at his saloon and lead them in a parade to Sportsman's Park, wearing a silk top hat and flanked by his greyhounds, Snoozer and Schnauzer. After the inevitable victory (his Browns dominated the 1880s), von der Ahe would lead another parade back to his saloon, where the drinks flowed. The Browns' fortunes changed in the "Gay Nineties" as von der Ahe got more involved with team affairs. The "Boss President" ran through a dozen managers between 1894 and 1896, including eight in 1895. Von der Ahe fancied himself a Rickeyesque judge of talent, but when confronted with a young John McGraw, who was trying out for the Browns, the boss ran the "Little Napoleon" off the field, suggesting he become a jockey instead. The innkeeper pioneered use of a Stadium Club decades before MacPhail, giving over a shaded area under the grandstand to his best consumers of ale and food. He also installed a water slide in center field, hired a Wild West show (one that included the legendary Sioux chief Sitting Bull) to perform before games, and built a racetrack inside the park. He eventually went bankrupt, was thrown in debtor's prison, and died of cirrhosis in 1913.

Sportsman's Park and its nearby right field fence (and screen) were catnip for lefty sluggers with an uppercut stroke. Babe Ruth in particular loved hitting there, slamming 58 homers, the most of any visiting player.

Perhaps Dr. Hyland's greatest feat was his cryogenic preservation of Musial's appendix in 1947. Musial was sick with appendicitis that summer, but Hyland was reluctant to operate, which meant losing the team's superstar for at least a month. So he froze the appendix with applied ice packs, a controversial treatment and one difficult to make effective. Musial sat for a week, then played the rest of the season, having the surgery afterward. He managed to hit .312, and called it a "lousy year."

Musial switched back and forth between first and the outfield several times in his career. Overall he would start 989 games at first base, 868 in left, 681 in right, and 351 in center. In 1947, '57, and '58, Musial played only at first, and he ended his career by sticking to the outfield. Otherwise, he shuttled to and fro as the team needed him.

Musial would lead the National League in doubles and triples in 1946 by a wide margin (50 doubles, 20 triples). Part of that was lethal hitting, and part was the fact that Musial ran very hard right out of the box.

The "Triple-Double-Inverted-Whammy" is as follows: The thumb, index finger, and pinky point outward, with the other fingers fisted and the hands stacked facing one another.

Chapter 22: "Bullseye!"

Fred Hutchinson appears in newsreel footage (along with Bob Feller) as he enlists in the navy in the movie *A League of Their Own*. Unlike Feller, Hutch joined Gene Tunney's physical fitness instruction detail and avoided combat.

Williams's epic homer was long estimated to travel roughly 450 feet, but in the mid-'80s the Red Sox used new technology to measure the blast at 502 feet, making it the longest home run in Sox history, one foot farther than a blast Manny Ramirez clubbed off a light tower in 2001.

Wally Moses was scouted by the New York Giants after he had been, according to legend, discovered by Ty Cobb after the Georgia Peach stumbled upon a sandlot game and took over as umpire. Moses impressed the scout, who had been dispatched mainly because John McGraw thought the kid was Jewish, and John J. was forever on the lookout for a Hebrew Hitter he could parlay into big box office in New York City. When Moses told the scout he was Scotch-Irish and not Jewish, the scout grumbled "ah, hell," and left without offering Moses a contract.

When Dickey took over as player-manager, he became the first Yankees skipper to wear a number on his uniform while managing. His number 8 would be retired after Yogi Berra sported it for eighteen memorable seasons.

Berra saw action in seven games in 1946, hitting .364 with a pair of homers in twenty-two at bats.

There have been two other seasons that saw three different men manage the Yankees: 1978 (Billy Martin, Dick Howser, and Bob Lemon) and 1982 (Lemon, Gene Michael, and Clyde King).

Dickey was upset in large part because MacPhail had hired journeyman manager Bucky Harris for a front-office position, with the rather apparent subtext being that Harris was ready to step in if Dickey made any waves about his contract. Already not liking MacPhail, and stung by the maneuver, Dickey quit, and Harris took over as skipper in 1947, winning the World Series in his initial season. Despite that success, Harris was a mediocrity as a manager, the ultimate retread who was a safe but unexciting hire. He lasted twenty-five seasons that way, with a .493 winning percentage. After the Yanks came in third in 1948, Harris was dumped in favor of Casey Stengel.

Joe DiMaggio would later lament the time he spent away from baseball, telling the *New York Daily News,* "It's obvious I was not the same player after the war. All you have to do is look at the record."

Chapter 23: All Things Eephus

Musial would become an All-Star Game fixture, making twenty overall and eighteen consecutive Midsummer Classics. He was even named a starter in 1957, when Cincinnati Reds fans infamously stuffed the ballot boxes for their players. Seven starters were Reds, but first base belonged to Stan the Man.

Williams would be named to seventeen All-Star Games. One assumes he would have been part of the four he missed due to service in World War II and Korea.

Other versions of the eephus pitch have been foisted on batters over the years. Boston's Bill "Spaceman" Lee threw an homage to Sewell's lob called the "Leephus" in Game Seven of the 1975 World Series. Tony Perez of the Reds golfed a towering two-run homer at Fenway Park that evoked Williams's 1946 blast, and the Reds beat the Sox 4–3 to win the championship.

Other floaters include Dave LaRoche's "LaLob," Vicente Padilla's "Soap Bubble," Dave Stieb's "Dead Fish," Casey Fossum's "Fossum Flip," and Steve Hamilton's "Folly Floater."

An exaggerated version of the Williams Shift was seen during an exhibition game Boston played in Dallas before the 1947 season. The Texas team put every fielder but the catcher into the right field stands when Ted came up to hit.

Bill Veeck differed from MacPhail in that he was more of a pure entrepreneur, while Mac was a forward-thinker and restless mind. Both had grand visions, but Veeck's were more of the retail variety. He wanted to reach every individual fan and better his or her ball-game experience. MacPhail was more interested in leaving his mark on the game.

Gaedel's first appearance featured him popping out of a cake that marked the party Veeck was throwing for the American League's fiftieth birthday. He then came to bat as a pinch hitter for Frank Saucier. Jim Delsing ran for Gaedel after he walked. Gaedel patted Delsing in the rear in his best baseball fashion on his way to the dugout. Three weeks later, Gaedel was arrested for disorderly conduct, a brush with the law that presaged his later problems in life. In June 1961, with his health in terrible shape, he was beaten and robbed, and died later that night. After the funeral, a con man showed up at Gaedel's mother's home, pretending to be from the Hall of Fame and asking for the bat and uniform Gaedel wore back in 1951. The man took the equipment and was never seen again.

Veeck staged a match race in August to determine the AL speed title. Cleveland's George Washington Case raced Senators rookie Gil Coan over one hundred yards on a soggy turf in full uniform. Case won, sprinting the distance in ten seconds flat, just six-tenths off the world record held by Jesse Owens. That earned Case a race with the man himself. Owens came to Cleveland in September to face Case. The Olympic great (there had not been an Olympiad since Berlin '36 due to the war, so Owens was still defending champion in the sprints and long jump) donned a baseball uniform and spikes, and blew Case away in 9.9 seconds.

The Veeck Orchestra was considered in play, with any ball landing inside the chicken wire surrounding the band worth two bases.

Jackie Price actually played in seven games in 1946, hitting .231.

Price finished the 1946 season with the Indians but was let go as both player and comic in 1947, after he let a pair of boa constrictors loose on a train to observe the reaction of some lady bowlers aboard. The snakes were part of his act (he would wrap them around him and then play catch), but proved his undoing after the railroad complained to Veeck.

Veeck was more than willing to swipe good ideas as well as innovate them. For example, a man named Marsh Samuel, a PR type in Chicago, created a media guide for the 1946 White Sox that he distributed to the Windy City writers, a seventeen-page pamphlet with all the players' and coaches' pertinent information. Veeck loved the idea so much he hired Samuel away from Chicago to create a more lavish version for the Tribe.

Chapter 24: Lucky

A pitcher named Forrest "Lefty" Brewer parachuted into Normandy on D-day six years to the day after pitching a no-hitter in the Florida International League. He was killed later that afternoon, near Sainte-Mère-Église. In addition to Brewer and Pinder, a third minor leaguer was killed on D-day, Elmer Wright.

Nine former players were killed at the Battle of the Bulge, counting Hank Nowak. The others were Ernie Holbrook, Bill Hansen, Elmer Wachtler, Alan Lightner, Ernie Hrovatic, Paul Mellblom, George Meyer, and Lamar Zimmerman.

Six ex-players were killed at Iwo Jima, including Harry O'Neill and Jimmy Trimble. The others are Jack Lummus (who posthumously was given the Medal of Honor for storming three Japanese pillboxes by himself), Bob Holmes, James Stewart, and Frank Ciaffone.

Trimble may be better known as the prep-school lover of the late writer Gore Vidal. The two carried on a torrid homosexual affair while at St. Albans before Trimble shipped off for war, at least according to Vidal.

The typhoon off the Philippines was Typhoon Cobra, aka "Halsey's Typhoon," a major storm that sank three US destroyers in Admiral Halsey's Third Fleet, killing 790 sailors. Nine other ships were damaged and more than one hundred aircraft swept overboard. Admiral Chester Nimitz compared the destruction to that sustained in a major operation. Author Herman Wouk survived the storm and later evoked his memories of Cobra to describe the typhoon that strikes the USS *Caine* in his book *The Caine Mutiny.*

The military transport plane Jack Lohrke was kicked off crashed in Ohio.

Lohrke's remarkable luck extended to his major league career, which was undistinguished except for 1951, when he was a reserve on the Miracle Giants.

Chapter 25: The Leo Beat

Durocher's slur was translated as "Nice guys finish eighth" by Lou Effrat in the *New York Times.*

Mel Ott wasn't that nice of a guy—about a month before Leo's famous backhanded compliment, Ott became the first manager to be thrown out of both ends of a doubleheader. Proving his worth, the Giants lost both games to Pittsburgh.

Memphis Engelberg was considered the top handicapper in New York, and the city's best bookmaker when such things were legal. He had the run of the Brooklyn clubhouse and would pick horses for Durocher, a fact that upset Rickey and Chandler. Durocher, in *Nice Guys Finish Last,* insists he didn't know whether Engelberg ever bet on baseball.

Laraine Day played a nurse in the Dr. Kildare films, which included:

> *Dr. Kildare's Victory*
> *Dr. Kildare's Wedding Day*
> *The People vs. Dr. Kildare*
> *Dr. Kildare's Crisis*
> *Dr. Kildare Goes Home*
> *Dr. Kildare's Strange Case*
> *Calling Dr. Kildare*
> *The Secret of Dr. Kildare*

There were two others, *Young Dr. Kildare* and *Interns Can't Take Money,* that Day did not appear in.

Durocher's first wife, Grace Dozier, claimed during their divorce proceedings that Leo had hit her and tied her up with a bed sheet.

Durocher would eventually divorce Laraine Day too, as well as his third wife, Lynne Goldblatt.

The Washington Senators were the last holdout in sending their announcers on the road. Not until 1955 did Arch McDonald and crew travel with the team.

Charley Paddock was the first to be called the "Fastest Man Alive," after he sprinted to two gold medals and a silver at the 1920 Olympic Games in Antwerp. He went on to win silver at the 1924 Games in Paris, edging Eric Liddell of *Chariots of Fire* fame in the 200-meter dash.

Paddock and other statisticians may have been cheered by the unveiling of the first fully automatic digital computer system, ENIAC, at Harvard that summer.

Some Brooklyn fans fluent in Morse code would be able to hear the telegraph reports coming in and, in the few seconds before Barber's call, would bet on the result with others in the bar, always collecting.

Dean was inducted into the Hall of Fame in 1953, but his career statistics are relatively puny, winning only 150 games in his twelve seasons. From 1934–36, when he won 30, 38, and 24 games, he was the best pitcher in baseball, but he doesn't have the longevity of most hurlers enshrined in Cooperstown. If his broadcasting is taken into account along with his playing, however, it's a no-brainer.

Dizzy's brother Paul made for a dominating brother act in 1934–35, when Paul won nineteen games in each season. But that was pretty much it for the younger Dean—he only won a dozen more games the rest of his career.

The TV tower added sixty-one feet to the Empire State Building, making the then-world's tallest building 1,250 feet high.

Wanamaker's wireless station was an important mode of communication in the early days of radio. News of the *Titanic*'s sinking was relayed to anxious crowds in New York City gathered outside the wireless station in 1912.

The plan had been for Chicago's WBKB to televise the opening-day game at Wrigley Field, but interference from the Wrigley Field elevator system kiboshed the transmission.

Herman retired just in time to miss the Braves' appearance in the 1948 World Series. Herman took the collar in the Fall Classic, losing all four Series he played in—three with the Cubs (1932, 1935, and 1938) and one with Brooklyn (1941).

Chapter 26: Red, Whitey, and "Four-Sack" Dusak

The Bikini "Able" test instantly killed a sizable portion of the animals left on board the naval ships that were in the harbor. The rest were destroyed in the "Baker" test three weeks later. Over the ensuing few years, there would be over twenty bombs exploded at Bikini, resulting in radiation exposure for inhabitants of nearby islands, an unlucky Japanese fishing boat that blundered into the area during one test in 1954, and the Bikini inhabitants, who were allowed back onto the island in 1957, only to be sickened at a rapid rate. As of this writing, the island remains uninhabitable.

Later in 1946, Klaus Fuchs and Johnny Von Neumann submitted a patent application for the first hydrogen bomb. One would imagine, in retrospect, that such a device would be immune from patent law due to state security, but apparently not.

A two-piece bathing suit named for the site of the Able test was all the rage on the runways of Paris in the spring of 1946. However, the "bikini" was banned in most places and wouldn't hit US shores until the early 1960s.

For all his excellence and longevity, it's fair to question Red Schoendienst's qualifications for Cooperstown. His induction was strongly benefited by Stan Musial's position on the Veterans Committee.

Elizabeth Avenue has been renamed Hall of Fame Place, and plaques mark the sidewalk outside the boyhood homes of Garagiola and Berra. Jack Buck, the Cardinals' legendary longtime broadcaster, lived at the corner of Elizabeth and Macklind for a time while he was calling games.

There are also plaques for the five members of the 1950 World Cup team that stunned

England. The Hill's Italian influence made St. Louis one of the few soccer-mad cities in the United States.

Garagiola's cuddly image as an NBC stalwart papered over his rather caustic time spent in baseball, where he never missed an opportunity to spike or taunt Jackie Robinson and was known for hard tags to the faces of enemy base runners. In 1970, he testified against Curt Flood and for the baseball owners in the landmark case that was the first step in erasing the Reserve Clause.

Ken Burkhart, the Cards pitcher who lent Garagiola his shoes, became an umpire and blew a famous call in the 1970 World Series. He got spun around and, with his back to the plate, called Cincinnati's Bernie Carbo out at home despite the fact that Baltimore catcher Elrod Hendricks tagged Carbo with the glove while holding the ball with his other hand. The play tied the game at three; the Orioles went on to win 4–3 and the Series in five games.

Chapter 27: CPO Feller

Feller's trip to the majors at such a young age was not without controversy. Cleveland general manager Cy Slapnicka forged transcripts and other paperwork in a transparent attempt to get Feller onto the Indians at age seventeen, in stark defiance of existing age rules. Commissioner Landis looked into the matter, but decided that since Feller (and his father) badly wanted to play for Cleveland, and since the Yankees and Tigers, Feller's other suitors, were already too good, Rapid Robert would become Indians property.

Of Feller's eighteen seasons, 1946 was almost certainly his finest. Besides his otherworldly strikeout total, he set career marks in ERA, innings, complete games, shutouts, K–BB ratio, and, funnily enough, saves, with four. Only in 1940 did he win more games, with twenty-seven to his twenty-six in '46.

Those that use the 107.6 mph measurement for Feller's 1946 fastball classify it as the second-fastest ever measured, behind a heater from Nolan Ryan clocked by similarly imprecise means at 108.1 mph (Ryan's pitch was measured by lasers crossing home plate). Aroldis Chapman of the Reds threw a pitch measured at 105 mph in 2010, the fastest ever recognized by MLB.

Admiral Halsey's command decisions of the carrier group that included *Alabama* at Leyte Gulf rank among the most controversial of the war. The Battle of Leyte Gulf was a last-ditch effort by the Japanese to repel General MacArthur's Philippine landings. A feint to the north by the Japanese fleet suckered the overenthusiastic Halsey and his Task Force 34 (which included *Alabama*), leaving the landings unguarded. Fortunately for the Americans, a powerful flotilla of Imperial Fleet carriers and battleships was turned away by a small group of American light cruisers (designated as Taffy 3) and the powerful fog of war, which obscured the fact that a determined Japanese thrust at the critical moment would have resulted in catastrophe for the US landing forces.

Some names—familiar to American baseball fans—who have won the Sawamura Award: Hideo Nomo, Koji Uehara (twice), Daisuke Matsuzaka, Kei Igawa, Kenshin Kawakami, and Yu Darvish.

Bobby Doerr broke up a Feller no-hitter in the ninth inning of a game in 1939 as well.

Feller would go on to throw twelve one-hitters, a record that has since been matched by Nolan Ryan, who amassed seven no-hitters as well.

Years later, researchers for the *Sporting News* revised Waddell's record upward, adding a pair of whiffs to give him 349 strikeouts.

The NL leader in strikeouts in 1946 was Johnny Schmitz of Chicago with 143. The colossal 213-strikeout difference is a major league record.

Surprisingly, Newhouser edged Feller in strikeouts per nine innings in 1946, 8.5 to 8.4. It was one of six categories in which Prince Hal paced the AL, including advanced numbers like ERA+, which adjusts for the home park. Feller led in ten, including walks allowed, shutouts (10), and complete games. Feller finished 36 of his 42 starts. Newhouser finished 29 of 34.

Feller was elected to the Hall of Fame in 1962, his first year of eligibility. Newhouser had to wait for thirty more years, 1992, until he was enshrined.

Amazingly for such a storied franchise, Newhouser is the sole Tigers pitcher enshrined in Cooperstown. Many would argue that Jack Morris, who starred for Detroit in the 1980s, should be in the Hall.

Koufax was bested by Nolan Ryan, who had 383 strikeouts for the 1973 California Angels. Randy Johnson had 372 and 364 whiffs in 1999 and 2001, respectively, and Ryan had 367 in 1974, so Waddell holds sixth place on the all-time list, and Feller seventh. This discounts a dozen seasons turned in by nineteenth-century pitchers.

Feller's push for the record seemed to take something out of him. He never again threw as many as 200 strikeouts in a season.

Chapter 28: The Jewel of Pigtown

Hilda Chester's unbridled enthusiasm is today saved for callers to sports talk radio, rather than actual paying customers at the ballpark. That must make the late Doris Bauer, aka "Doris from Rego Park," an obsessed Mets fan whose late-night phone calls to WFAN in New York were a symphony of baseball expertise and coughing fits, the evolutionary Hilda Chester. Thank you for your time and courtesy, Doris.

Prior to "Dodgers," the Brooklyn side was known as the "Grays," the "Grooms," the "Bridegrooms," the "Superbas," and the "Robins." At all times the official name of the team was simply the Brooklyn Base Ball Club.

In another example of the popularity of the Dodgers in Brooklyn, a man named Robert Russell Bennett wrote an opera in 1941 about the team. There were four parts: *Allegro con brio* (Brooklyn Wins), *Andante lamentosa* (Brooklyn Loses), *Scherzo* (Larry MacPhail Tries to Give Cleveland the Brooklyn Bridge for Bob Feller), and *Finale* (The Giants Come to Town).

Reiser would go on to be a minor league manager after his playing days ended. Coincidentally, one of the teams he skippered was the Spokane Indians, rebuilt after the horrible tragedy at Snoqualmie Pass two decades earlier.

Thanks to excellent fielding from Dixie Walker and especially Carl Furillo, Abe Stark gave away very few suits. One he definitely did give was to Furillo, in gratitude. The only known player to have hit the sign on the fly was Mel Ott. The sign served its purpose—Stark's name recognition was so high he was able to become Brooklyn Borough President from 1962–1970. There is an ice skating rink on Surf Avenue in Stark's name.

Records are sketchy, but it appears the 1912 New York Giants inaugurated the separate admission doubleheader.

Bama Rowell was promised a free watch from Bulova for hitting the clock, but due to one snafu or another, he didn't get it until forty-one years had gone by. Bama finally got his timepiece on a day thrown for him back in Citronelle, Alabama, in 1987.

Rowell was traded to the Dodgers two seasons later, part of a package that sent Eddie
Stanky to Boston. After a mere eleven days as a Bum, Rowell was sold to the Phillies.

Chapter 29: Fighting Retreat

Here's the full list of original player representatives. Each team could have had two reps
apiece, but except for the Yankees and Browns, no AL team did.

NATIONAL LEAGUE

    STL—Marty Marion, Terry Moore
    BROOK—Augie Galan, Dixie Walker
    CHI—Phil Cavarretta, Billy Jurges
    BOS—Billy Herman, Bill Lee (not the Spaceman)
    CIN—Joe Beggs, Bucky Walters
    PHI—Roland Hemsley, Ry Hughes
    NYG—Buddy Blattner, Hal Schumaker
    PIT—Rip Sewell, Lee Handley

AMERICAN LEAGUE

    NYY—Tommy Henrich, Johnny Murphy
    STL—Johnny Berardino, Babe Dahlgren
    BOS—Pinky Higgins
    WAS—Bobo Newsom
    DET—Hank Greenberg
    CHI—Joe Kuhel
    PHI—Gene Desautels
    CLEV—Mel Harder

Today, the owners, who cannot take advantage of the players, instead take advantage of the fans and, often, the taxpayers.

Chapter 30: Here's to You, Mrs. Robinson

In addition to Robinson, Wright, and Partlow, Don Newcombe and Roy Campanella
were signed to minor league contracts in 1946. Newk and Campy played for the
Nashua Pride of the Class B New England League. There was little racial prejudice
in the small town, and Nashua won the league championship, in no small part thanks
to its Negro stars.

Jackie wasn't the only pioneer in 1946. The Phillies hired the first female scout, Edith
Haughton, a former WAVE who grew up with the game. The *Sporting News* welcomed her with some backhanded misogyny—"Who knows more about human
nature than the weaker sex?" the paper asked. "Whom does the male, ballplayer or
banker, find it most difficult to fool? Who knows more about the workings of the
male mind and that collection of oddments in the male cerebellum? In short, why
not a female scout?"

Chapter 31: The Autumn of Their Discontent

Jim Bagby Jr., who pitched for Boston in 1946, was the son of Jim Bagby Sr., who pitched
for the Indians from 1916–1922. He won thirty-one games in 1920 and helped the

Tribe win the World Series over the Brooklyn Robins. That year, Bagby hit the first ever home run by a pitcher in the World Series, and was on the mound when Bill Wambsganss turned in an unassisted triple play, the only one in Series history.

Marty Marion hit a home run off Bagby that gave Tech High of Atlanta the 1934 Georgia State High School championship over Bagby's Boys High.

Bobo Newsom is one of only two pitchers to amass over two hundred wins while sporting a losing record (211–222). He also set a record in 1938 for the highest ERA of any twenty-game winner, 5.08.

Newsom had talent, but was so annoying to teammates and management that he played for seventeen teams in his career and never was on the same team for more than two consecutive years. Eight times he was traded in midseason, as teams couldn't wait to dump him. He got the nickname "Bobo" because that was what he called everyone he met.

Newsom played for both Joe Cronin and Leo Durocher. He would chase Cro back to shortstop when the player-manager made visits to the mound. And he was the cause of a team revolt against Durocher in '43, after Leo accused him of throwing a spitter that resulted in a wild pitch that cost the Dodgers a ball game.

Marchildon's sixteen losses in '46 tied him for the most in the AL with teammates Dick Fowler and Lou Knerr.

In 1947, Marchildon would win nineteen games for the seventy-eight-win A's.

The inside-the-park homer was one of Williams's seven game-winning home runs of 1946.

Doc Cramer was nicknamed "Flit," the name of a popular insecticide, for his excellence at fielding fly balls—hence, he was "death to flies," just like the bug killer. He led the AL in putouts in 1936 and 1938.

The 1945 World Series was the progenitor of the so-called Billy Goat Curse that has prevented the Cubs from capturing a title. Bill Sianis, the owner of the Billy Goat Tavern and proud owner of a *Capra aegagrus hircus,* was booted from a Series game at Wrigley Field due to the foul odor emanating from his goat. "Them Cubs, they aren't gonna win no more," Sianis supposedly said on his way out. As of 2012, he has been proven correct.

The year 1946 may have ended triumphantly for Hank Greenberg, but it was his last season in Detroit. Hank wanted to transition from the field into the executive offices and become the Tigers' general manager, but owner Walter Briggs turned him down and, in a fit of pique, released him. Briggs convinced his fellow American League owners not to sign Greenberg. The slugger wasn't hurting for money, however, as he married Caral Gimbel, the heiress to the Gimbels department store fortune, that winter. Rumor had it that Hank's new in-laws were going to buy the Tigers from Briggs and install Greenberg as GM, but that never happened. Instead, Hank went to Pittsburgh, where he hit twenty-five homers and mentored the Pirates young slugger, Ralph Kiner, before calling it quits for good after 1947. He became GM in Cleveland and later with the Chicago White Sox.

Chapter 32: *Victoire*

Somehow, despite his numbers and historical significance, Robinson only finished fourth in the International League MVP vote. Eddie Robinson of Baltimore won the award. The two Robinsons had an encounter during the '46 season—Eddie slammed hard into Jackie, breaking up a double play, and Jackie responded by holding the ball up to Eddie's face and warning, "Next time I'll put this right between your eyes."

Even as Robinson was ending his triumphant first season playing with whites, the National Football League was welcoming its first African-American player. Kenny Washington was a teammate of Robinson's at UCLA, and his proximity to baseball's first black player helped earn him a job with the L.A. Rams.

Chapter 33: The Stretch Run

Munger would go 2–2 with a 3.33 ERA in his ten starts upon returning from Germany, where he took over running the Third Army's sports leagues from Harry Walker.

Ed Stevens was held out of the service due to his recurring nightmares. He told the recruiting officer that he also was prone to sleepwalking, which was frowned upon on the front lines.

The Joe Louis–Billy Conn fight of June 19, 1946, was of course a rematch of their famous first bout in 1941, when Conn was en route to upsetting Louis before the Brown Bomber caught up to Conn with a dramatic thirteenth-round knockout, thus fulfilling his pre-fight prophecy, "He can run, but he can't hide."

The war and poor financial management had left Louis heavily in debt, so after besting Conn he was back in the ring to demolish Mariello a mere three months later. It was the last great performance of the Brown Bomber's career.

The previous record for longest scoreless tie was an eighteen-inning game back in 1909 between Detroit and Washington.

The Dodgers won a replay of the scoreless tie on September 20, 5–3 over the Reds. Dixie Walker's three-run homer off Johnny Vander Meer was the big blow.

During the stretch run, Dyer's native state of Louisiana bestowed an official colonelship upon the manager.

Roy Rogers's film slate in 1946 included *My Pal Trigger, Heldorado,* and the western state shoutouts *Out California Way, Home in Oklahoma, Roll On Texas Moon, Rainbow over Texas, Under Nevada Skies,* and *Song of Arizona.*

Chapter 34: The First Playoff

Ralph Branca sports an 0–3 record in tiebreaker playoff games, losing Games One and Three in 1951 along with Game One in 1946.

Branca pitched twelve times in the first four months of the 1946 season, with no decisions and a 7.12 ERA. In August and September, he pitched eleven times, going 3–0 with a 1.55 ERA.

Those premature World Series programs are probably worth a fortune today, if anyone has them.

Cookie Lavagetto would become famous the following season, when his pinch-hit double in Game Four of the World Series against the Yankees simultaneously broke up Bill Bevens's no-hit bid and drove in the two winning runs in a breathless 3–2 Dodgers win. Lavagetto was hitting for Eddie Stanky. The Yanks won the Series in seven games, however.

Lavagetto missed four full seasons to the war. Although he was classified 3-A, and could have put off enlistment for at least a year, Cookie joined up with his brother right after Pearl Harbor. He served as a navy air machinist for the duration, albeit never overseas. When he at last returned to baseball, he wasn't nearly the same player. Cookie hit but .236 with three homers in nearly three hundred at bats in 1946, and the 1947 Series was his final hurrah—he retired after the season.

Pollet would go 5–2, 2.30 against the Brooks.

Cronin by default would have won the AL version of the Manager of the Year, unless Boudreau got it for the shift brainstorm.

Sadly, a Boston–Brooklyn World Series never happened—that would have been exceptionally fun, regardless of the results.

Clyde Kluttz is not to be confused as a relative of Mickey Klutts, who was an infielder with the Yankees and A's in the 1970s and '80s. Nevertheless, both men overcame the handicap of their surname to make the majors. Clyde was also a longtime scout, including a stint as scouting director with the Yankees in the mid-1970s.

Chapter 35: Splintered

Earl Johnson's brother, Chet Johnson, was one of baseball's foremost characters. A St. Louis Brown for all of five games in 1946, Chet mostly toiled in the minors, including a stint with the Hollywood Stars of the Pacific Coast League, where his comedic act went over like gangbusters. He would throw blooped, "eephus"-like pitches, use underhanded deliveries and triple-windups, and talk to the ball, à la Mark Fidrych, only thirty years earlier. During warm-ups, he would soft toss the ball to his catcher, who would return it harder and harder. On the final return, Johnson would scream in pain, yanking off his glove to reveal a (fake) bloody thumb. He took the mound wearing oversized glasses, coonskin caps, fake mustaches. Former PCL pitcher Bud Watkins described one of Johnson's classic bits to minorleaguebaseball.com: "He would pretend to not be able to see the catcher's sign. So he would creep in closer and closer and squint and shake his head until he finally was right in front of home plate, which is pretty funny in and of itself.

"Then he would get down on all fours and stare at the catcher's crotch for a couple seconds, then stand up and shout 'Eureka! I got it!' and run back to the mound. OK, very funny, right? But Chet's topper was the classic. He would then take his position on the rubber and, very seriously and deliberately, shake off the sign. If you weren't laughing by then, you weren't human." Comedians like the Marx Brothers, Jack Benny, and George Burns were regulars during Johnson's stint with the Stars. "About the only thing he kept up on a wall of his home was a fan letter from Groucho Marx, in which Groucho complimented Chet on his routines," said Earl. "That's like Babe Ruth complimenting you on your hitting, don't you think?"

DiMaggio's fifty-six-game hitting streak warrants his 1941 MVP Award over Williams, in the same manner that you can't argue that the Houston Rockets erred badly by picking (H)akeem Olajuwon in the 1984 NBA Draft instead of Michael Jordan. Houston and Hakeem won two titles, after all. But the 1942 vote is a *shonda*. Williams went .356/36/137 to Gordon's .322/18/103, and his OPS was .247 points higher, 1.147 to .900. Gordon had a career year on a pennant-winning Yankees team, but clearly the writers did Williams a disservice. Still, that was not as great a screw job as was 1947, when an (unnamed) writer left Ted completely off his ballot. Williams thus lost the award to DiMaggio, 202–201.

Here is the final result of the 1946 balloting:

1. Williams 224 points
2. Newhouser 197
3. Doerr 158
4. Pesky 141

5. Vernon 134
6. Feller 105
7. Ferriss 94
8. Greenberg 91
9. Dom DiMaggio 56
10. Boudreau 37

York finished eleventh, Hughson thirteenth, and Hal Wagner mysteriously received a single vote. Joe DiMaggio got six, and Phil Marchildon five.

The NL balloting:

1. Musial 319
2. Dixie Walker 159
3. Slaughter 144
4. Pollet 116
5. Sain 95
6. Reese 79
7. Stanky 67
8. Del Ennis (PHIL) 61
9. Reiser 58
10. Cavarretta 49

Ol' Hig was fifteenth, Harry the Hat Walker twenty-second. Carl Furillo received a single vote.

Chapter 36: The World Series

In understanding the trauma of the national beef shortage, it's important to remember that this was still a time when food, including meat, was mostly seasonal. Beef, especially steak, was considered "fall food," coming off a spring and summer of livestock grazing on the plains, fattening for slaughter. The food industrial complex and globalization of the dinner table was only just being conceptualized. So for autumn to arrive without steak was more upsetting than it might otherwise have been.

Days after the Series ended, Truman removed price controls on meat, and the steak shortage eased.

Pinky Higgins was in his last year as a player in 1946, after a long career whose highlight was twelve consecutive hits in 1938, the AL record (since tied by Walt Dropo). He would later become the Red Sox manager from 1955–1962. As the years went by and the Sox failed to integrate, Higgins, a well-known racist, became the team's totemic figure. At one point writer Clif Keane opined that he thought Cuban-born outfielder Minnie Minoso was the league's best player, and Higgins replied that Keane was "nothing but a fucking nigger-lover." After he was fired, Higgins was driving while drunk in Louisiana and struck and killed a highway worker. He got four years in prison for that. Days after his parole, he died of a heart attack at fifty-nine.

Game One of the '46 Series was the first extra-inning contest to begin a Series since 1924.

The interference play at third base continued a recent tradition of important doings at the Hot Corner for the Redbirds in the World Series. In the 1942 Classic, Slaughter threw out a runner, Tuck Stainback, in the ninth inning of Game Two against the Yankees to ice a win for St. Louis. They would go on to win in five games. The next year, in the rematch between the two teams, New York's Johnny Lindell ran over Kurowski to force an error, which started a decisive five-run rally in the eighth inning of Game Three. The Yanks got revenge, winning in five games as well.

Few historians give the Magda Goebbels/Hitler affair much credence, but the papers reported the fact that Frau Meissner told the tale, including, notably, the *St. Louis Post-Dispatch* and most subscribers to the Associated Press.

The first NBA game was played on November 1, 1946. The Toronto Huskies beat the New York Knicks 68–66 at Maple Leaf Gardens.

In a ghoulish twist, Rice died while attending a benefit dinner in his honor, in Garden Grove, California, in 1983. He was sixty.

Doc Blanchard was Army's "Mr. Inside" to Glenn Davis's "Mr. Outside." Blanchard won the Heisman Trophy in 1945, and Davis won it in 1946. In '46 Army won its third consecutive national championship under coach Earl "Red" Blaik. The Black Knights were 27–0–1 in the span.

The Joe Dimaggio–for–Ted Williams trade talks would be revived that winter, with a deal reportedly made one drunken evening between MacPhail and Yawkey. But when they sobered up, Mac squawked over including a promising catching prospect, Yogi Berra, in the deal, and it fell apart.

The 1946 midterm elections were a historic rout in favor of the Republicans, and a repudiation of President Truman. The meat shortage played a large role in the erosion of support for the Democrats, as did the yearlong labor crisis. Among those elected to Congress for the first time were a senator from Wisconsin, Joe McCarthy, and a California representative named Richard Nixon.

Chapter 37: The Series Comes to the Hub

Ralph Slater wrote the classic hypnotist's guide, *Hypnotism and Self Hypnosis*. His real name was Joseph Bolsky, and he ran afoul of the FDA for selling a phonograph that promised to cure insomnia. On it was his voice over catchy tunes, which was deemed by one expert as "too close to Frank Sinatra's music to put anyone to sleep." He had more luck with his stage performances, regularly selling out Carnegie Hall and putting audience members, often ex-GIs or nubile young women, under hypnosis. He had a lively stage career until 1952, when a young girl he hypnotized in London fell and broke her ankle. Stage hypnosis was swiftly banned in the United Kingdom, and the United States, Canada, and Australia followed suit. Slater's career was abruptly over.

Arch McDonald was actually nicknamed "the Old Pine Tree" for his signature call. It was from a country song, recorded by Gene Autry, among others: "They cut down the old pine tree, and they hauled it away to the mill / To make a coffin of pine, for that sweetheart of mine."

The three Cardinals with four hits were joined by Sox right fielder Wally Moses, who had four singles of his own. But he neither scored nor drove in a run in the contest.

Gutteridge was voted a half-share of the Series profits for his efforts, which Yawkey sweetened with a bonus that made up the other half.

Ferriss's shutout in Game Three was the third in Sox Series history. Future umpire Bill Dineen blanked the Pirates twice in 1903, and Babe Ruth shut out Chicago in Game One of the 1918 Series.

The photo of Williams slumped against the left field wall during the Game Four pitching change evokes a similar shot of his successor, Carl Yastrzemski, doing much the same during the "Boston Massacre" of 1978, when the Yankees bombarded the Sox in a four-game series at Fenway that keyed the Bombers' rally to win the AL East and, ultimately, the World Series.

Munger had an interesting post-baseball career, as a private investigator with the Pinkerton Detective Agency in Houston.

One of the Boston pitchers tattooed by the Cards in Game Four was Mace Brown. He is most famous for surrendering the fabled "Homer in the Gloamin'" to Gabby Hartnett in 1938, while pitching for Pittsburgh. Hartnett's homer at Wrigley Field, with darkness fast approaching, won a critical late-season game for the Cubs and propelled them to the pennant.

It should be remembered when considering Schmidt's account of his exchanges with Pollet and Dyer that Freddy disliked his manager, feeling Dyer buried him in the bullpen. So his memories tend to have an anti-Eddie tinge. It doesn't seem likely that Pollet, who was very close to Dyer, would have an intermediary tell his friend and manager that he felt poorly, but it is possible—certainly Pollet would be loath to let Dyer down and may not have felt up to telling him the truth about his condition.

Dobson went 13–7 with a 3.24 ERA in 1946.

Beazley pitched a scoreless inning in Game Five, although he told the team in September he wanted to quit, as he was exhausted. Dyer talked him into staying on to see the season through.

Chapter 38: Cat Scratch Fever

The tough-as-nails talk from Country Slaughter on the eve of Game Six may need to be taken with a grain or two of salt, as it was "reported" by Arthur Daley of the *Times*, an unabashed Slaughter worshipper.

The meager shares came to $3,742.33 for the winners, $2,140.89 for the losers. By contrast, the shares from the year before, when Detroit and Chicago tangled, were $6,443.34 and $3,930.22, respectively. In 1947 the shares would go back up to $5,830.03 and $4,081.19. That the Series shares were so low after a season in which attendance went through the roof was a bitter irony.

The pension plan would be formally ratified in February, and put into place on April 1, 1947. It called for retired players with five years in the bigs to get $50 per month, and those with ten years to get $100 per month. Today, players become vested after a mere forty-three days of big league service, which earns each one $34,000 annually and a lifetime health plan. Ten years in the show means $100,000 annually.

Game Six wasn't the first time Cronin made an unusual pitching decision that cost him. In the 1933 World Series, while player-manager of the Senators, Cro tried to pull a fast one. Instead of aces Earl Whitehill or Alvin Crowder, both twenty-game winners, his Game One starter was Walter Stewart, who was solid but much less highly regarded. The New York Giants pounded Stewart for four runs in two innings, and they went on to win in five games.

Chapter 39: The Mad Dash

Stivers told the *Los Angeles Times* he had stayed silent about his complicity in Goering's suicide for six decades because he feared (probably correctly) that he would be charged in the matter by the US Army.

Other theories on the manner by which Goering managed to cheat the hangman included a cyanide capsule in a filling, bribed guards, and a "kiss of death" from his wife, Emmy, on her final visit, supposedly passing some form of poison from mouth to mouth.

Whirlaway won the 1941 Triple Crown with fabled jockey Eddie Arcaro aboard, and is considered one of the great thoroughbred horses of all time.

Before Brecheen, the last pitcher to win three World Series games was Stan Covaleskie in 1920. The Cat was the first lefty to do it.

With the win in 1946, the Cards remained undefeated in Game Sevens. This was their fourth in a row. The Redbirds would win two more, in 1964 and 1967, before finally dropping a Series decider in 1968 to Detroit. They are 2–2 since, including the 2011 Series against Texas. Eleven of St. Louis's eighteen Series appearances have gone the full seven games.

Game Seven continued a trend of tight wins for the Cards in 1946—it was the team's thirty-fifth one-run win of the season.

Pesky's moment of indecision as Slaughter rounded the bases had a recent Series antecedent. In 1940, Dick Bartell of the Tigers held a relay throw a beat too long as Frank McCormick scored from second in the seventh inning of Game Seven. The play tied the game at one—moments later, Cincinnati scored again and won the game and the Series.

Chapter 40: Aftermath

Grover Cleveland Alexander won 373 games in his twenty-year career and was inducted into the Hall of Fame in the third-ever class, in 1938.

Pesky's death in August 2012 didn't earn him any alleviation of his crime against Red Sox Nation. Mostly, however, his "holding the ball" was acknowledged, then outweighed by his lifetime of service to the franchise. A minor controversy surrounded his funeral when it was revealed that only four members of the current Sox team attended. Many of the 2012 Red Sox were unloaded soon afterward.

There can be little doubt that if Williams played today, ESPN's Skip Bayless would be his biggest antagonist.

Epilogue

Harry Walker's first managing job in the bigs was in St. Louis. The man he replaced? Eddie Stanky, who had taken over for Terry Moore.

In nine years of managing three teams, Walker was 630–604. He never won a pennant at the helm. Two other managers in *Ball Four* were players in 1946. Ted Williams ("of the Major Fucking Leagues") comes off well in the book. Joe Schultz, who was a catcher with the Browns and managed Bouton in Seattle before he was traded to Walker's Houston Astros, not so much.

The 1946 World Series share was the lowest since 1918, the last time Boston and Fenway Park were involved.

The MacPhail-Durocher feud stemmed from Mac's hiring of a pair of Durocher's coaches, Chuck Dressen and Red Corriden, for the Yankees, and escalated from there.

The active player who supposedly lost big money in a rigged craps game run by

Durocher and Raft was never officially named, but Elden Auker, in his memoir *Sleeper Cars and Flannel Uniforms,* said it was Tigers pitcher Dizzy Trout.

Before Durocher was suspended, he welcomed Jackie Robinson to the team. Famously, he squashed any talk of a job action by Jackie's new Dodgers teammates, saying, "I don't care if the guy is yellow or black, or if he has stripes like a fucking zebra. I'm the manager of this team and I say he plays."

Perhaps that's a bit of historical whitewashing, however, as some sources from the time claim Durocher didn't want or like Robinson. Most signficant among them is Ed Stevens, who, it should be noted, despised Leo in turn. Most likely is that Durocher, similar to many of his contemporaries, was conditioned from youth to distrust, if not outright dislike, Negroes. But once he got a gander at Robinson's brilliance, the cash register in his head started ringing, drowning out all other thoughts.

Clyde Sukeforth managed the first two games of Brooklyn's 1947 season but refused to take the job full-time, opening the door for Shotton.

Besides Eddie Dyer, the other managers to win it all in their rookie season are Bucky Harris of the 1924 Senators, Ralph Houk of the 1961 Yankees, and Bob Brenly of the 2001 Diamondbacks. Six others have won the Series in their first full season at the helm, including Tris Speaker (1920 Indians), Rogers Hornsby (1926 Cardinals), Bill Terry (1933 Giants), Frankie Frisch (1934 Cardinals), Dallas Green (1980 Phillies), and Tom Kelly (1987 Twins).

Robinson was, of course, one of a trio of black players given a tryout by the Red Sox in 1945, along with Sam Jethroe of the Cleveland Buckeyes and Marvin Williams of the Philadelphia Stars. The workout, which took place on April 12, the same day FDR died, was mere window dressing—no one in the Sox organization, from Tom Yawkey on down, had any intention of signing a black player. "It's not up to us," Cronin told Jackie and the others lamely after the workout.

Robinson's breakout season in 1949 was aided by batting tips from George Sisler, Dick's father.

Jackie Robinson Jr. was diagnosed with emotional problems at an early age. He served in Vietnam and was wounded there in 1965, at just eighteen years old. Upon returning to the States, Jackie Jr. struggled with addiction, which turned his father into an outspoken antidrug advocate. Jackie Jr. had just completed treatment at a rehab facility when he was killed in an auto accident on June 17, 1971, at the age of twenty-four.

Perhaps the movie about Jackie Robinson's debut season, *42,* to be released in April 2013, will help raise his profile among a new generation, and Rachel's museum project will be a beneficiary.

For the statistically inclined, it should be noted that Williams trails Musial in career WAR (wins above replacement), 123.4 to 119.8. They rank twelfth and thirteenth on the all-time list, respectively (Babe Ruth is first, of course, at 178.3).

Updike's classic story from *The New Yorker* is entitled "Hub Fans Bid Kid Adieu." Its famous final line is often misquoted as "Gods don't answer letters," and as any fan of literature or Commander Data from *Star Trek: The Next Generation* will tell you, contractions (and the lack of them) are vitally important.

Williams's home run in his final at bat, his 521st, did not, contrary to memory, win the game for Boston. His solo blast pulled the Sox to within 4–3 of the Baltimore Orioles. Boston then scored two in the ninth to win 5–4, minus any heroics from Ted.

The homer was Williams's 248th at Fenway, compared to 273 on the road, proof that his lefty swing was probably better suited to a differently configured park. He might have hit 800 at Sportsman's Park, for example.

Musial, whose hit in his final at bat was the 3,630th of his career, went 2–3 in that final game against the Reds, a 3–2 Cards victory. Pete Rose retrieved the ball from the outfield and handed it to Musial as Stan was pulled from the game to a standing ovation.

That moment between rookie and retiree represents 7,886 hits, rapped out by the first and fourth men on the all-time list.

Musial's final two singles gave him precisely 1,815 hits at home and 1,815 hits on the road.

Mickey Owen spent the 1953 season managing in the Class B Piedmont League, where the ever-ornery former catcher presaged Mike Tyson by allegedly biting a chunk out of an opponent's ear during a brawl, an act that cost him $2,500 in fines.

Owen never did live down his dropped third strike in the 1941 World Series, or his self-imposed departure from the bigs, but he did give back to the game with a baseball school named for him in Missouri, his home state. Among the campers to pass through the Mickey Owen Baseball School—Michael Jordan and Charlie Sheen.

In case you were wondering, DiMaggio, Williams, Feller, and Robinson all made Richard Nixon's all-time All-Star teams—Joe D. on the 1925–45 squad, the others on the 1945–65 team.

Of the parks in use in 1946, only Fenway and Wrigley Field still stand.

The Department of Veterans Affairs doesn't keep track of everyone who fought in World War II. It estimates the number of vets who pass each day by actuarial tables that are based on the 1990 census.

Bibliography

Ahrens, Art. "The Old Brawl Game." *The National Pastime,* August 2003.

Allen, Lee. *The Hot Stove League.* Kingston, NY: Total Sports, 2000.

Anderson, Dave. *Pennant Races: Baseball at Its Best.* New York: Doubleday, 1994.

Anderson, William L., and Derek W. Little. "All's Fair: War and Other Causes of Divorce." Statistical breakdown of divorce rates. http://findarticles.com/p/articles/mi_m0254/is_4_58/ai_58496765/ (accessed February 14, 2012).

Appleton, Sheldon. "Frank McCormick." SABR bio of the former Reds and Phillies star. http://sabr.org/bioproj/person/ff6ce012 (accessed December 19, 2011).

Aronoff, Jason, and Dave Anderson. *Going, Going . . . Caught!* Jefferson, NC: McFarland, 2009.

Auker, Elden. *Sleeper Cars and Flannel Uniforms.* Chicago: Triumph Books, 2001.

Bedingfield, Gary. *Baseball's Dead of World War II.* Jefferson, NC: McFarland, 2009.

Berg, A. Scott. *Lindbergh.* New York: Putnam, 1998.

Berger, Ralph. "Paul Derringer." SABR bio of the former Reds pitcher. http://sabr.org/bioproj/person/01f0b3b3 (accessed July 11, 2012).

Bjarkman, Peter C., ed. *Encyclopedia of Major League Baseball Team Histories.* Westport, CT: Meckler Publishing, 1991.

Breslin, Jimmy. *Branch Rickey.* New York: Viking, 2011.

Broeg, Bob. "Keep Your Eye on the Cat." *Sport,* October 1947.

———. *The Man Stan: Musial . . . Then and Now.* St. Louis: Bethany Press, 1977.

———. *Redbirds: A Century of Cardinals' Baseball.* St. Louis: River City Publishers, 1987.

Brown, William. *Baseball's Fabulous Montreal Royals.* Montreal: Robert Davies Publishing, 1996.

Bruce, Janet. *The Kansas City Monarchs.* Lawrence, KS: University of Kansas Press, 1985.

Bullock, Steven R. *Playing for Their Nation: Baseball and the American Military During World War II.* Lincoln, NE: University of Nebraska Press, 2004.

Carnes, Mark C., and John A. Garraty. *Mapping America's Past.* New York: Henry Holt, 1996.

Cisco, Dan. *Hawai'i Sports: History, Facts, and Statistics.* Honolulu: University of Hawaii Press, 1999.

Cleveland, Rick. "David 'Boo' Ferriss: A Baseball Great." Bio of the Red Sox pitcher. http://mshistory.k12.ms.us/articles/78/david-boo-ferriss-a-baseball-great (accessed March 4, 2012).

Cockcroft, James D. *Latinos in Béisbol.* New York: Franklin Watts, 1996.

Cohen, Stan. *V for Victory.* Missoula, MT: Pictorial Histories Publishing, 1991.

Conot, Robert E. *Justice at Nuremberg.* New York: HarperCollins, 1983.

Corbett, Warren. "Eddie Dyer." SABR bio of the Cardinals manager. http://sabr.org/bioproj/person/b3e94581 (accessed April 14, 2012).

———. "Tiny Bonham." SABR bio of the Yankees pitcher. http://sabr.org/bioproj/person/d7503bf4 (accessed March 9, 2012).

Costello, Rory. "Willard Brown." SABR bio of the Negro Leaguer and OISE All-Star. http://sabr.org/bioproj/person/49784799 (accessed August 15, 2012).

Cramer, Richard Ben. *Joe DiMaggio: The Hero's Life.* New York: Simon and Schuster, 2000.

"The Crash of the XF-11." Details of Howard Hughes's crash in his experimental plane. http://www.check-six.com/Crash_Sites/XF-11_crash_site.htm (accessed February 18, 2012).

Davisson, Budd. "The Widow Maker Made Good." History of the B-26 Marauder. http://www.airbum.com/pireps/PirepPeanutB-26.html (accessed April 12, 2012).

Day, Laraine. *Day with the Giants.* New York: Doubleday, 1952.

Dewey, Donald, and Nicholas Acocella. *The New Biographical History of Baseball.* Chicago: Triumph Books, 1992.

Dickey, Glenn. *The History of the World Series Since 1903.* Briarcliff Manor, NY: Stein and Day, 1984.

Dickson, Paul. "Playing with All Their Heart." *Memories and Dreams* (official publication of the National Baseball Hall of Fame), fall 2012.

Durocher, Leo. *The Dodgers and Me.* Chicago: Ziff-Davis, 1948.

Durocher, Leo, with Ed Linn. *Nice Guys Finish Last.* New York: Simon and Schuster, 1975.

Eisenbath, Mike. *The Cardinals Encyclopedia.* Philadelphia: Temple University Press, 1999.

Eskenazi, Gerald. *The Lip.* New York: William Morrow, 1993.

Feller, Bob, with Bill Gilbert. *Now Pitching, Bob Feller.* New York: Birch Lane Press, 1990.

Fimrite, Ron. "O Lucky Man." *Sports Illustrated,* November 14, 1994.

Freese, Mel. *The St. Louis Cardinals in the 1940s.* Jefferson, NC: McFarland, 1997.

Frommer, Harvey. *Baseball's Greatest Managers.* New York: Franklin Watts, 1985.

———. "Joe Page." Bio of the former Yankees hurler. http://theyplayedthegame.tripod.com/id5.htm (accessed February 21, 2012).

———. *Rickey & Robinson.* New York: MacMillan, 1982.

Gibbons, Frank. "Seventh Son Guidance for Tribe." *Baseball Digest,* February 1951.

Goldblatt, Andrew. *The Giants and the Dodgers.* Jefferson, NC: McFarland, 1993.

Golenbock, Peter. *Bums: An Oral History of the Brooklyn Dodgers.* New York: G. P. Putnam's Sons, 1984.

———. *Fenway: An Unexpurgated History of the Boston Red Sox.* New York: Putnam, 1992.

———. *The Spirit of St. Louis.* New York: HarperCollins, 2000.

Gould, Paul. "Unionism's Bid in Baseball." *New Republic,* August 5, 1946.

Graham, Frank. "The Great Mexican War of 1946." *Sports Illustrated,* September 19, 1966.

———. *The New York Giants.* New York: G. P. Putnam's Sons, 1952.

Gross, Milton. "The Yankees' Angry Ace." *Saturday Evening Post,* July 13, 1946.

Gutman, Dan. *Baseball Babylon.* New York: Penguin, 1992.

Halberstam, David. *Sports on New York Radio.* Chicago: Master's Press, 1999.

Hill, Benjamin. "Forgotten Members of the 'Great Experiment.'" Story about John Wright and Roy Partlow, the other black players on the 1946 Montreal Royals. http://www.milb.com/news/article.jsp?ymd=20070214&content_id=176859&vkey =news_milb&fext=.jsp (accessed March 2, 2012).

Holland, Gerald. "Who in the World but Larry?" *Sports Illustrated,* August 17, 1959.

Honig, Donald. *Baseball When the Grass Was Real.* New York: Coward, McCann and Geoghegan, 1975.

Hynd, Noel. *The Giants of the Polo Grounds.* New York: Doubleday, 1988.

Jacobson, Sidney. *Pete Reiser.* Jefferson, NC: McFarland, 2004.

James, Bill. *The Baseball Book 1991.* New York: Random House, 1991.

——. *The Bill James Guide to Baseball Managers.* New York: Scribner, 1997.

James, Bill, with Rob Neyer. *The Neyer/James Guide to Pitchers.* New York: Touchstone, 2004.

Jenkinson, Bill. *The Year Babe Ruth Hit 104 Home Runs.* New York: Carroll and Graf, 2007.

Johnson, Garrett. "The Great Strike Wave of 1946." Recap of the year's strikes. http://www.bitsofnews.com/content/view/6638/ (accessed August 15, 2012).

Johnson, Paul. *Modern Times.* New York: Harper and Row, 1983.

Kaese, Harold. "What's the Matter with the Red Sox?" *Saturday Evening Post,* March 23, 1946.

Kahn, Roger. *The Boys of Summer.* New York: Harper and Row, 1972.

——. *The Head Game.* New York: Harcourt, 2000.

——. "The Ten Years of Jackie Robinson." *Sport,* October 12–21, 1955.

Kelley, Brent. *The Pastime in Turbulence.* Jefferson, NC: McFarland, 2001.

Kinkead, Eugene. "That Was the War." *The New Yorker,* May 11, 1946.

Korr, Charles P. *The End of Baseball as We Knew It: The Players Union, 1960–81.* Champaign, IL: University of Illinois Press, 2002.

Leck, Charlie. "1946 World Series." Video of the 1946 World Series. http://chasblogs .blogspot.com/2011/06/1946-world-series.html (accessed February 1, 2012).

Lieb, Frederick G. *The Boston Red Sox.* New York: G. P. Putnam's Sons, 1947.

Linn, Ed. *Hitter.* New York: Harcourt Brace Jovanovich, 1993.

Manchester, William. *The Glory and the Dream.* New York: Little, Brown, 1974.

Mann, Arthur. "The Truth About the Jackie Robinson Case." *Saturday Evening Post,* May 13, 1950.

Marchildon, Phil, with Brian Kendall. *Ace.* New York: Penguin, 1993.

Marshall, William. *Baseball's Pivotal Era, 1945–1951.* Lexington, KY: University of Kentucky Press, 1999.

Marzano, Rudy. *The Brooklyn Dodgers in the 1940s.* Jefferson, NC: McFarland, 2005.

McCullough, David. *Truman.* New York: Simon and Schuster, 1992.

McKelvey, G. Richard. *The MacPhails.* Jefferson, NC: McFarland, 2000.

Montville, Leigh. *Ted Williams.* New York: Doubleday, 2004.

Morris, Peter. *A Game of Inches.* Chicago: Ivan R. Dee, 2006.

Musial, Stan. *Stan Musial: "The Man's" Own Story.* New York: Doubleday, 1964.

Nathan, David. *The McFarland Baseball Quotations Dictionary.* Jefferson, NC: McFarland, 1991.

Nathanson, Mitchell. *A People's History of Baseball.* Springfield, IL: University of Illinois Press, 2012.

Nemec, David. *The Great American Baseball Team Book.* New York: Penguin, 1992.

New York Daily News. *Joe DiMaggio: An American Icon.* Champaign, IL: Sports Publishing LLC, 1999.

Neyer, Rob. *Rob Neyer's Big Book of Baseball Lineups.* New York: Fireside, 2003.

Nicholson, William. "Bleacher Bums of Yesteryear." History of baseball superfans. http://research.sabr.org/journals/bleacher-bums (accessed April 1, 2012).

Nowlin, Bill. "Bobby Doerr." SABR bio of the Red Sox second baseman. http://sabr.org/bioproj/person/afad9e3d (accessed March 22, 2012).

———. "Dave Ferriss." SABR bio of the pitcher. http://sabr.org/bioproj/person/ee5565cb (accessed March 4, 2012).

———. "Johnny Pesky." SABR bio of the Red Sox shortstop. http://sabr.org/bioproj/person/23baaef3 (accessed March 4, 2012).

———. *Ted Williams at War.* Burlington, MA: Rounder Books, 2007.

Oakley, J. Ronald. *Baseball's Last Golden Age, 1946–1960.* Jefferson, NC: McFarland, 1994.

Oliphant, Thomas. *Praying for Gil Hodges.* New York: St. Martin's Press, 2005.

Parrott, Harold. *The Lords of Baseball.* Westport, CT: Praeger Publishers, 1976.

Pepe, Phil. "Scooter's World." *Memories and Dreams* (official publication of the National Baseball Hall of Fame), summer 2012.

"Plane Crash Info 1946." Details of plane crashes in 1946. http://planecrashinfo.com/1946/1946.htm (accessed November 22, 2011).

Pomerance, Benjamin. "More Than Black and White." Details of Robinson's season in Montreal. http://www.apnmag.com/fall_2009/pomerance_JackieRobinson.php (accessed March 9, 2012).

Pool, Bob. "Former GI Claims Role in Goering's Death." Seventy-eight-year-old sheet worker says he passed Nazi poison in Nuremberg prison. http://articles.latimes.com/2005/feb/07/local/me-goering7 (accessed January 31, 2012).

Powell, Larry. *Bottom of the Ninth: An Oral History on the Life of Harry "The Hat" Walker.* Lincoln, NE: iUniverse.com, 2000.

Price, Cadet Bryan C. "More Than a Game: Baseball Diplomacy in World War II and the Cold War, 1941–1958." Paper submitted to History Department. West Point, NY, May 7, 1998.

Primm, James Neal. *Lion of the Valley.* St. Louis: Missouri Historical Society Press, 1981.

Riley, James A. *Dandy, Day, and the Devil.* Cocoa, FL: TK Publishers, 1997.

Robinson, Eddie. *Lucky Me: My 65 Years in Baseball.* Dallas: SMU Press, 2011.

Rosengren, John. *Hank Greenberg.* New York: Penguin, 2013.

———. "Opening Day, 1946." *History Channel Magazine,* May–June 2003.

Sargent, Jim. "Tom McBride." SABR bio of the Red Sox outfielder. http://sabr.org/

bioproj/person/512a26d9 (accessed January 11, 2012).

Schoor, Gene. *The History of the World Series.* New York: William Morrow, 1990.

Shaughnessy, Dan. *The Curse of the Bambino.* New York: Penguin, 1990.

Sheed, Wilfrid. *My Life as a Fan.* New York: Simon and Schuster, 1993.

Sickels, John. *Bob Feller: Ace of the Greatest Generation.* Dulles, VA: Brassey's Inc., 2008.

Silber, Irwin. *Press Box Red.* Philadelphia: Temple University Press, 2003.

Skipper, Doug. "Wally Moses." SABR bio of the Sox right fielder. http://sabr.org/bioproj/person/4be0756d (accessed July 2, 2012).

Slaughter, Enos, with Kevin Reid. *Country Hardball.* Greensboro, NC: Tudor Publishers, 1991.

Spatz, Lyle. *Dixie Walker.* Jefferson, NC: McFarland, 2011.

Spatz, Lyle, ed. *The Team That Forever Changed Baseball and America.* Lincoln, NE: University of Nebraska Press, 2012.

Stadler, Frances Hurd. *St. Louis Day by Day.* St. Louis: Patrice Press, 1989.

Stevens, Ed. *The Other Side of the Jackie Robinson Story.* Mustang, OK: Tate Publishing and Enterprises, 2009.

Sugar, Bert Randolph. *Hit the Sign and Win a Free Suit of Clothes from Harry Finklestein.* Chicago: Contemporary Books, 1978.

Swaine, Rick. "Whitey Kurowski." SABR bio of the Cards third baseman. http://sabr.org/bioproj/person/2c2e4e20 (accessed February 25, 2012).

Szalontai, James. *Close Shave: The Life and Times of Baseball's Sal Maglie.* Jefferson, NC: McFarland, 2002.

Thorn, John, and Jules Tygiel. "Jackie Robinson's Signing: The Real Story." *Sport,* June 1988.

Trager, James. *The People's Chronology.* New York: Henry Holt, 1992.

Trouppe, Quincy. *20 Years Too Soon.* St. Louis: Missouri Historical Society Press, 1977.

Turner, Frederick. *When the Boys Came Back.* New York: Henry Holt, 1996.

Tygiel, Jules. *Baseball's Great Experiment.* New York: Oxford University Press, 1983.

———. "The Court-Martial of Jackie Robinson." *American Heritage,* August–September, 1984.

Updike, John. "Hub Fans Bid Kid Adieu." *The New Yorker,* October 22, 1960.

Van Blair, Rick. *Dugout to Foxhole.* Jefferson, NC: McFarland, 1994.

van Mensvoort, Martijn. "Barack Obama is the 7th Left-Handed US President." A rundown of the presidential handedness. http://www.handresearch.com/news/barack-obama-left-handed-us-president.htm (accessed February 12, 2012).

Vecsey, George. *Stan Musial: An American Life.* New York: Ballantine, 2011.

Veeck, Bill, and Ed Linn. *Veeck—As in Wreck.* Evanston, IL: Holtzman Press, 1962.

Virtue, John. *South of the Color Barrier.* Jefferson, NC: McFarland, 2008.

Wancho, Joseph. "Enos Slaughter." SABR bio of Country Slaughter. http://sabr.org/bioproj/person/fd6550d9 (accessed July 17, 2011).

Weintraub, Robert. *The House That Ruth Built: A New Stadium, the First Yankees Championship, and the Redemption of 1923.* New York: Little, Brown, 2011.

West, Jean. "The Unconquerable Doing the Impossible." A history of Jackie Robinson's first spring training. http://www.jimcrowhistory.org/resources/lessonplans/hs_es_jackie

_robinson.htm (accessed March 29, 2012).

Wexler, Laura. *Fire in a Canebrake: The Last Mass Lynching in America.* New York: Scribner, 2003.

Yergin, Daniel. *The Prize: The Epic Quest for Oil, Money, and Power.* New York: Simon and Schuster, 1991.

Young, Dick. "Oh, Those Broken Pledges." *Baseball Digest,* October 1950.

Zoss, Joel, and John Bowman. *Diamonds in the Rough.* New York: MacMillan, 1989.

The following sources were also consulted:

Newspapers: *Boston Globe, Boston Herald, Boston Record, Brooklyn Eagle, Chicago Defender, Cleveland Plain Dealer, Harvard Crimson, Los Angeles Times, Montreal Gazette, Montreal Star, New York Daily News, New York Herald Tribune, New York Post, New York Sun, New York Times, Pittsburgh Courier, Providence Journal, Richmond Afro-American, San Francisco Chronicle, Stars and Stripes, St. Louis Post-Dispatch, St. Louis Star-Times, Syracuse Post-Dispatch, Washington Post*

Magazines: *Collier's, Fortune, Life, Newsweek, Sporting News, Time*

Websites: BallparksofBaseball.com, Baseball-Almanac.com, Baseball-Reference.com, MiLB.com, Retrosheet.org, SABR.org

Index